RADIANT

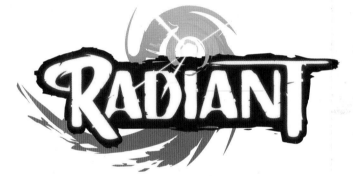

TONY VALENTE

CONTENTS

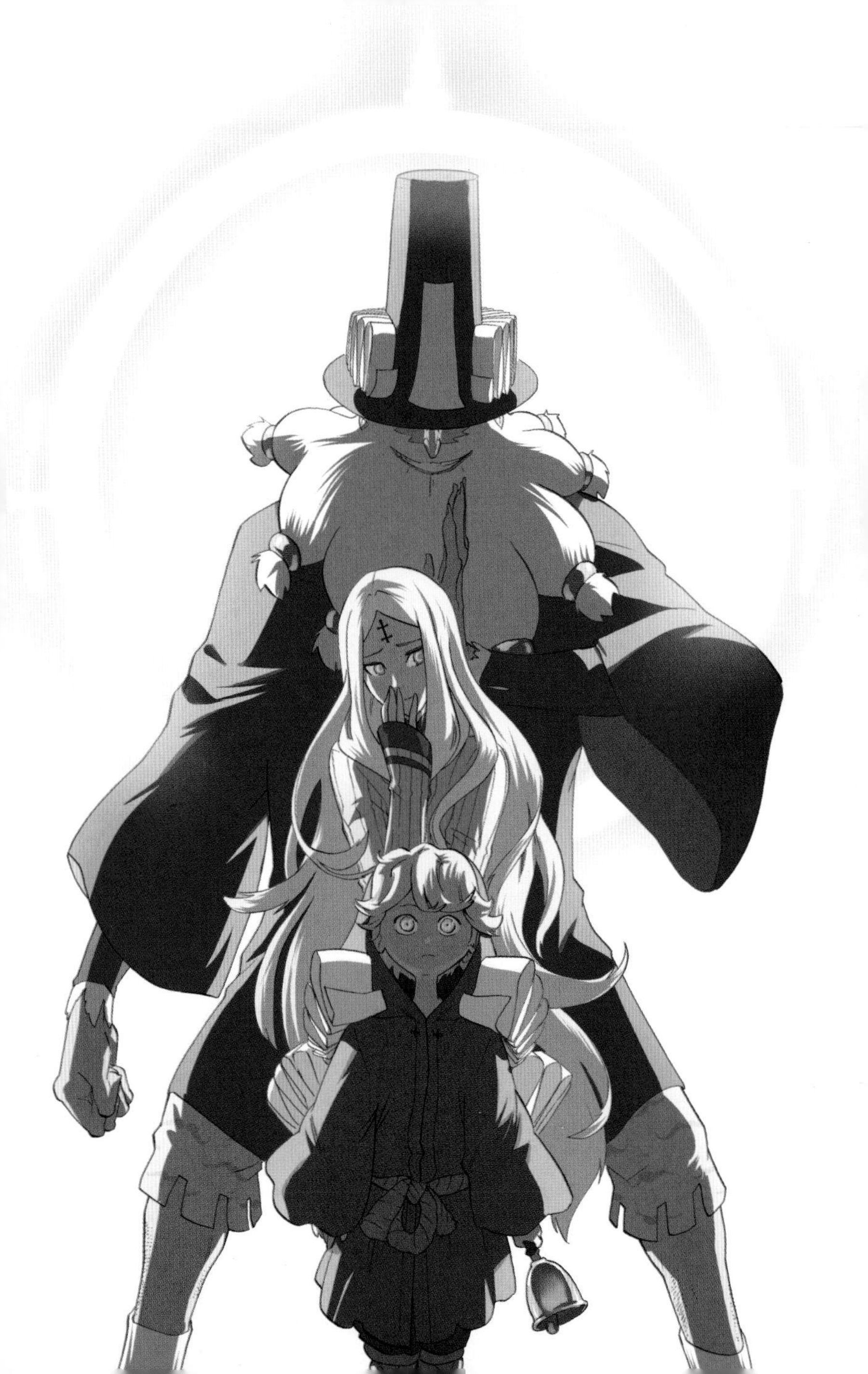

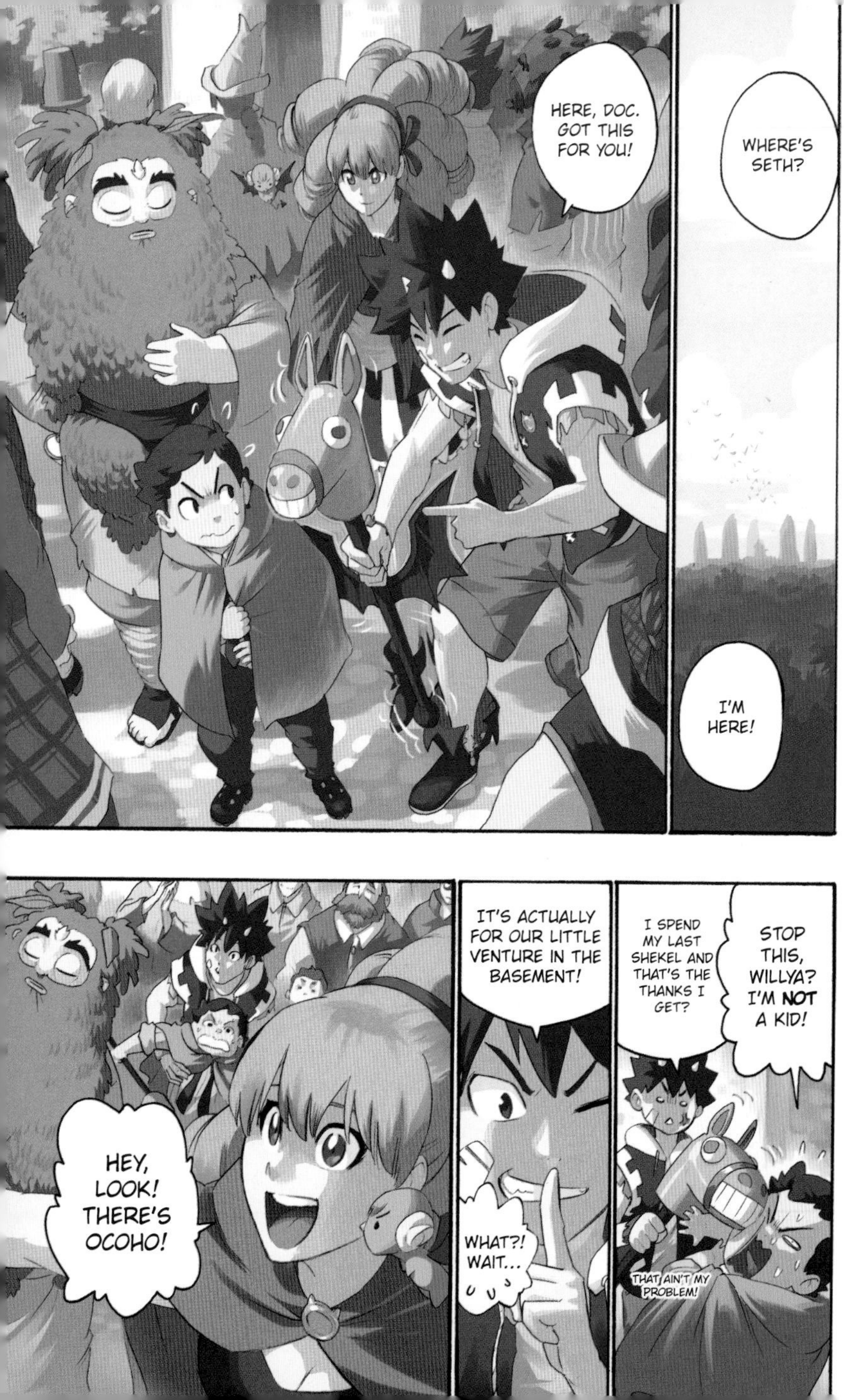
WHERE'S SETH?
I'M HERE!
HERE, DOC. GOT THIS FOR YOU!
STOP THIS, WILLYA? I'M **NOT** A KID!
I SPEND MY LAST SHEKEL AND THAT'S THE THANKS I GET?
THAT AIN'T MY PROBLEM!
IT'S ACTUALLY FOR OUR LITTLE VENTURE IN THE BASEMENT!
WHAT?! WAIT...
HEY, LOOK! THERE'S OCOHO!

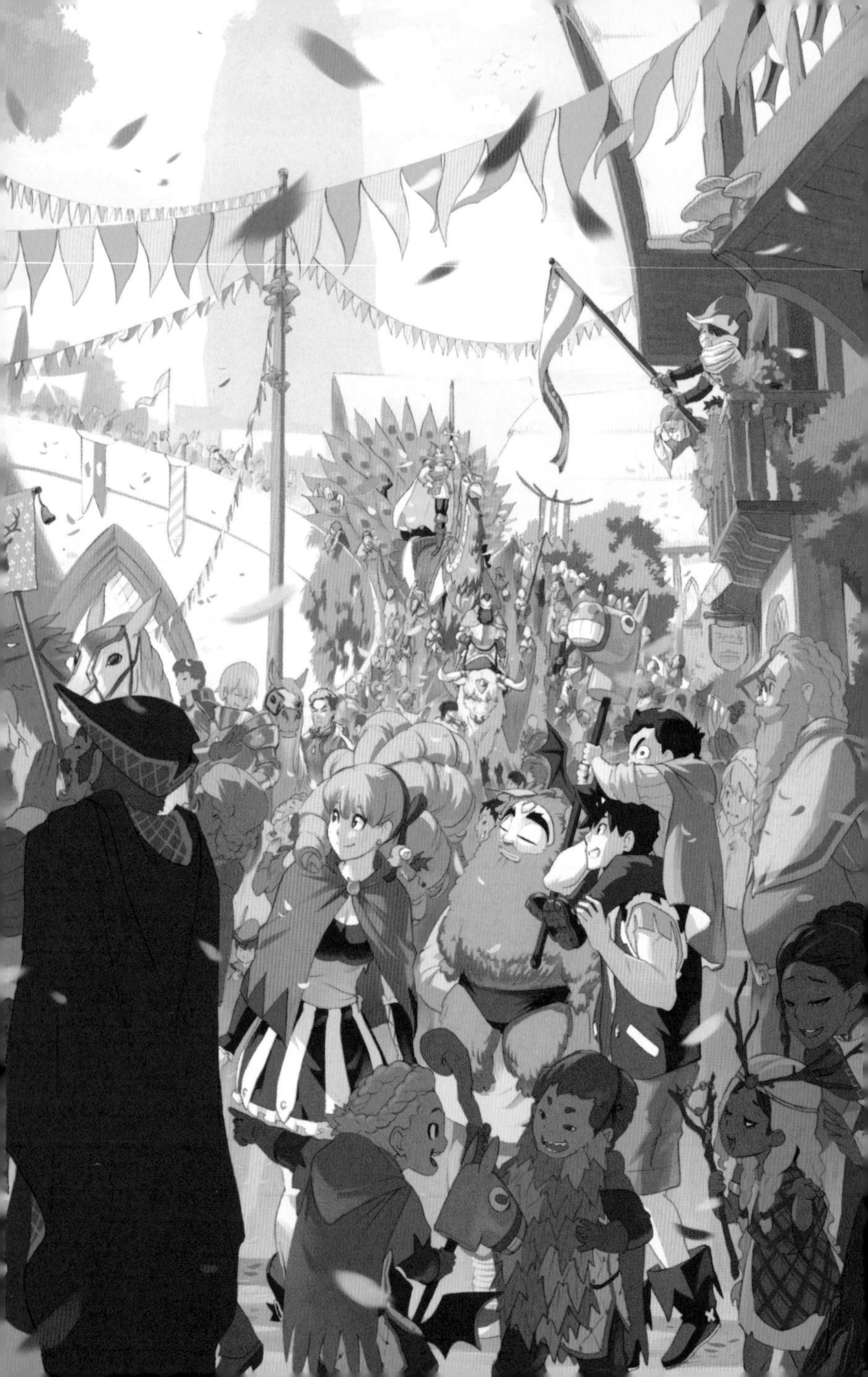

Chapter 53
Untamable Heir

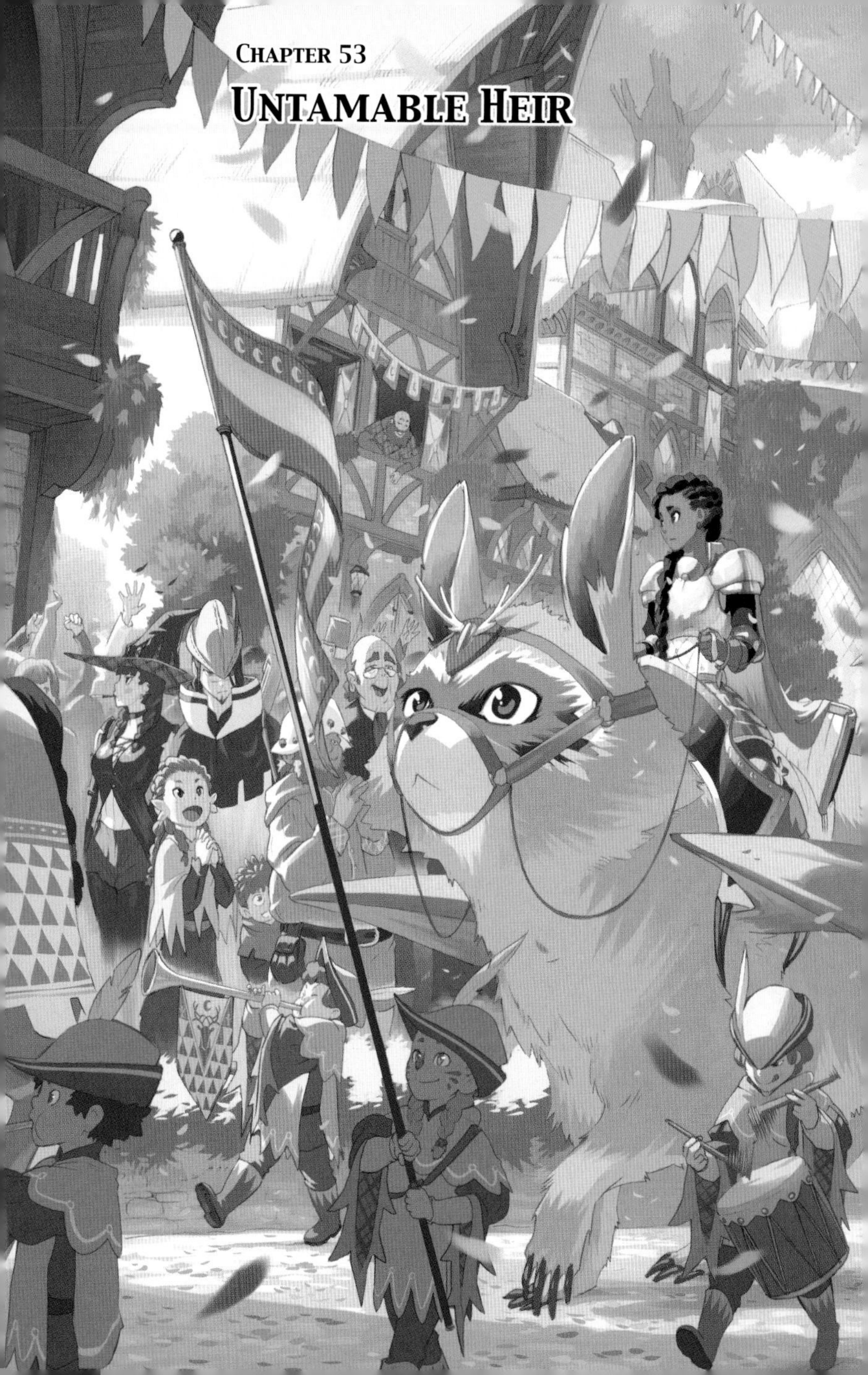

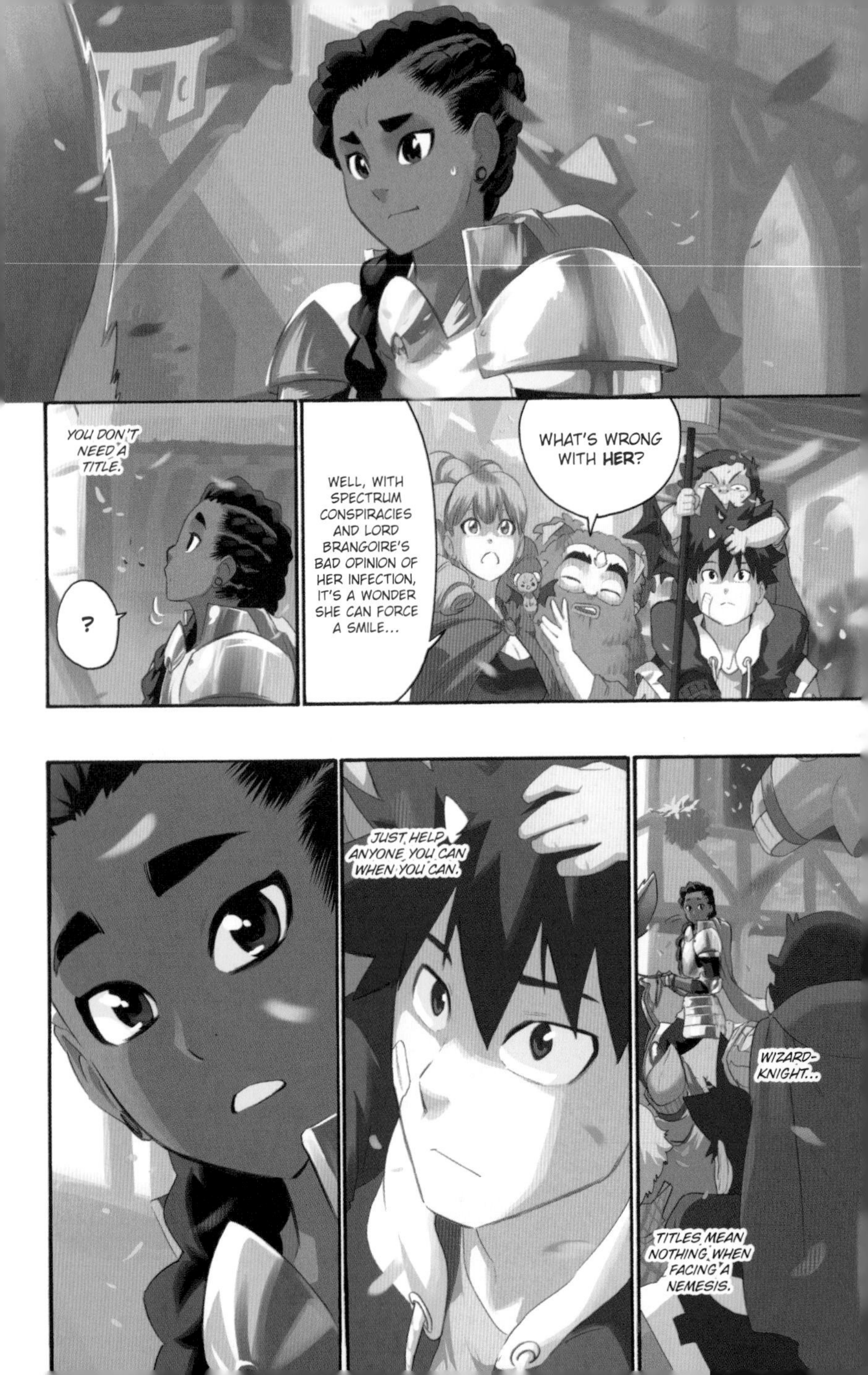
YOU DON'T NEED A TITLE.
?
WHAT'S WRONG WITH **HER**?
WELL, WITH SPECTRUM CONSPIRACIES AND LORD BRANGOIRE'S BAD OPINION OF HER INFECTION, IT'S A WONDER SHE CAN FORCE A SMILE...
JUST HELP ANYONE YOU CAN WHEN YOU CAN.
WIZARD-KNIGHT...
TITLES MEAN NOTHING WHEN FACING A NEMESIS.

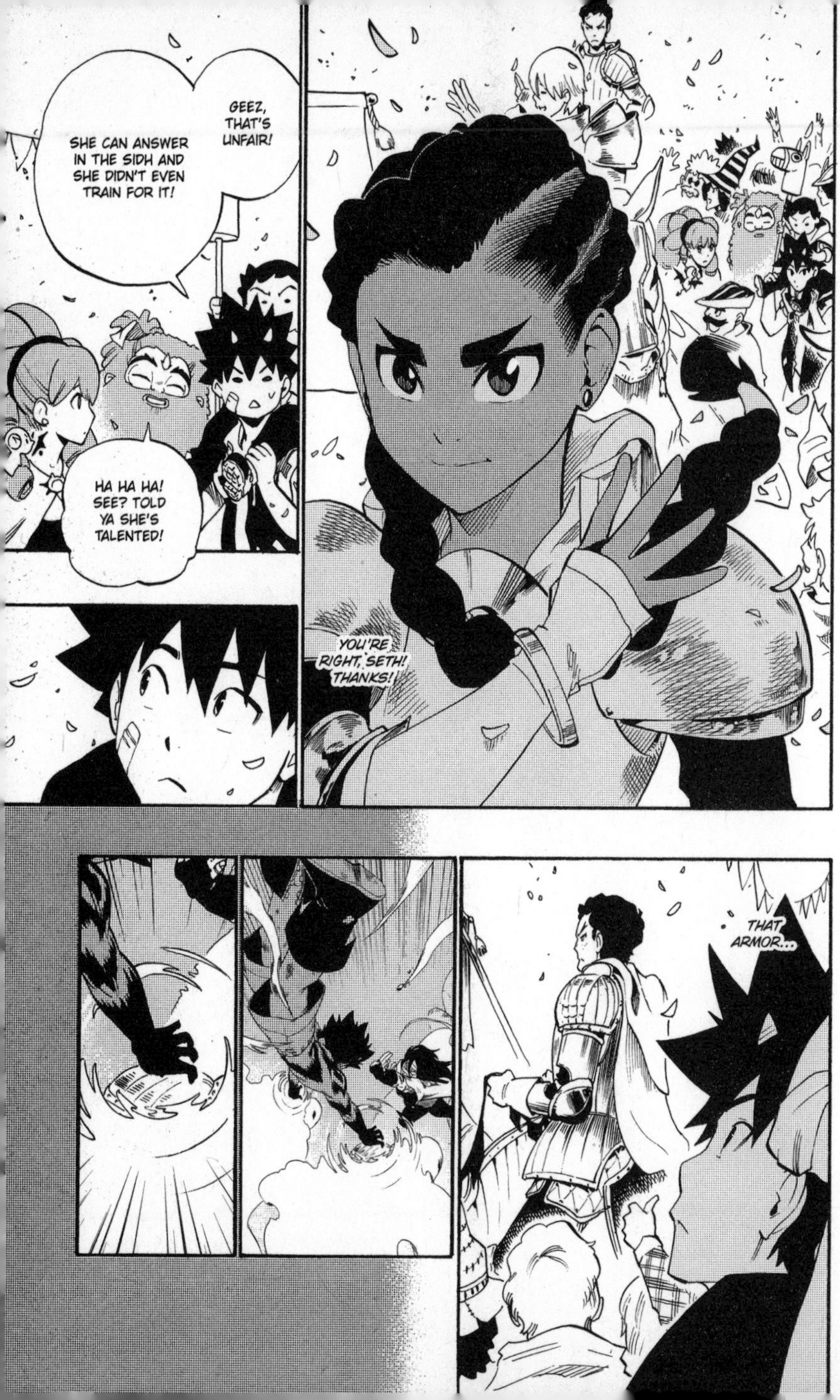
SHE CAN ANSWER IN THE SIDH AND SHE DIDN'T EVEN TRAIN FOR IT!
GEEZ, THAT'S UNFAIR!
HA HA HA! SEE? TOLD YA SHE'S TALENTED!
YOU'RE RIGHT, SETH! THANKS!
THAT ARMOR...

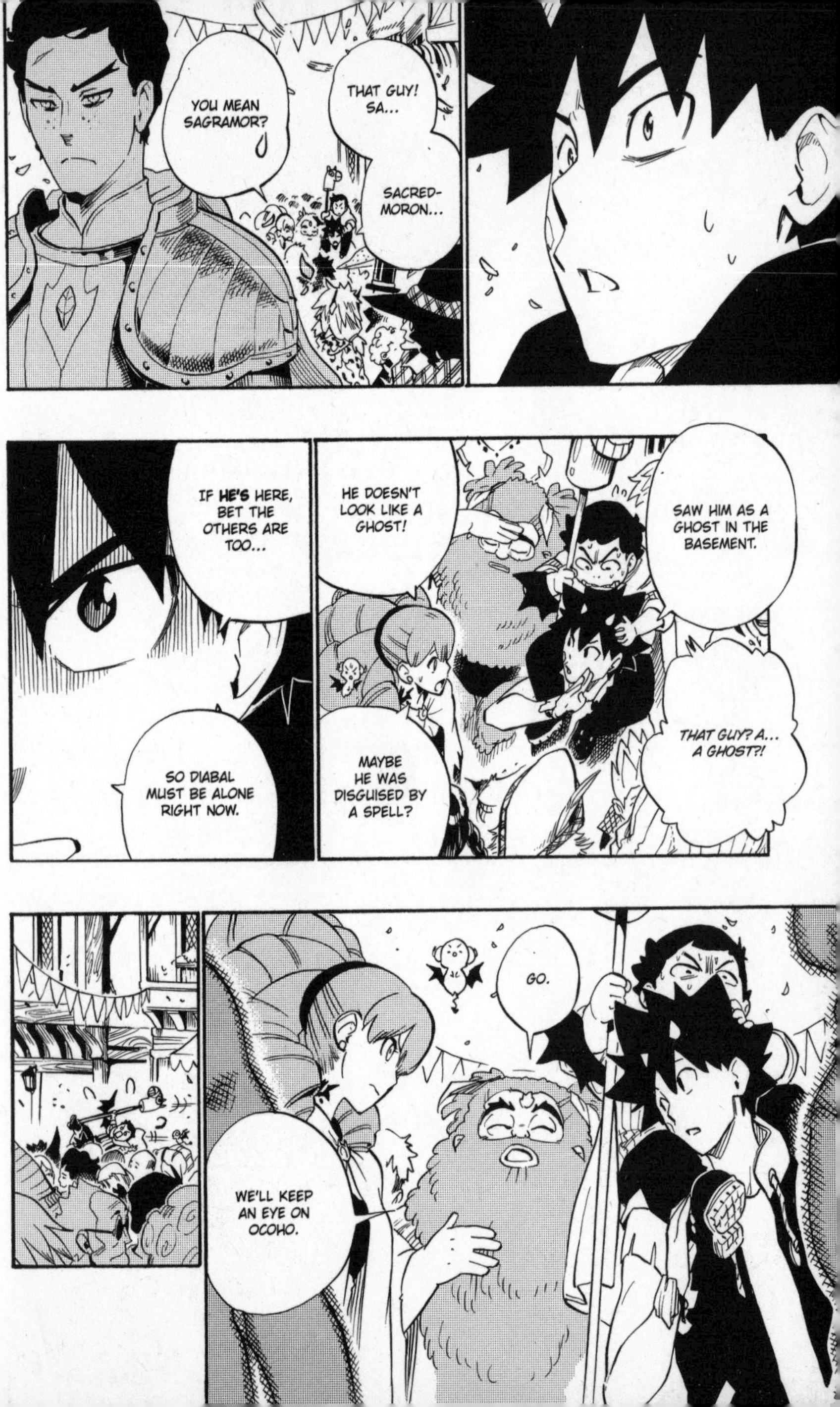
THAT GUY! SA...
SACRED-MORON...
YOU MEAN SAGRAMOR?
SAW HIM AS A GHOST IN THE BASEMENT.
THAT GUY? A... A GHOST?!
HE DOESN'T LOOK LIKE A GHOST!
MAYBE HE WAS DISGUISED BY A SPELL?
IF HE'S HERE, BET THE OTHERS ARE TOO...
SO DIABAL MUST BE ALONE RIGHT NOW.
GO.
WE'LL KEEP AN EYE ON OCOHO.

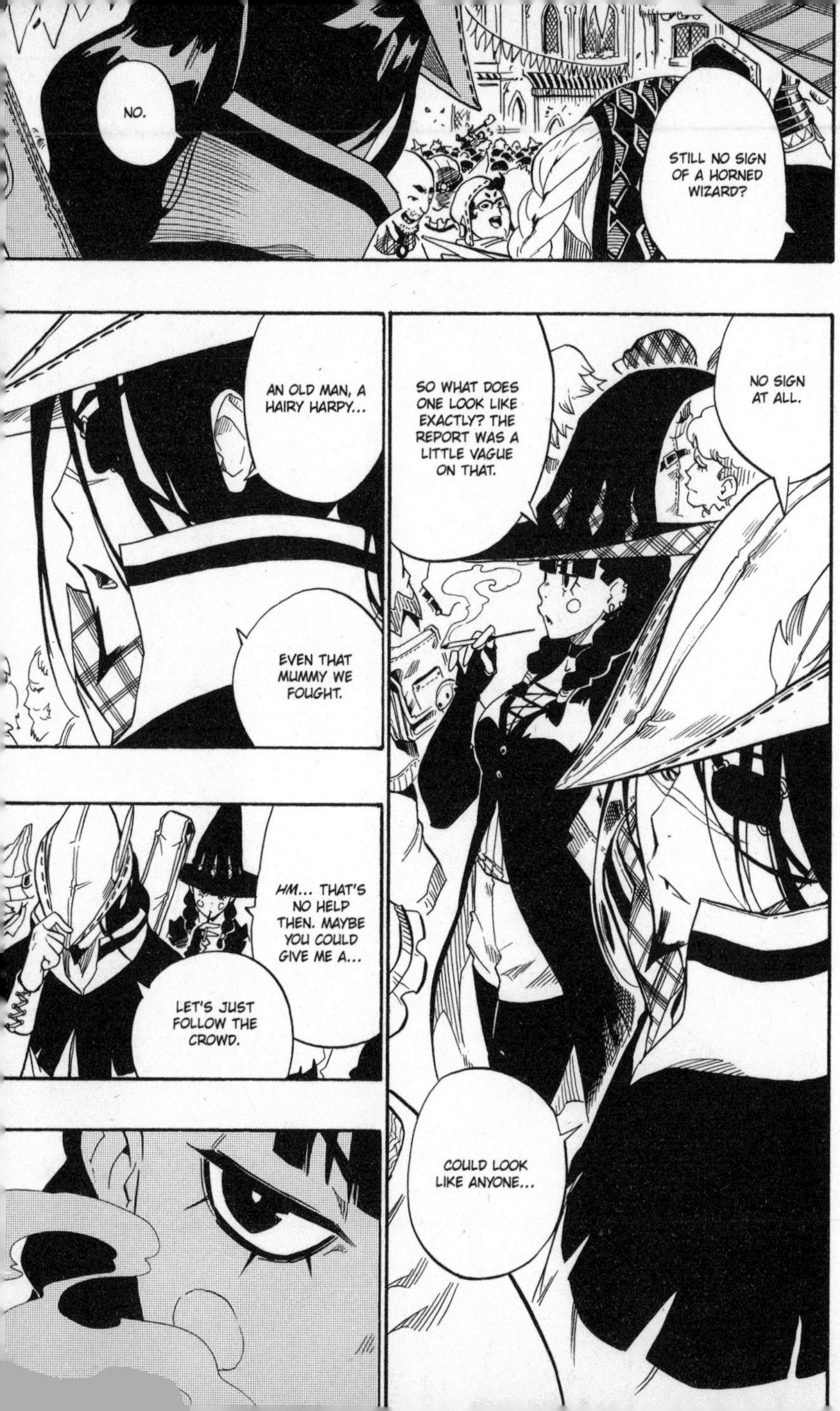
STILL NO SIGN OF A HORNED WIZARD?
NO.
NO SIGN AT ALL.
SO WHAT DOES ONE LOOK LIKE EXACTLY? THE REPORT WAS A LITTLE VAGUE ON THAT.
COULD LOOK LIKE ANYONE...
AN OLD MAN, A HAIRY HARPY...
EVEN THAT MUMMY WE FOUGHT.
HM... THAT'S NO HELP THEN. MAYBE YOU COULD GIVE ME A...
LET'S JUST FOLLOW THE CROWD.

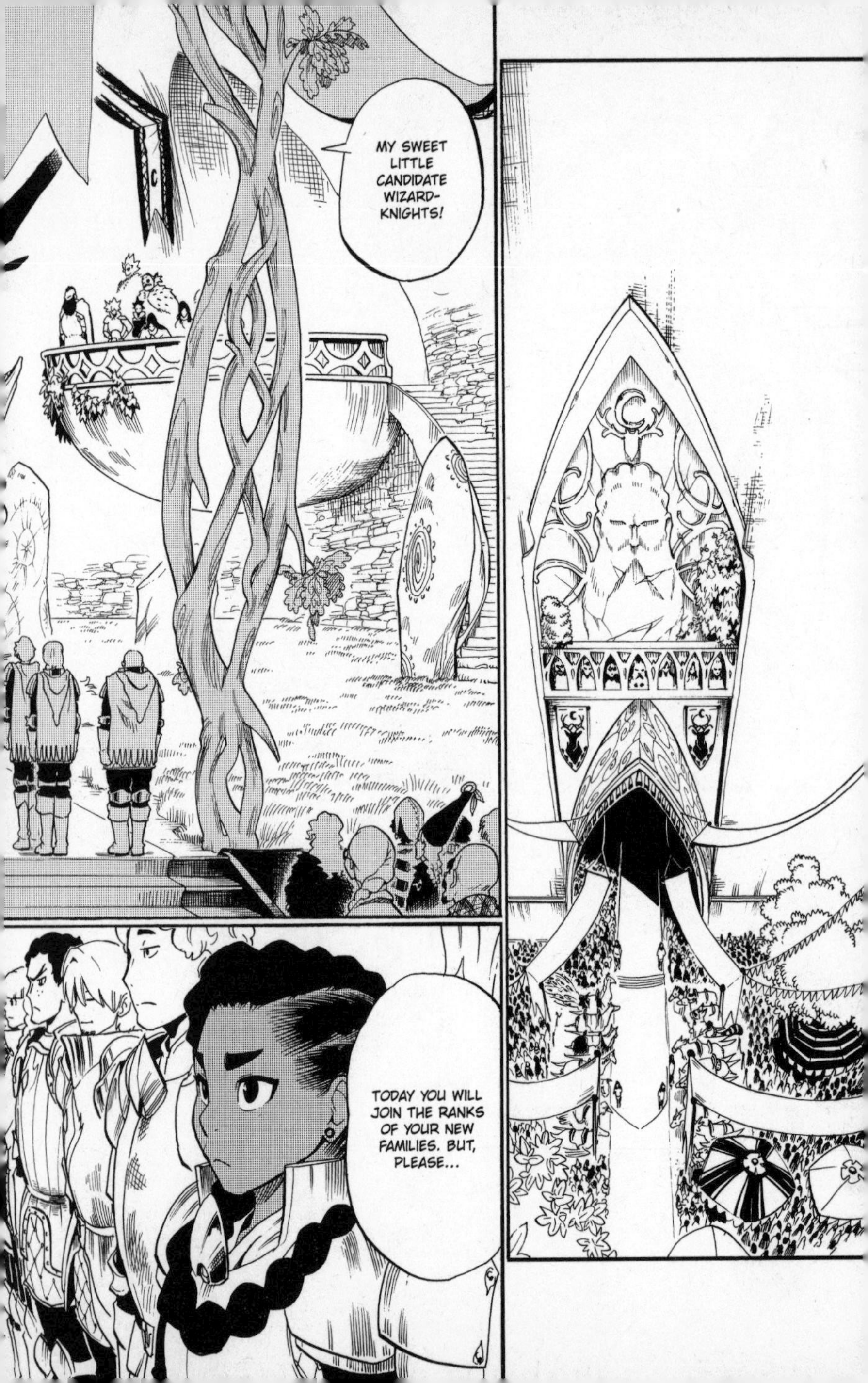
MY SWEET LITTLE CANDIDATE WIZARD-KNIGHTS!
TODAY YOU WILL JOIN THE RANKS OF YOUR NEW FAMILIES. BUT, PLEASE...

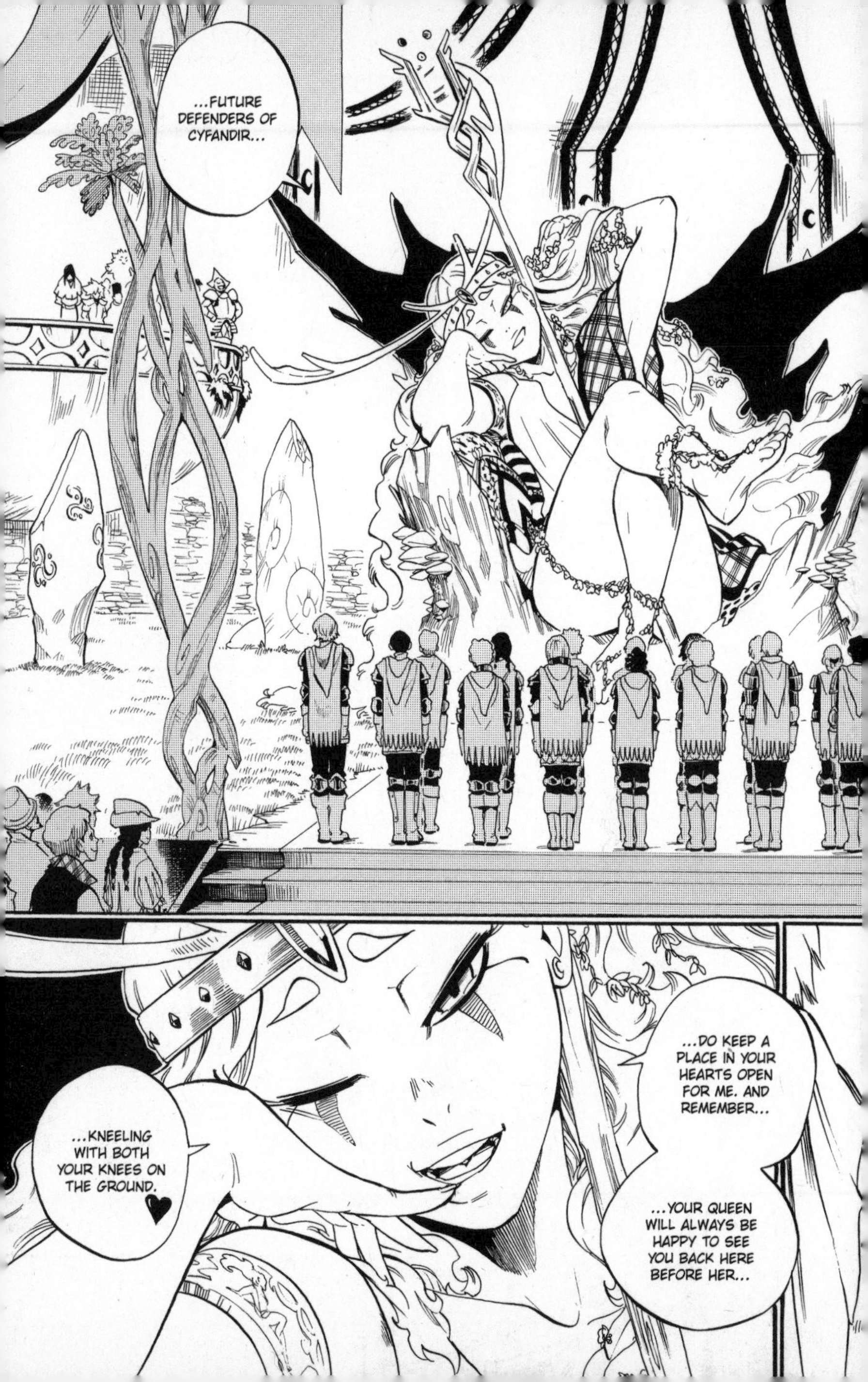
...FUTURE DEFENDERS OF CYFANDIR...
...DO KEEP A PLACE IN YOUR HEARTS OPEN FOR ME. AND REMEMBER...
...YOUR QUEEN WILL ALWAYS BE HAPPY TO SEE YOU BACK HERE BEFORE HER...
...KNEELING WITH BOTH YOUR KNEES ON THE GROUND. ♥

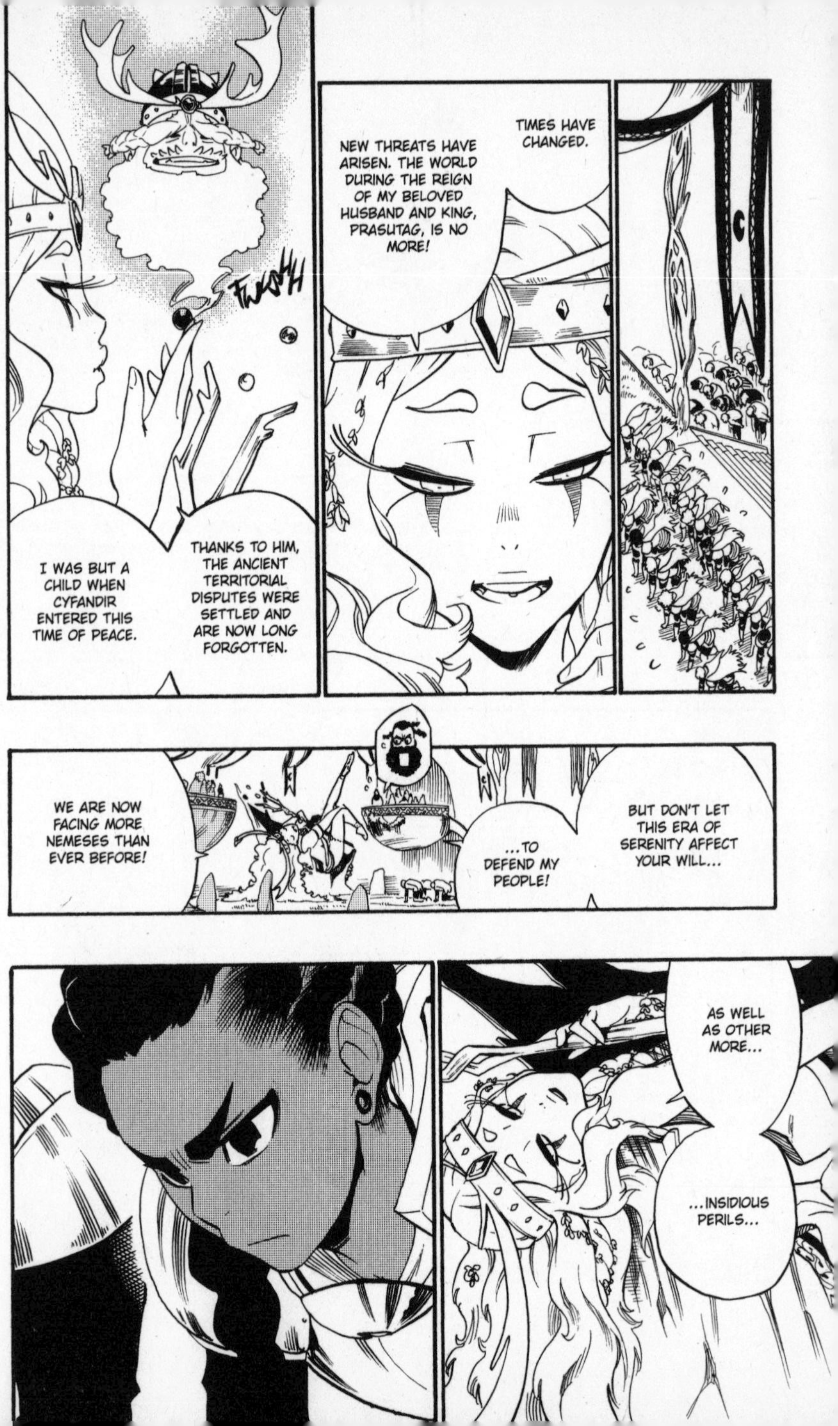
TIMES HAVE CHANGED.
NEW THREATS HAVE ARISEN. THE WORLD DURING THE REIGN OF MY BELOVED HUSBAND AND KING, PRASUTAG, IS NO MORE!
THANKS TO HIM, THE ANCIENT TERRITORIAL DISPUTES WERE SETTLED AND ARE NOW LONG FORGOTTEN.
I WAS BUT A CHILD WHEN CYFANDIR ENTERED THIS TIME OF PEACE.
BUT DON'T LET THIS ERA OF SERENITY AFFECT YOUR WILL...
...TO DEFEND MY PEOPLE!
WE ARE NOW FACING MORE NEMESES THAN EVER BEFORE!
AS WELL AS OTHER MORE...
...INSIDIOUS PERILS...

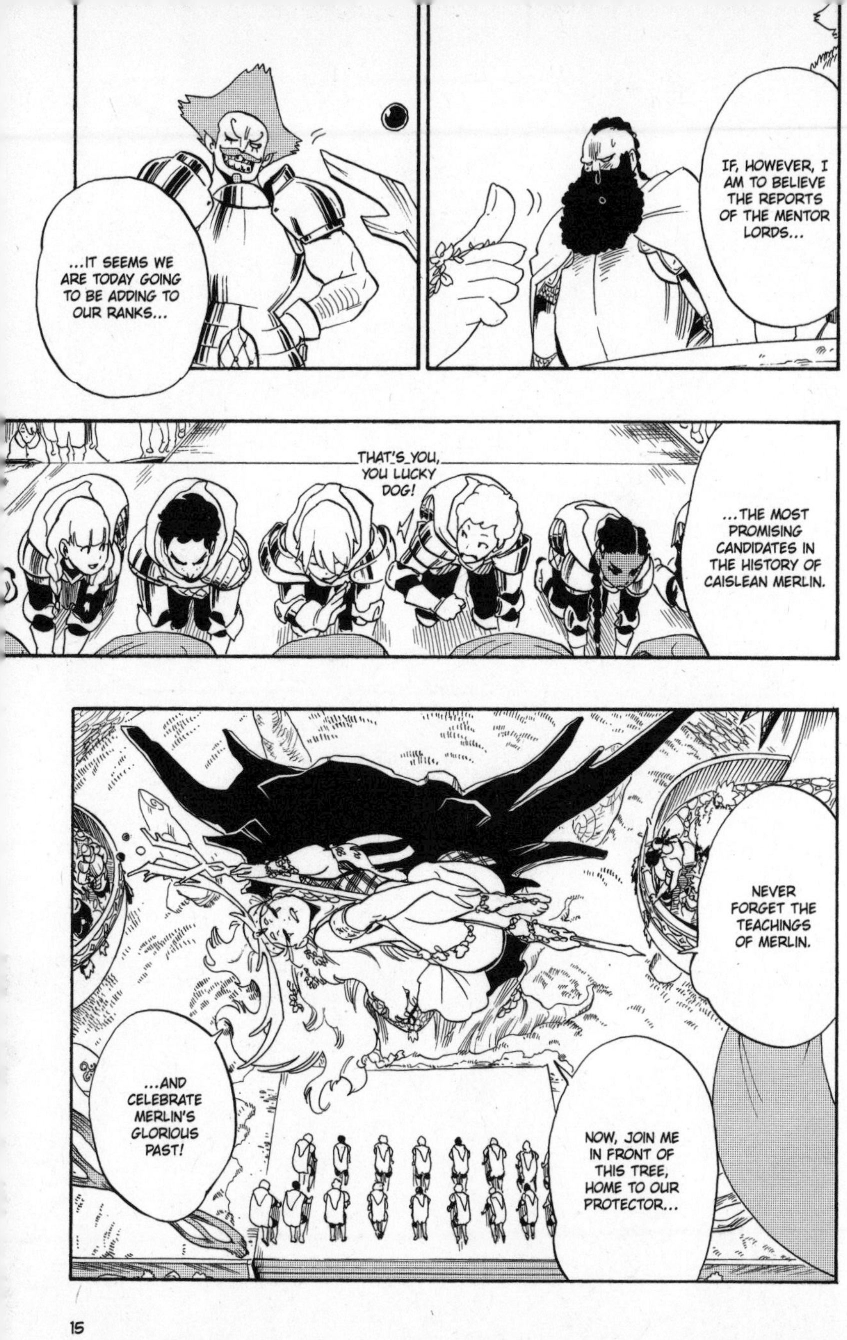
IF, HOWEVER, I AM TO BELIEVE THE REPORTS OF THE MENTOR LORDS...
...IT SEEMS WE ARE TODAY GOING TO BE ADDING TO OUR RANKS...
...THE MOST PROMISING CANDIDATES IN THE HISTORY OF CAISLEAN MERLIN.
THAT'S YOU, YOU LUCKY DOG!
NEVER FORGET THE TEACHINGS OF MERLIN.
NOW, JOIN ME IN FRONT OF THIS TREE, HOME TO OUR PROTECTOR...
...AND CELEBRATE MERLIN'S GLORIOUS PAST!

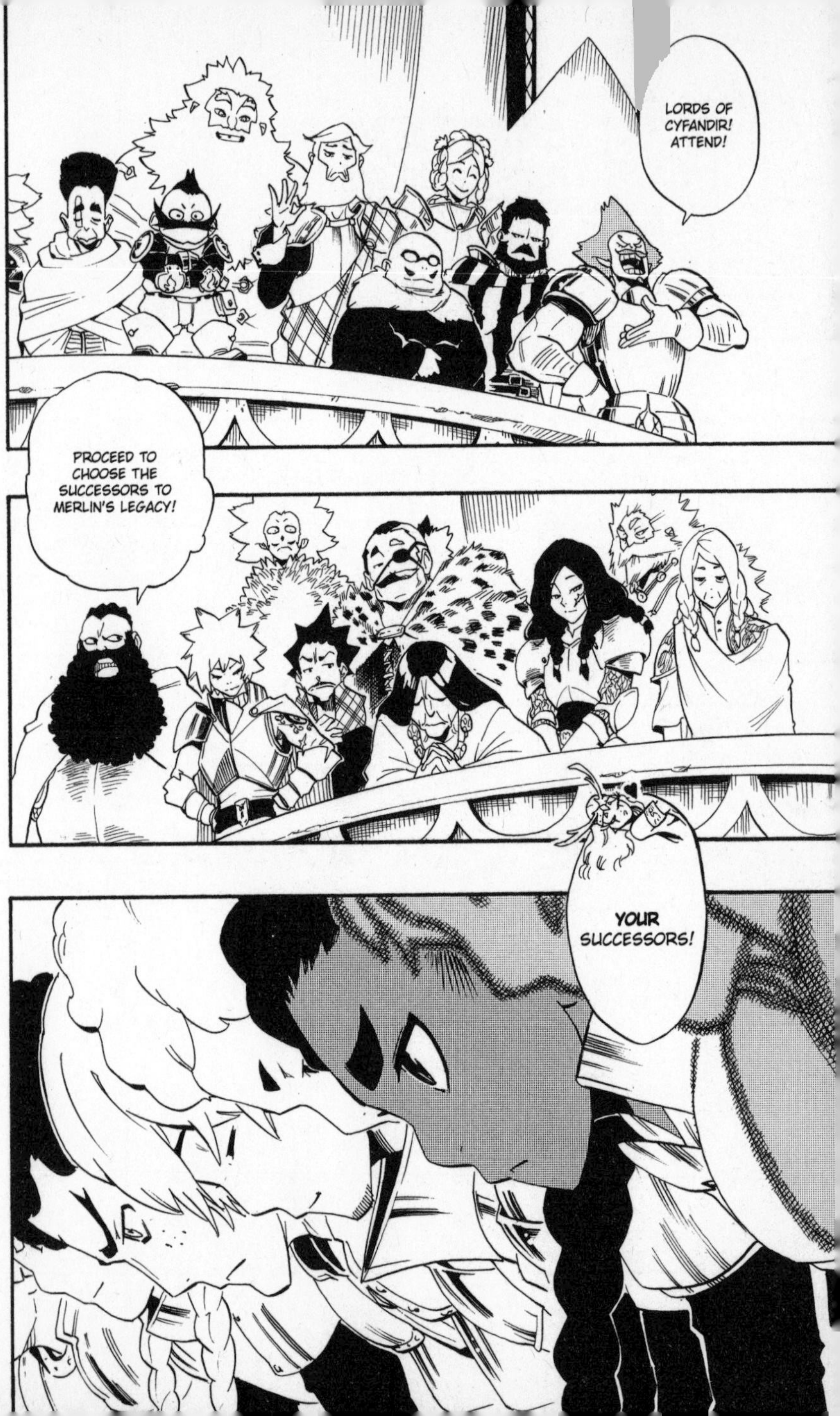
LORDS OF CYFANDIR! ATTEND!
PROCEED TO CHOOSE THE SUCCESSORS TO MERLIN'S LEGACY!
YOUR SUCCESSORS!

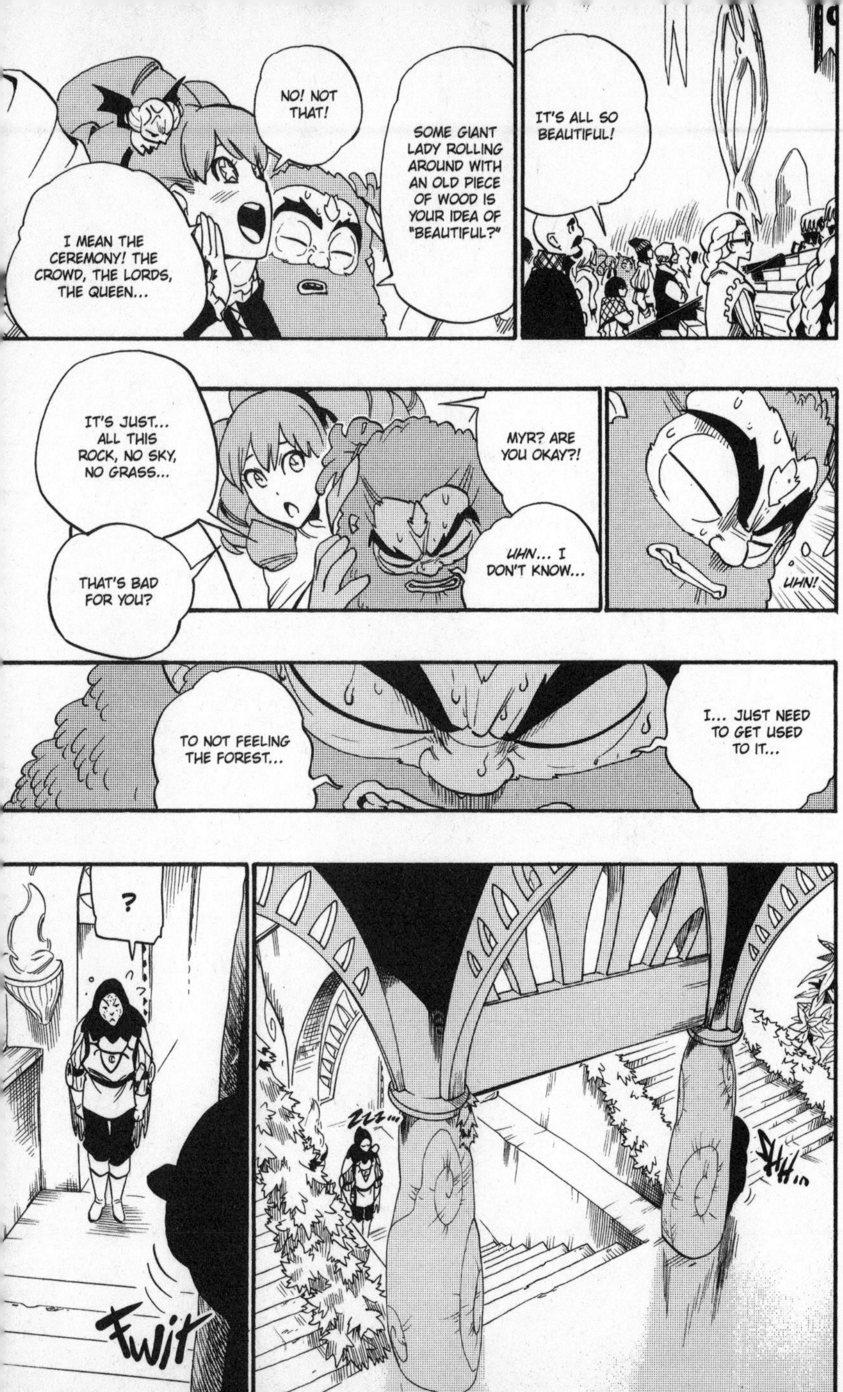
IT'S ALL SO BEAUTIFUL!
SOME GIANT LADY ROLLING AROUND WITH AN OLD PIECE OF WOOD IS YOUR IDEA OF "BEAUTIFUL?"
NO! NOT THAT!
I MEAN THE CEREMONY! THE CROWD, THE LORDS, THE QUEEN...
UHN!
MYR? ARE YOU OKAY?!
UHN... I DON'T KNOW...
IT'S JUST... ALL THIS ROCK, NO SKY, NO GRASS...
THAT'S BAD FOR YOU?
I... JUST NEED TO GET USED TO IT...
TO NOT FEELING THE FOREST...
ZZZ...
SHH...
?
FWIT

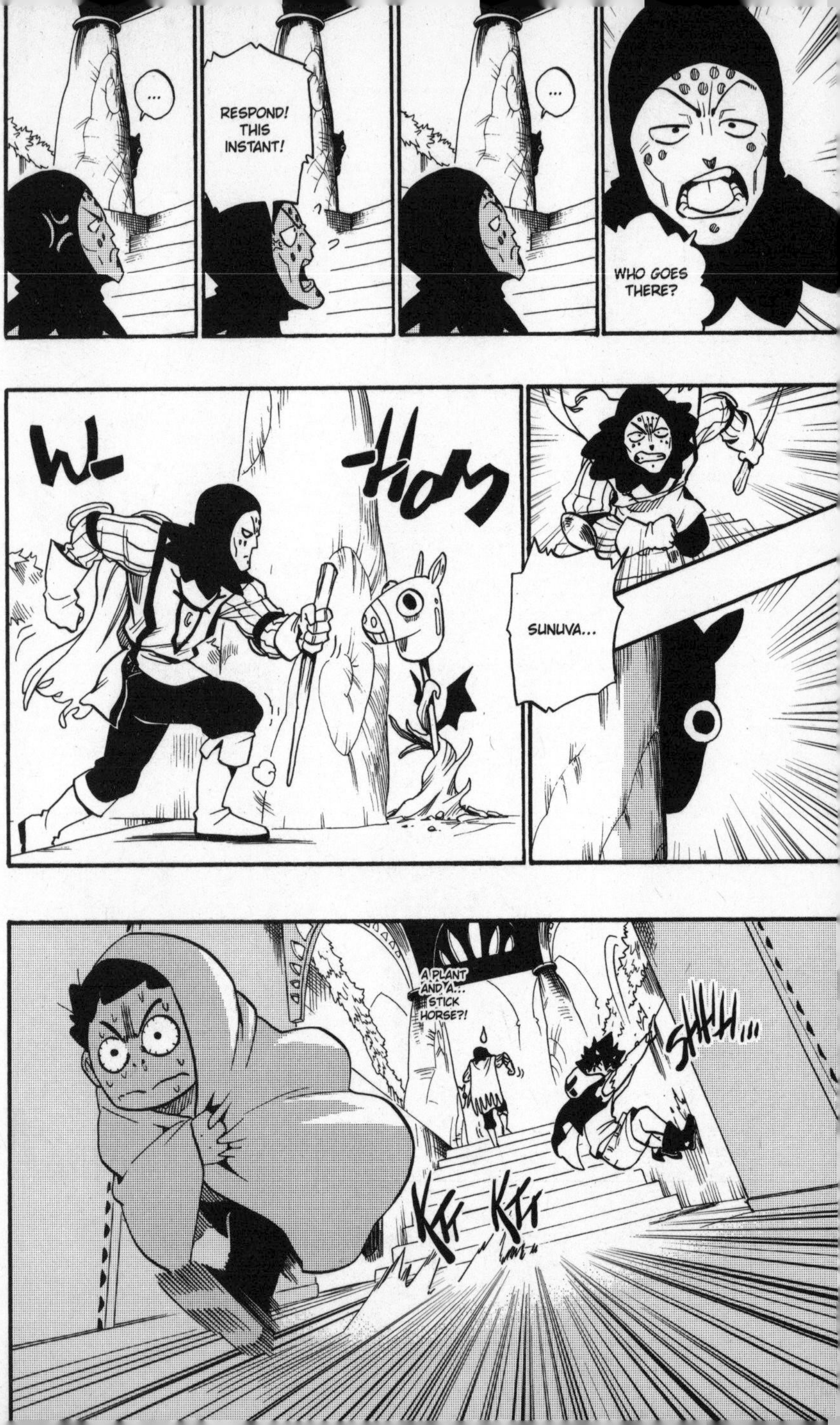
WHO GOES THERE?
...
RESPOND! THIS INSTANT!
...
SUNUVA...
A PLANT AND A... STICK HORSE?!

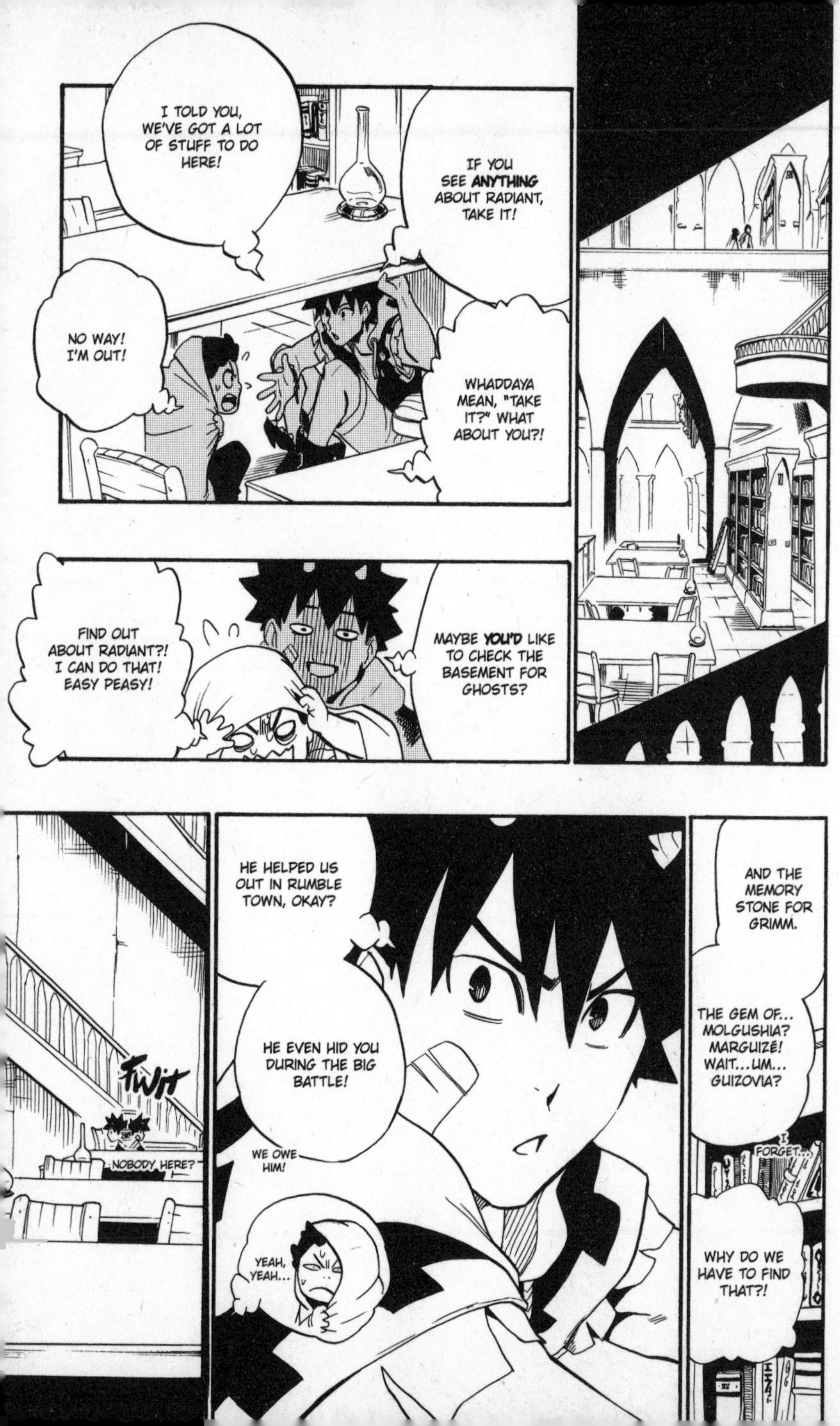
IF YOU SEE ANYTHING ABOUT RADIANT, TAKE IT!
WHADDAYA MEAN, "TAKE IT?" WHAT ABOUT YOU?!
I TOLD YOU, WE'VE GOT A LOT OF STUFF TO DO HERE!
NO WAY! I'M OUT!
MAYBE YOU'D LIKE TO CHECK THE BASEMENT FOR GHOSTS?
FIND OUT ABOUT RADIANT?! I CAN DO THAT! EASY PEASY!
AND THE MEMORY STONE FOR GRIMM.
THE GEM OF... MOLGUSHIA? MARGUIZÉ! WAIT...UM... GUIZOVIA?
I FORGET...
WHY DO WE HAVE TO FIND THAT?!
HE HELPED US OUT IN RUMBLE TOWN, OKAY?
HE EVEN HID YOU DURING THE BIG BATTLE!
WE OWE HIM!
YEAH, YEAH...
FWIT
NOBODY HERE?

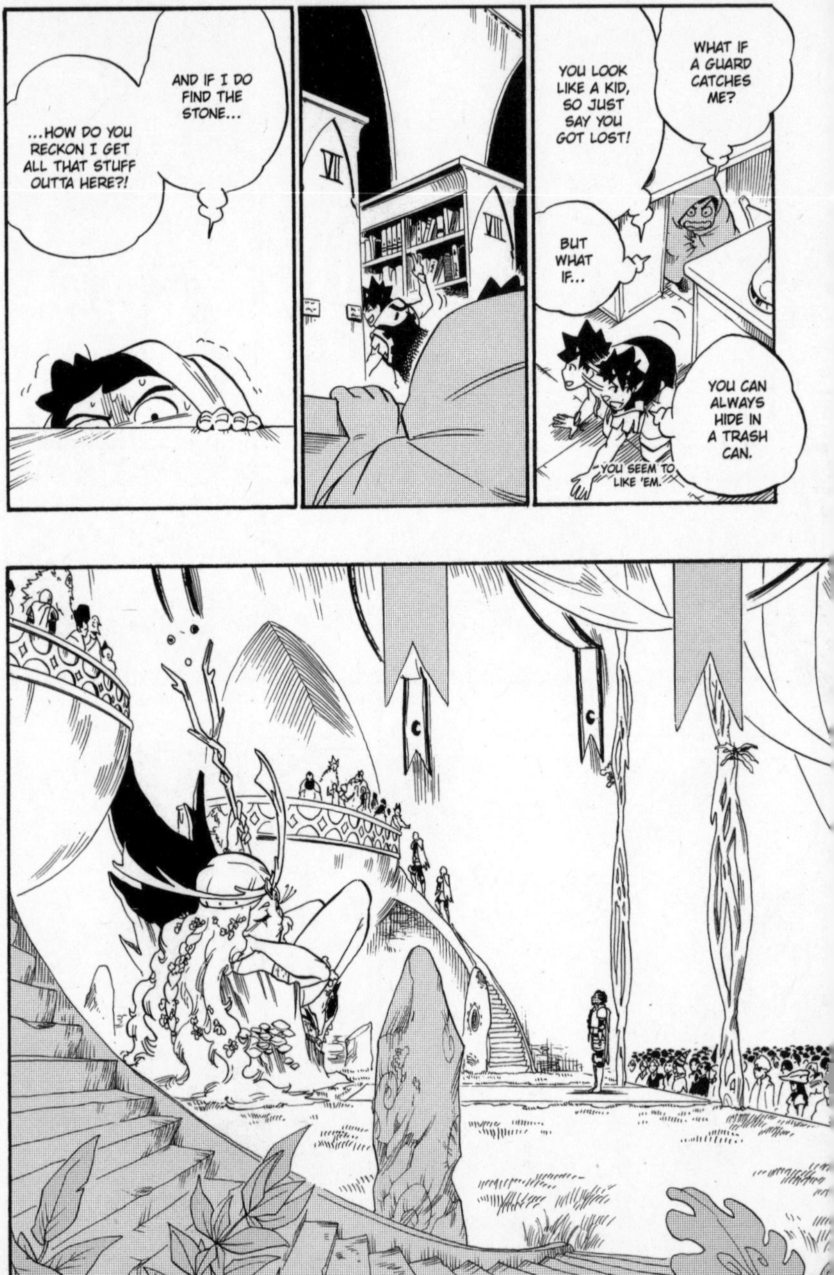
WHAT IF A GUARD CATCHES ME?
YOU LOOK LIKE A KID, SO JUST SAY YOU GOT LOST!
BUT WHAT IF...
YOU CAN ALWAYS HIDE IN A TRASH CAN.
YOU SEEM TO LIKE 'EM.
AND IF I DO FIND THE STONE...
...HOW DO YOU RECKON I GET ALL THAT STUFF OUTTA HERE?!

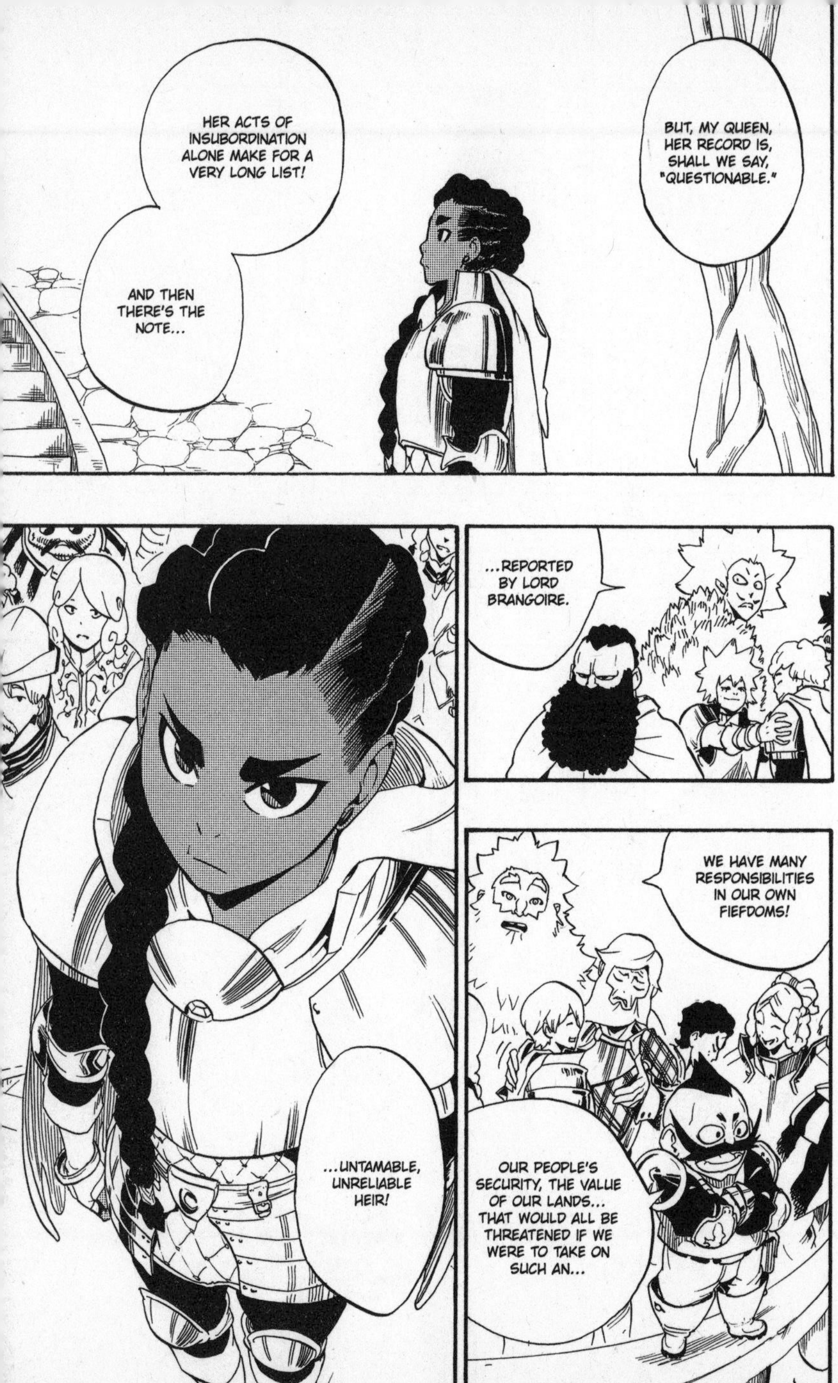
BUT, MY QUEEN, HER RECORD IS, SHALL WE SAY, "QUESTIONABLE."
HER ACTS OF INSUBORDINATION ALONE MAKE FOR A VERY LONG LIST!
AND THEN THERE'S THE NOTE...
...REPORTED BY LORD BRANGOIRE.
WE HAVE MANY RESPONSIBILITIES IN OUR OWN FIEFDOMS!
OUR PEOPLE'S SECURITY, THE VALUE OF OUR LANDS... THAT WOULD ALL BE THREATENED IF WE WERE TO TAKE ON SUCH AN...
...UNTAMABLE, UNRELIABLE HEIR!

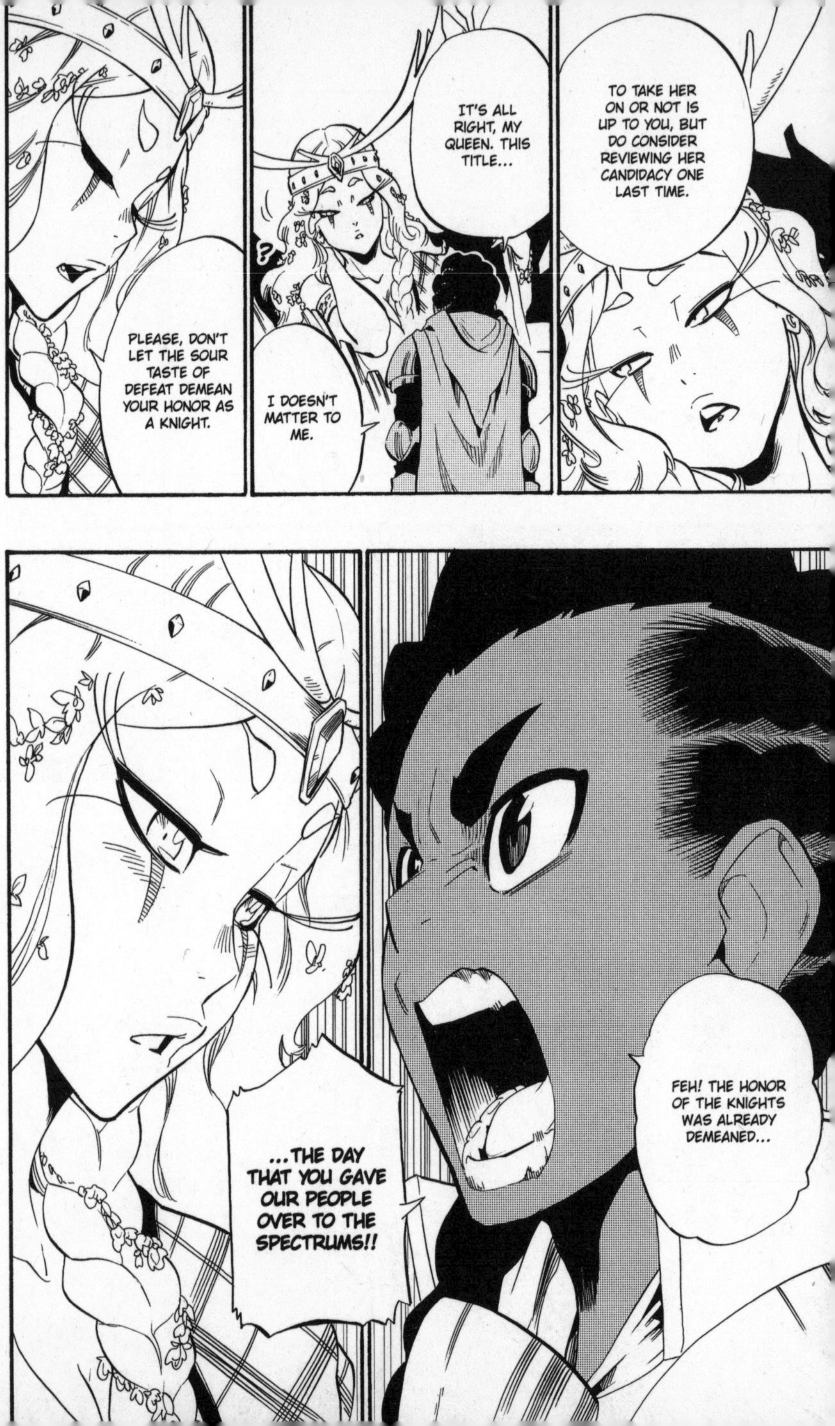
TO TAKE HER ON OR NOT IS UP TO YOU, BUT DO CONSIDER REVIEWING HER CANDIDACY ONE LAST TIME.
IT'S ALL RIGHT, MY QUEEN. THIS TITLE...
I DOESN'T MATTER TO ME.
PLEASE, DON'T LET THE SOUR TASTE OF DEFEAT DEMEAN YOUR HONOR AS A KNIGHT.
FEH! THE HONOR OF THE KNIGHTS WAS ALREADY DEMEANED...
...THE DAY THAT YOU GAVE OUR PEOPLE OVER TO THE SPECTRUMS!!

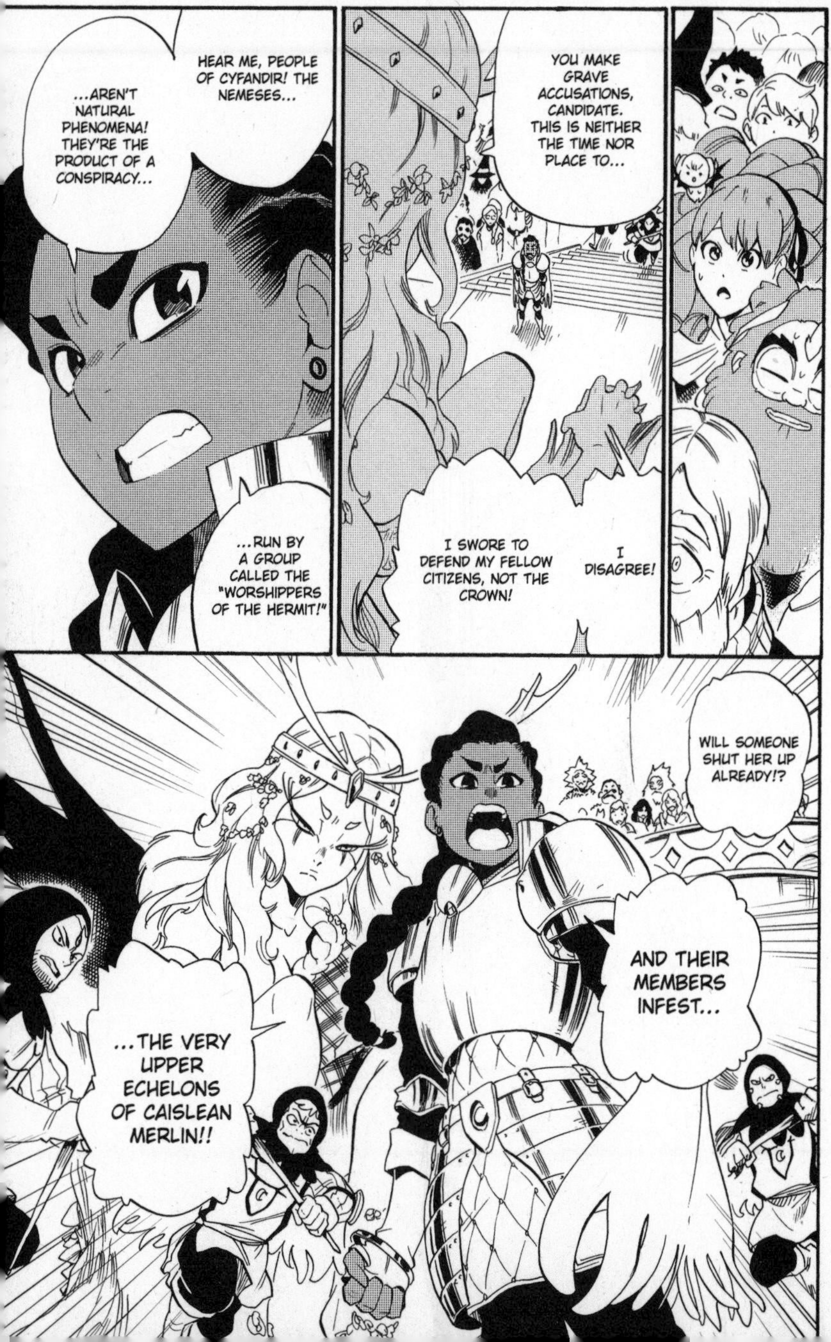
HEAR ME, PEOPLE OF CYFANDIR! THE NEMESES...
...AREN'T NATURAL PHENOMENA! THEY'RE THE PRODUCT OF A CONSPIRACY...
...RUN BY A GROUP CALLED THE "WORSHIPPERS OF THE HERMIT!"
YOU MAKE GRAVE ACCUSATIONS, CANDIDATE. THIS IS NEITHER THE TIME NOR PLACE TO...
I DISAGREE!
I SWORE TO DEFEND MY FELLOW CITIZENS, NOT THE CROWN!
AND THEIR MEMBERS INFEST...
...THE VERY UPPER ECHELONS OF CAISLEAN MERLIN!!
WILL SOMEONE SHUT HER UP ALREADY!?

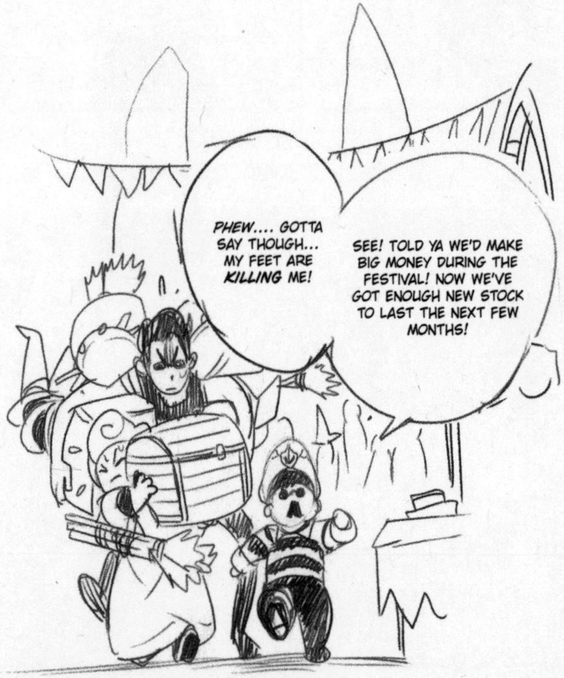
SEE! TOLD YA WE'D MAKE BIG MONEY DURING THE FESTIVAL! NOW WE'VE GOT ENOUGH NEW STOCK TO LAST THE NEXT FEW MONTHS!
PHEW.... GOTTA SAY THOUGH... MY FEET ARE *KILLING* ME!

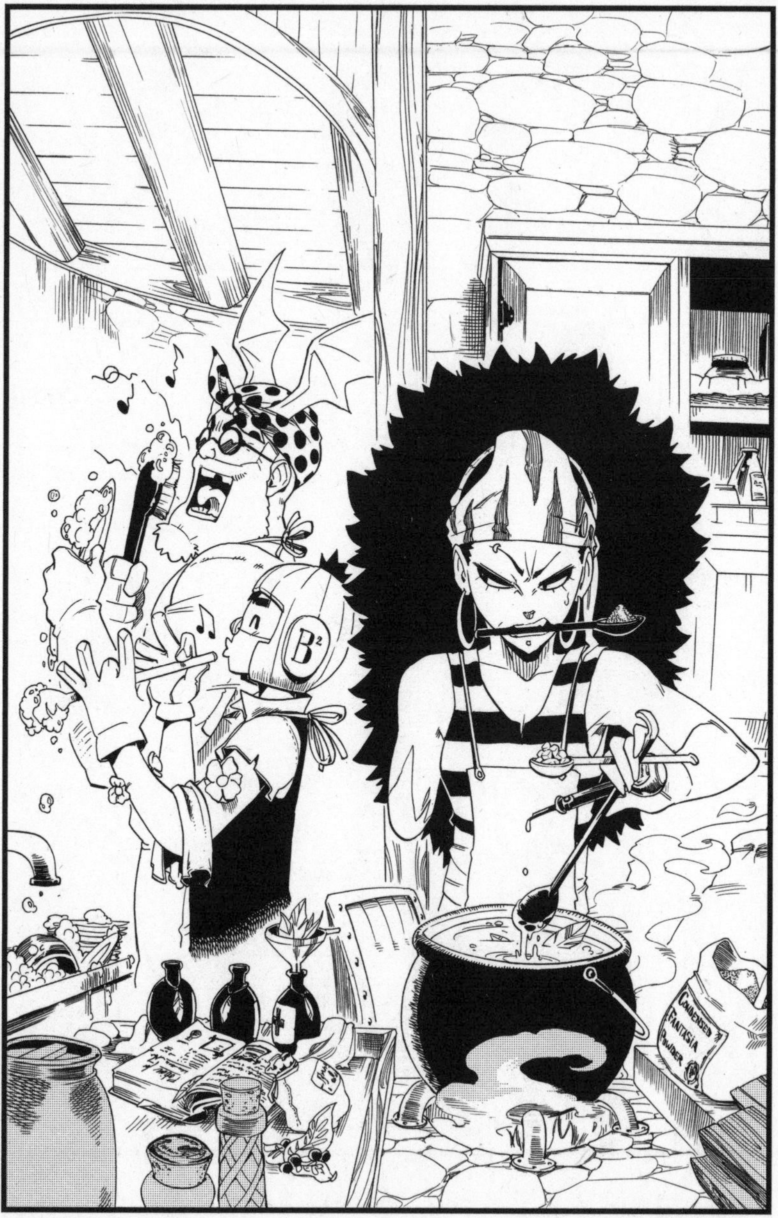
B²
CONDENSED FANTASIA POWDER

CHAPTER 54 **B.O.T.**

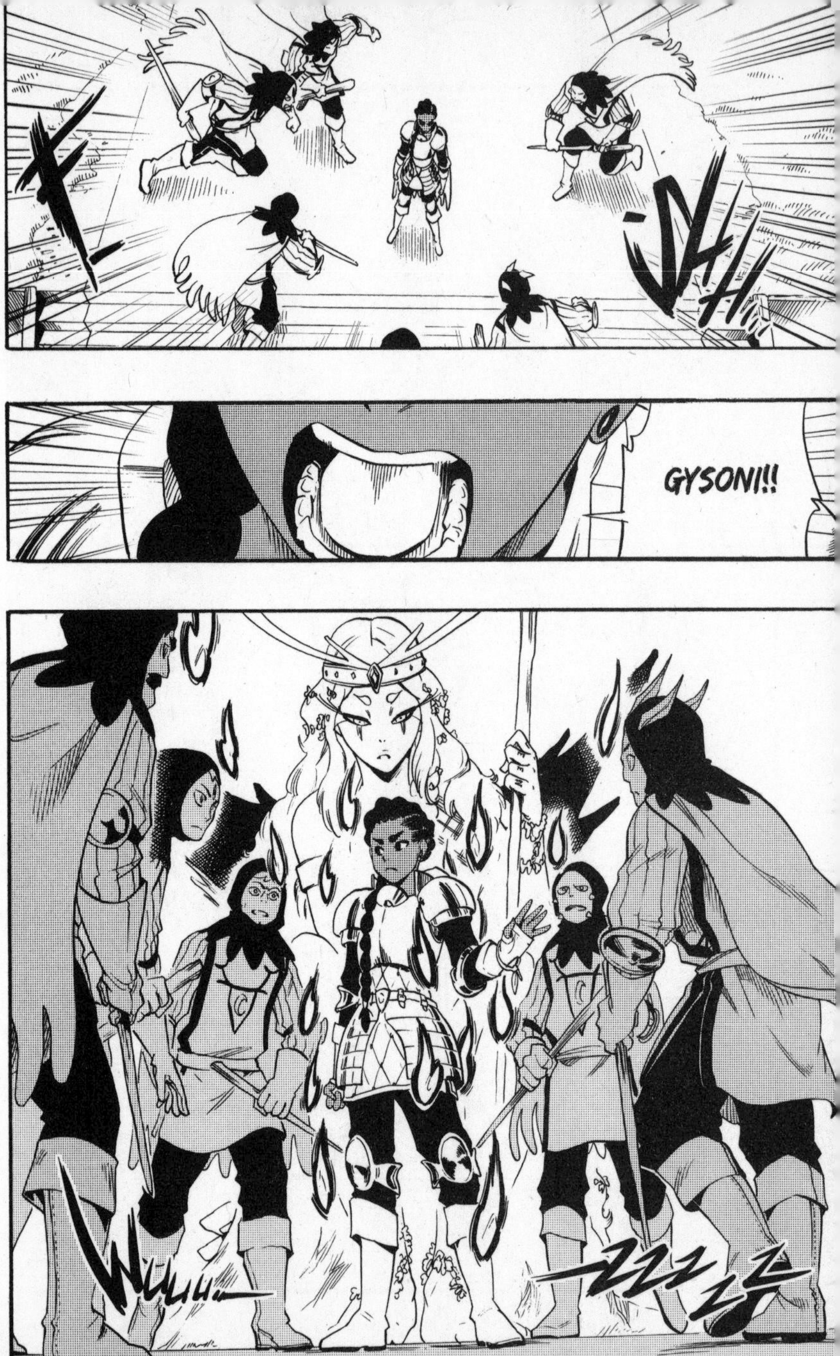
GYSONI!!

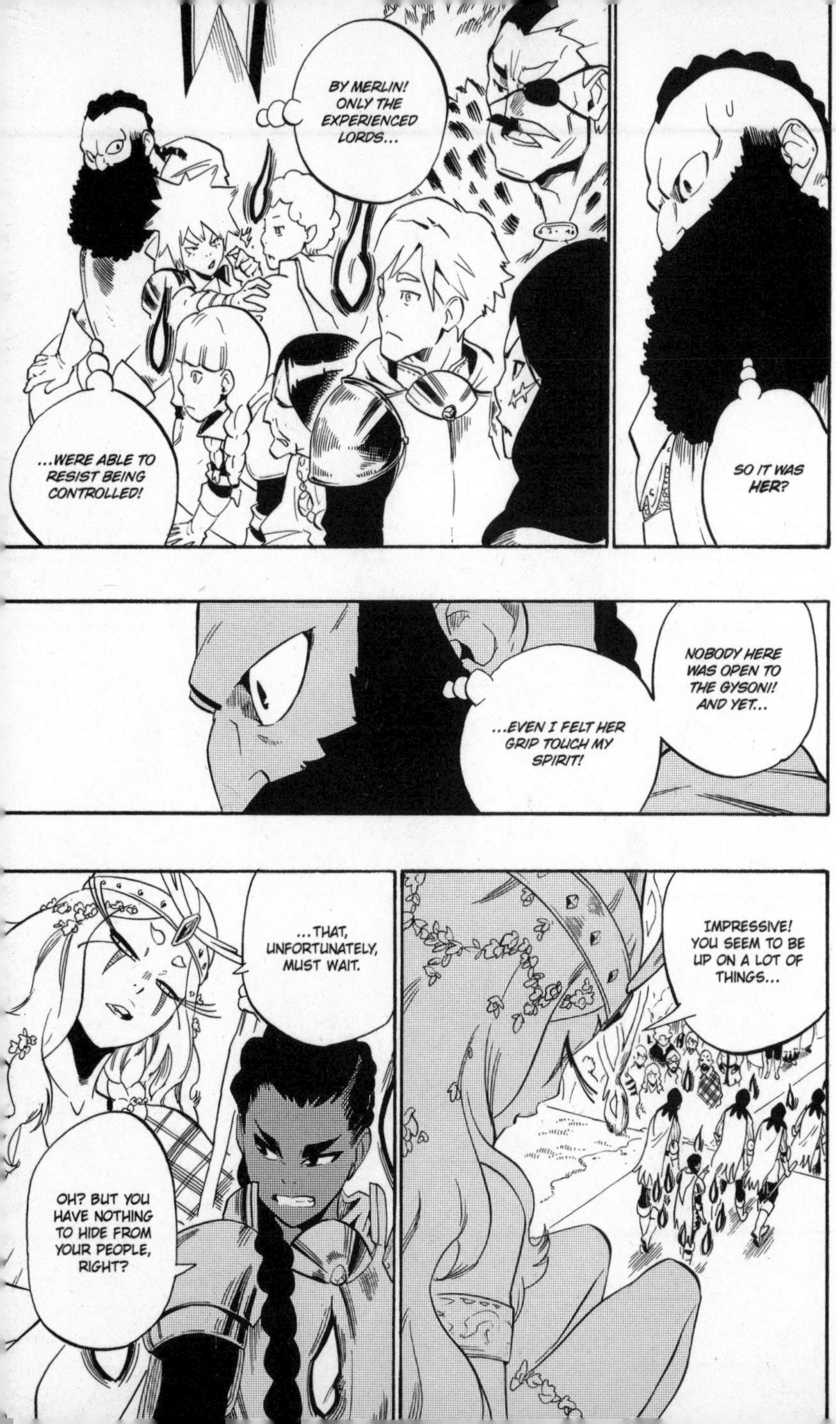
SO IT WAS HER?
BY MERLIN! ONLY THE EXPERIENCED LORDS...
...WERE ABLE TO RESIST BEING CONTROLLED!
NOBODY HERE WAS OPEN TO THE GYSONI! AND YET...
...EVEN I FELT HER GRIP TOUCH MY SPIRIT!
IMPRESSIVE! YOU SEEM TO BE UP ON A LOT OF THINGS...
...THAT, UNFORTUNATELY, MUST WAIT.
OH? BUT YOU HAVE NOTHING TO HIDE FROM YOUR PEOPLE, RIGHT?

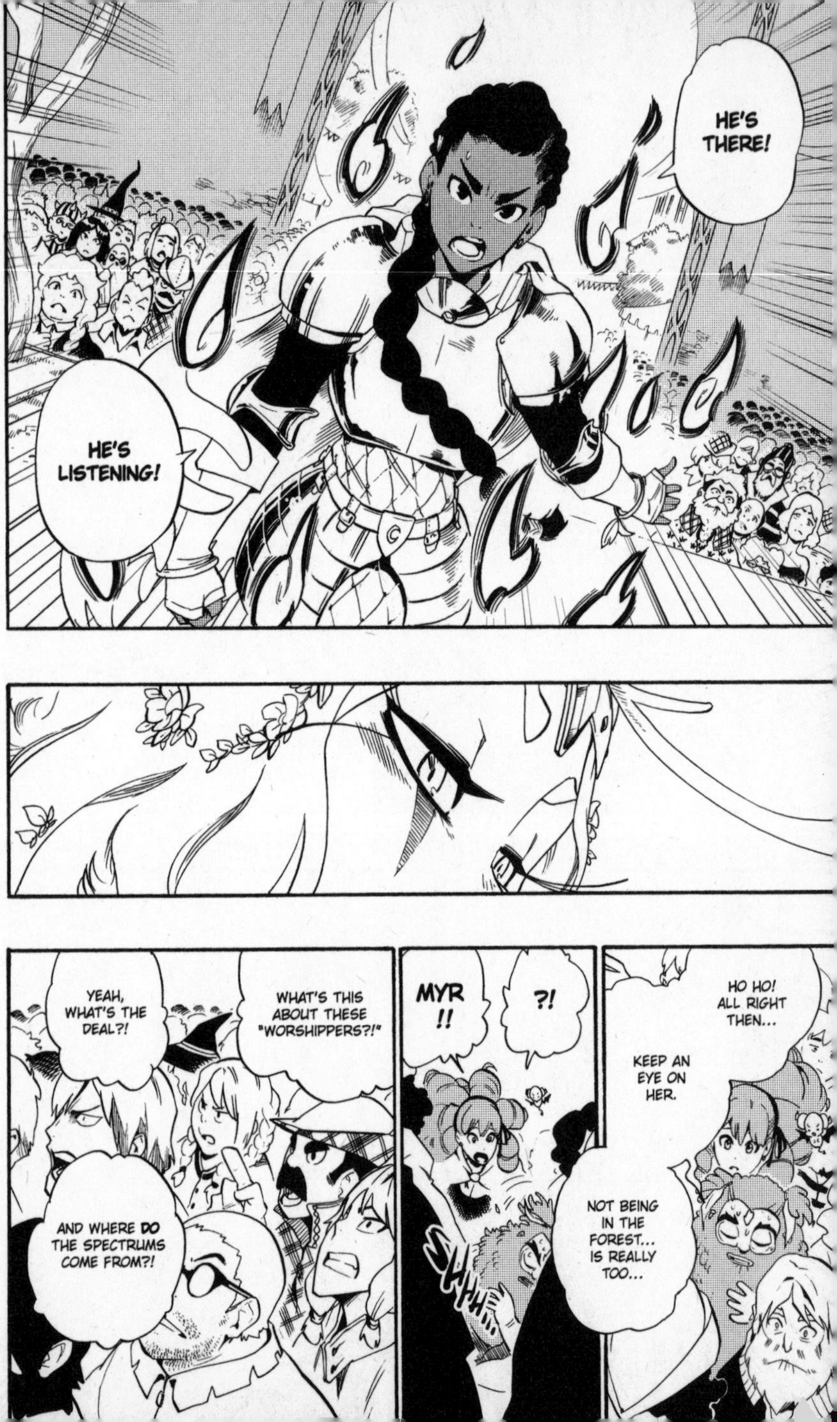
HE'S THERE!
HE'S LISTENING!
HO HO! ALL RIGHT THEN...
KEEP AN EYE ON HER.
NOT BEING IN THE FOREST... IS REALLY TOO...
?!
MYR !!
SHHH
WHAT'S THIS ABOUT THESE "WORSHIPPERS?!"
YEAH, WHAT'S THE DEAL?!
AND WHERE DO THE SPECTRUMS COME FROM?!

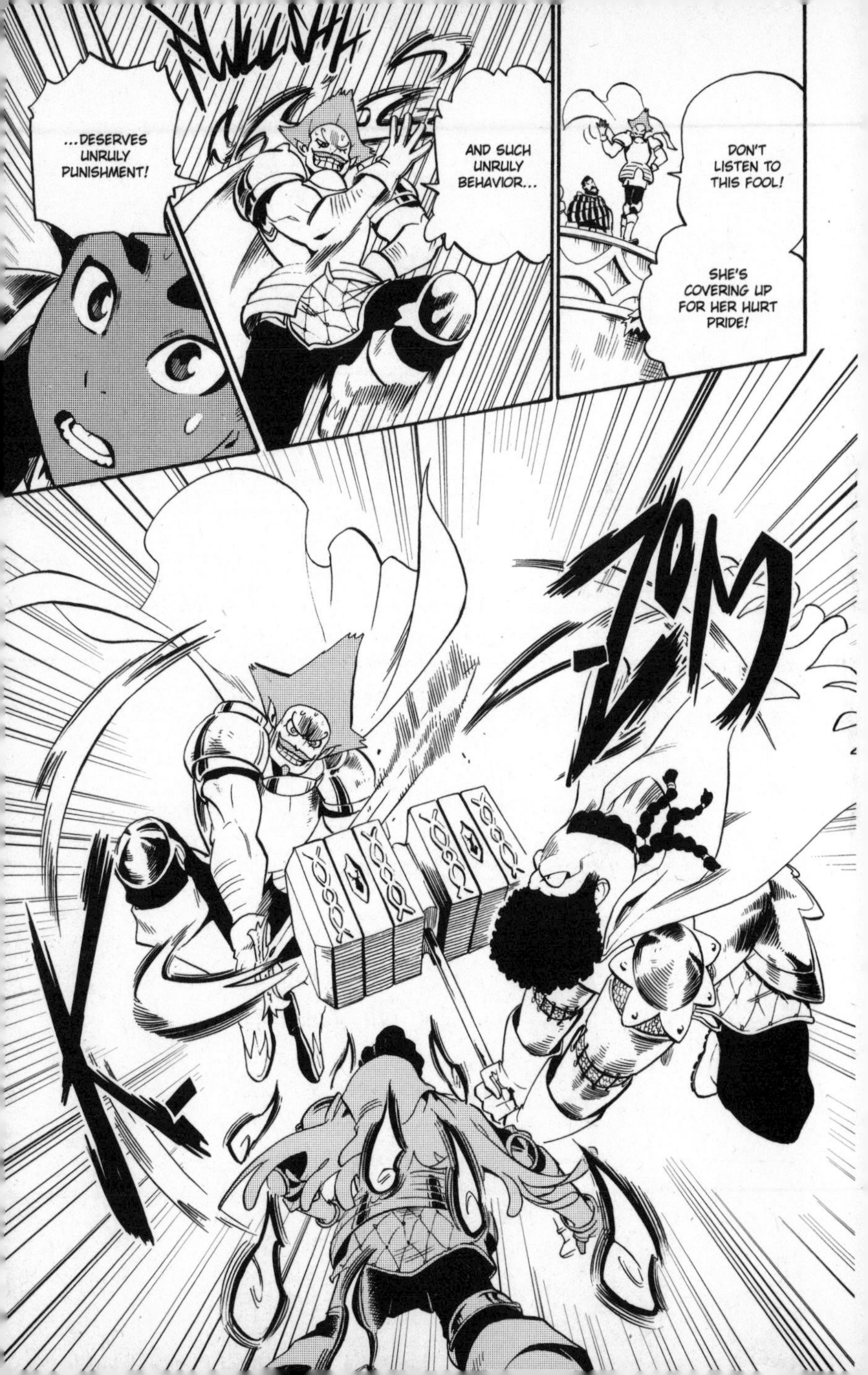
DON'T LISTEN TO THIS FOOL!
SHE'S COVERING UP FOR HER HURT PRIDE!
AND SUCH UNRULY BEHAVIOR...
...DESERVES UNRULY PUNISHMENT!

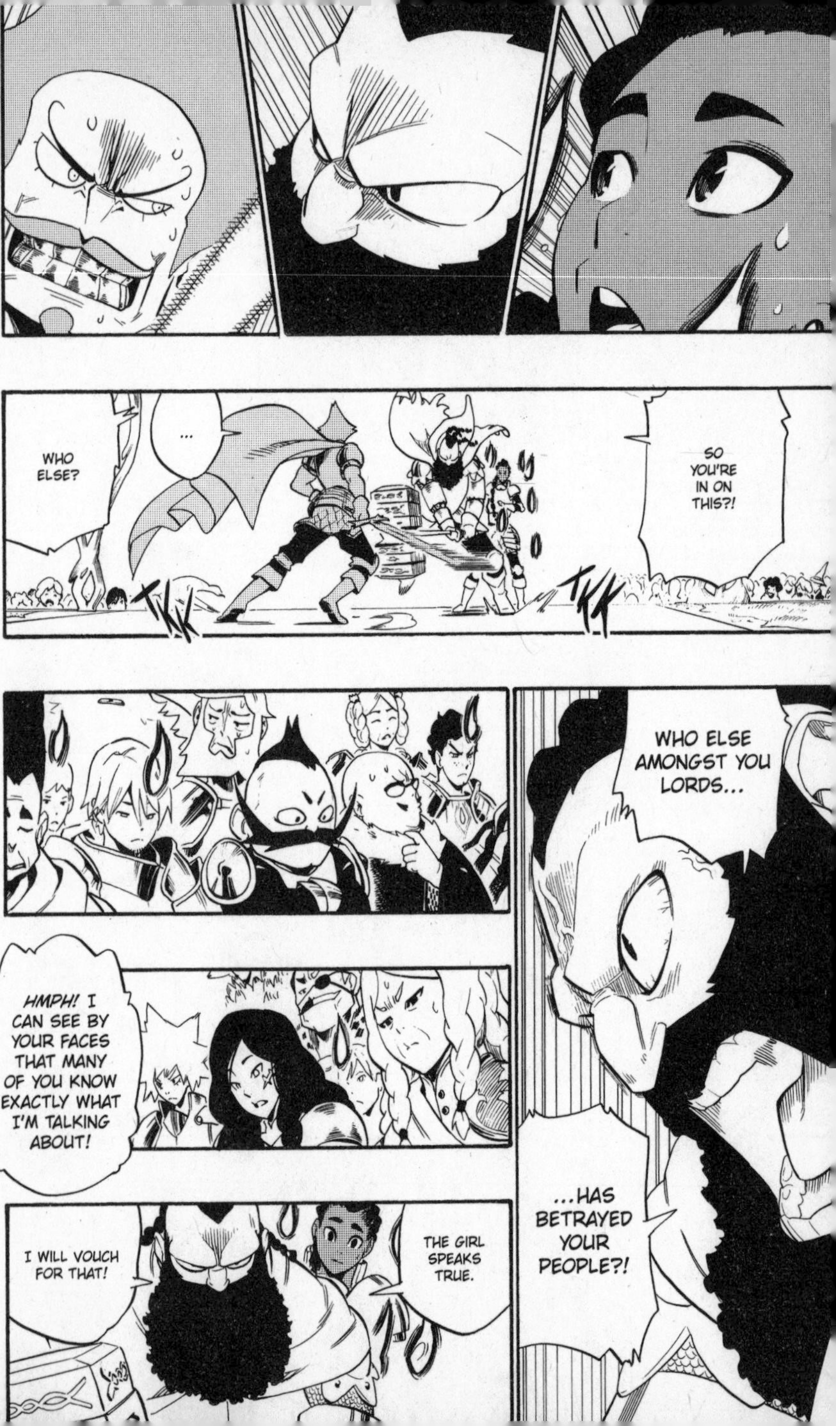
SO YOU'RE IN ON THIS?!
...
WHO ELSE?
WHO ELSE AMONGST YOU LORDS...
...HAS BETRAYED YOUR PEOPLE?!
HMPH! I CAN SEE BY YOUR FACES THAT MANY OF YOU KNOW EXACTLY WHAT I'M TALKING ABOUT!
THE GIRL SPEAKS TRUE.
I WILL VOUCH FOR THAT!

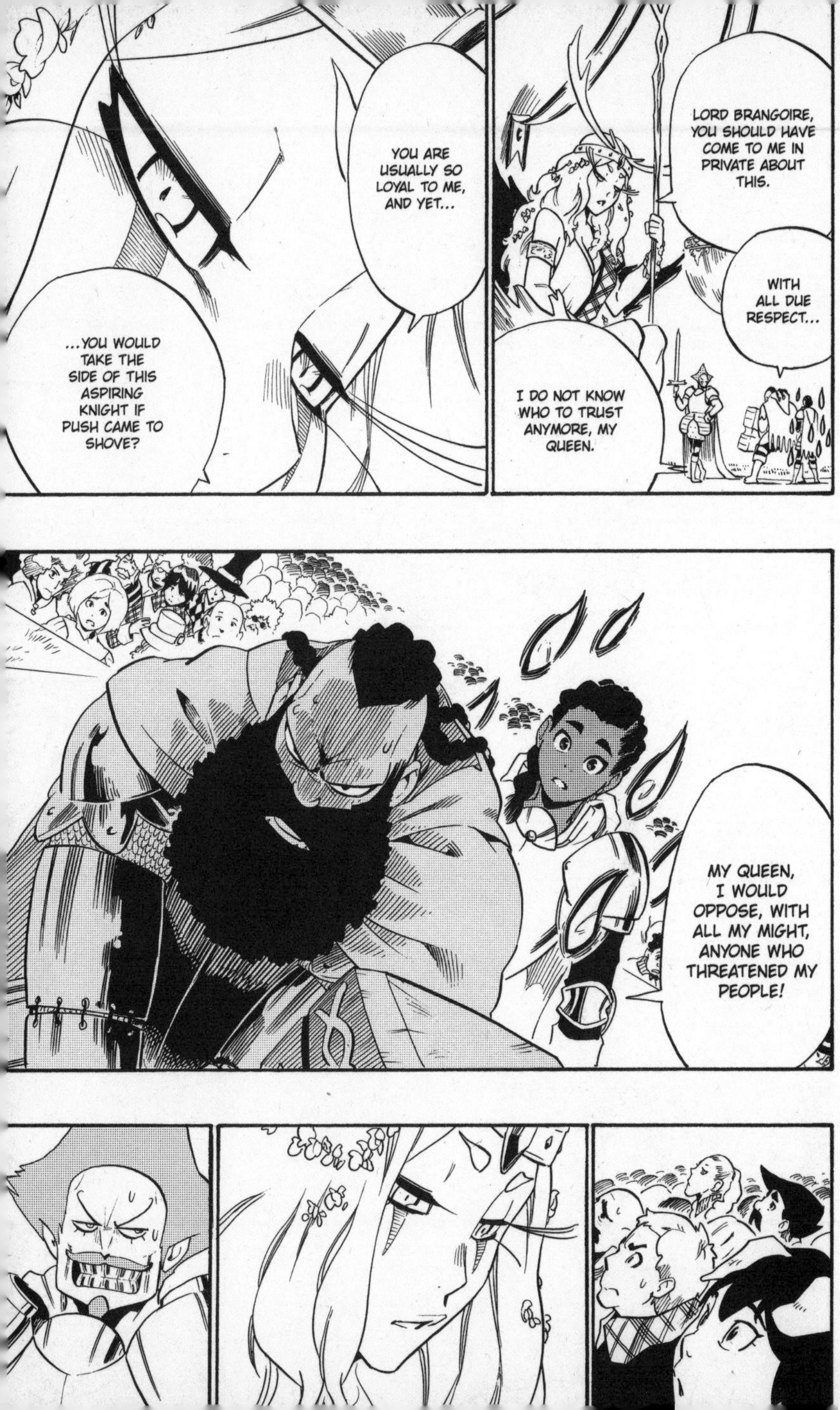

LORD BRANGOIRE, YOU SHOULD HAVE COME TO ME IN PRIVATE ABOUT THIS.
WITH ALL DUE RESPECT...
I DO NOT KNOW WHO TO TRUST ANYMORE, MY QUEEN.
YOU ARE USUALLY SO LOYAL TO ME, AND YET...
...YOU WOULD TAKE THE SIDE OF THIS ASPIRING KNIGHT IF PUSH CAME TO SHOVE?
MY QUEEN, I WOULD OPPOSE, WITH ALL MY MIGHT, ANYONE WHO THREATENED MY PEOPLE!

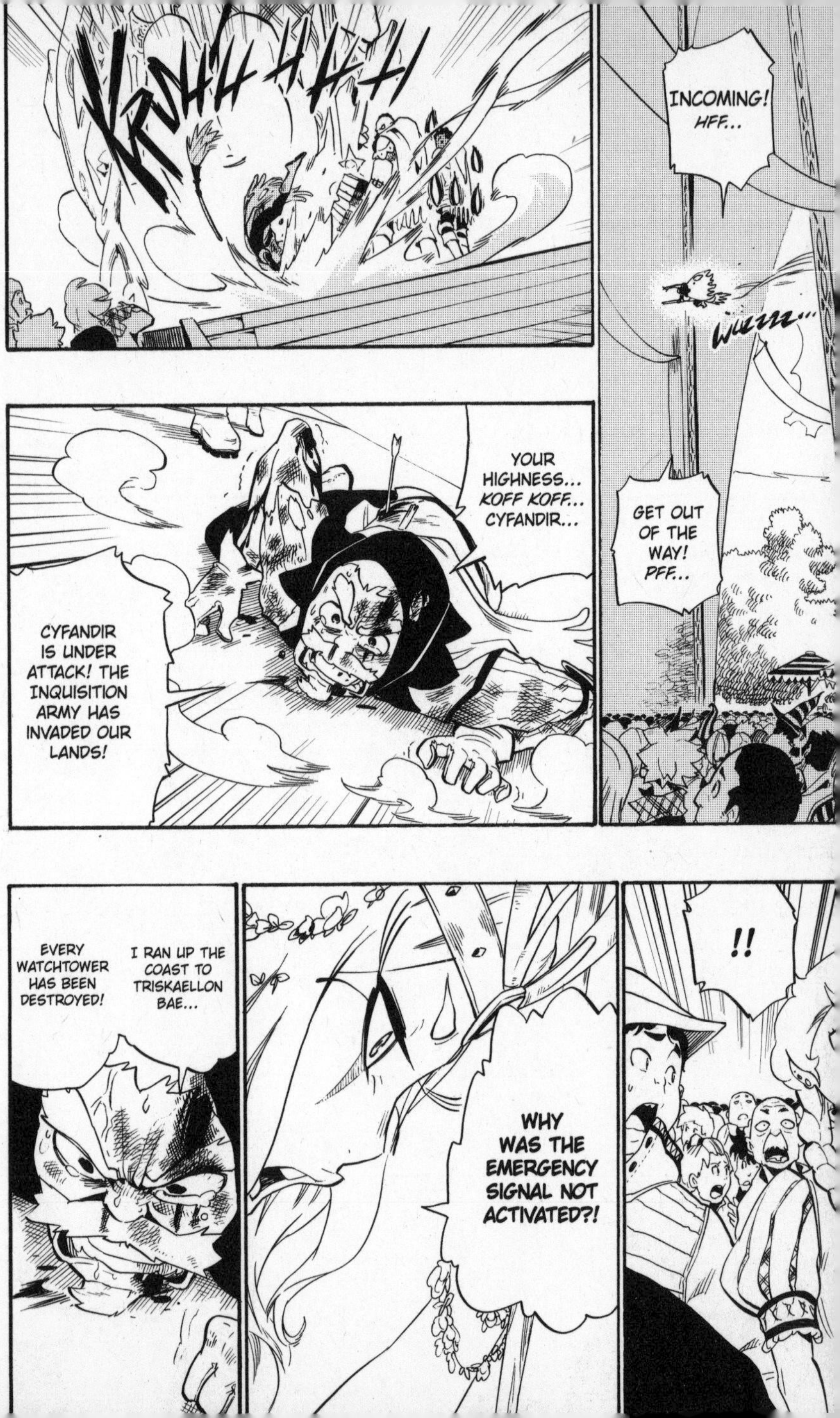
INCOMING! HFF...
WUZZZZ...
GET OUT OF THE WAY! PFF...
YOUR HIGHNESS... KOFF KOFF... CYFANDIR...
CYFANDIR IS UNDER ATTACK! THE INQUISITION ARMY HAS INVADED OUR LANDS!
!!
WHY WAS THE EMERGENCY SIGNAL NOT ACTIVATED?!
I RAN UP THE COAST TO TRISKAELLON BAE...
EVERY WATCHTOWER HAS BEEN DESTROYED!

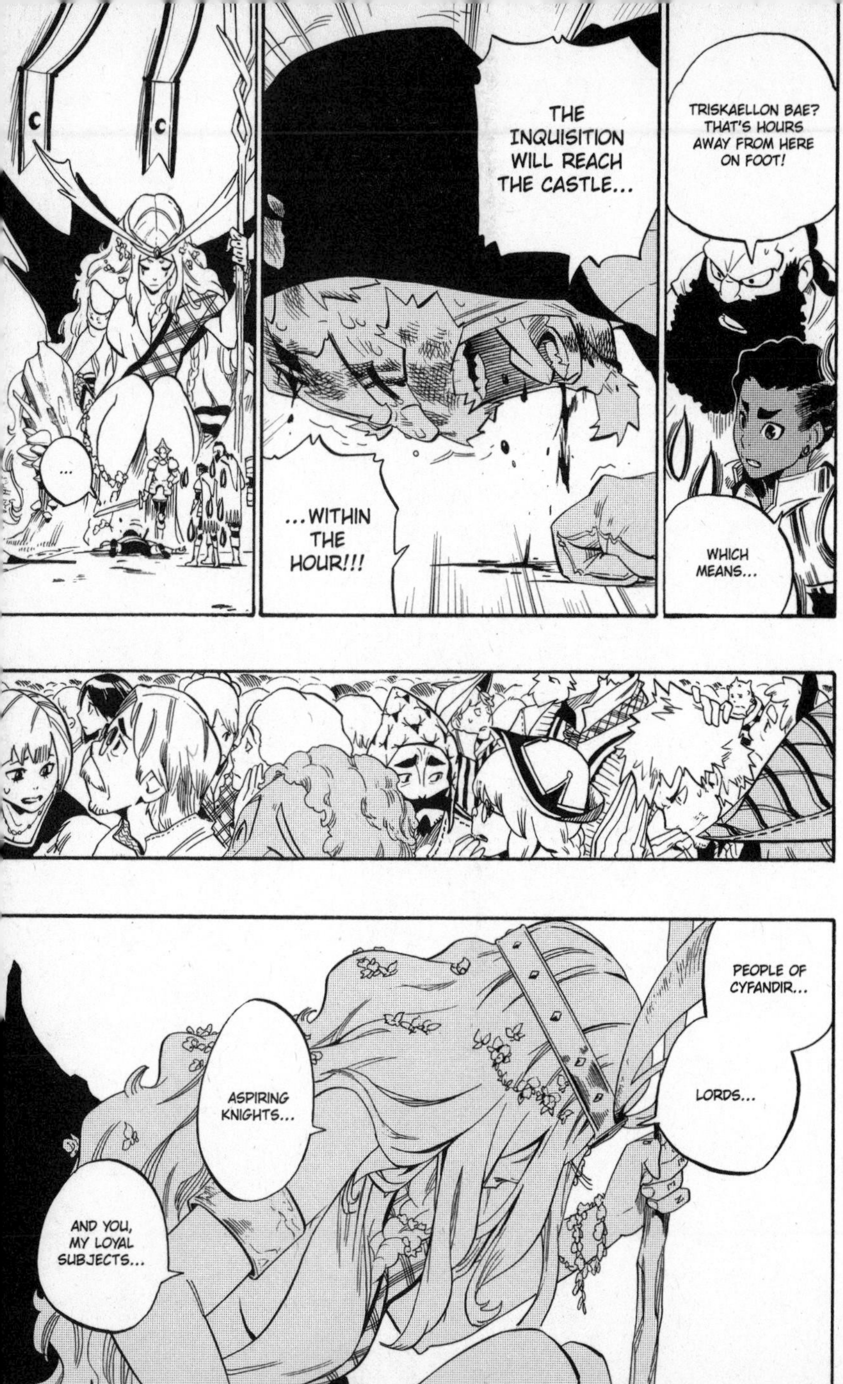
TRISKAELLON BAE? THAT'S HOURS AWAY FROM HERE ON FOOT!
WHICH MEANS...
THE INQUISITION WILL REACH THE CASTLE...
...WITHIN THE HOUR!!!
...
PEOPLE OF CYFANDIR...
LORDS...
ASPIRING KNIGHTS...
AND YOU, MY LOYAL SUBJECTS...

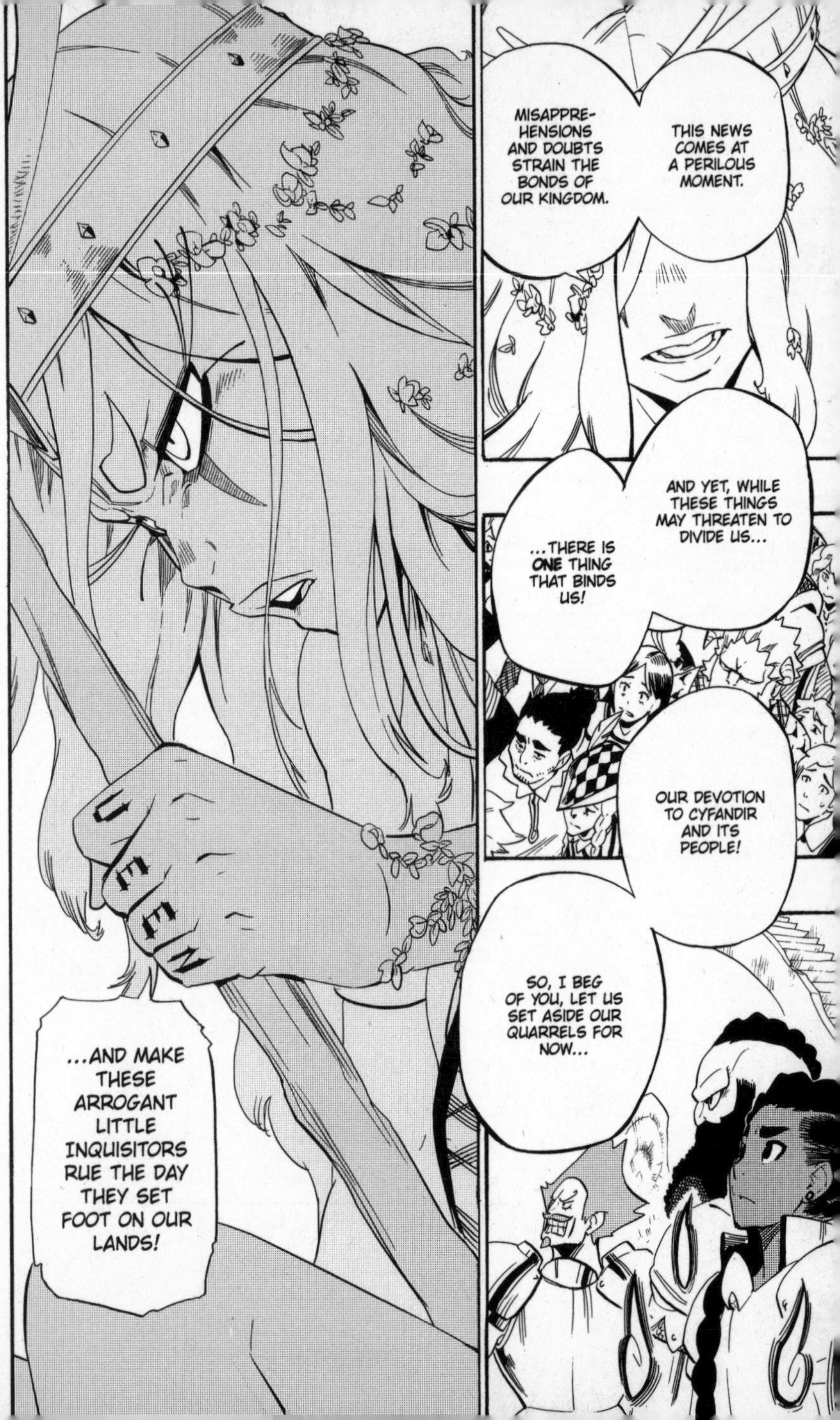
THIS NEWS COMES AT A PERILOUS MOMENT.
MISAPPREHENSIONS AND DOUBTS STRAIN THE BONDS OF OUR KINGDOM.
AND YET, WHILE THESE THINGS MAY THREATEN TO DIVIDE US...
...THERE IS **ONE** THING THAT BINDS US!
OUR DEVOTION TO CYFANDIR AND ITS PEOPLE!
SO, I BEG OF YOU, LET US SET ASIDE OUR QUARRELS FOR NOW...
...AND MAKE THESE ARROGANT LITTLE INQUISITORS RUE THE DAY THEY SET FOOT ON OUR LANDS!

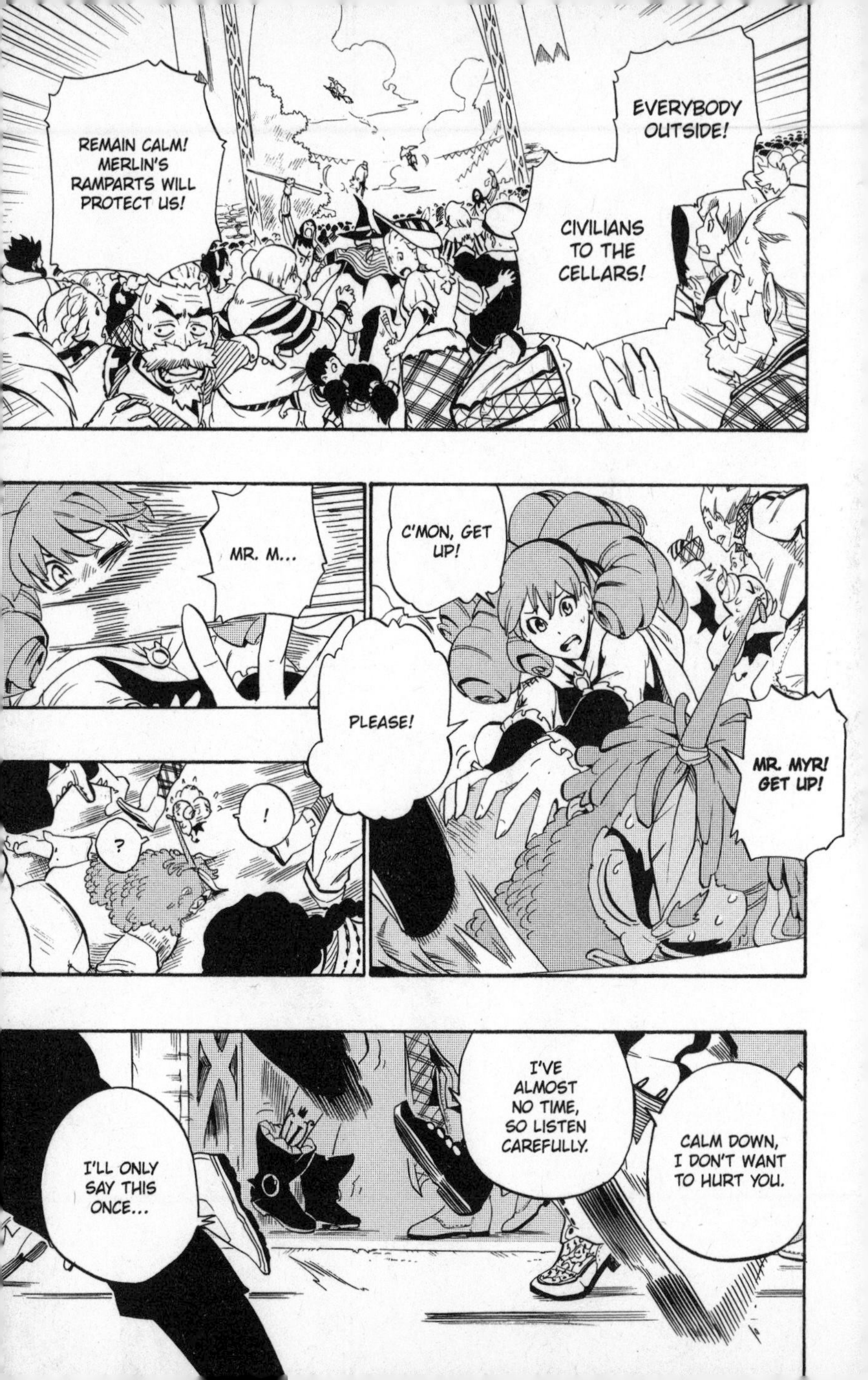
EVERYBODY OUTSIDE!
CIVILIANS TO THE CELLARS!
REMAIN CALM! MERLIN'S RAMPARTS WILL PROTECT US!
C'MON, GET UP!
MR. MYR! GET UP!
PLEASE!
MR. M...
!
?
CALM DOWN, I DON'T WANT TO HURT YOU.
I'VE ALMOST NO TIME, SO LISTEN CAREFULLY.
I'LL ONLY SAY THIS ONCE...

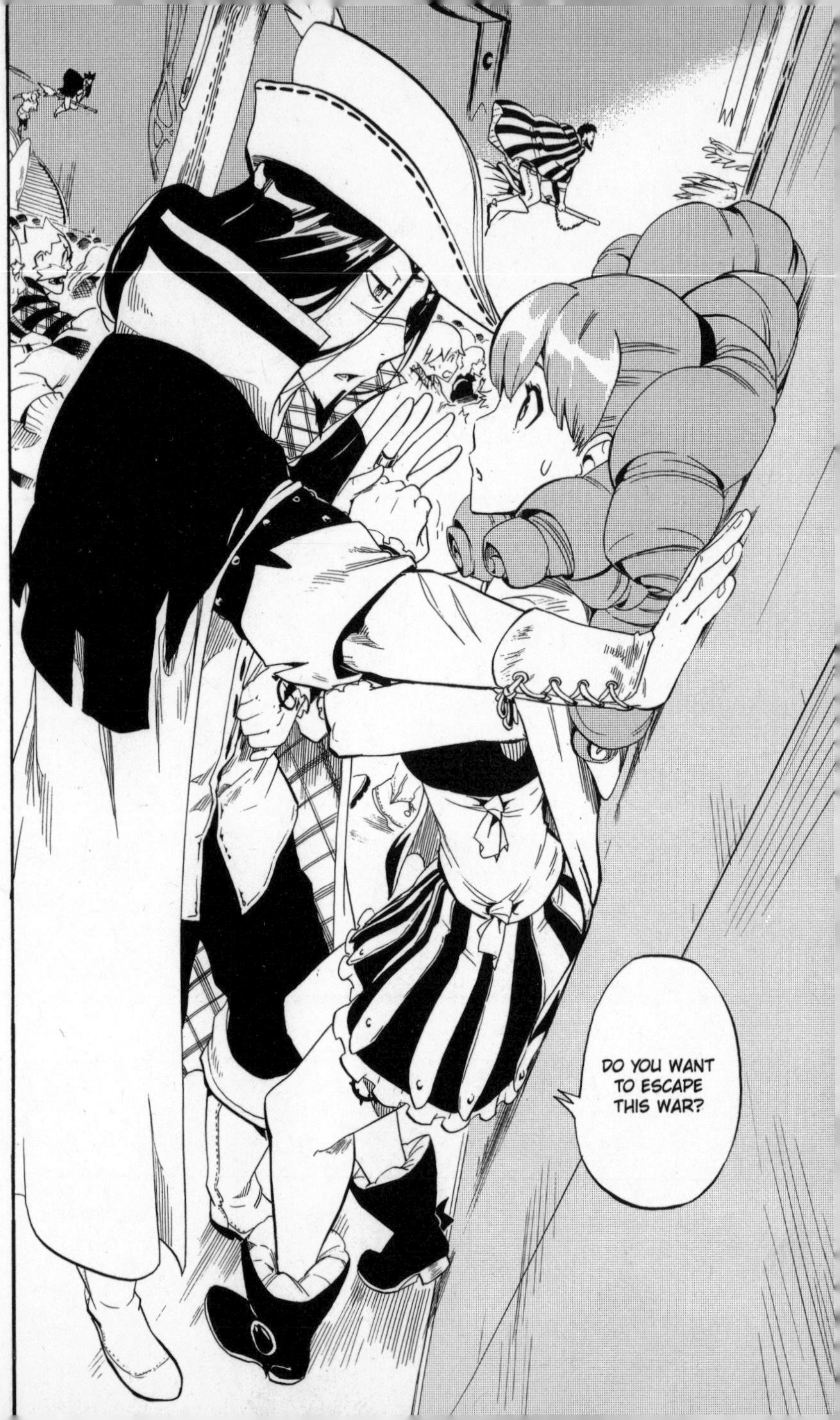
DO YOU WANT TO ESCAPE THIS WAR?

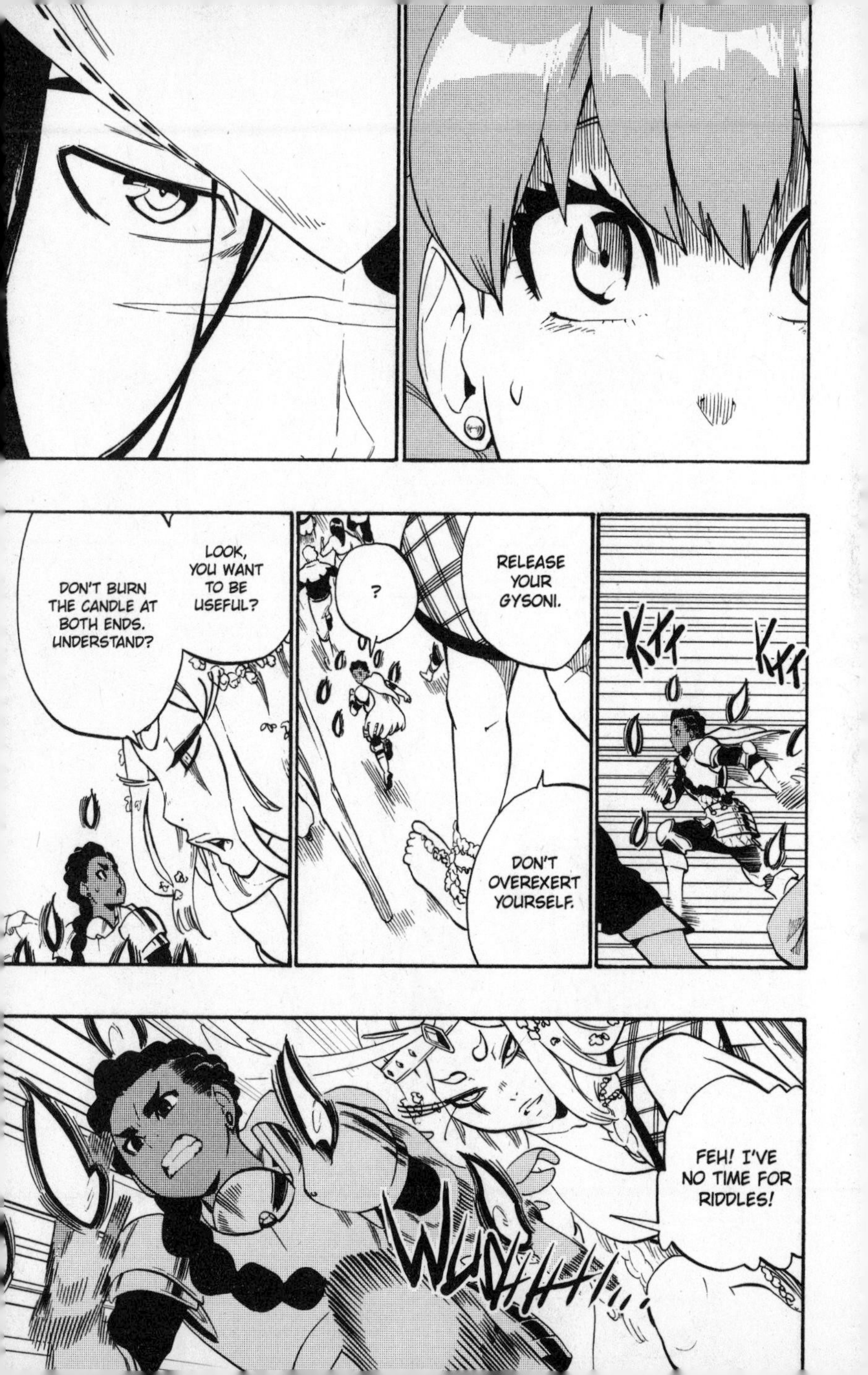
RELEASE YOUR GYSONI.
?
DON'T OVEREXERT YOURSELF.
LOOK, YOU WANT TO BE USEFUL?
DON'T BURN THE CANDLE AT BOTH ENDS. UNDERSTAND?
FEH! I'VE NO TIME FOR RIDDLES!
WUSHHH!..

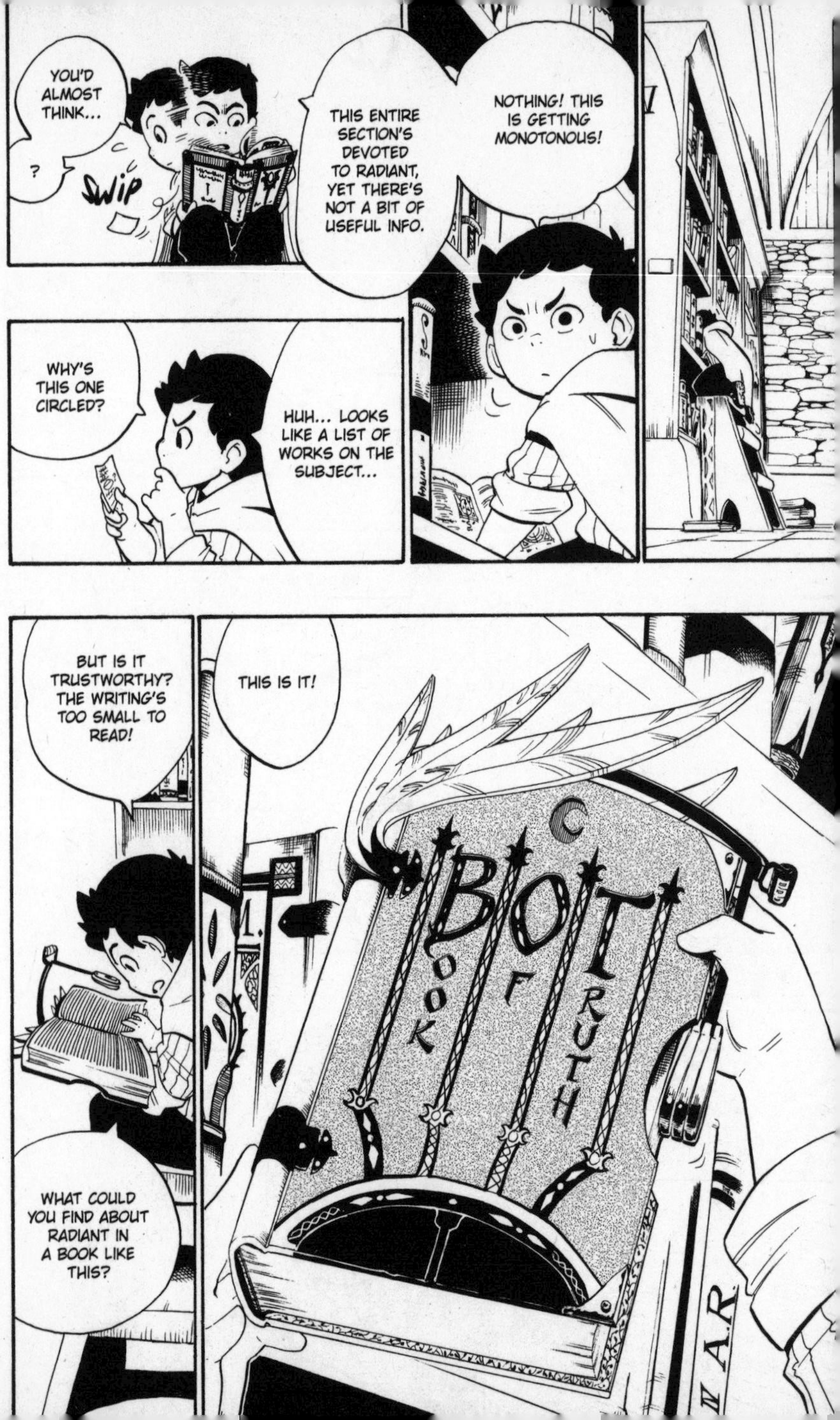
NOTHING! THIS IS GETTING MONOTONOUS!
THIS ENTIRE SECTION'S DEVOTED TO RADIANT, YET THERE'S NOT A BIT OF USEFUL INFO.
YOU'D ALMOST THINK...
?
SWIP
HUH... LOOKS LIKE A LIST OF WORKS ON THE SUBJECT...
WHY'S THIS ONE CIRCLED?
THIS IS IT!
BOOK OF TRUTH
BUT IS IT TRUSTWORTHY? THE WRITING'S TOO SMALL TO READ!
WHAT COULD YOU FIND ABOUT RADIANT IN A BOOK LIKE THIS?

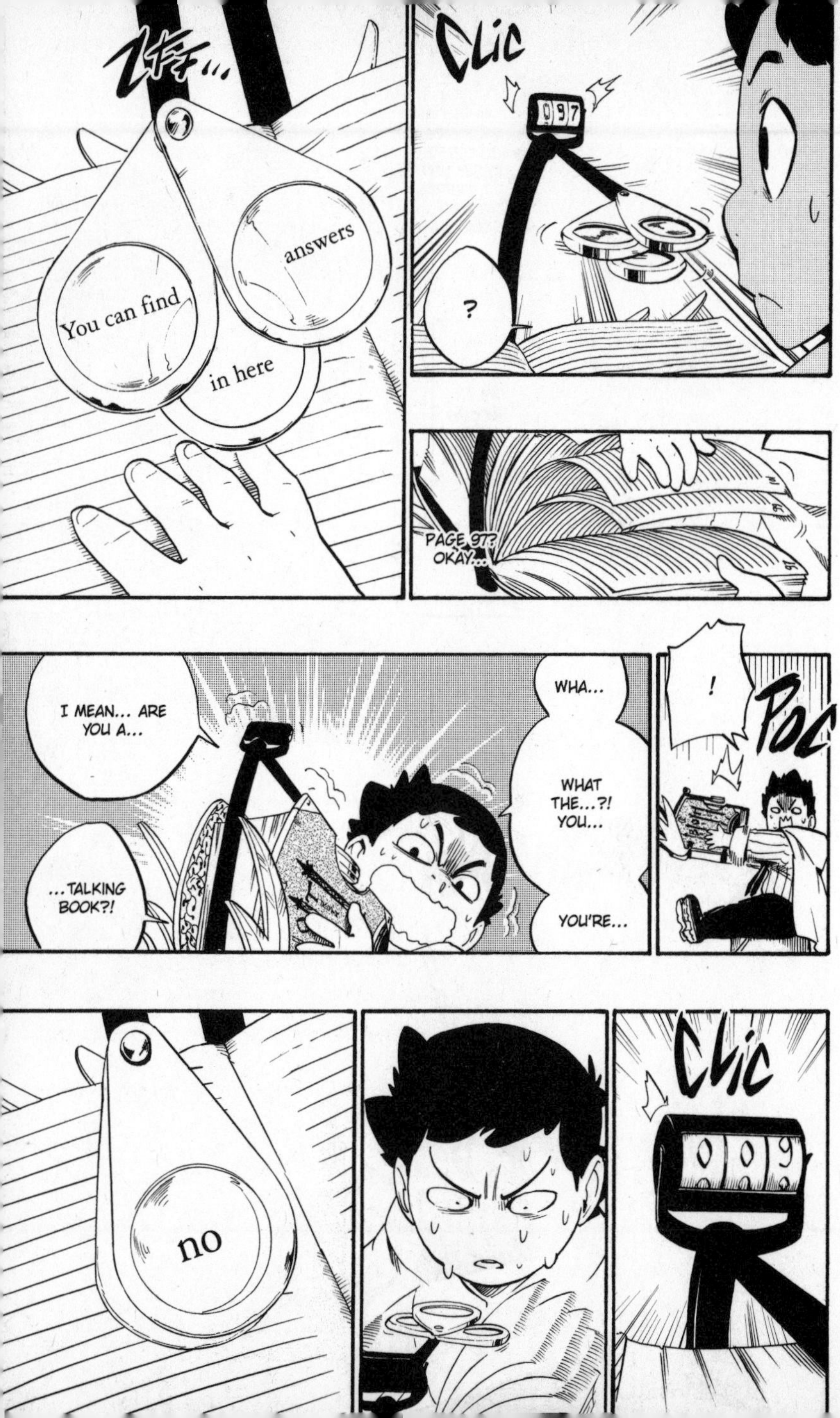
CLIC
097
?
PAGE 97? OKAY...
You can find
answers
in here
!
POC
WHA...
WHAT THE...?! YOU...
YOU'RE...
I MEAN... ARE YOU A...
...TALKING BOOK?!
CLIC
009
no

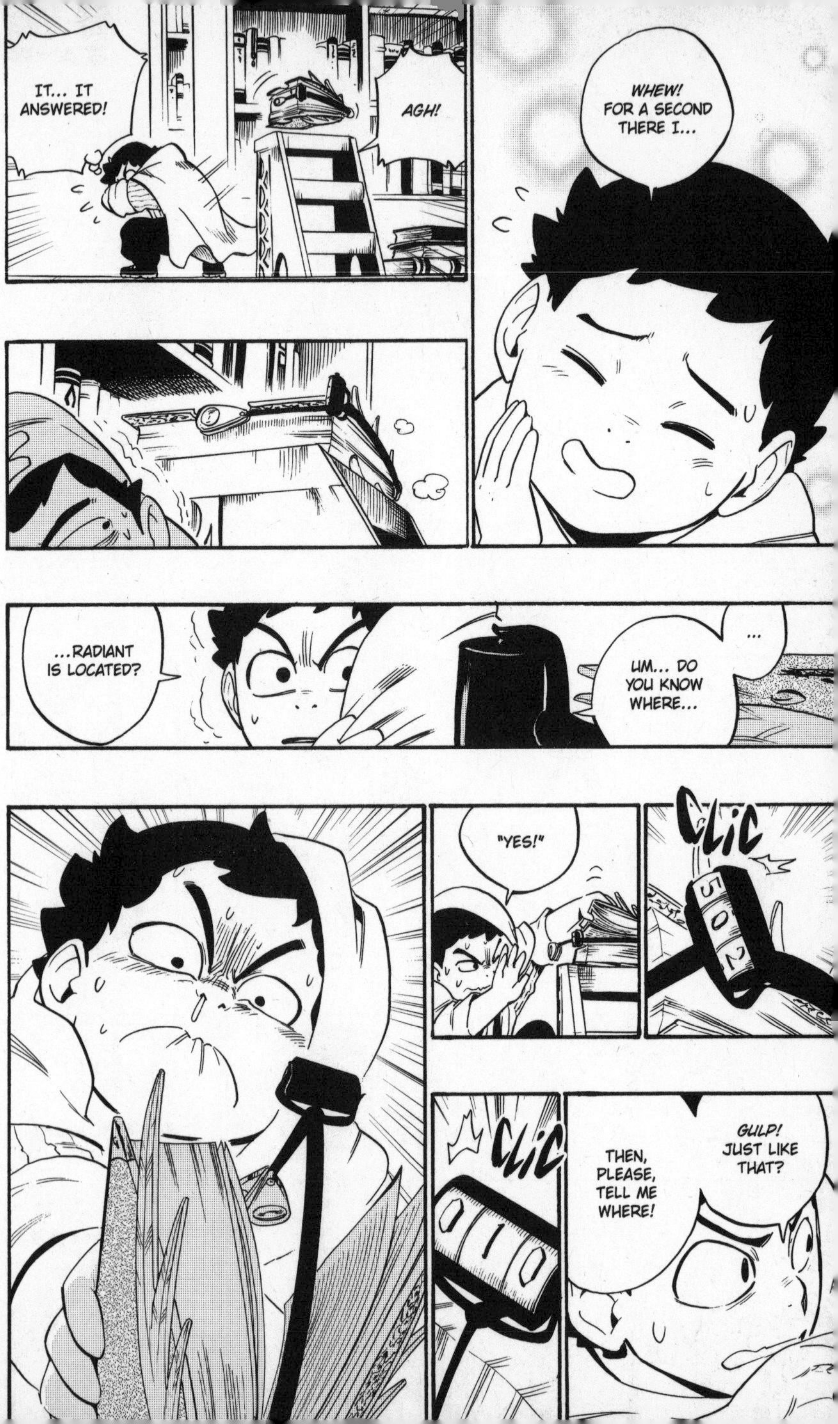
WHEW! FOR A SECOND THERE I...
AGH!
IT... IT ANSWERED!
...
UM... DO YOU KNOW WHERE...
...RADIANT IS LOCATED?
CLIC
"YES!"
GULP! JUST LIKE THAT?
THEN, PLEASE, TELL ME WHERE!
CLIC

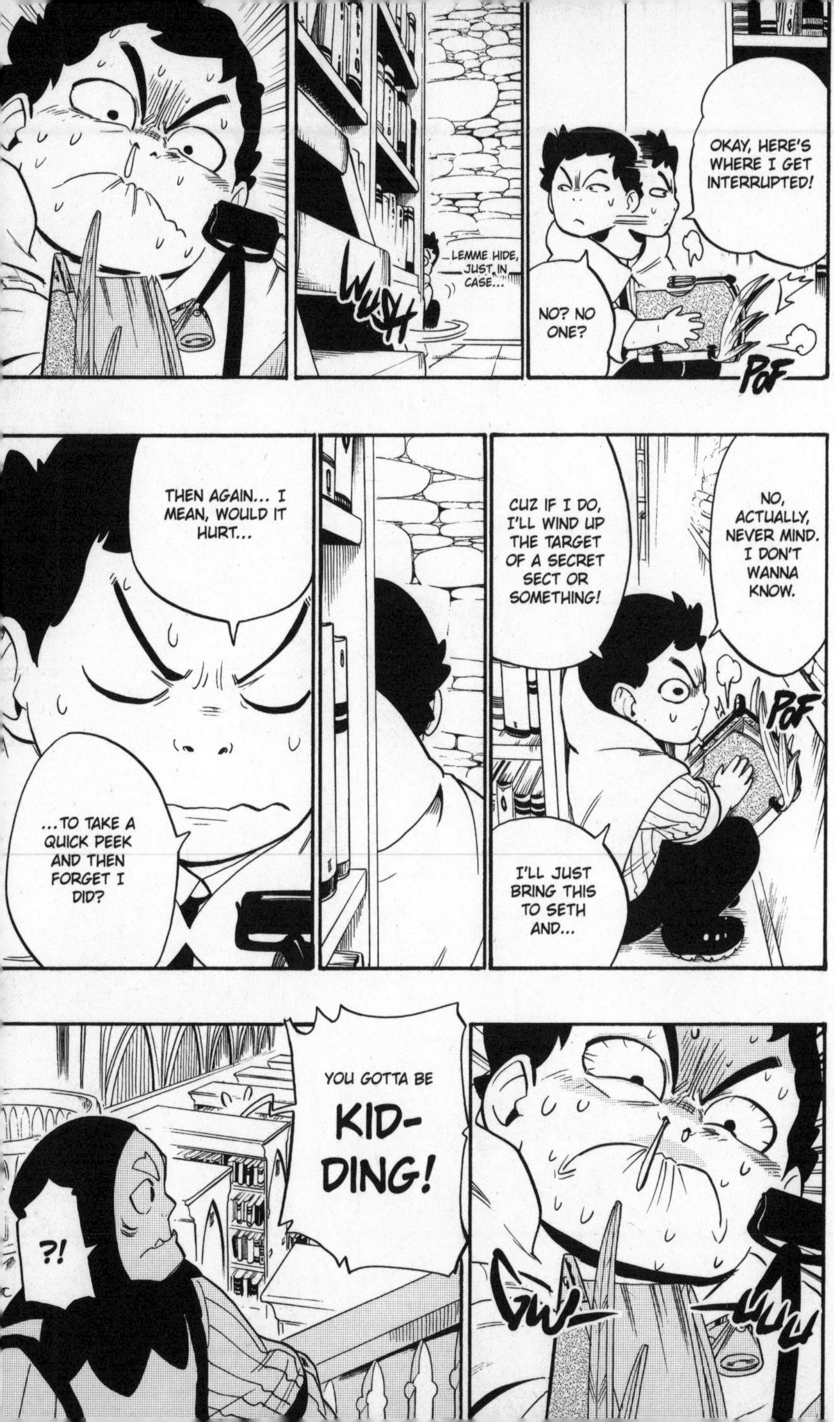
OKAY, HERE'S WHERE I GET INTERRUPTED!
NO? NO ONE?
POF
LEMME HIDE, JUST IN CASE...
WUSH
NO, ACTUALLY, NEVER MIND. I DON'T WANNA KNOW.
POF
CUZ IF I DO, I'LL WIND UP THE TARGET OF A SECRET SECT OR SOMETHING!
I'LL JUST BRING THIS TO SETH AND...
THEN AGAIN... I MEAN, WOULD IT HURT...
...TO TAKE A QUICK PEEK AND THEN FORGET I DID?
GWUUU
YOU GOTTA BE KID-DING!
?!

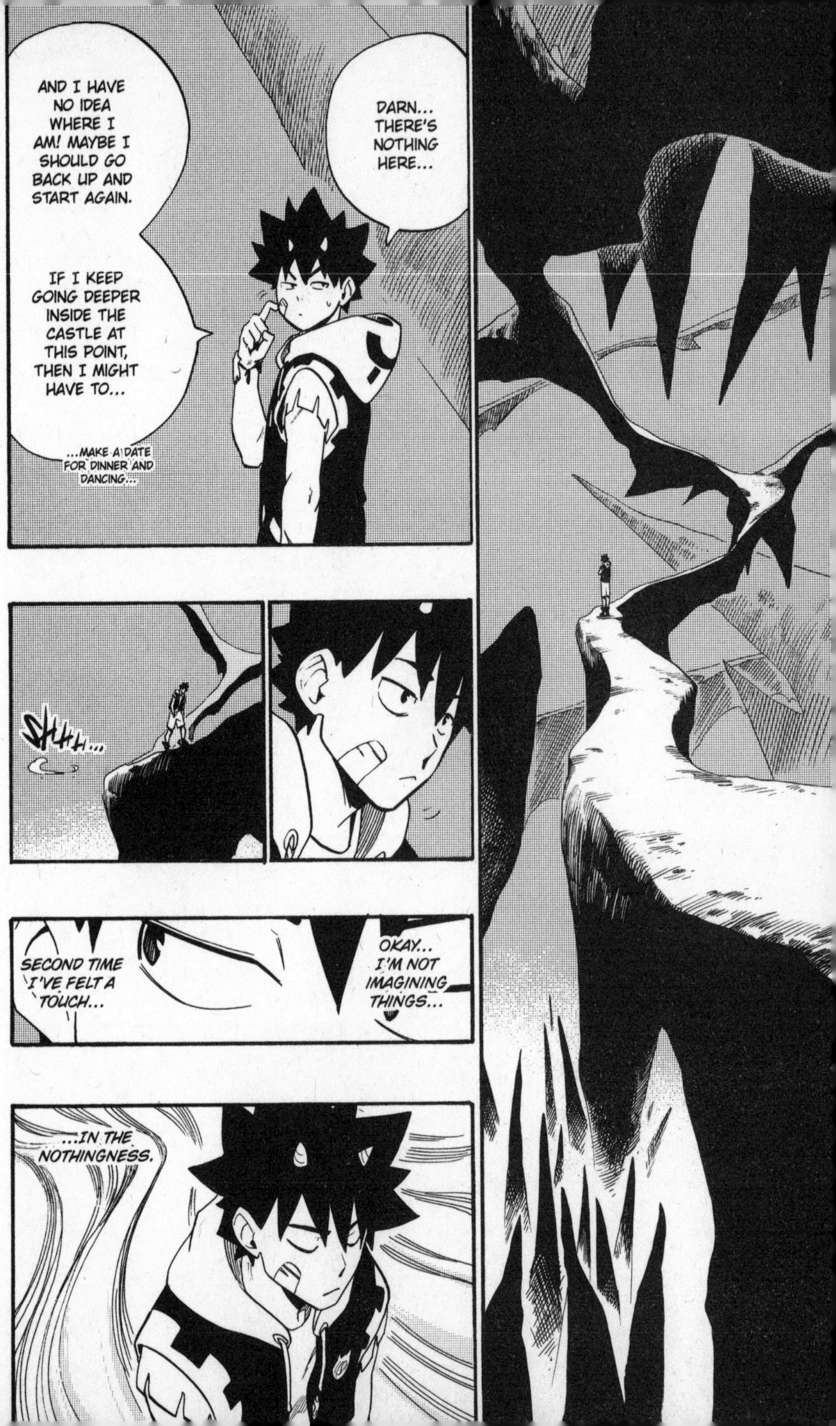
DARN... THERE'S NOTHING HERE...
AND I HAVE NO IDEA WHERE I AM! MAYBE I SHOULD GO BACK UP AND START AGAIN.
IF I KEEP GOING DEEPER INSIDE THE CASTLE AT THIS POINT, THEN I MIGHT HAVE TO...
...MAKE A DATE FOR DINNER AND DANCING...
SHHH...
OKAY... I'M NOT IMAGINING THINGS...
SECOND TIME I'VE FELT A TOUCH...
...IN THE NOTHINGNESS.

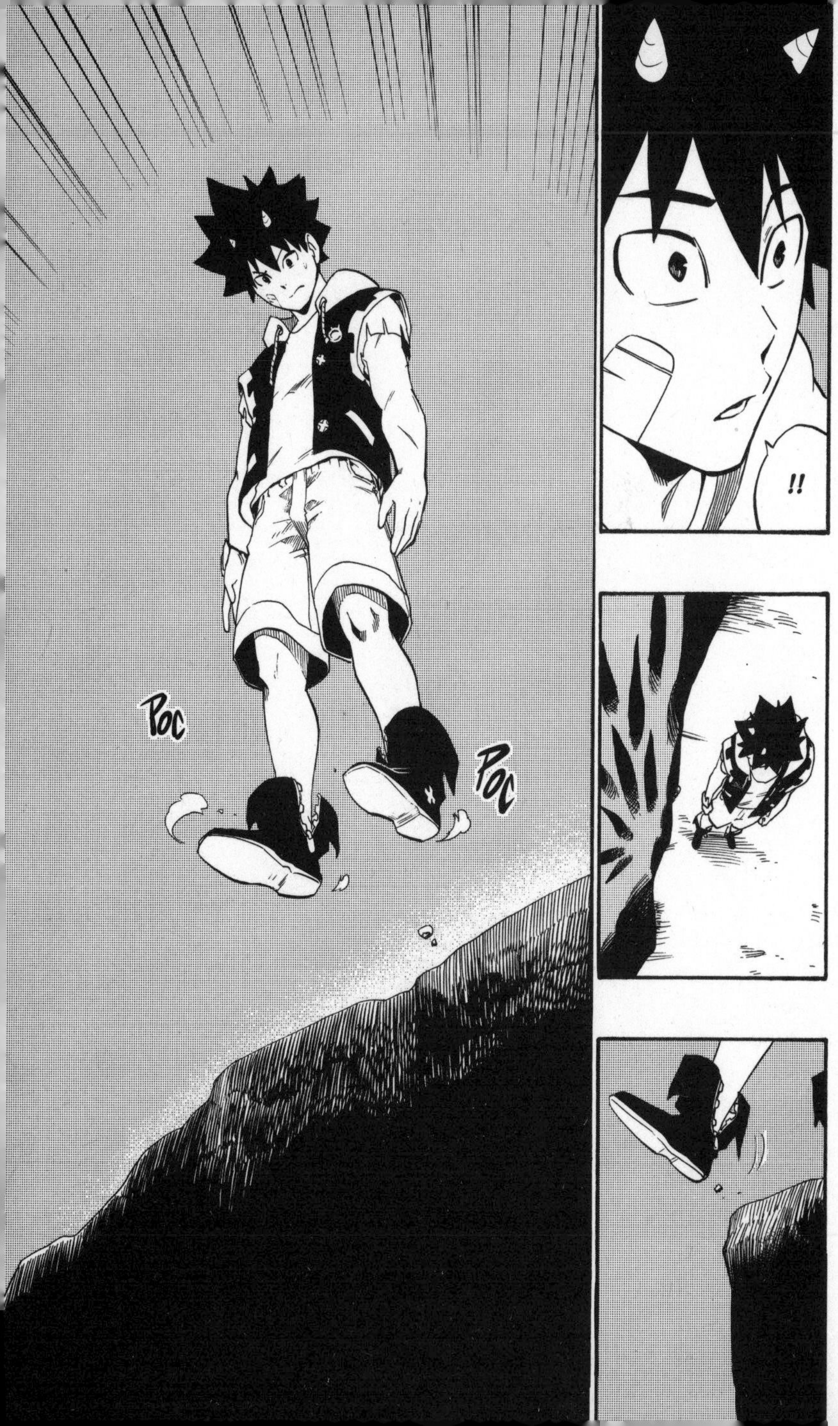
!!
POC
POC

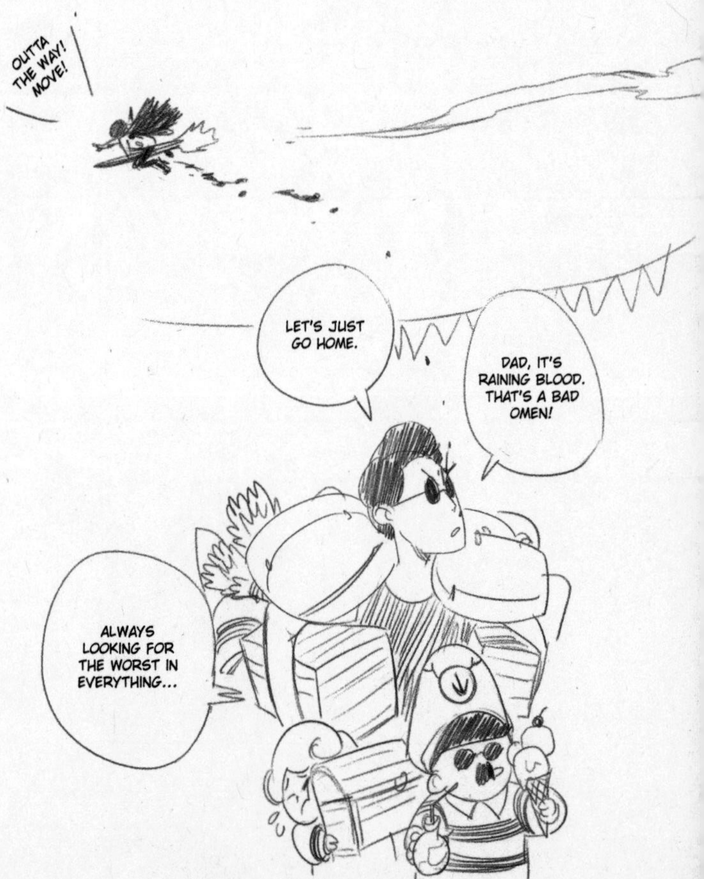

OUTTA THE WAY! MOVE!
DAD, IT'S RAINING BLOOD. THAT'S A BAD OMEN!
LET'S JUST GO HOME.
ALWAYS LOOKING FOR THE WORST IN EVERYTHING...

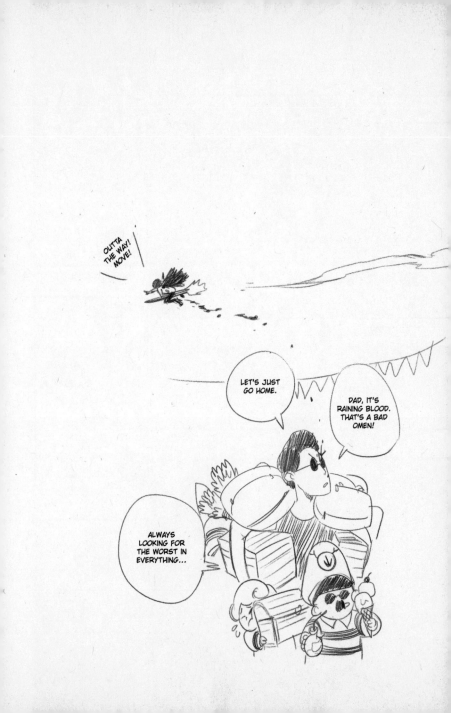

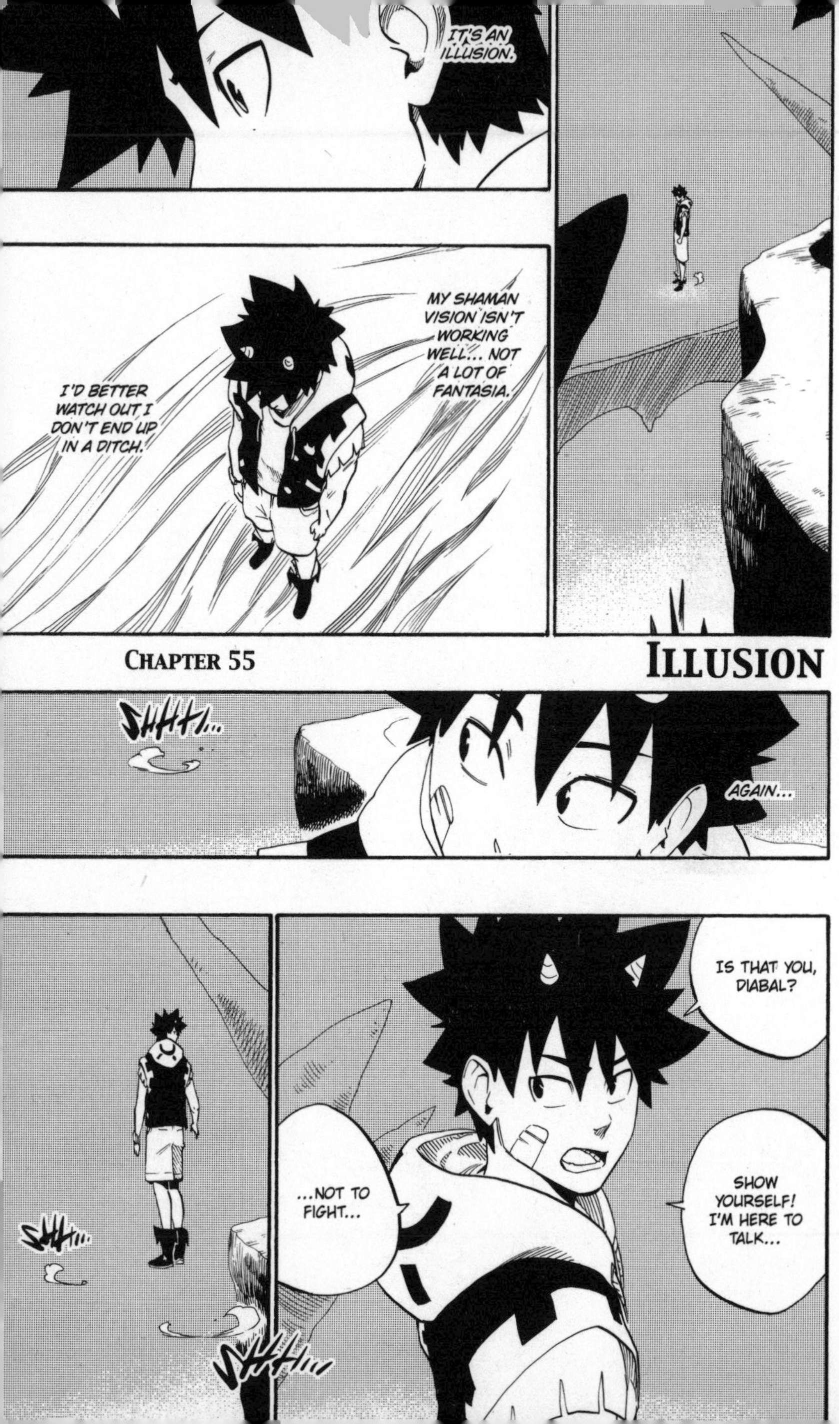
IT'S AN ILLUSION.
MY SHAMAN VISION ISN'T WORKING WELL... NOT A LOT OF FANTASIA.
I'D BETTER WATCH OUT I DON'T END UP IN A DITCH.
CHAPTER 55
ILLUSION
AGAIN...
SHHH...
IS THAT YOU, DIABAL?
SHOW YOURSELF! I'M HERE TO TALK...
...NOT TO FIGHT...
SHHH...
SHHH...

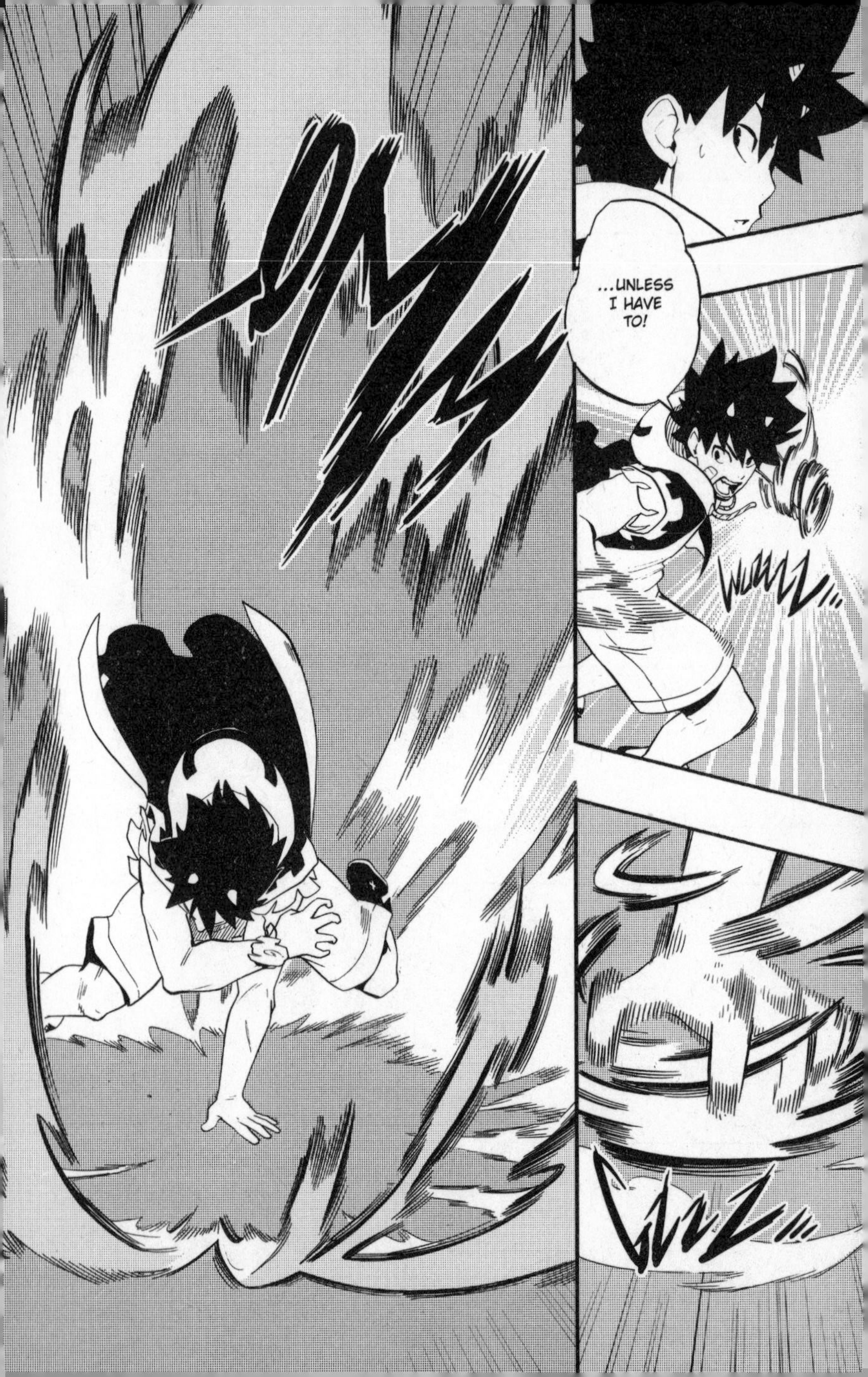
...UNLESS I HAVE TO!
WUMMM...

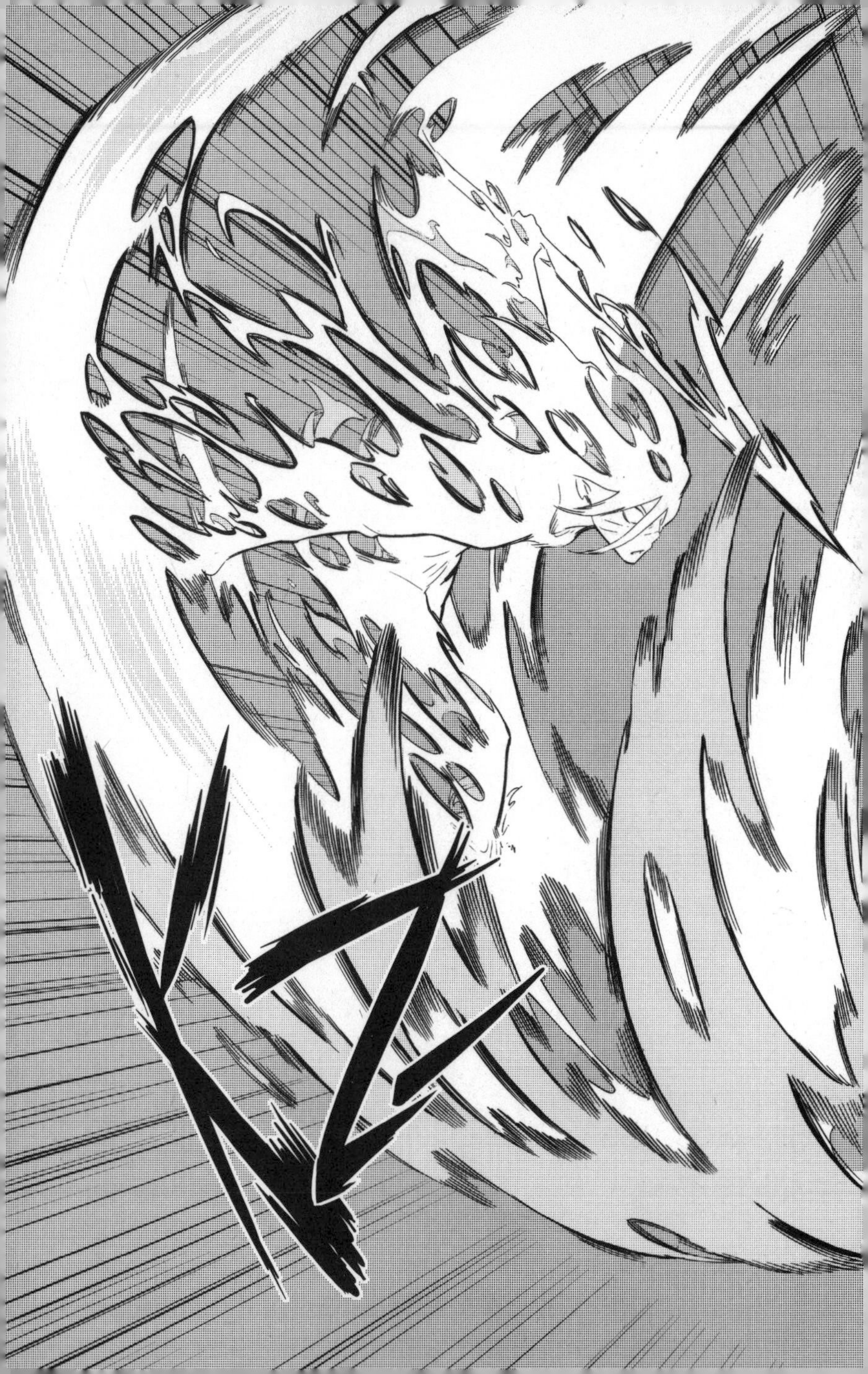

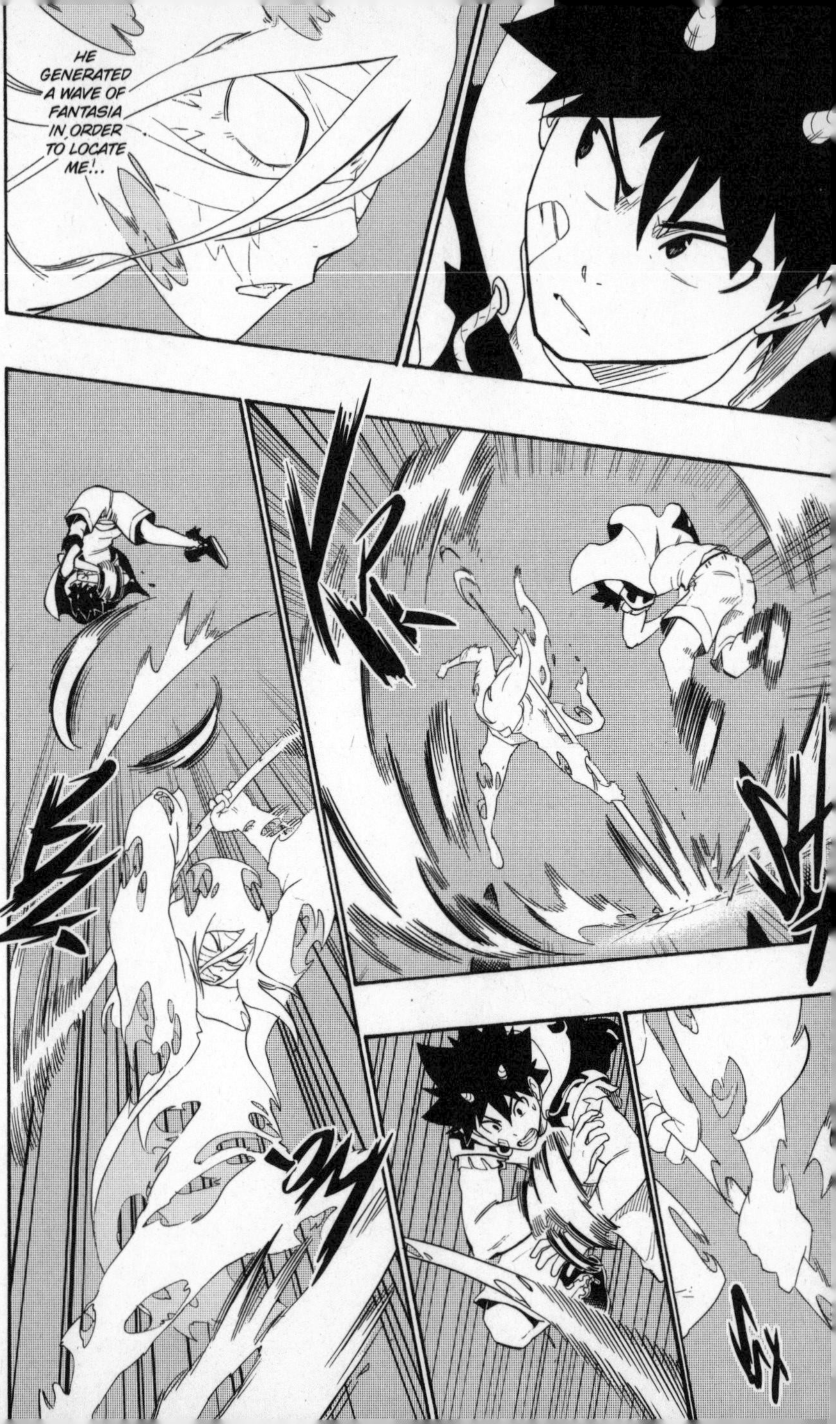
HE GENERATED A WAVE OF FANTASIA IN ORDER TO LOCATE ME!...

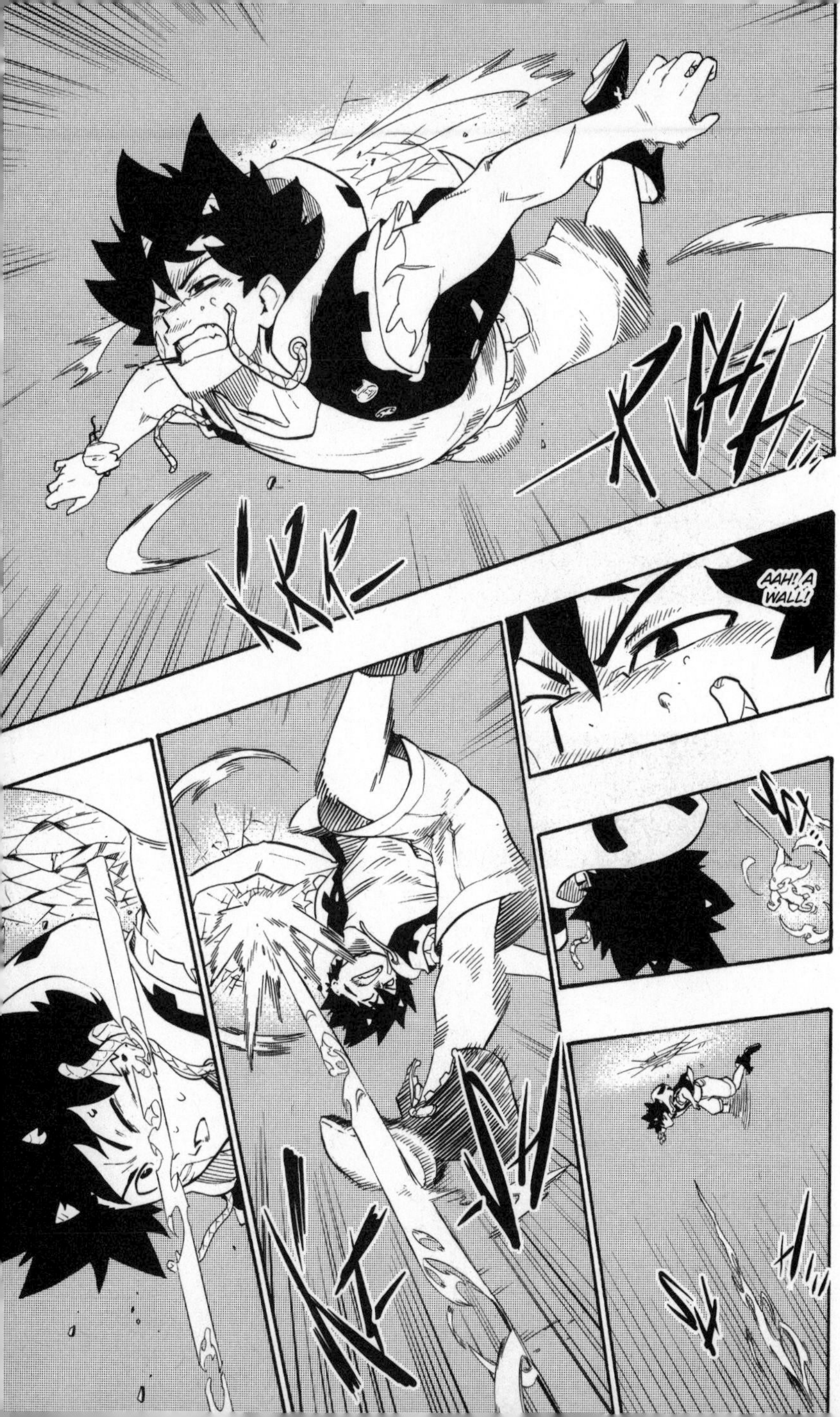
AAH! A WALL!

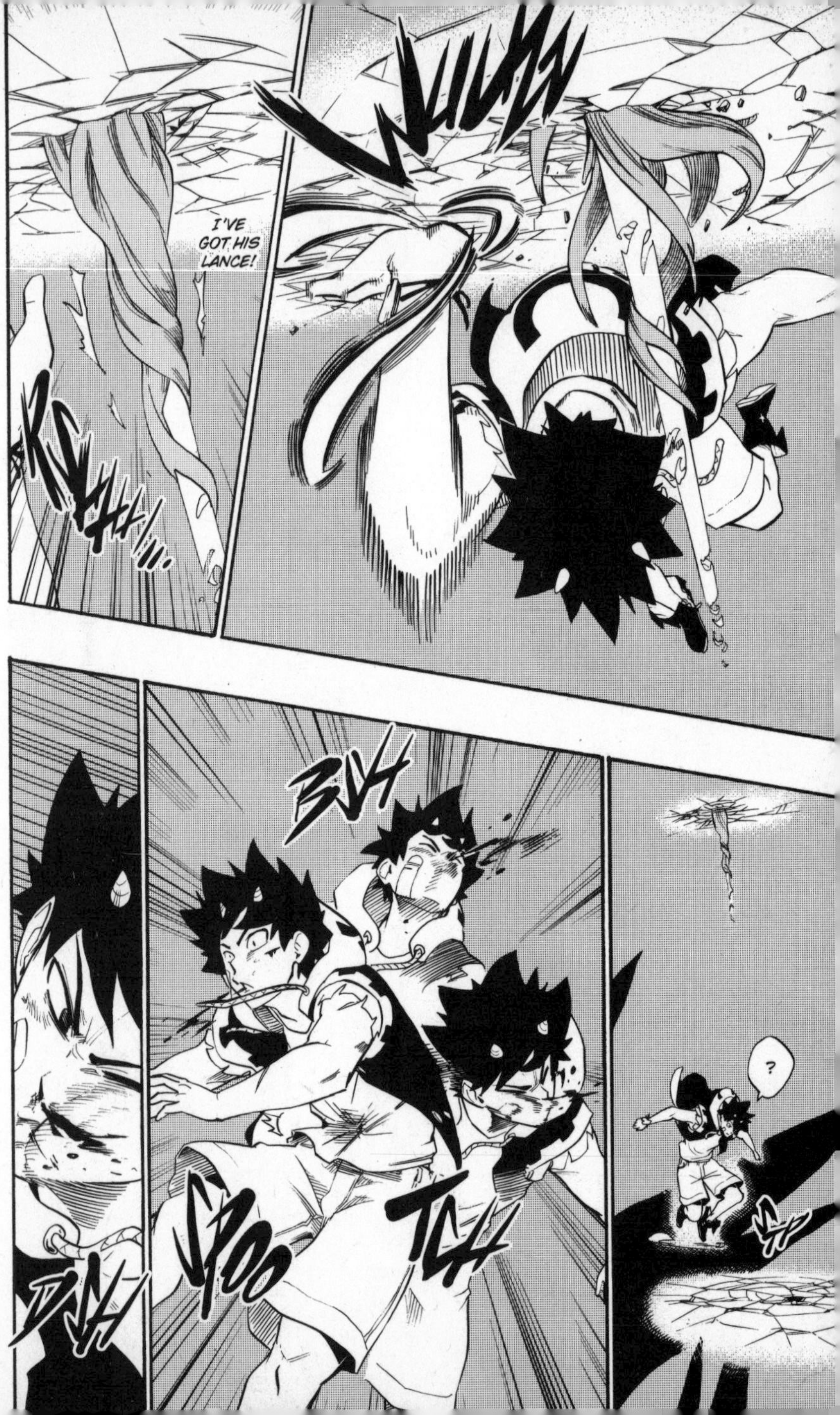
I'VE GOT HIS LANCE!
?
BSH
TCH
SPOO

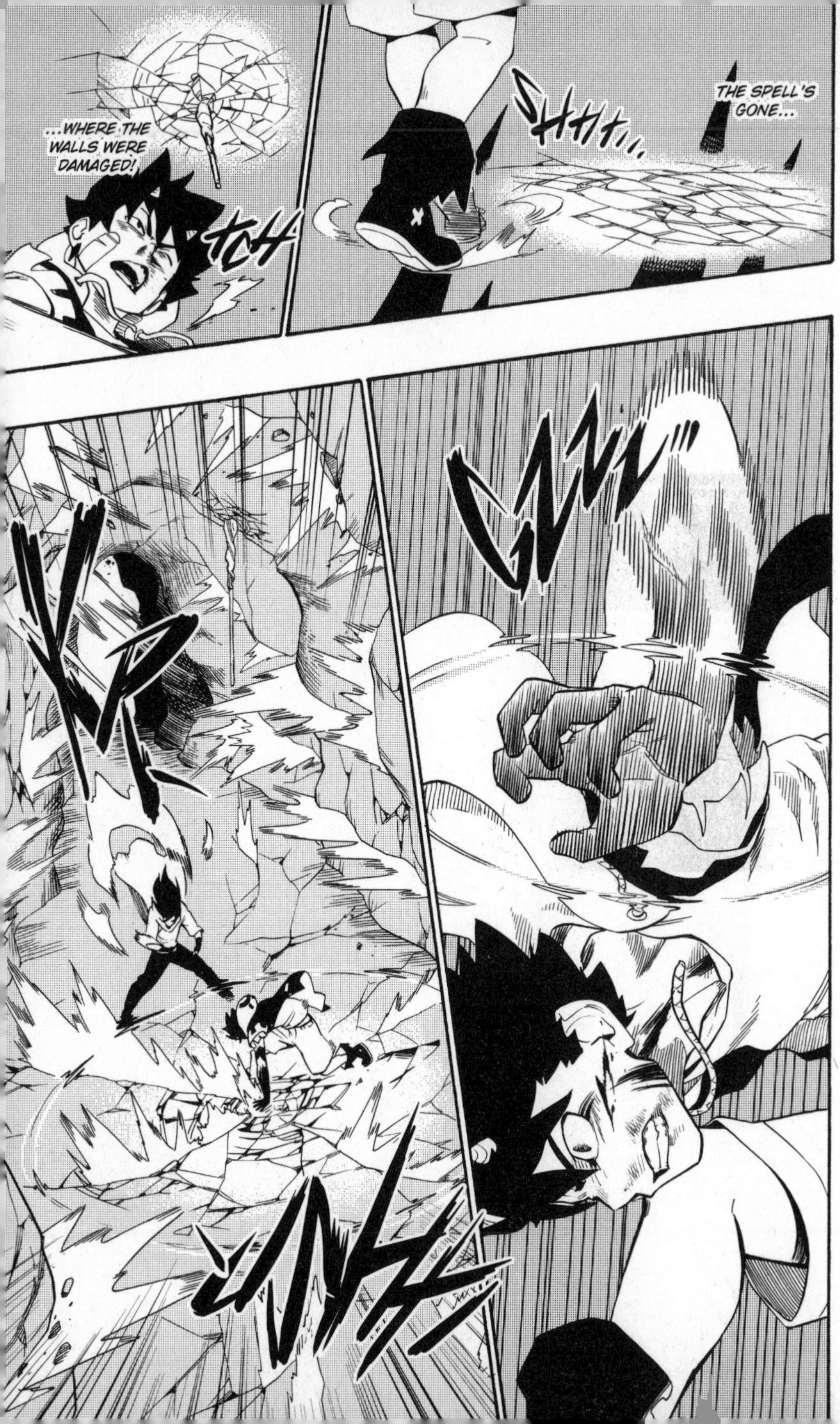
THE SPELL'S GONE...
...WHERE THE WALLS WERE DAMAGED!
TCH

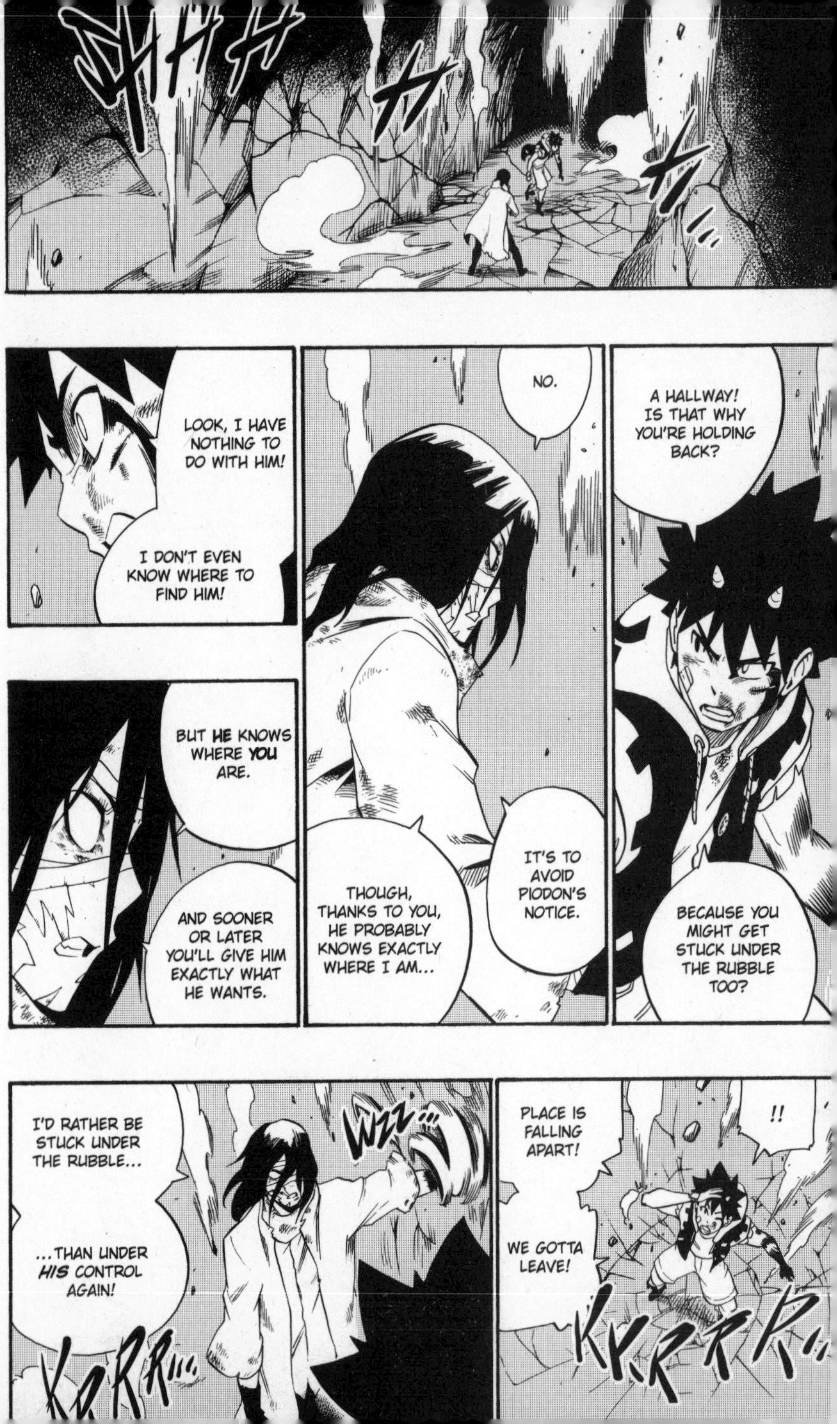
A HALLWAY! IS THAT WHY YOU'RE HOLDING BACK?
BECAUSE YOU MIGHT GET STUCK UNDER THE RUBBLE TOO?
NO.
IT'S TO AVOID PIODON'S NOTICE.
THOUGH, THANKS TO YOU, HE PROBABLY KNOWS EXACTLY WHERE I AM...
LOOK, I HAVE NOTHING TO DO WITH HIM!
I DON'T EVEN KNOW WHERE TO FIND HIM!
BUT **HE** KNOWS WHERE **YOU** ARE.
AND SOONER OR LATER YOU'LL GIVE HIM EXACTLY WHAT HE WANTS.
!!
PLACE IS FALLING APART!
WE GOTTA LEAVE!
I'D RATHER BE STUCK UNDER THE RUBBLE...
...THAN UNDER *HIS* CONTROL AGAIN!

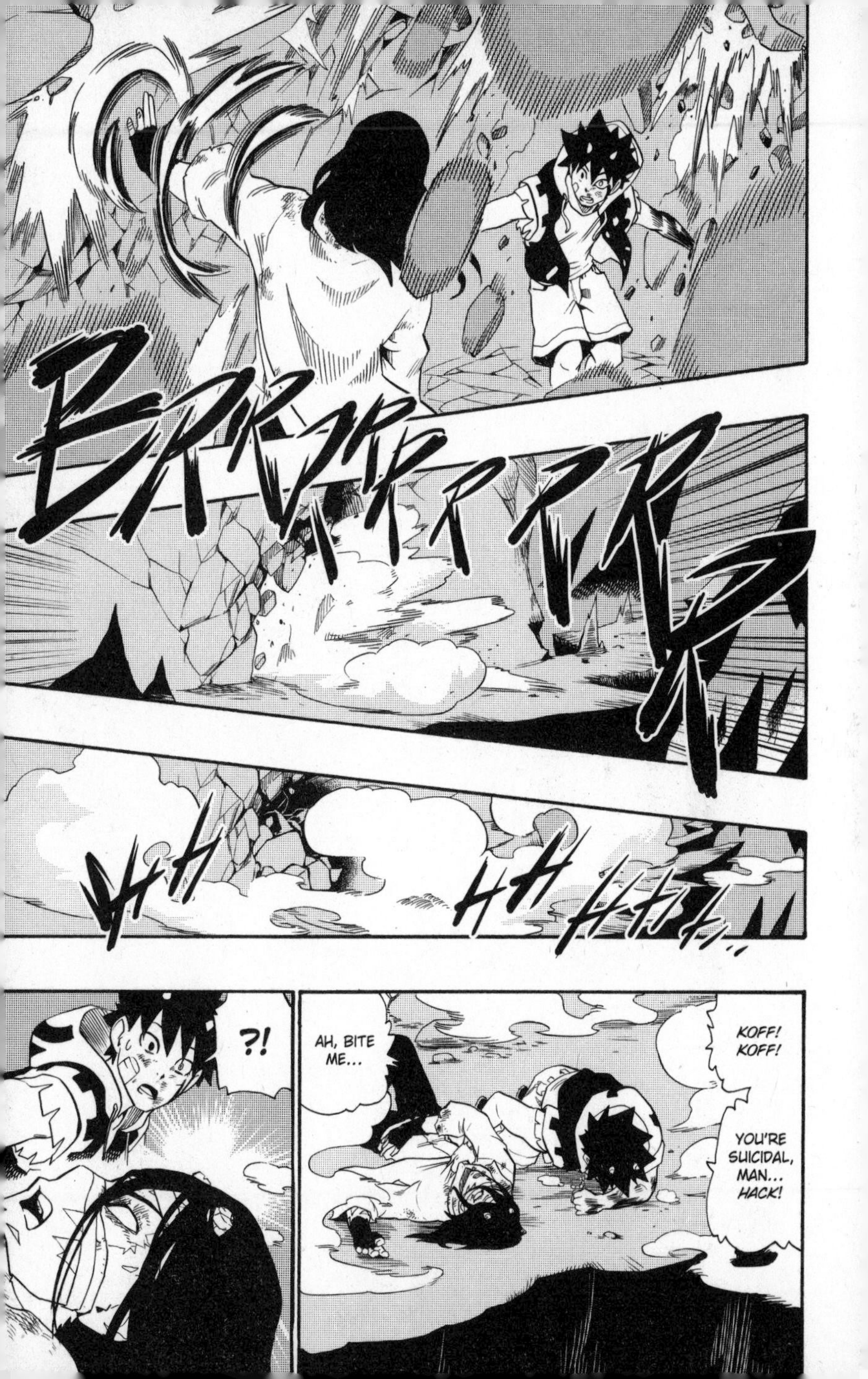
KOFF! KOFF!
YOU'RE SUICIDAL, MAN... HACK!
AH, BITE ME...
?!

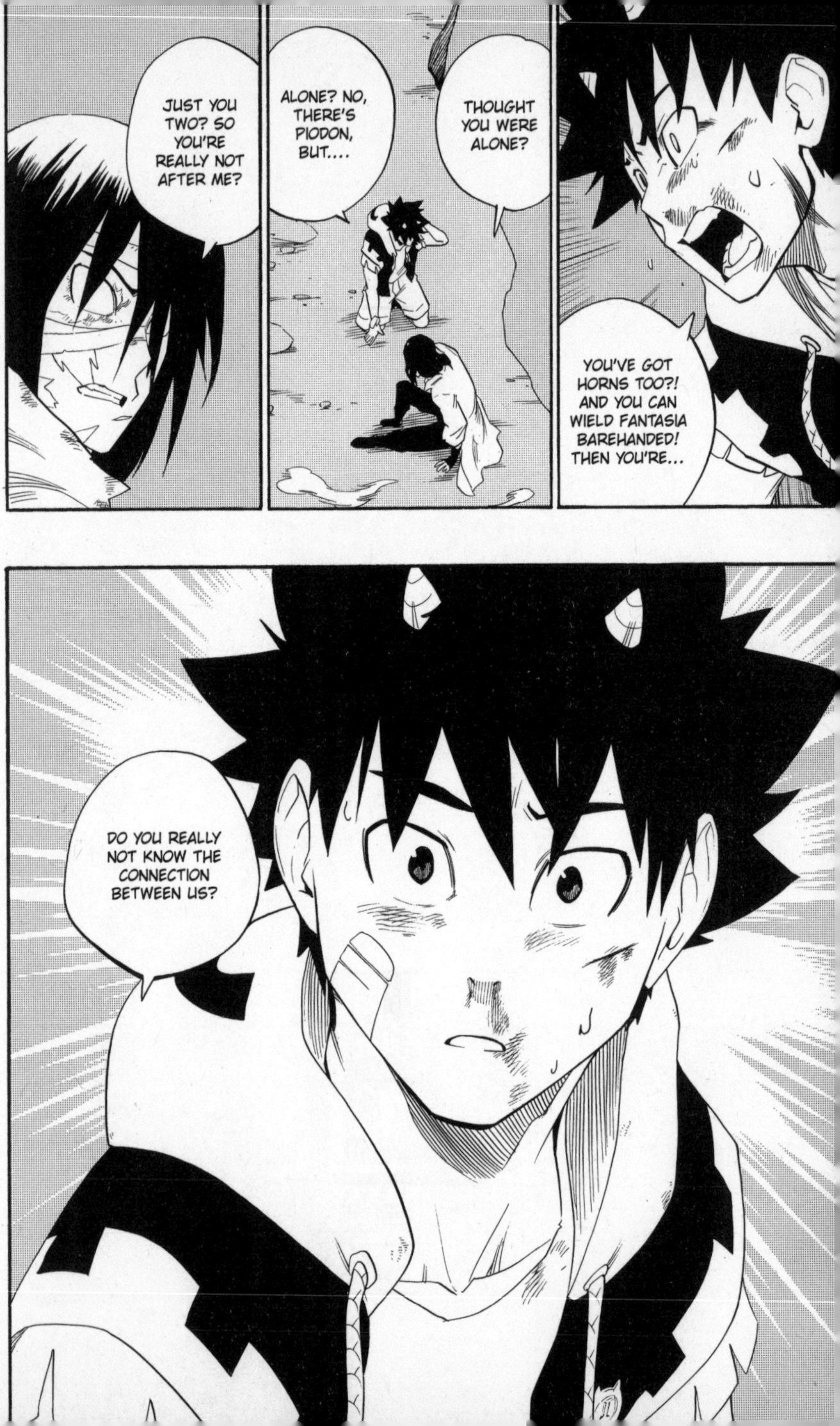
YOU'VE GOT HORNS TOO?! AND YOU CAN WIELD FANTASIA BAREHANDED! THEN YOU'RE...
THOUGHT YOU WERE ALONE?
ALONE? NO, THERE'S PIODON, BUT....
JUST YOU TWO? SO YOU'RE REALLY NOT AFTER ME?
DO YOU REALLY NOT KNOW THE CONNECTION BETWEEN US?

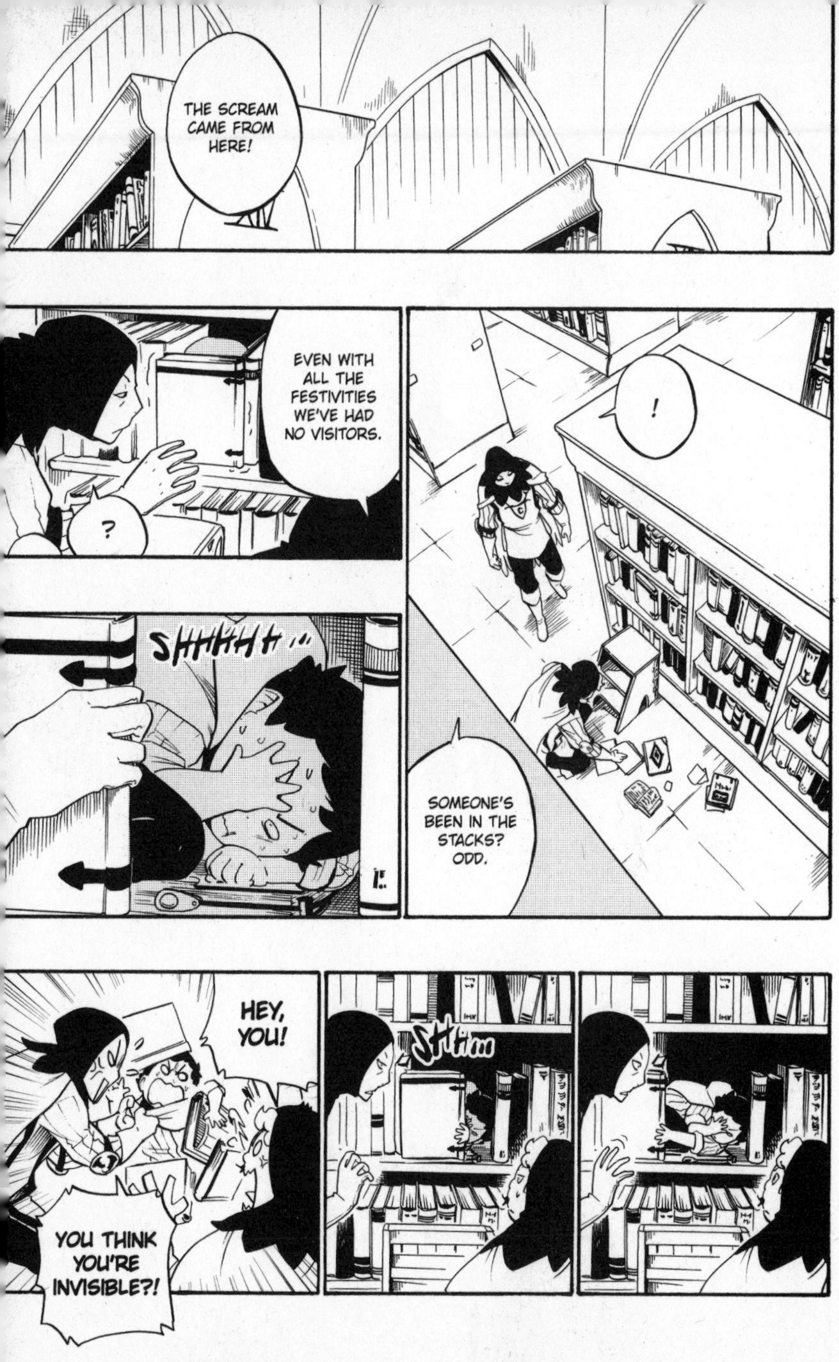
THE SCREAM CAME FROM HERE!
!
SOMEONE'S BEEN IN THE STACKS? ODD.
EVEN WITH ALL THE FESTIVITIES WE'VE HAD NO VISITORS.
?
SHHHHH...
SHH...
HEY, YOU!
YOU THINK YOU'RE INVISIBLE?!

WHAT'RE YOU DOING HERE?
I'M A KID!
WHERE ARE YOUR PARENTS!?
A KID!
'ELP!
ALERT! ALERT!
EVERYONE UPSTAIRS! NOW!
THE LORDS WANT ALL GUARDS FRONT AND CENTER!
BY MERLIN, WHAT'S GOING ON?
AND WHAT ABOUT THIS KI-
...!
FORGET 'IM!
THE LORDS WON'T WAIT!

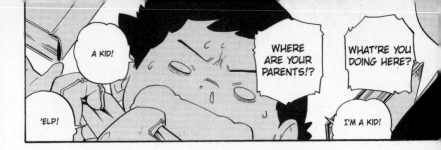

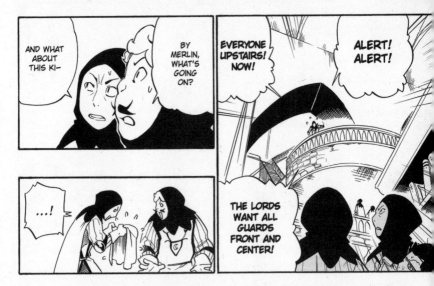

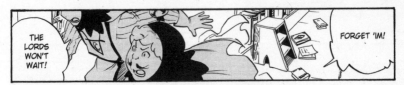

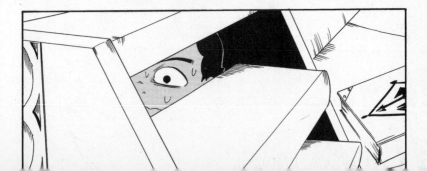

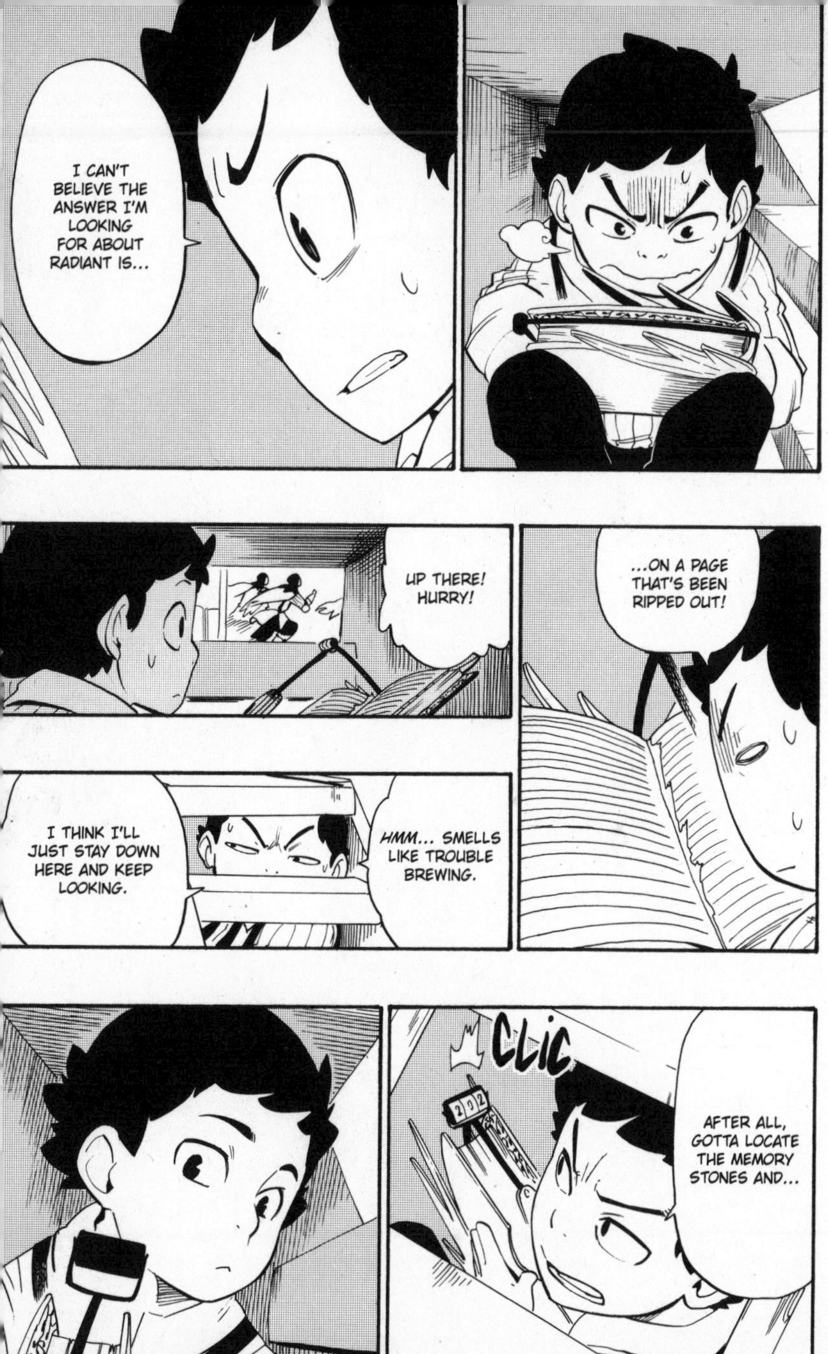
I CAN'T BELIEVE THE ANSWER I'M LOOKING FOR ABOUT RADIANT IS...
...ON A PAGE THAT'S BEEN RIPPED OUT!
UP THERE! HURRY!
HMM... SMELLS LIKE TROUBLE BREWING.
I THINK I'LL JUST STAY DOWN HERE AND KEEP LOOKING.
CLIC
AFTER ALL, GOTTA LOCATE THE MEMORY STONES AND...

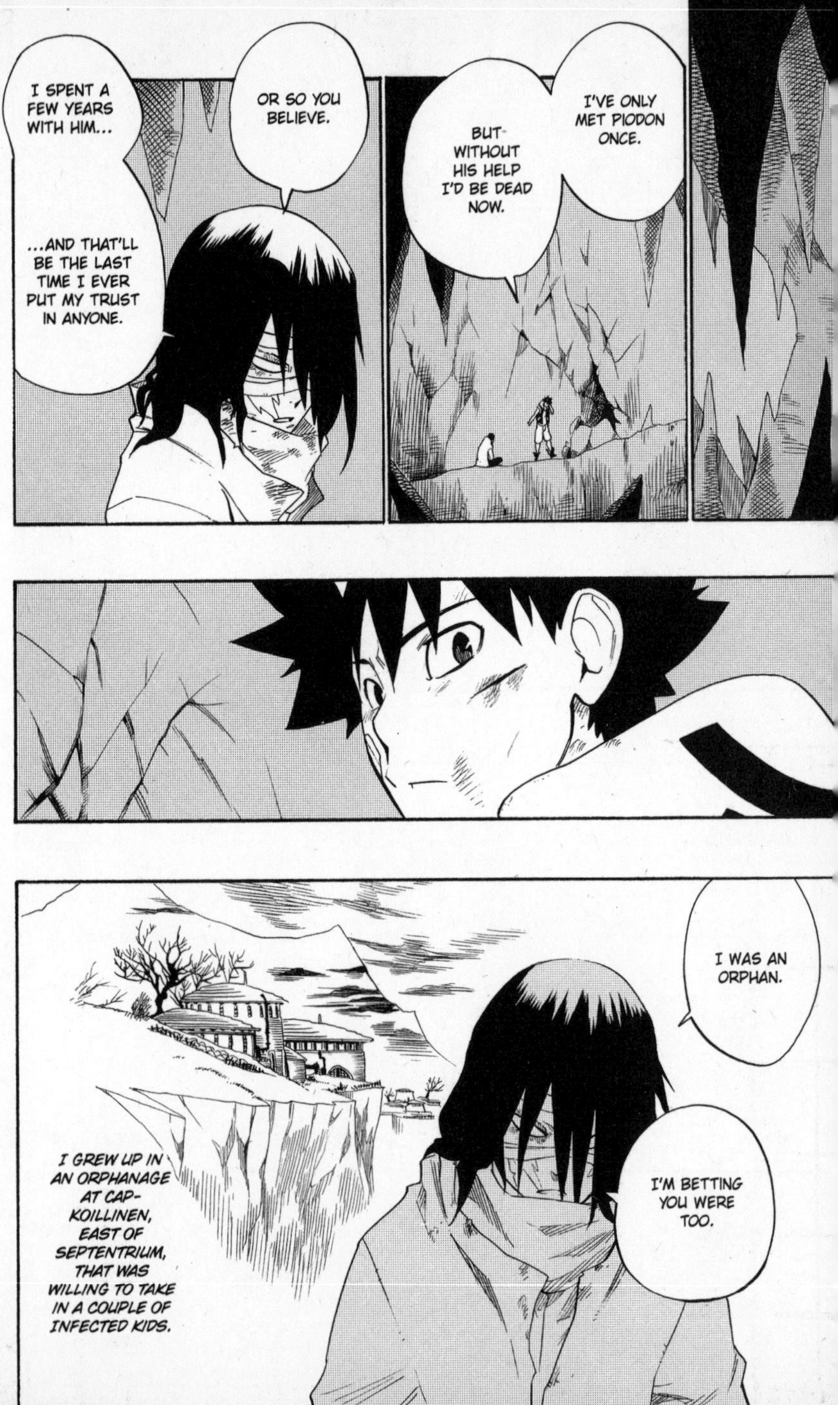
I'VE ONLY MET PIODON ONCE.
BUT WITHOUT HIS HELP I'D BE DEAD NOW.
OR SO YOU BELIEVE.
I SPENT A FEW YEARS WITH HIM...
...AND THAT'LL BE THE LAST TIME I EVER PUT MY TRUST IN ANYONE.
I WAS AN ORPHAN.
I'M BETTING YOU WERE TOO.
I GREW UP IN AN ORPHANAGE AT CAP-KOILLINEN, EAST OF SEPTENTRIUM, THAT WAS WILLING TO TAKE IN A COUPLE OF INFECTED KIDS.

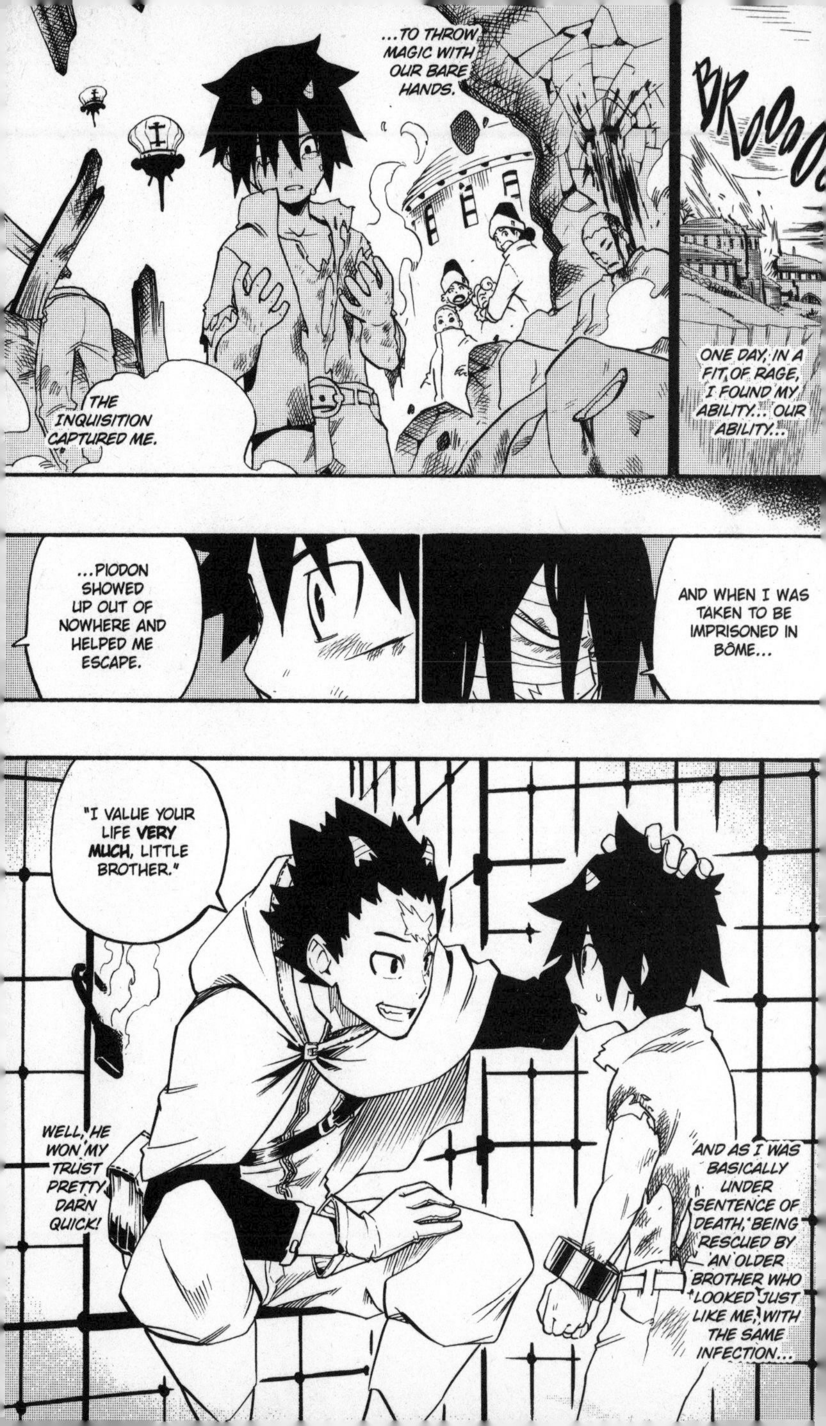
BROOOOO
ONE DAY, IN A FIT OF RAGE, I FOUND MY ABILITY... OUR ABILITY...
...TO THROW MAGIC WITH OUR BARE HANDS.
THE INQUISITION CAPTURED ME.
AND WHEN I WAS TAKEN TO BE IMPRISONED IN BÔME...
...PIODON SHOWED UP OUT OF NOWHERE AND HELPED ME ESCAPE.
AND AS I WAS BASICALLY UNDER SENTENCE OF DEATH, BEING RESCUED BY AN OLDER BROTHER WHO LOOKED JUST LIKE ME, WITH THE SAME INFECTION...
"I VALUE YOUR LIFE **VERY MUCH**, LITTLE BROTHER."
WELL, HE WON MY TRUST PRETTY DARN QUICK!

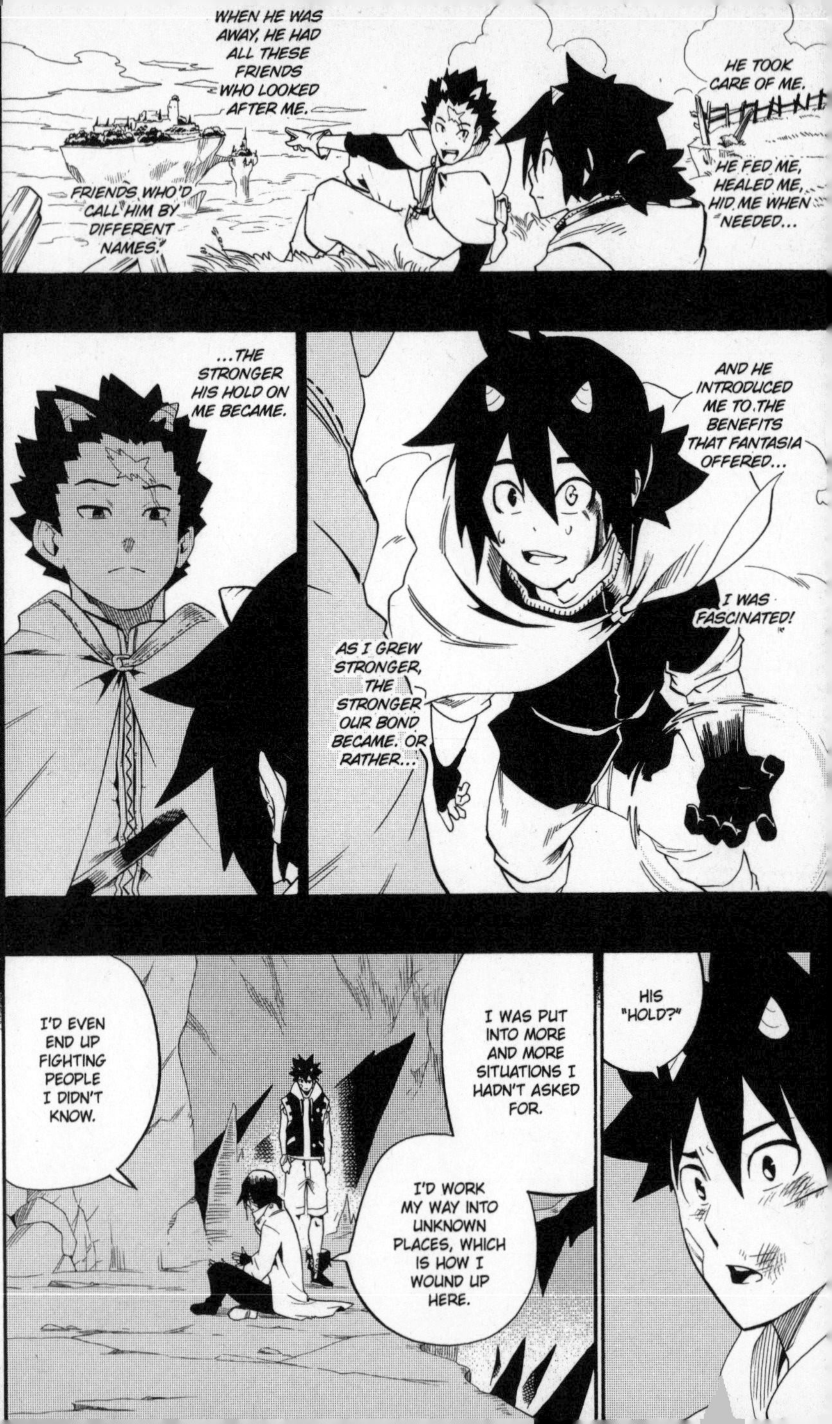
HE TOOK CARE OF ME.
HE FED ME, HEALED ME, HID ME WHEN NEEDED...
WHEN HE WAS AWAY, HE HAD ALL THESE FRIENDS WHO LOOKED AFTER ME.
FRIENDS WHO'D CALL HIM BY DIFFERENT NAMES.
AND HE INTRODUCED ME TO THE BENEFITS THAT FANTASIA OFFERED...
I WAS FASCINATED!
AS I GREW STRONGER, THE STRONGER OUR BOND BECAME. OR RATHER...
...THE STRONGER HIS HOLD ON ME BECAME.
HIS "HOLD?"
I WAS PUT INTO MORE AND MORE SITUATIONS I HADN'T ASKED FOR.
I'D EVEN END UP FIGHTING PEOPLE I DIDN'T KNOW.
I'D WORK MY WAY INTO UNKNOWN PLACES, WHICH IS HOW I WOUND UP HERE.

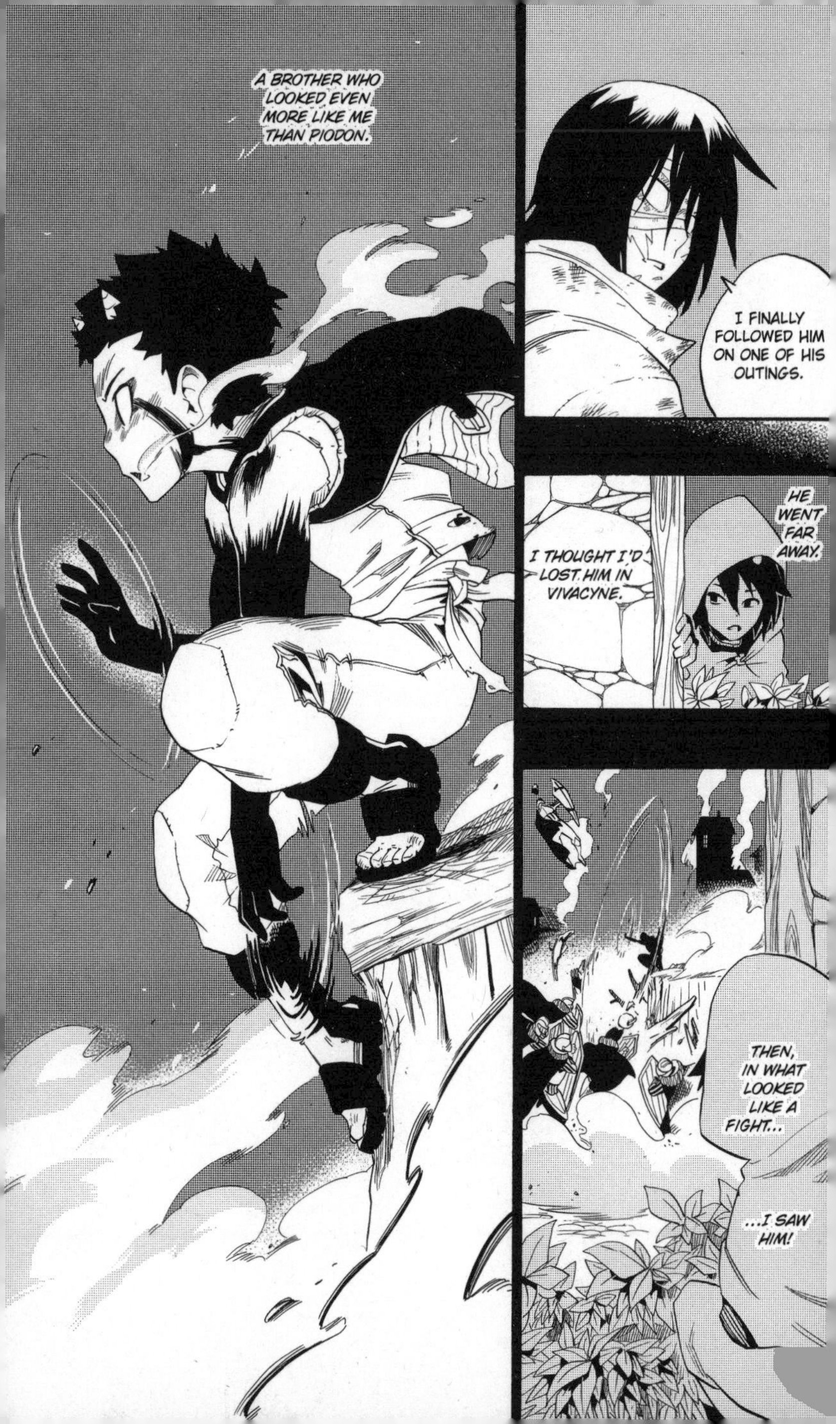
I FINALLY FOLLOWED HIM ON ONE OF HIS OUTINGS.
HE WENT FAR AWAY.
I THOUGHT I'D LOST HIM IN VIVACYNE.
THEN, IN WHAT LOOKED LIKE A FIGHT...
...I SAW HIM!
A BROTHER WHO LOOKED EVEN MORE LIKE ME THAN PIODON.

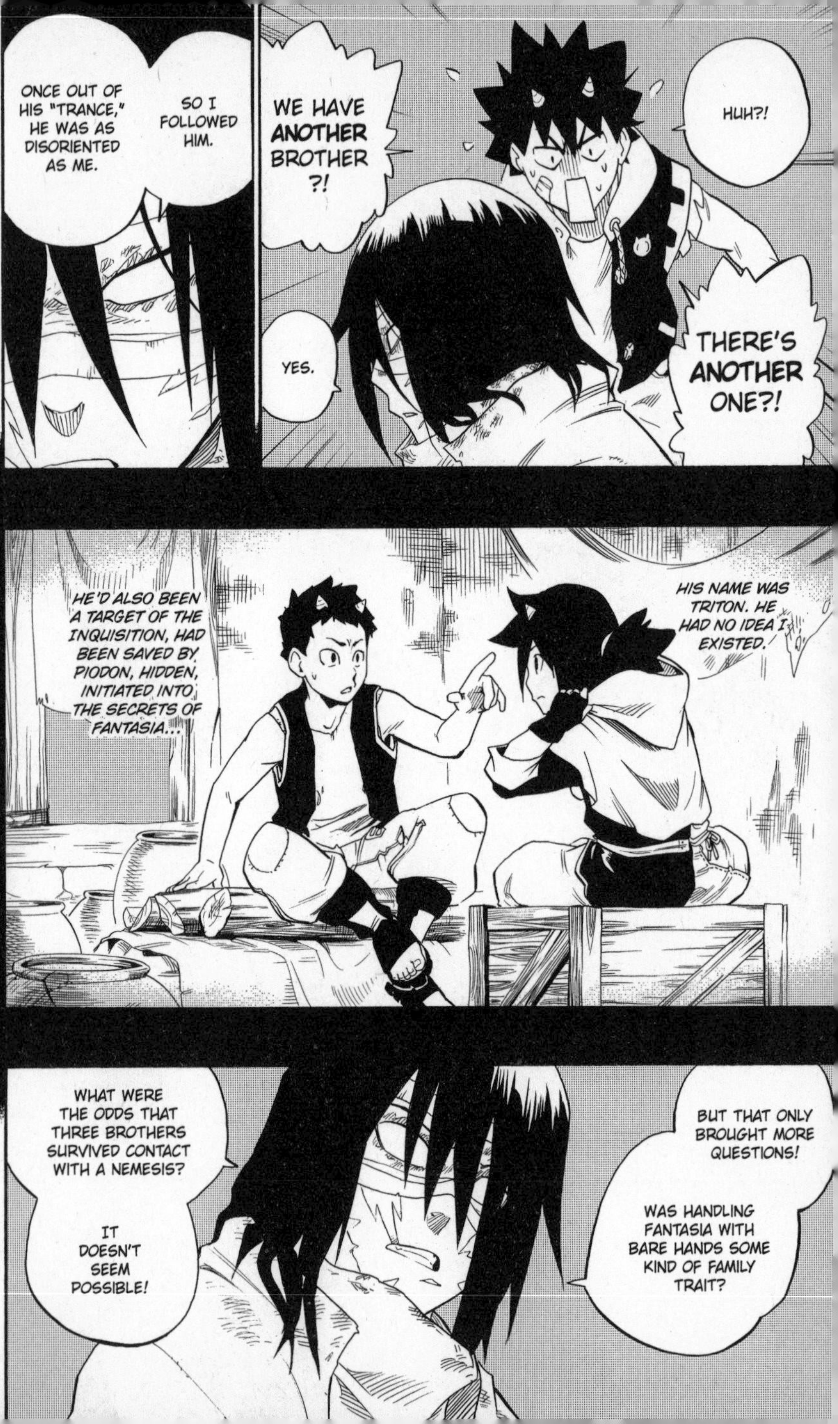
HUH?!
THERE'S ANOTHER ONE?!
WE HAVE ANOTHER BROTHER?!
YES.
ONCE OUT OF HIS "TRANCE," HE WAS AS DISORIENTED AS ME.
SO I FOLLOWED HIM.
HIS NAME WAS TRITON. HE HAD NO IDEA I EXISTED.
HE'D ALSO BEEN A TARGET OF THE INQUISITION, HAD BEEN SAVED BY PIODON, HIDDEN, INITIATED INTO THE SECRETS OF FANTASIA...
BUT THAT ONLY BROUGHT MORE QUESTIONS!
WAS HANDLING FANTASIA WITH BARE HANDS SOME KIND OF FAMILY TRAIT?
WHAT WERE THE ODDS THAT THREE BROTHERS SURVIVED CONTACT WITH A NEMESIS?
IT DOESN'T SEEM POSSIBLE!

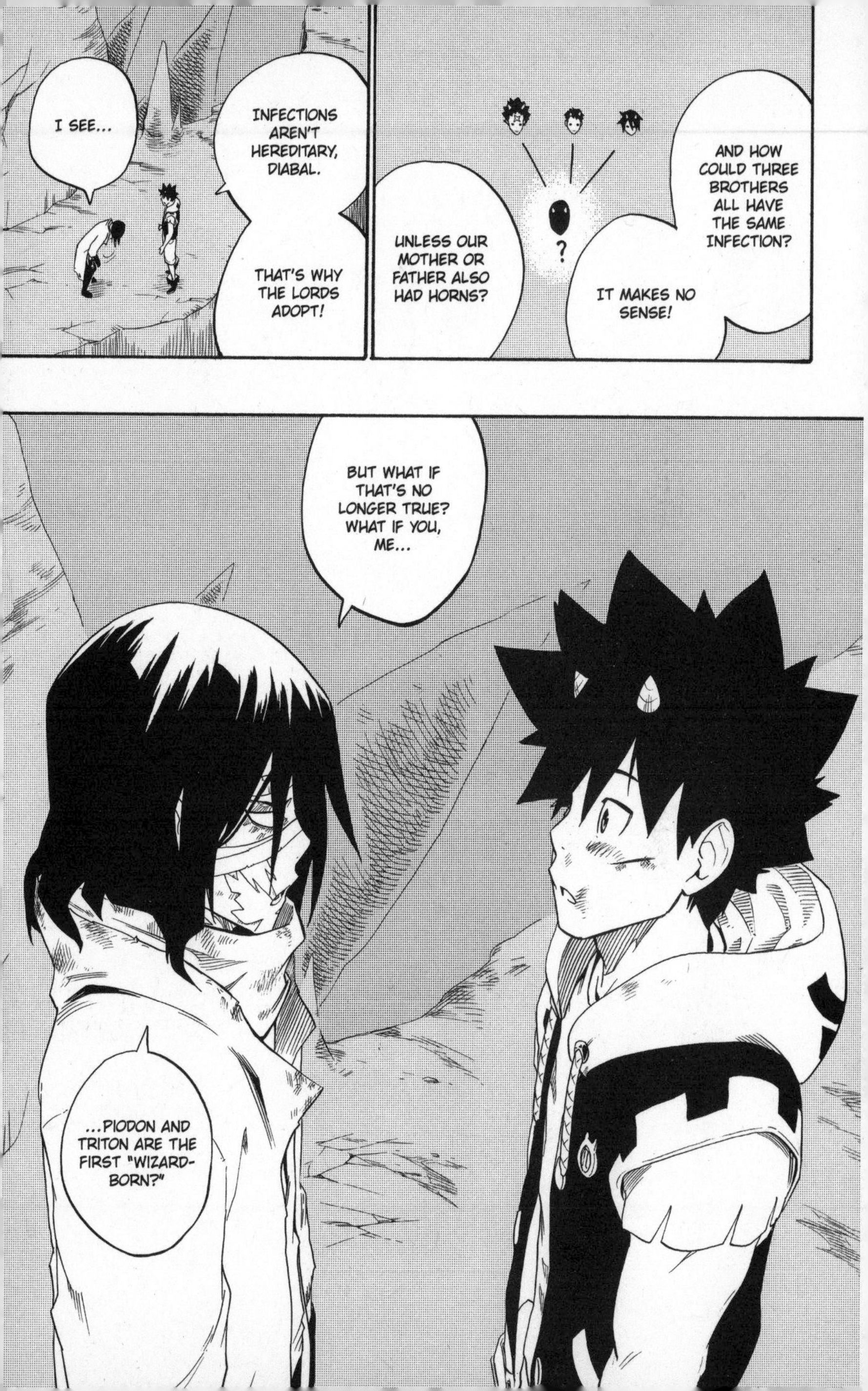
AND HOW COULD THREE BROTHERS ALL HAVE THE SAME INFECTION?
IT MAKES NO SENSE!
UNLESS OUR MOTHER OR FATHER ALSO HAD HORNS?
?
INFECTIONS AREN'T HEREDITARY, DIABAL.
THAT'S WHY THE LORDS ADOPT!
I SEE...
BUT WHAT IF THAT'S NO LONGER TRUE? WHAT IF YOU, ME...
...PIODON AND TRITON ARE THE FIRST "WIZARD-BORN?"

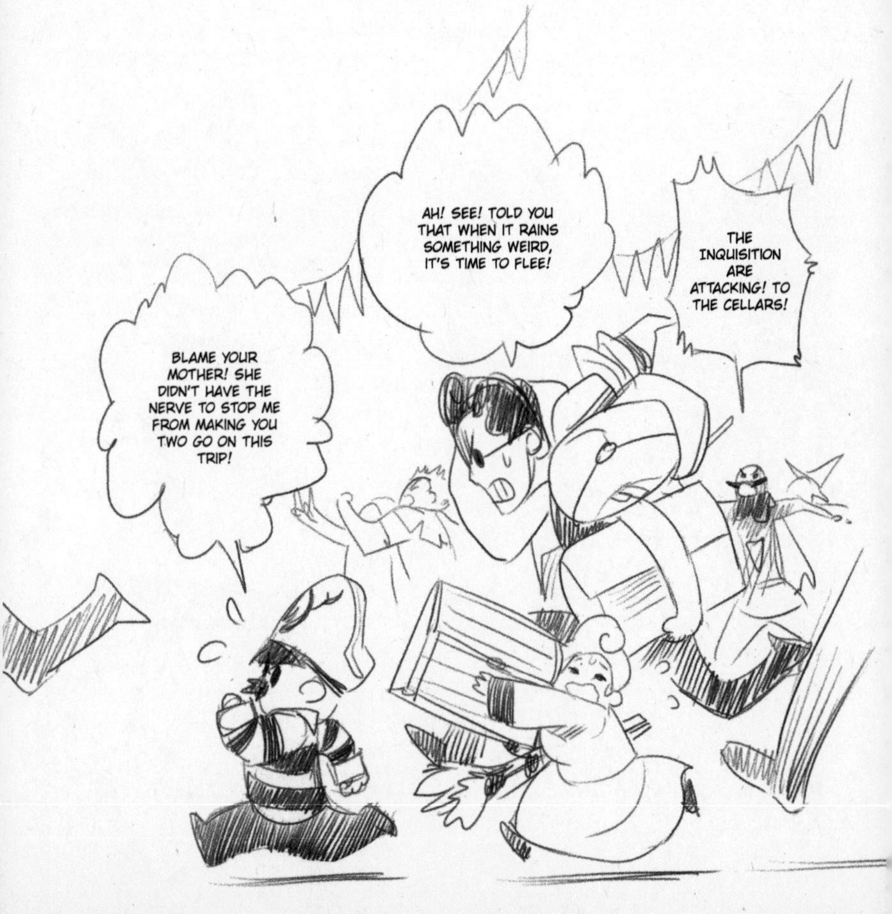
THE INQUISITION ARE ATTACKING! TO THE CELLARS!
AH! SEE! TOLD YOU THAT WHEN IT RAINS SOMETHING WEIRD, IT'S TIME TO FLEE!
BLAME YOUR MOTHER! SHE DIDN'T HAVE THE NERVE TO STOP ME FROM MAKING YOU TWO GO ON THIS TRIP!

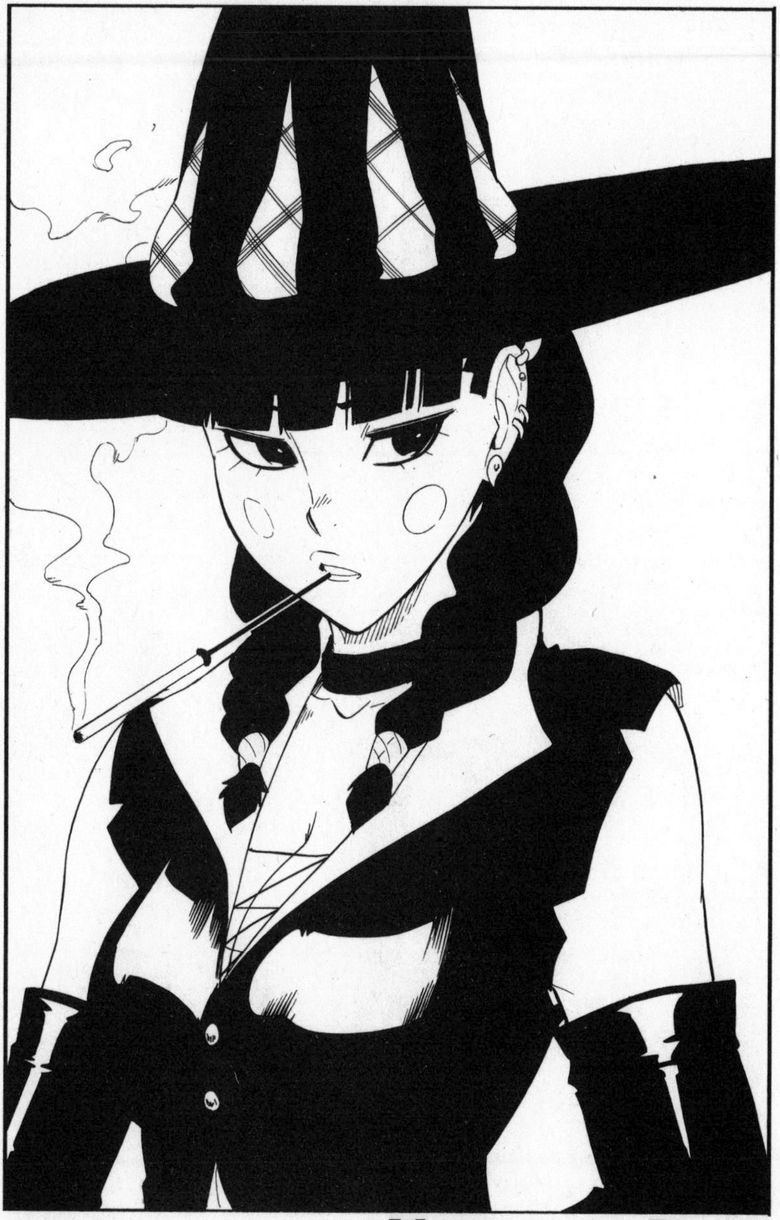

Chapter 56

Message of Peace

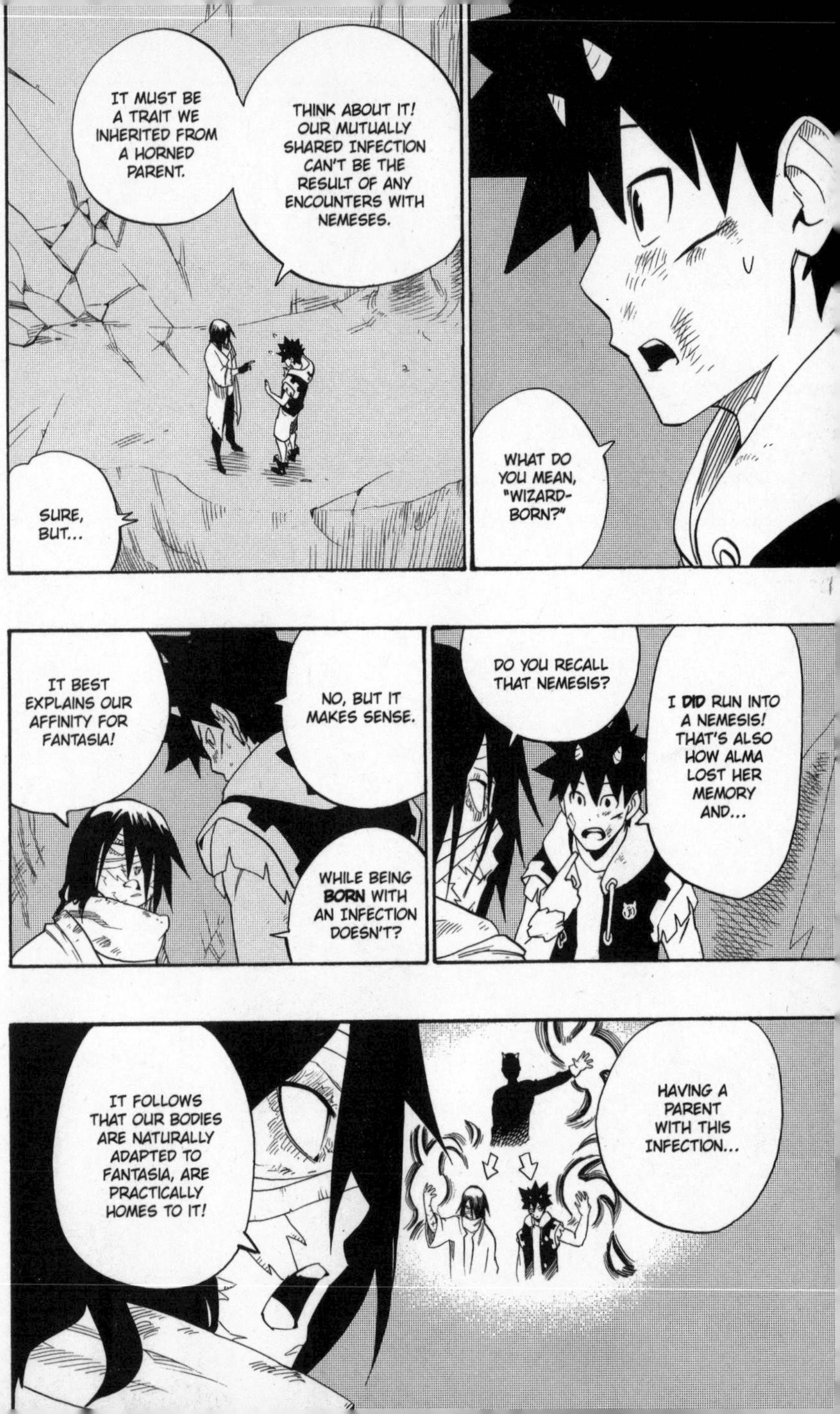
WHAT DO YOU MEAN, "WIZARD-BORN?"
IT MUST BE A TRAIT WE INHERITED FROM A HORNED PARENT.
SURE, BUT...
THINK ABOUT IT! OUR MUTUALLY SHARED INFECTION CAN'T BE THE RESULT OF ANY ENCOUNTERS WITH NEMESES.
I **DID** RUN INTO A NEMESIS! THAT'S ALSO HOW ALMA LOST HER MEMORY AND...
DO YOU RECALL THAT NEMESIS?
NO, BUT IT MAKES SENSE.
WHILE BEING **BORN** WITH AN INFECTION DOESN'T?
IT BEST EXPLAINS OUR AFFINITY FOR FANTASIA!
HAVING A PARENT WITH THIS INFECTION...
IT FOLLOWS THAT OUR BODIES ARE NATURALLY ADAPTED TO FANTASIA, ARE PRACTICALLY HOMES TO IT!

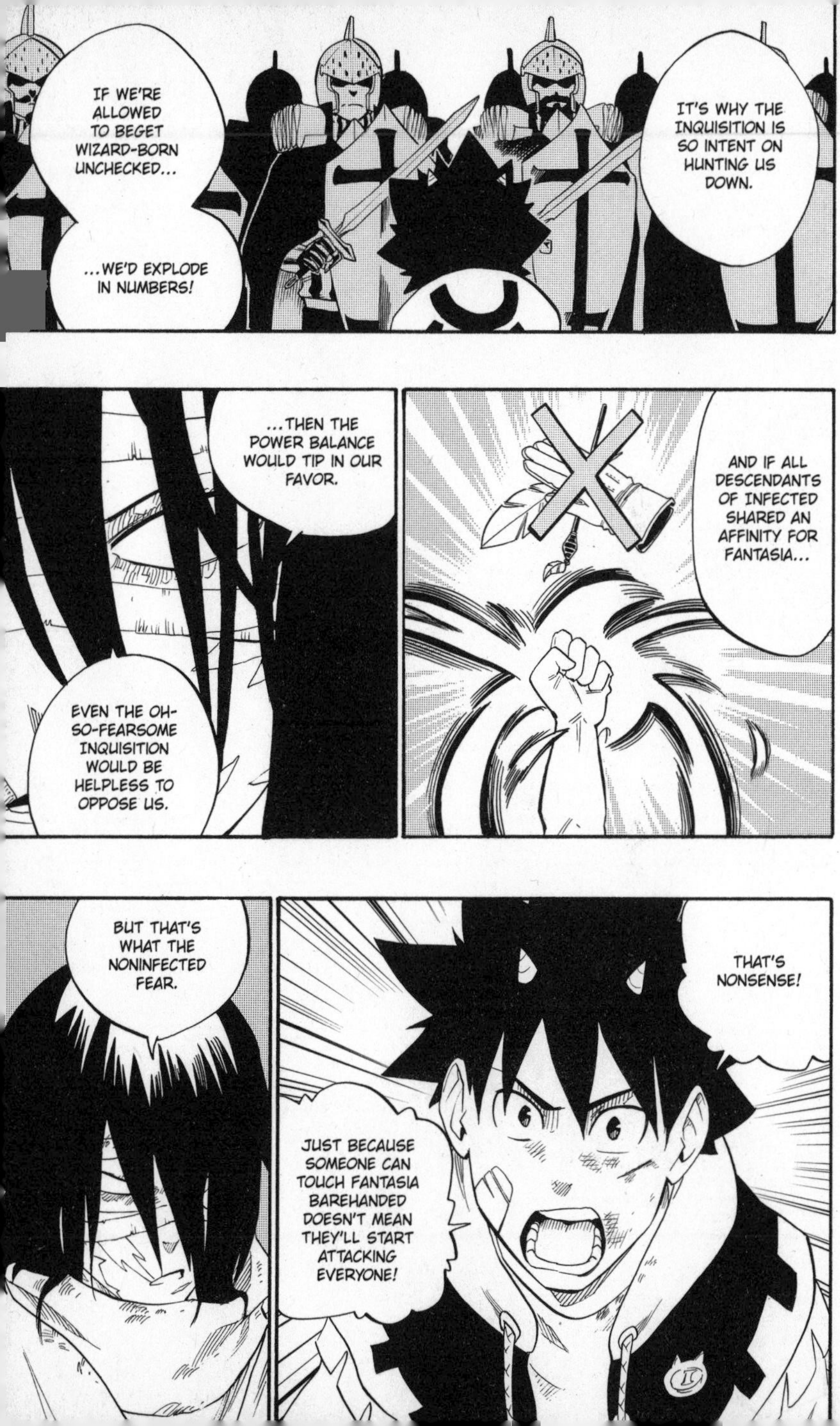
IT'S WHY THE INQUISITION IS SO INTENT ON HUNTING US DOWN.
IF WE'RE ALLOWED TO BEGET WIZARD-BORN UNCHECKED...
...WE'D EXPLODE IN NUMBERS!
AND IF ALL DESCENDANTS OF INFECTED SHARED AN AFFINITY FOR FANTASIA...
...THEN THE POWER BALANCE WOULD TIP IN OUR FAVOR.
EVEN THE OH-SO-FEARSOME INQUISITION WOULD BE HELPLESS TO OPPOSE US.
THAT'S NONSENSE!
JUST BECAUSE SOMEONE CAN TOUCH FANTASIA BAREHANDED DOESN'T MEAN THEY'LL START ATTACKING EVERYONE!
BUT THAT'S WHAT THE NONINFECTED FEAR.

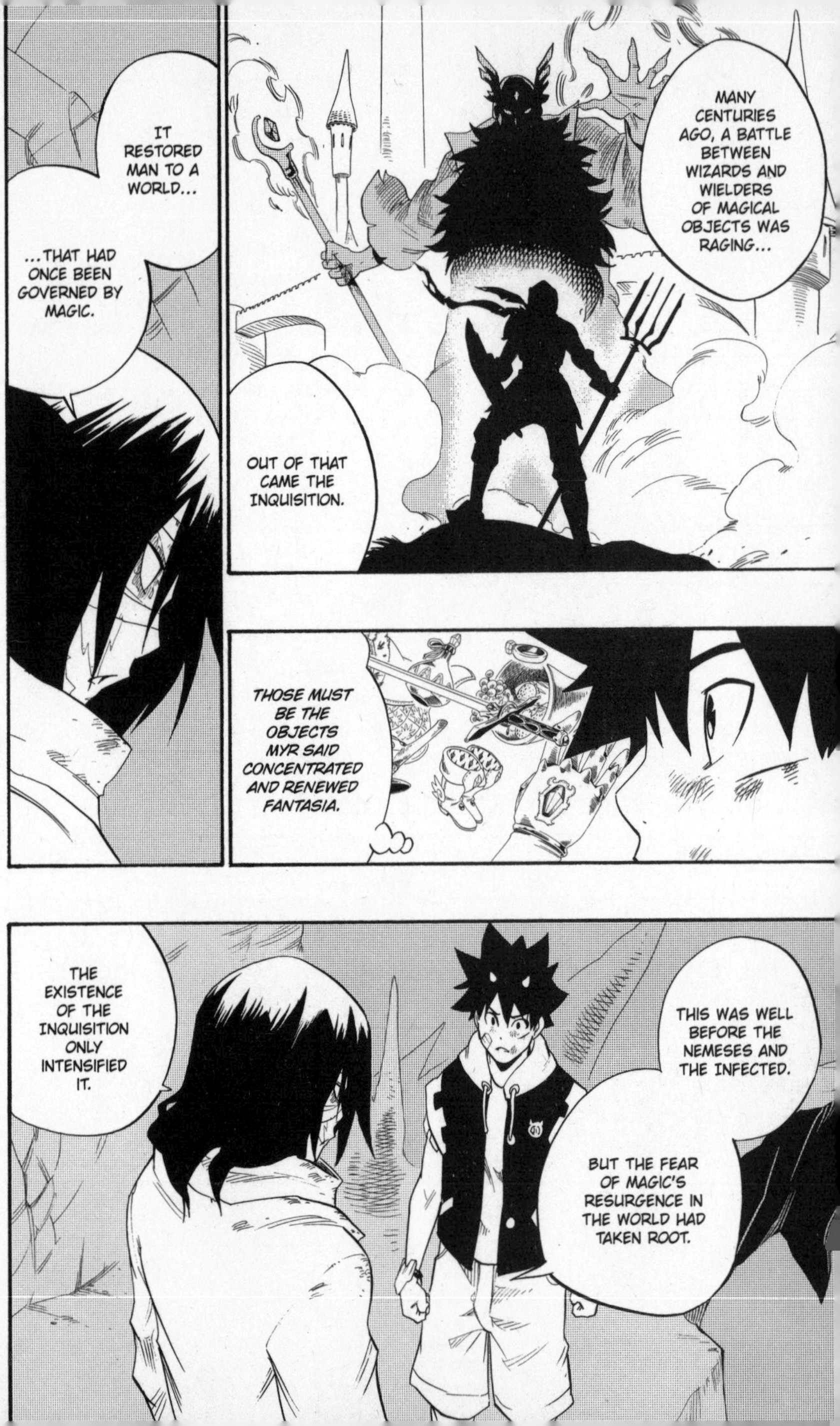
MANY CENTURIES AGO, A BATTLE BETWEEN WIZARDS AND WIELDERS OF MAGICAL OBJECTS WAS RAGING...
OUT OF THAT CAME THE INQUISITION.
THOSE MUST BE THE OBJECTS MYR SAID CONCENTRATED AND RENEWED FANTASIA.
IT RESTORED MAN TO A WORLD...
...THAT HAD ONCE BEEN GOVERNED BY MAGIC.
THIS WAS WELL BEFORE THE NEMESES AND THE INFECTED.
BUT THE FEAR OF MAGIC'S RESURGENCE IN THE WORLD HAD TAKEN ROOT.
THE EXISTENCE OF THE INQUISITION ONLY INTENSIFIED IT.

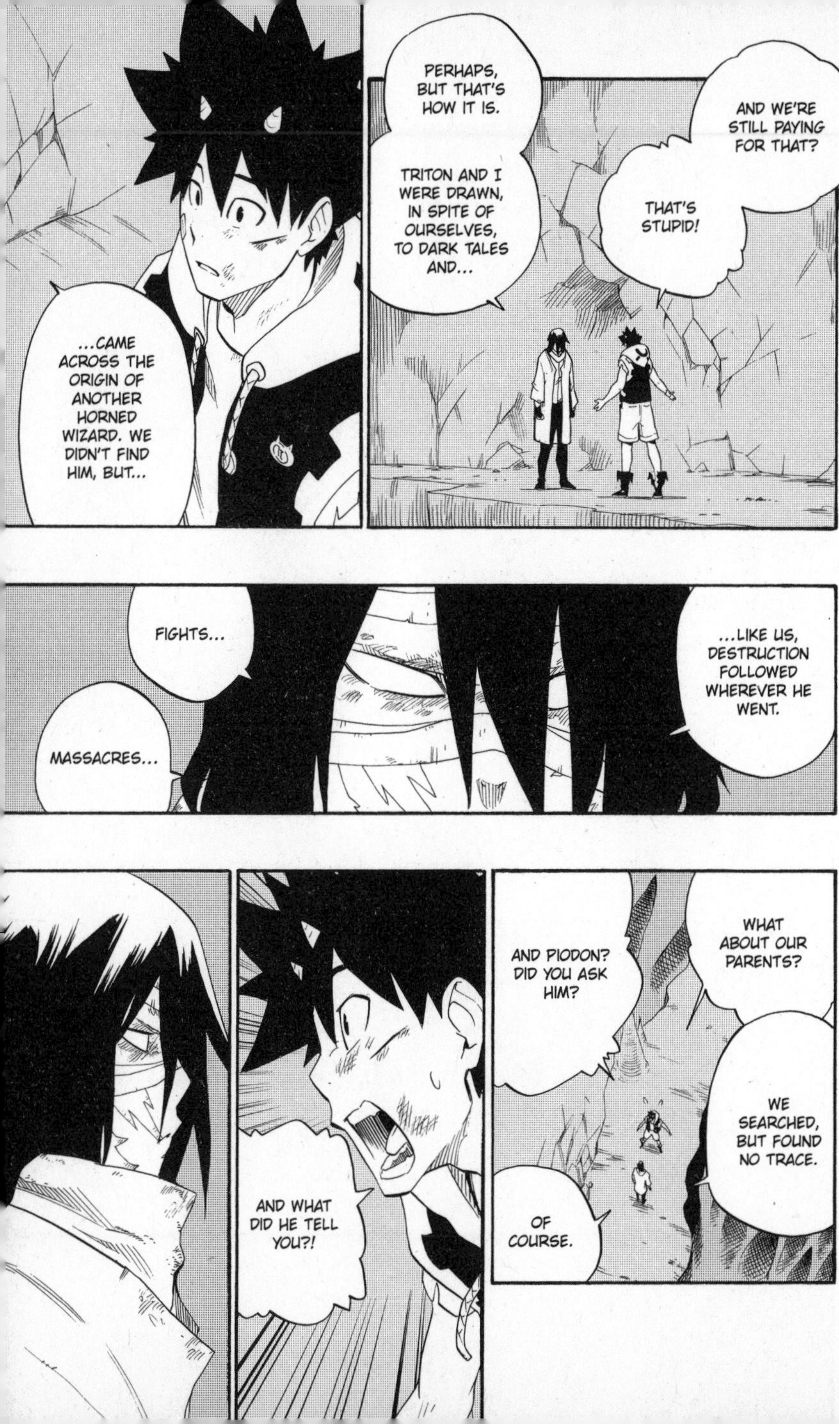
AND WE'RE STILL PAYING FOR THAT?
THAT'S STUPID!
PERHAPS, BUT THAT'S HOW IT IS.
TRITON AND I WERE DRAWN, IN SPITE OF OURSELVES, TO DARK TALES AND...
...CAME ACROSS THE ORIGIN OF ANOTHER HORNED WIZARD. WE DIDN'T FIND HIM, BUT...
...LIKE US, DESTRUCTION FOLLOWED WHEREVER HE WENT.
FIGHTS...
MASSACRES...
WHAT ABOUT OUR PARENTS?
WE SEARCHED, BUT FOUND NO TRACE.
AND PIODON? DID YOU ASK HIM?
OF COURSE.
AND WHAT DID HE TELL YOU?!

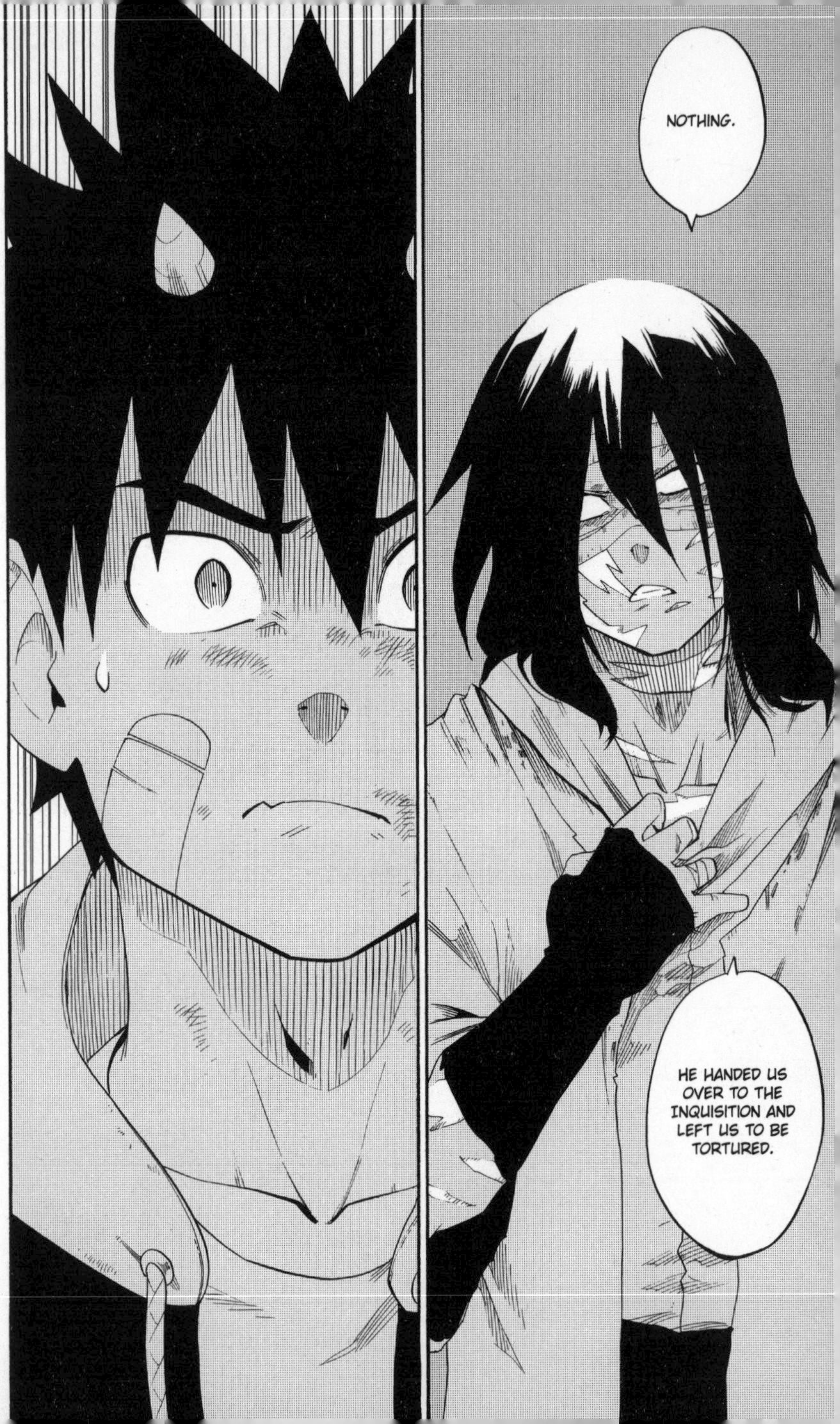
NOTHING.
HE HANDED US OVER TO THE INQUISITION AND LEFT US TO BE TORTURED.

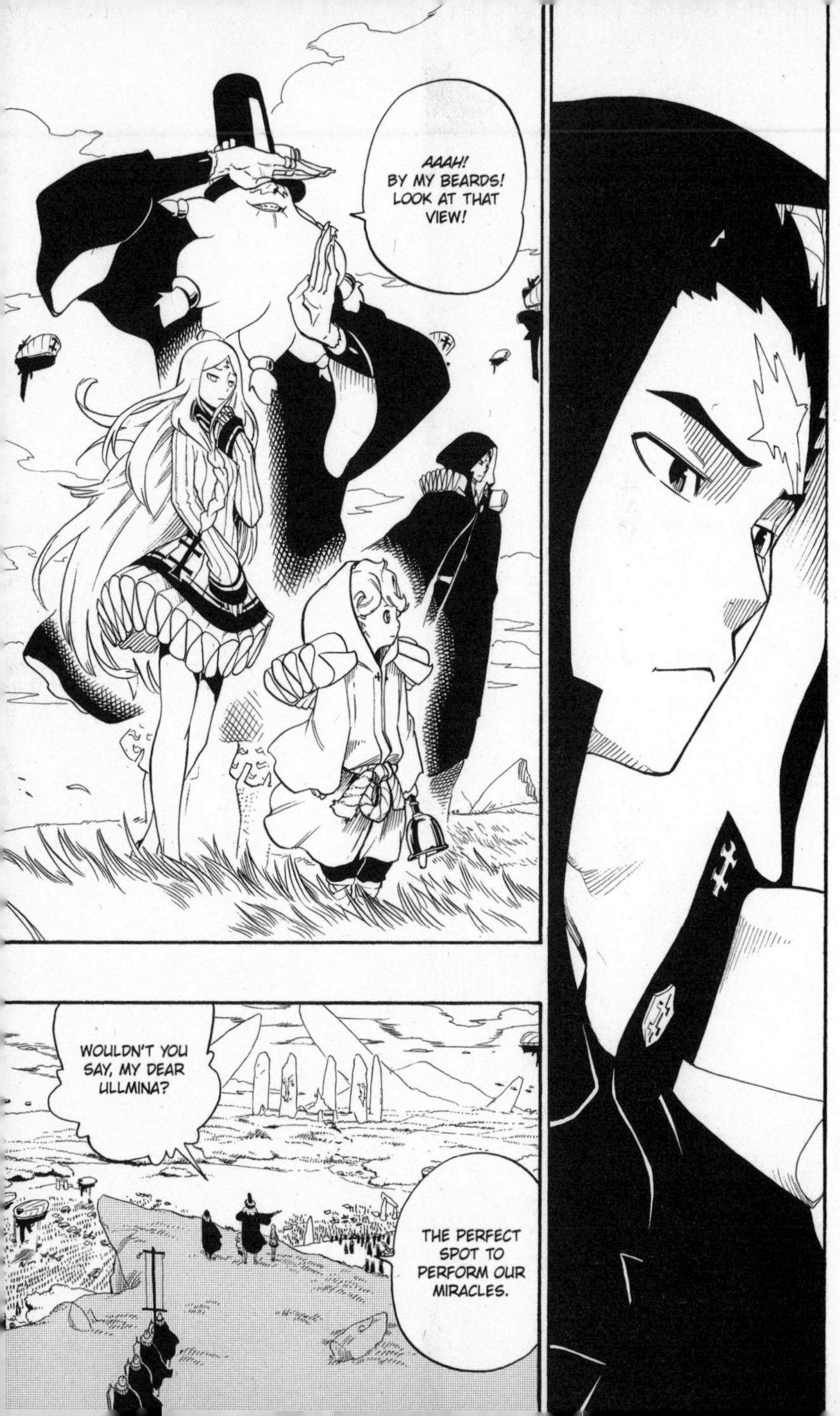
AAAH! BY MY BEARDS! LOOK AT THAT VIEW!
WOULDN'T YOU SAY, MY DEAR ULLMINA?
THE PERFECT SPOT TO PERFORM OUR MIRACLES.

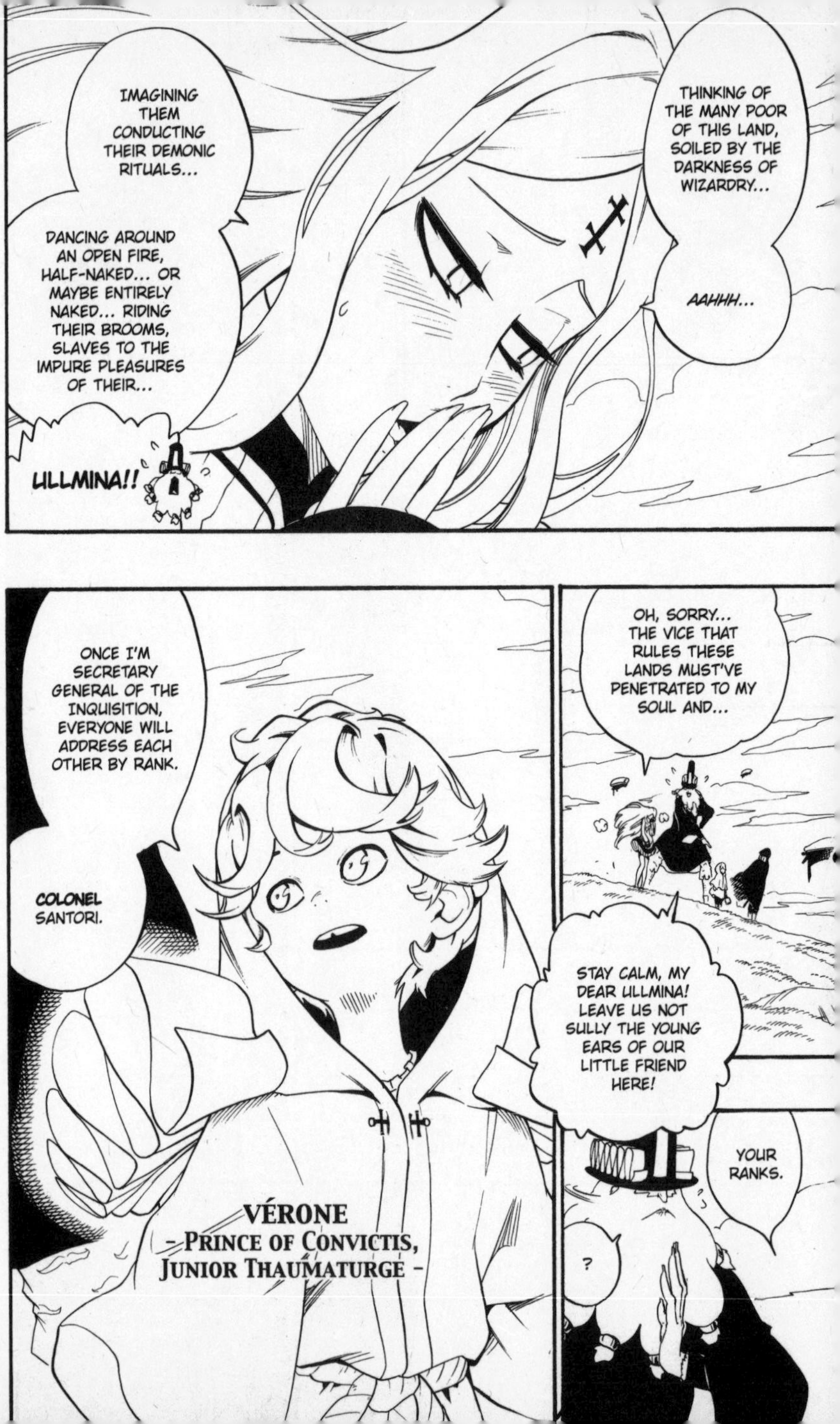
THINKING OF THE MANY POOR OF THIS LAND, SOILED BY THE DARKNESS OF WIZARDRY...
AAHHH...
IMAGINING THEM CONDUCTING THEIR DEMONIC RITUALS...
DANCING AROUND AN OPEN FIRE, HALF-NAKED... OR MAYBE ENTIRELY NAKED... RIDING THEIR BROOMS, SLAVES TO THE IMPURE PLEASURES OF THEIR...
ULLMINA!!
OH, SORRY... THE VICE THAT RULES THESE LANDS MUST'VE PENETRATED TO MY SOUL AND...
STAY CALM, MY DEAR ULLMINA! LEAVE US NOT SULLY THE YOUNG EARS OF OUR LITTLE FRIEND HERE!
YOUR RANKS.
?
ONCE I'M SECRETARY GENERAL OF THE INQUISITION, EVERYONE WILL ADDRESS EACH OTHER BY RANK.
COLONEL SANTORI.
VÉRONE
- PRINCE OF CONVICTIS, JUNIOR THAUMATURGE -

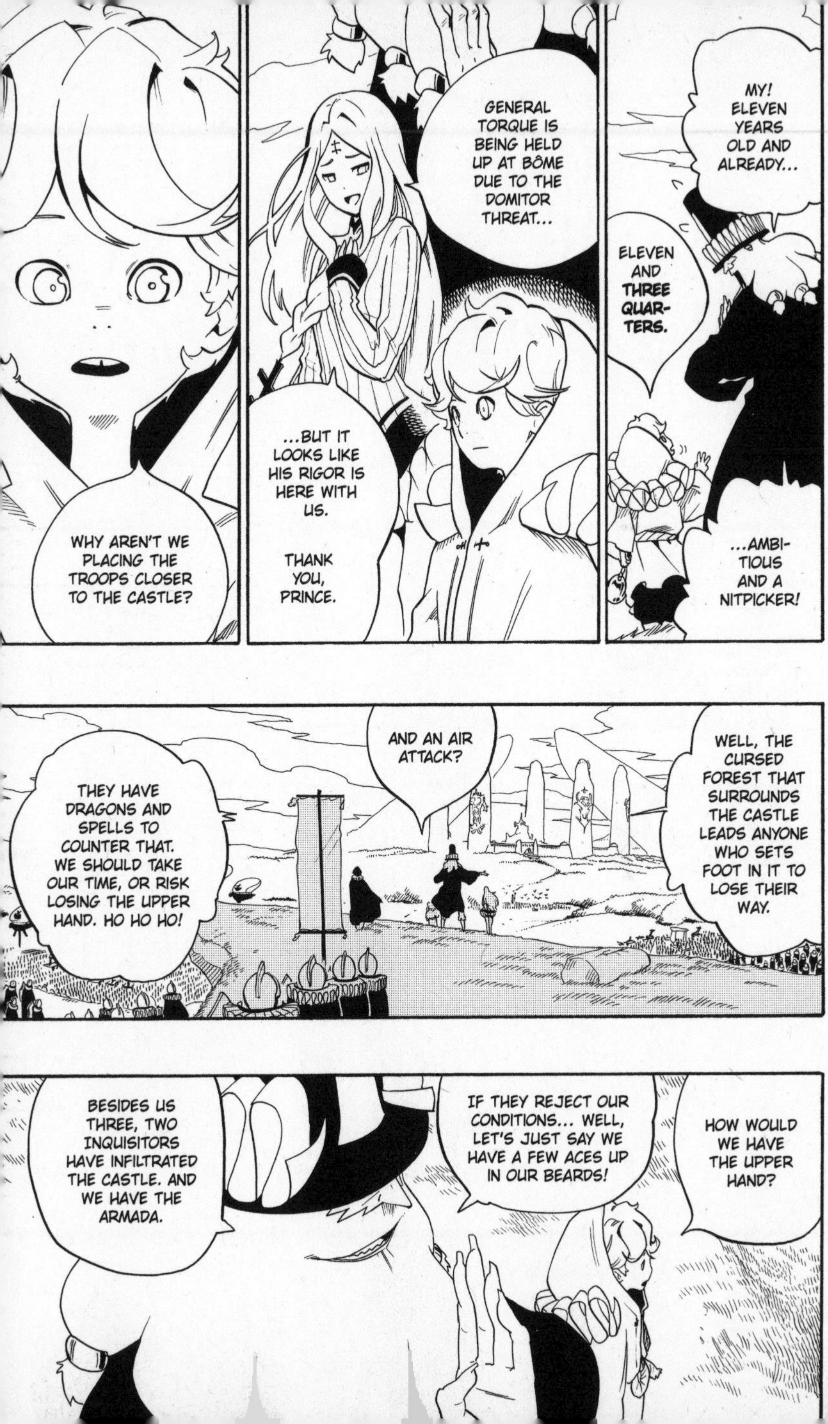
MY! ELEVEN YEARS OLD AND ALREADY...
ELEVEN AND THREE QUARTERS.
...AMBITIOUS AND A NITPICKER!
GENERAL TORQUE IS BEING HELD UP AT BÔME DUE TO THE DOMITOR THREAT...
...BUT IT LOOKS LIKE HIS RIGOR IS HERE WITH US.
THANK YOU, PRINCE.
WHY AREN'T WE PLACING THE TROOPS CLOSER TO THE CASTLE?
WELL, THE CURSED FOREST THAT SURROUNDS THE CASTLE LEADS ANYONE WHO SETS FOOT IN IT TO LOSE THEIR WAY.
AND AN AIR ATTACK?
THEY HAVE DRAGONS AND SPELLS TO COUNTER THAT. WE SHOULD TAKE OUR TIME, OR RISK LOSING THE UPPER HAND. HO HO HO!
HOW WOULD WE HAVE THE UPPER HAND?
BESIDES US THREE, TWO INQUISITORS HAVE INFILTRATED THE CASTLE. AND WE HAVE THE ARMADA.
IF THEY REJECT OUR CONDITIONS... WELL, LET'S JUST SAY WE HAVE A FEW ACES UP IN OUR BEARDS!

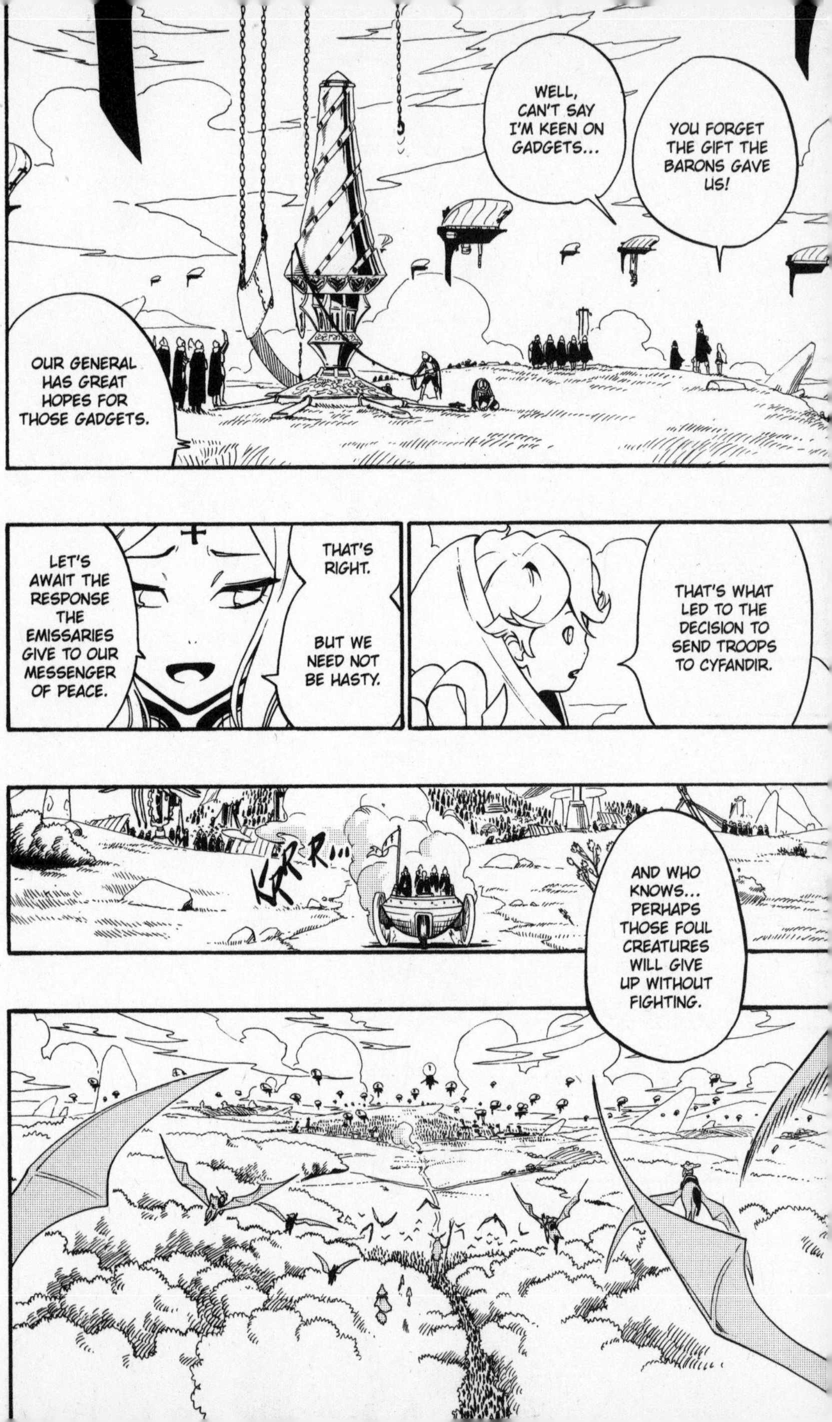
YOU FORGET THE GIFT THE BARONS GAVE US!
WELL, CAN'T SAY I'M KEEN ON GADGETS...
OUR GENERAL HAS GREAT HOPES FOR THOSE GADGETS.
THAT'S WHAT LED TO THE DECISION TO SEND TROOPS TO CYFANDIR.
THAT'S RIGHT.
BUT WE NEED NOT BE HASTY.
LET'S AWAIT THE RESPONSE THE EMISSARIES GIVE TO OUR MESSENGER OF PEACE.
AND WHO KNOWS... PERHAPS THOSE FOUL CREATURES WILL GIVE UP WITHOUT FIGHTING.
KRRR!!!

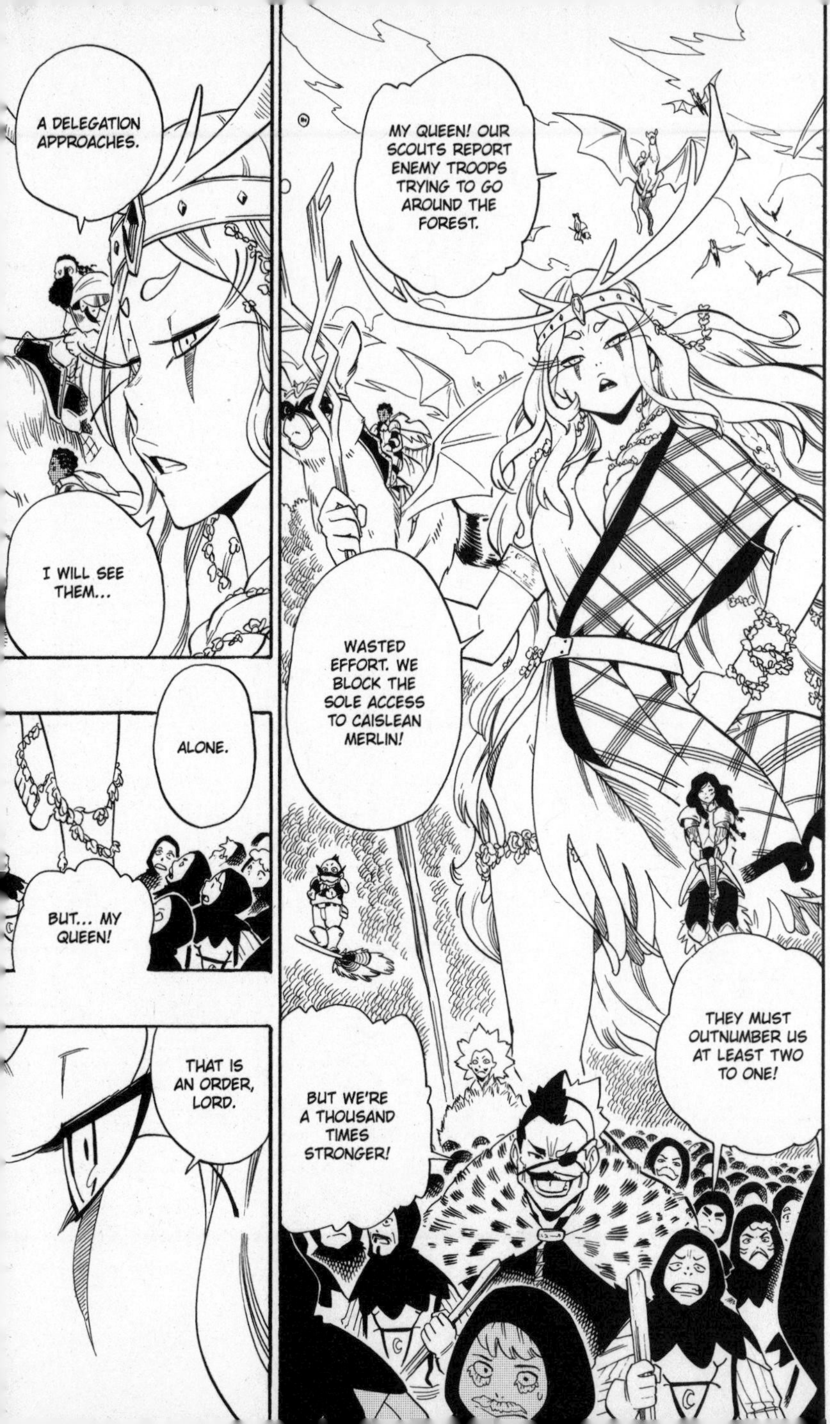
MY QUEEN! OUR SCOUTS REPORT ENEMY TROOPS TRYING TO GO AROUND THE FOREST.
WASTED EFFORT. WE BLOCK THE SOLE ACCESS TO CAISLEAN MERLIN!
THEY MUST OUTNUMBER US AT LEAST TWO TO ONE!
BUT WE'RE A THOUSAND TIMES STRONGER!
A DELEGATION APPROACHES.
I WILL SEE THEM...
ALONE.
BUT... MY QUEEN!
THAT IS AN ORDER, LORD.

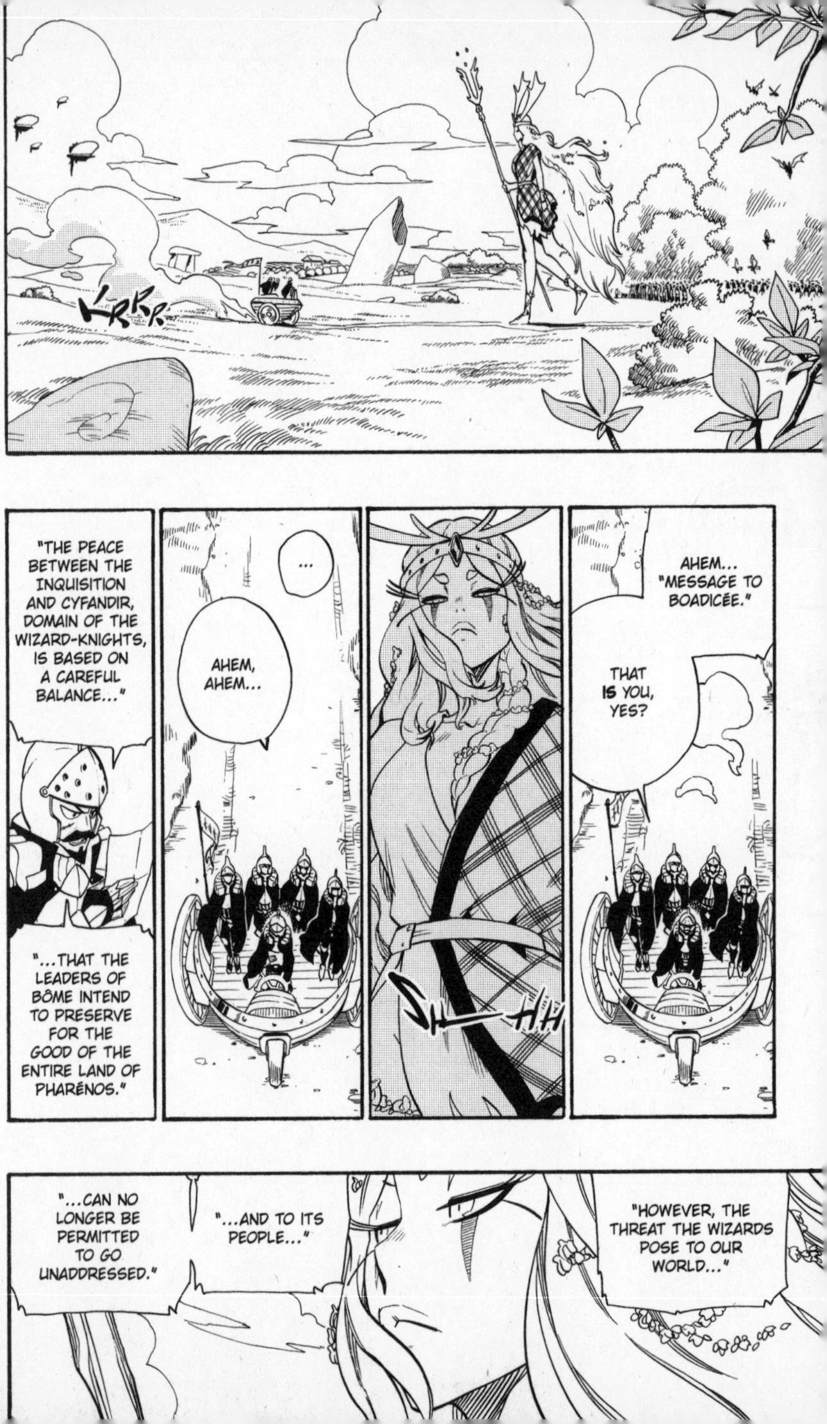
KRRR
AHEM... "MESSAGE TO BOADICÉE."
THAT IS YOU, YES?
SHHH
...
AHEM, AHEM...
"THE PEACE BETWEEN THE INQUISITION AND CYFANDIR, DOMAIN OF THE WIZARD-KNIGHTS, IS BASED ON A CAREFUL BALANCE..."
"...THAT THE LEADERS OF BÔME INTEND TO PRESERVE FOR THE GOOD OF THE ENTIRE LAND OF PHARÉNOS."
"HOWEVER, THE THREAT THE WIZARDS POSE TO OUR WORLD..."
"...AND TO ITS PEOPLE..."
"...CAN NO LONGER BE PERMITTED TO GO UNADDRESSED."

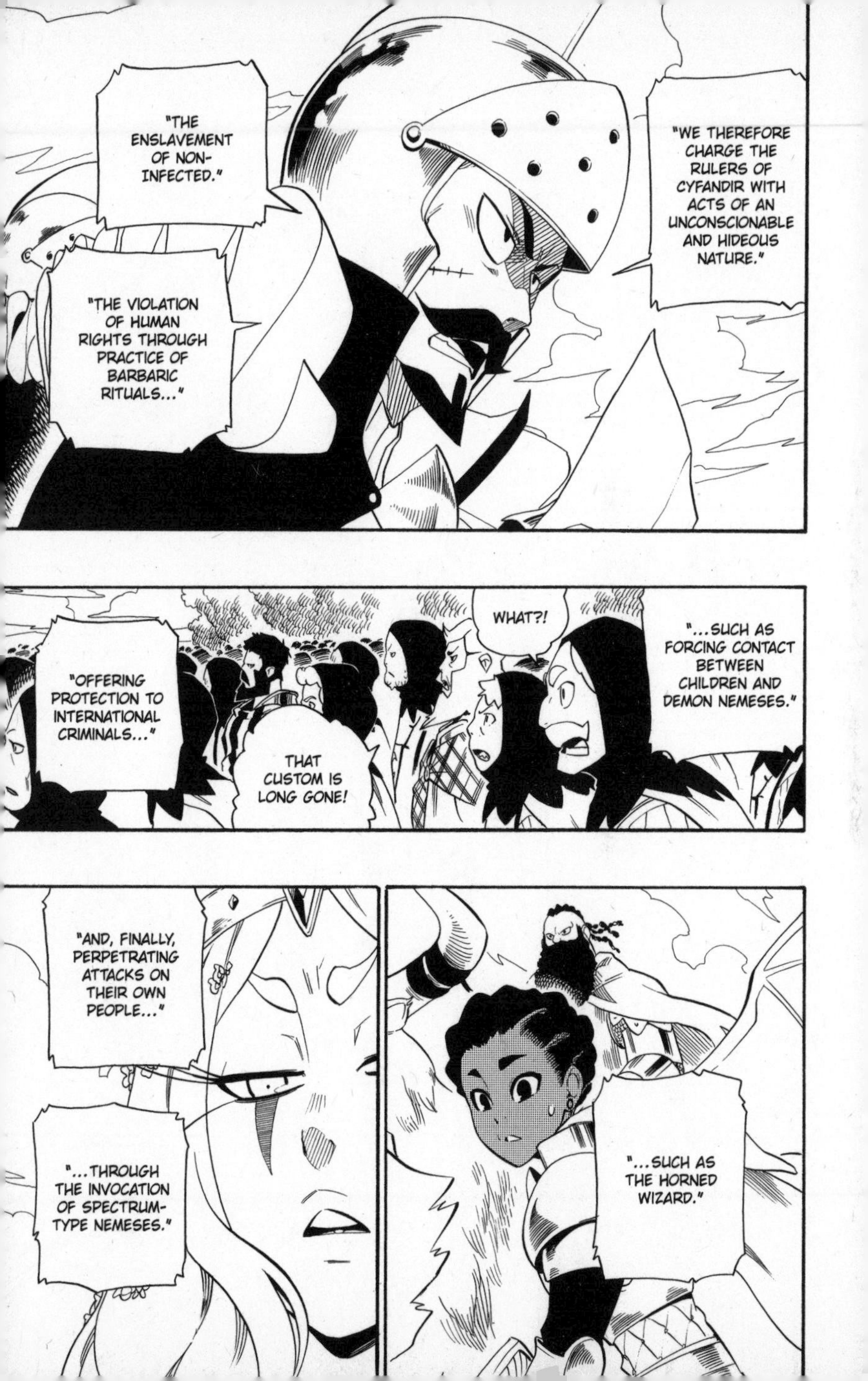
"WE THEREFORE CHARGE THE RULERS OF CYFANDIR WITH ACTS OF AN UNCONSCIONABLE AND HIDEOUS NATURE."
"THE ENSLAVEMENT OF NON-INFECTED."
"THE VIOLATION OF HUMAN RIGHTS THROUGH PRACTICE OF BARBARIC RITUALS..."
"...SUCH AS FORCING CONTACT BETWEEN CHILDREN AND DEMON NEMESES."
WHAT?!
THAT CUSTOM IS LONG GONE!
"OFFERING PROTECTION TO INTERNATIONAL CRIMINALS..."
"AND, FINALLY, PERPETRATING ATTACKS ON THEIR OWN PEOPLE..."
"...THROUGH THE INVOCATION OF SPECTRUM-TYPE NEMESES."
"...SUCH AS THE HORNED WIZARD."

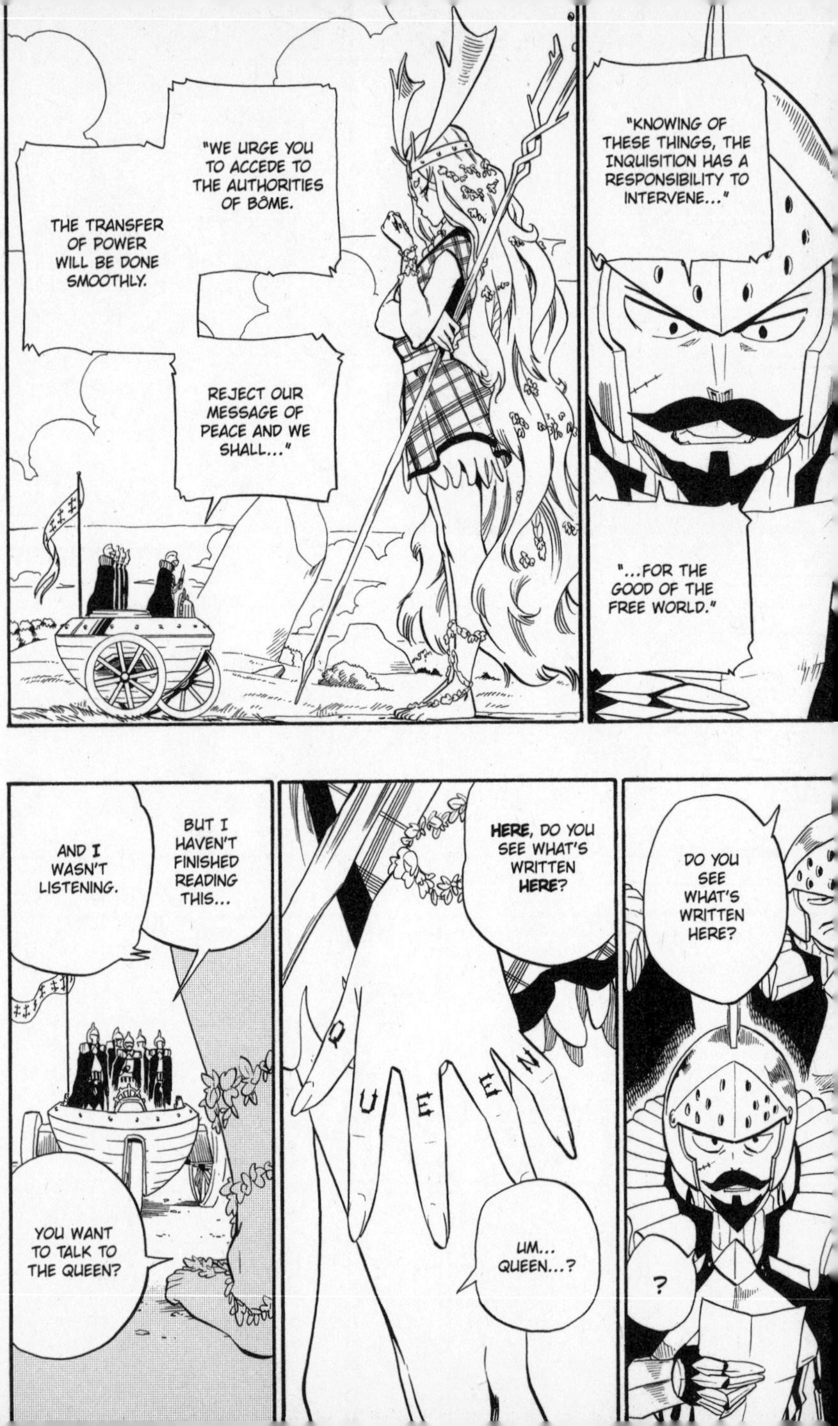
"KNOWING OF THESE THINGS, THE INQUISITION HAS A RESPONSIBILITY TO INTERVENE..."
"...FOR THE GOOD OF THE FREE WORLD."
"WE URGE YOU TO ACCEDE TO THE AUTHORITIES OF BÔME.
THE TRANSFER OF POWER WILL BE DONE SMOOTHLY.
REJECT OUR MESSAGE OF PEACE AND WE SHALL..."
DO YOU SEE WHAT'S WRITTEN HERE?
?
HERE, DO YOU SEE WHAT'S WRITTEN HERE?
QUEEN
UM... QUEEN...?
BUT I HAVEN'T FINISHED READING THIS...
AND I WASN'T LISTENING.
YOU WANT TO TALK TO THE QUEEN?

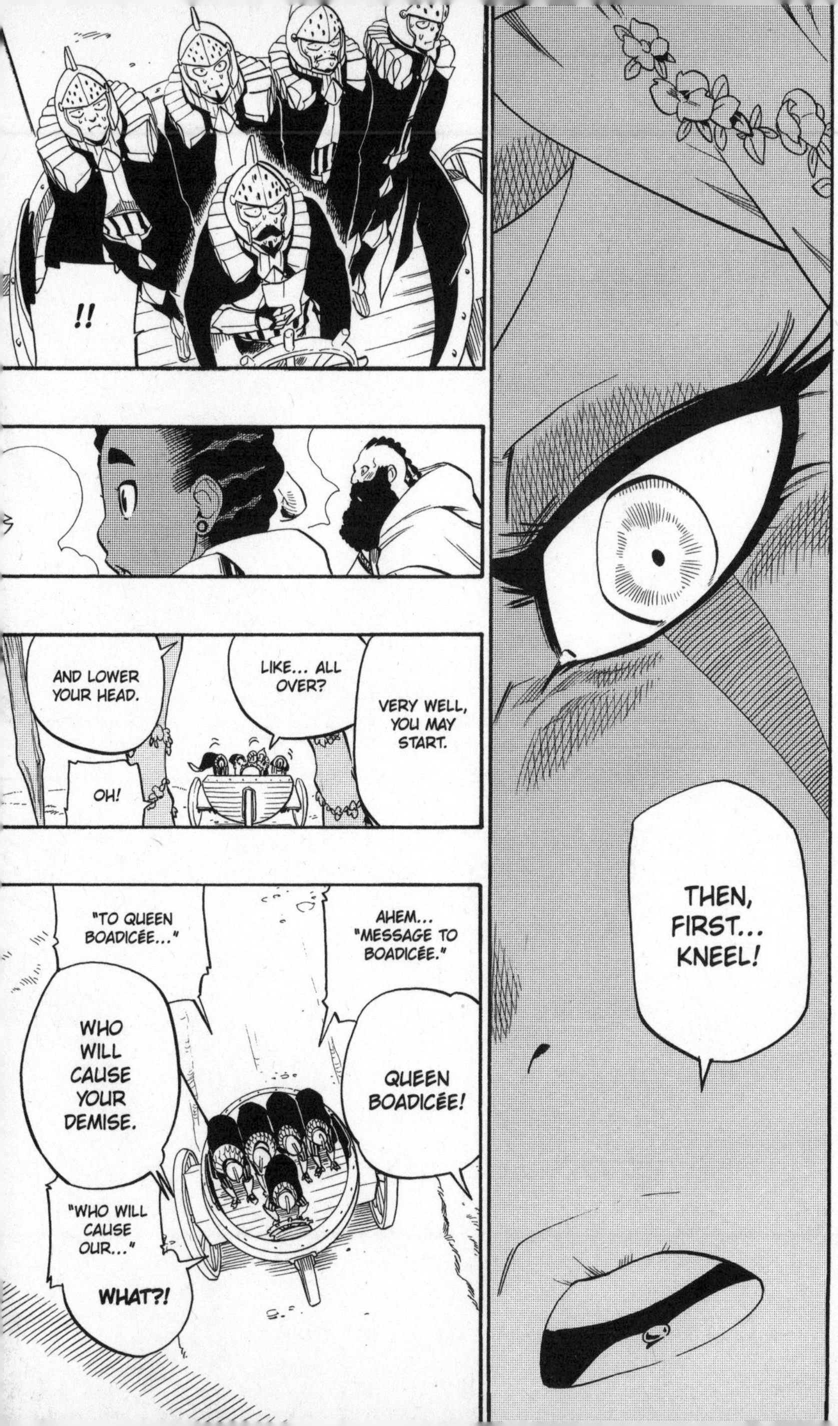
THEN, FIRST... KNEEL!
!!
LIKE... ALL OVER?
AND LOWER YOUR HEAD.
OH!
VERY WELL, YOU MAY START.
AHEM... "MESSAGE TO BOADICÉE."
QUEEN BOADICÉE!
"TO QUEEN BOADICÉE..."
WHO WILL CAUSE YOUR DEMISE.
"WHO WILL CAUSE OUR..."
WHAT?!

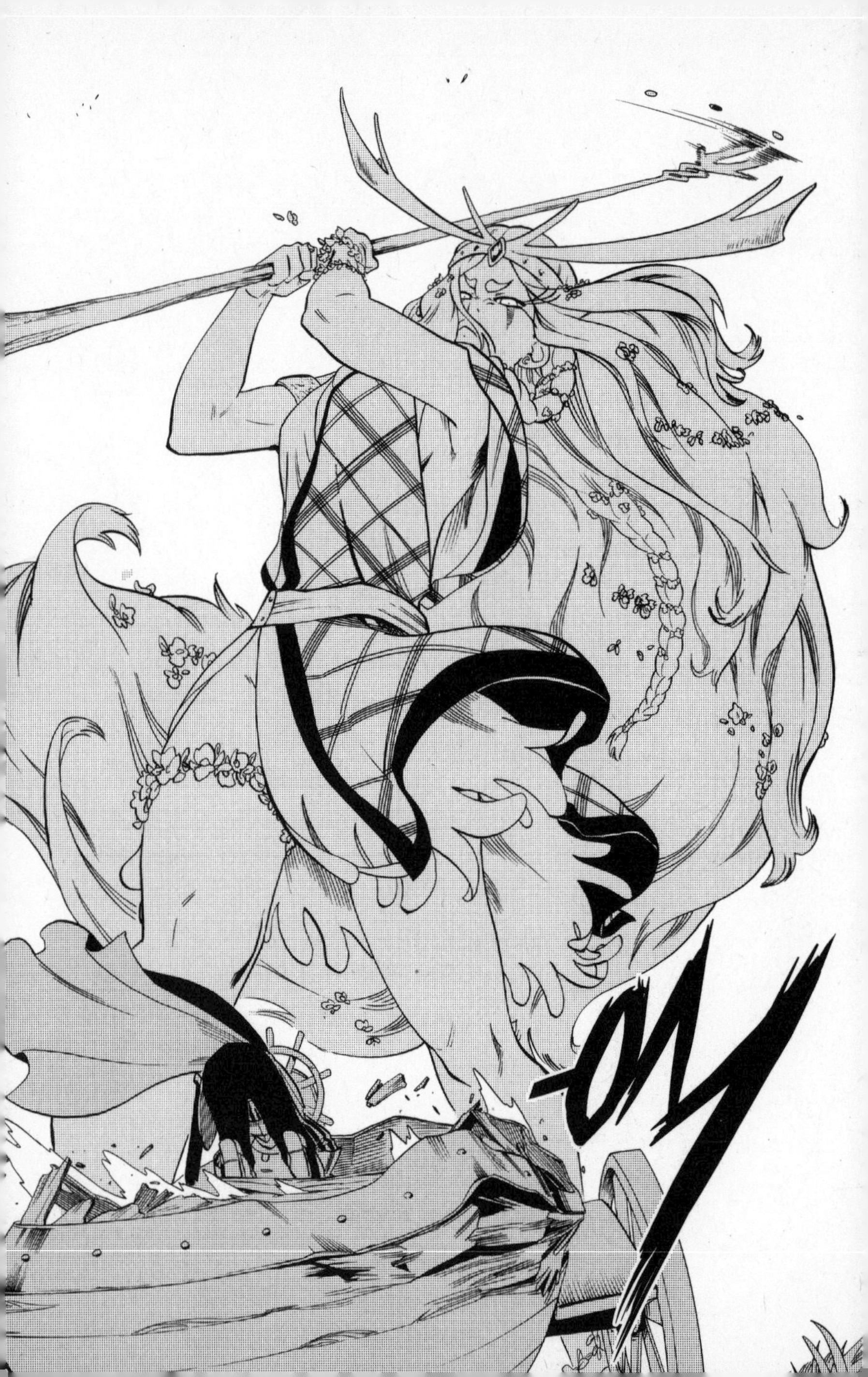

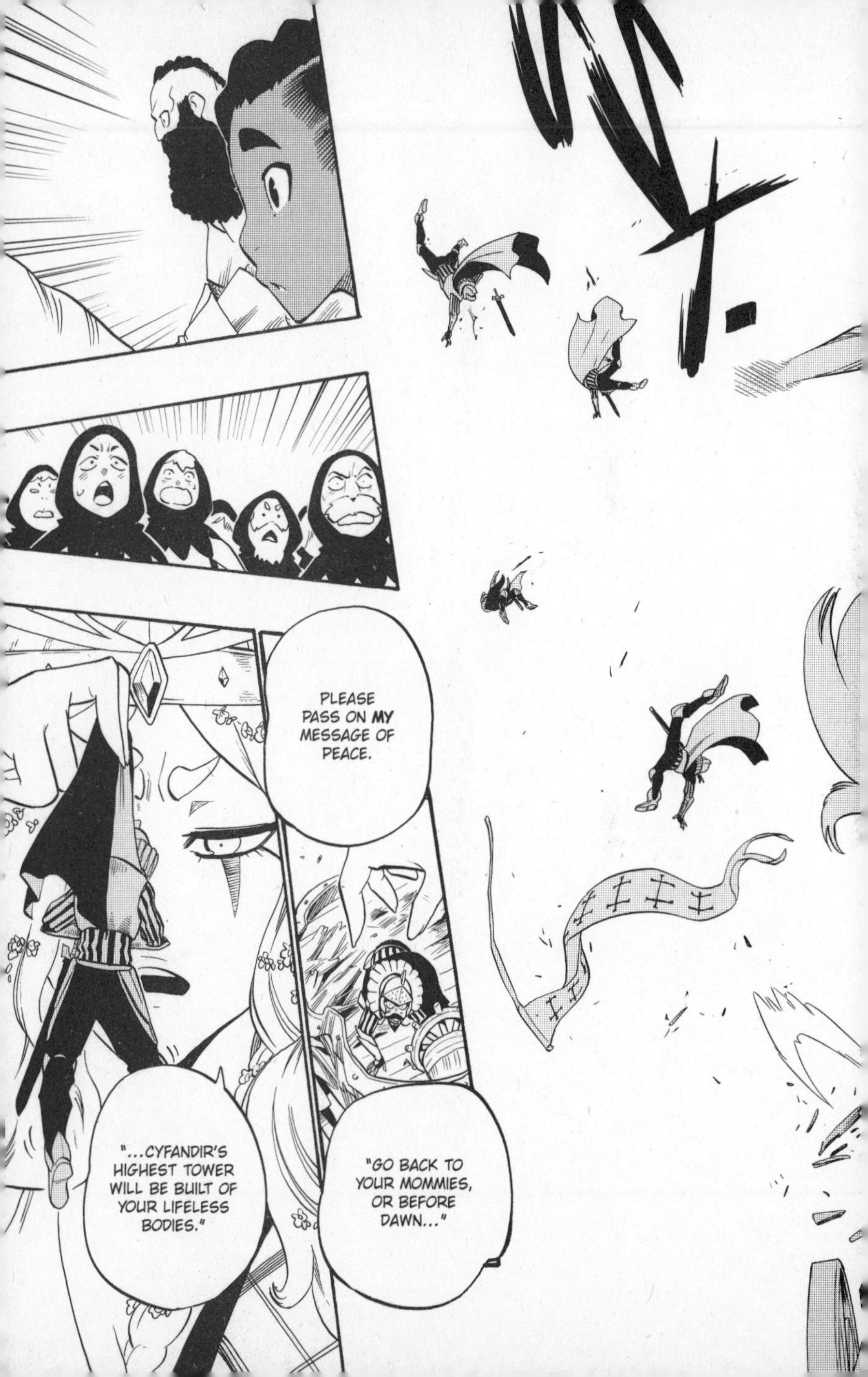
PLEASE PASS ON MY MESSAGE OF PEACE.
"GO BACK TO YOUR MOMMIES, OR BEFORE DAWN..."
"...CYFANDIR'S HIGHEST TOWER WILL BE BUILT OF YOUR LIFELESS BODIES."

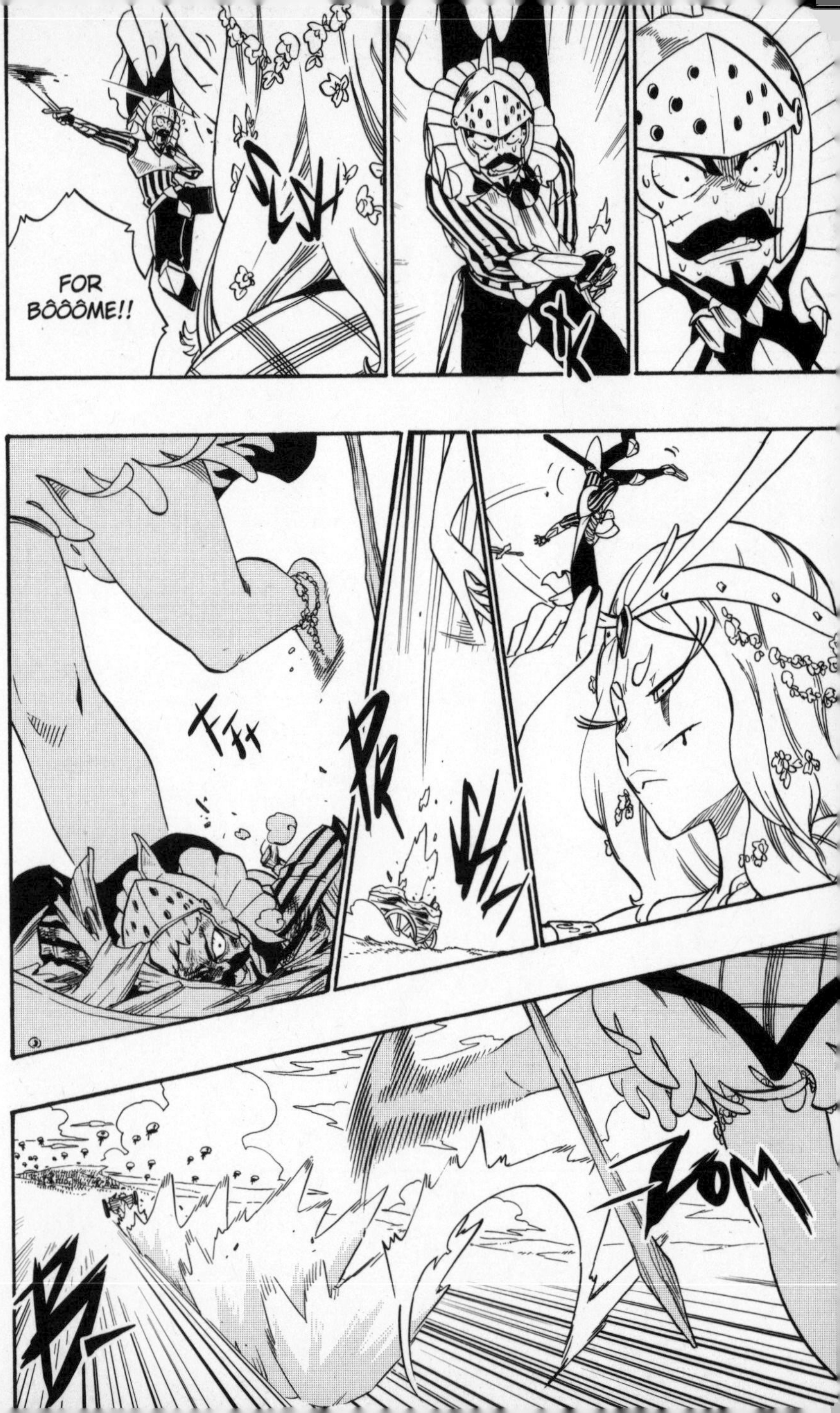
FOR BÔÔÔME!!
ZOM

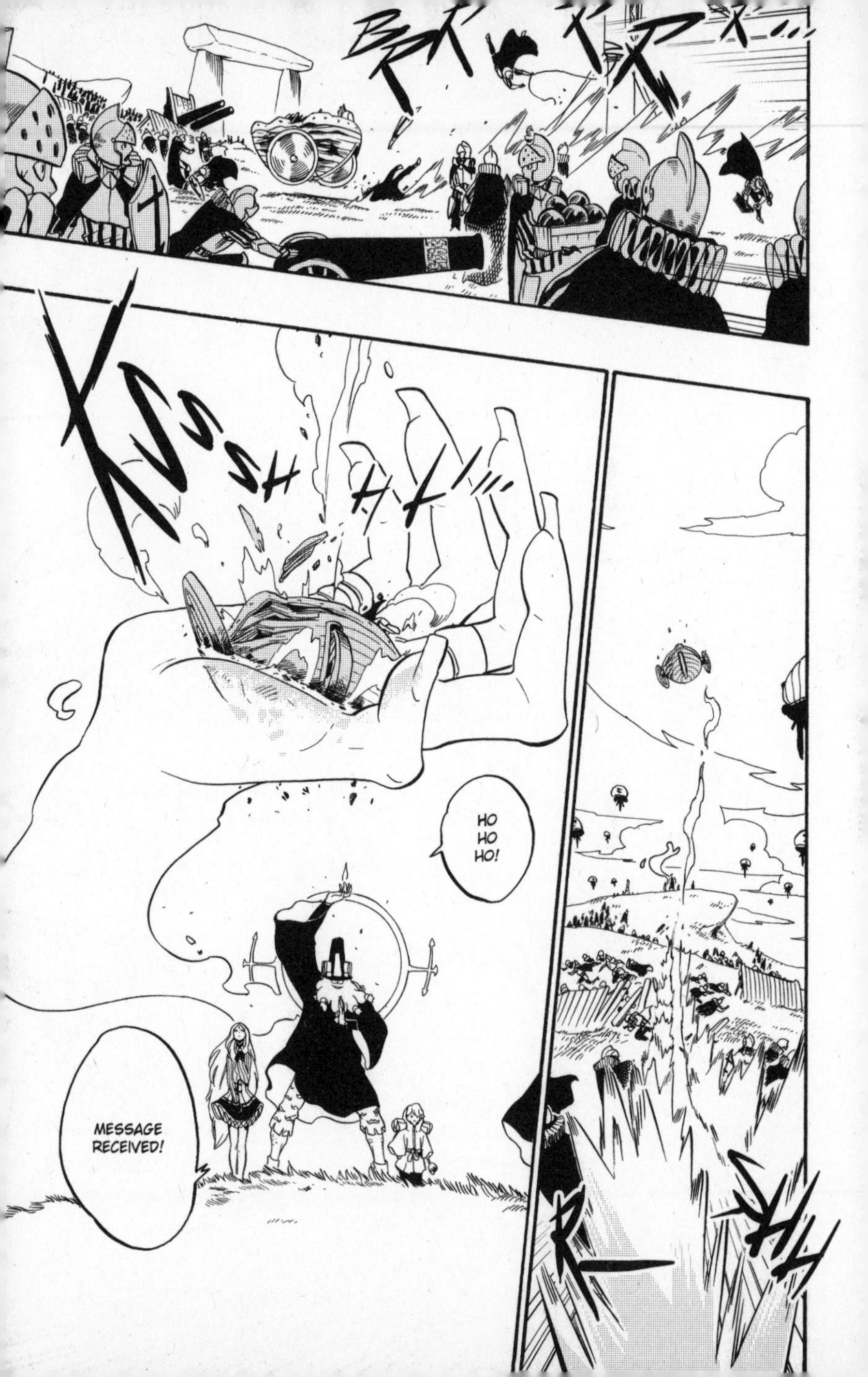
HO HO HO!
MESSAGE RECEIVED!

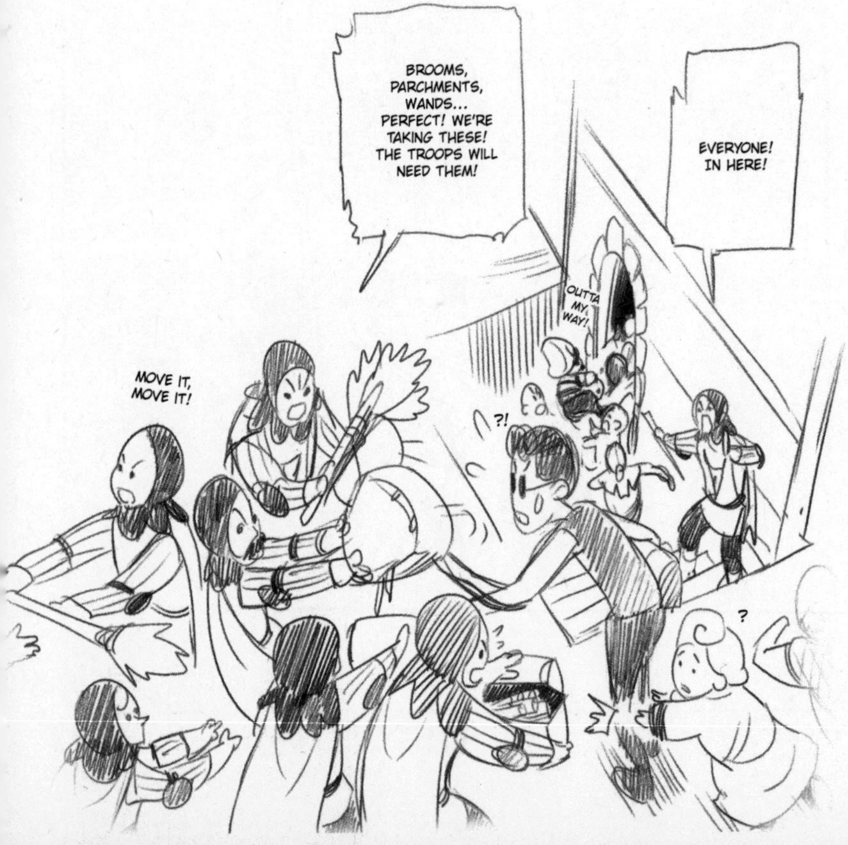
EVERYONE! IN HERE!
BROOMS, PARCHMENTS, WANDS... PERFECT! WE'RE TAKING THESE! THE TROOPS WILL NEED THEM!
OUTTA MY WAY!
?!
MOVE IT, MOVE IT!
?

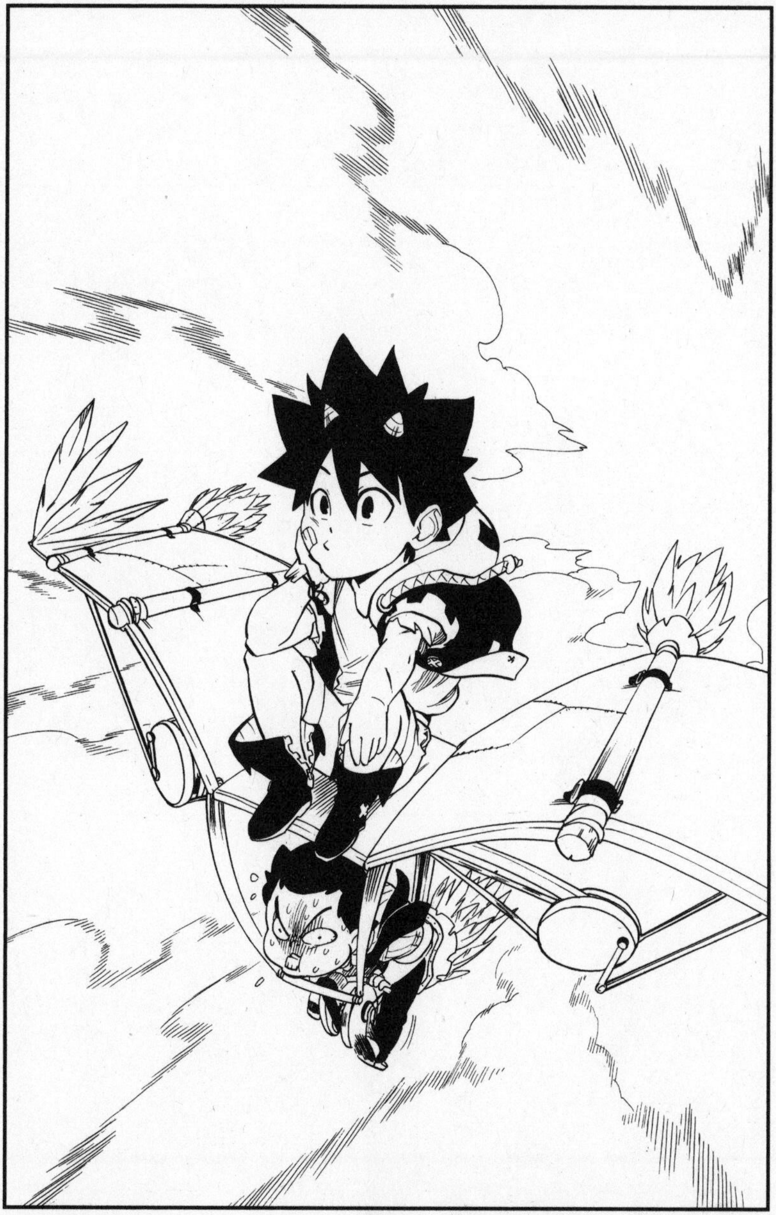

CHAPTER 57

THE WIZARD-KINGS

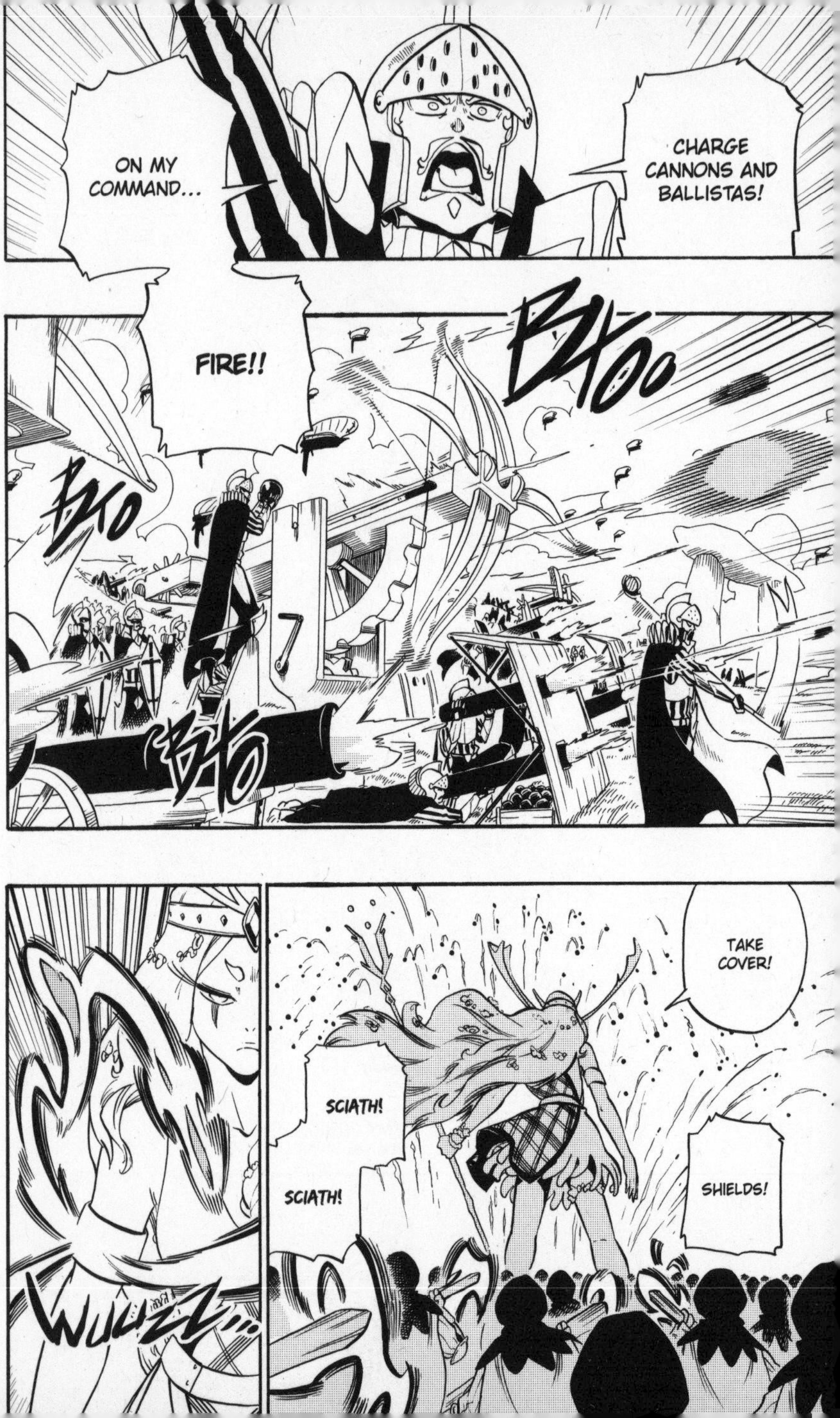
CHARGE CANNONS AND BALLISTAS!
ON MY COMMAND...
FIRE!!
TAKE COVER!
SCIATH!
SHIELDS!
SCIATH!

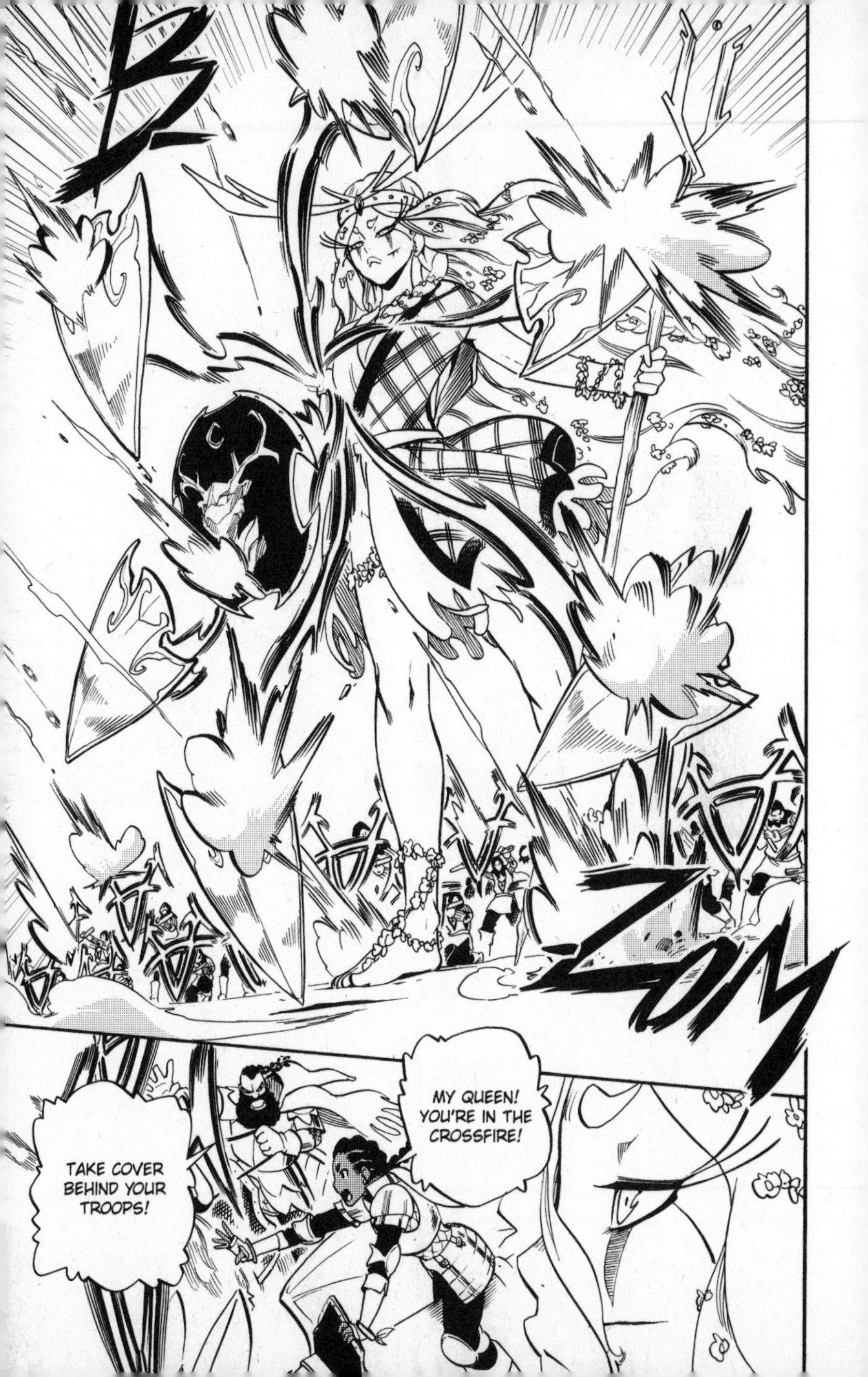
MY QUEEN! YOU'RE IN THE CROSSFIRE!
TAKE COVER BEHIND YOUR TROOPS!

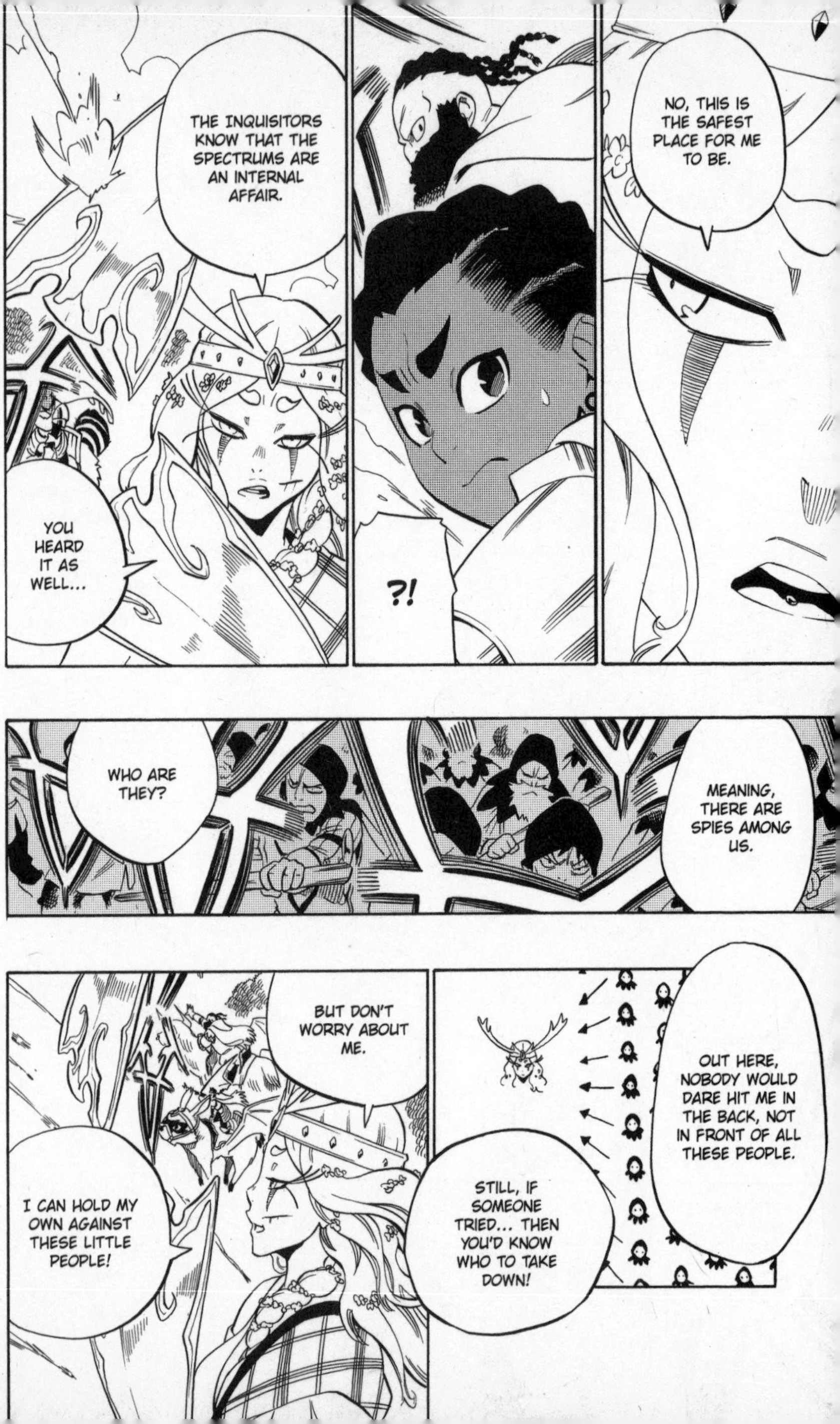
NO, THIS IS THE SAFEST PLACE FOR ME TO BE.
?!
THE INQUISITORS KNOW THAT THE SPECTRUMS ARE AN INTERNAL AFFAIR.
YOU HEARD IT AS WELL...
MEANING, THERE ARE SPIES AMONG US.
WHO ARE THEY?
OUT HERE, NOBODY WOULD DARE HIT ME IN THE BACK, NOT IN FRONT OF ALL THESE PEOPLE.
STILL, IF SOMEONE TRIED... THEN YOU'D KNOW WHO TO TAKE DOWN!
BUT DON'T WORRY ABOUT ME.
I CAN HOLD MY OWN AGAINST THESE LITTLE PEOPLE!

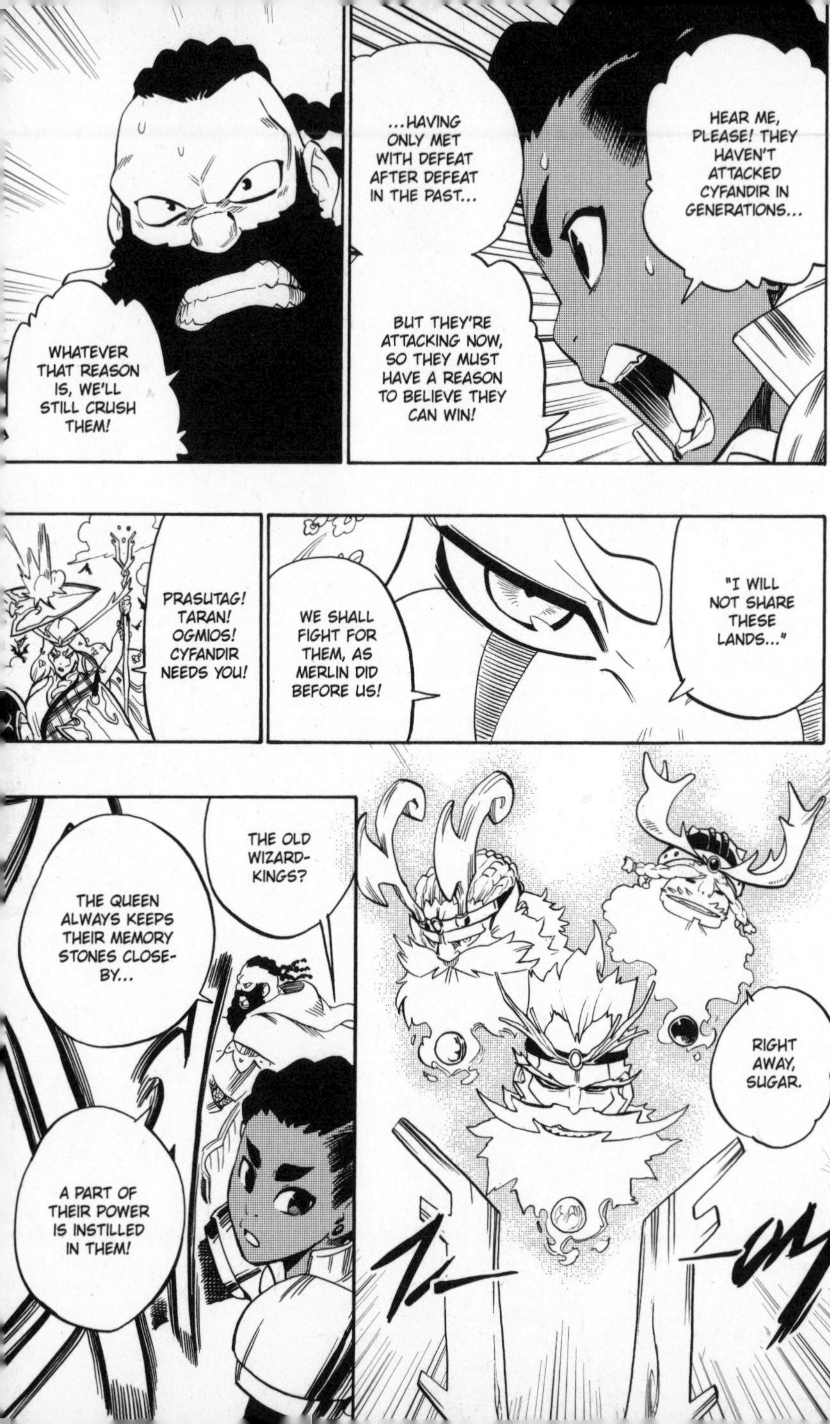
HEAR ME, PLEASE! THEY HAVEN'T ATTACKED CYFANDIR IN GENERATIONS...
...HAVING ONLY MET WITH DEFEAT AFTER DEFEAT IN THE PAST...
BUT THEY'RE ATTACKING NOW, SO THEY MUST HAVE A REASON TO BELIEVE THEY CAN WIN!
WHATEVER THAT REASON IS, WE'LL STILL CRUSH THEM!
"I WILL NOT SHARE THESE LANDS..."
WE SHALL FIGHT FOR THEM, AS MERLIN DID BEFORE US!
PRASUTAG! TARAN! OGMIOS! CYFANDIR NEEDS YOU!
RIGHT AWAY, SUGAR.
THE OLD WIZARD-KINGS?
THE QUEEN ALWAYS KEEPS THEIR MEMORY STONES CLOSE-BY...
A PART OF THEIR POWER IS INSTILLED IN THEM!

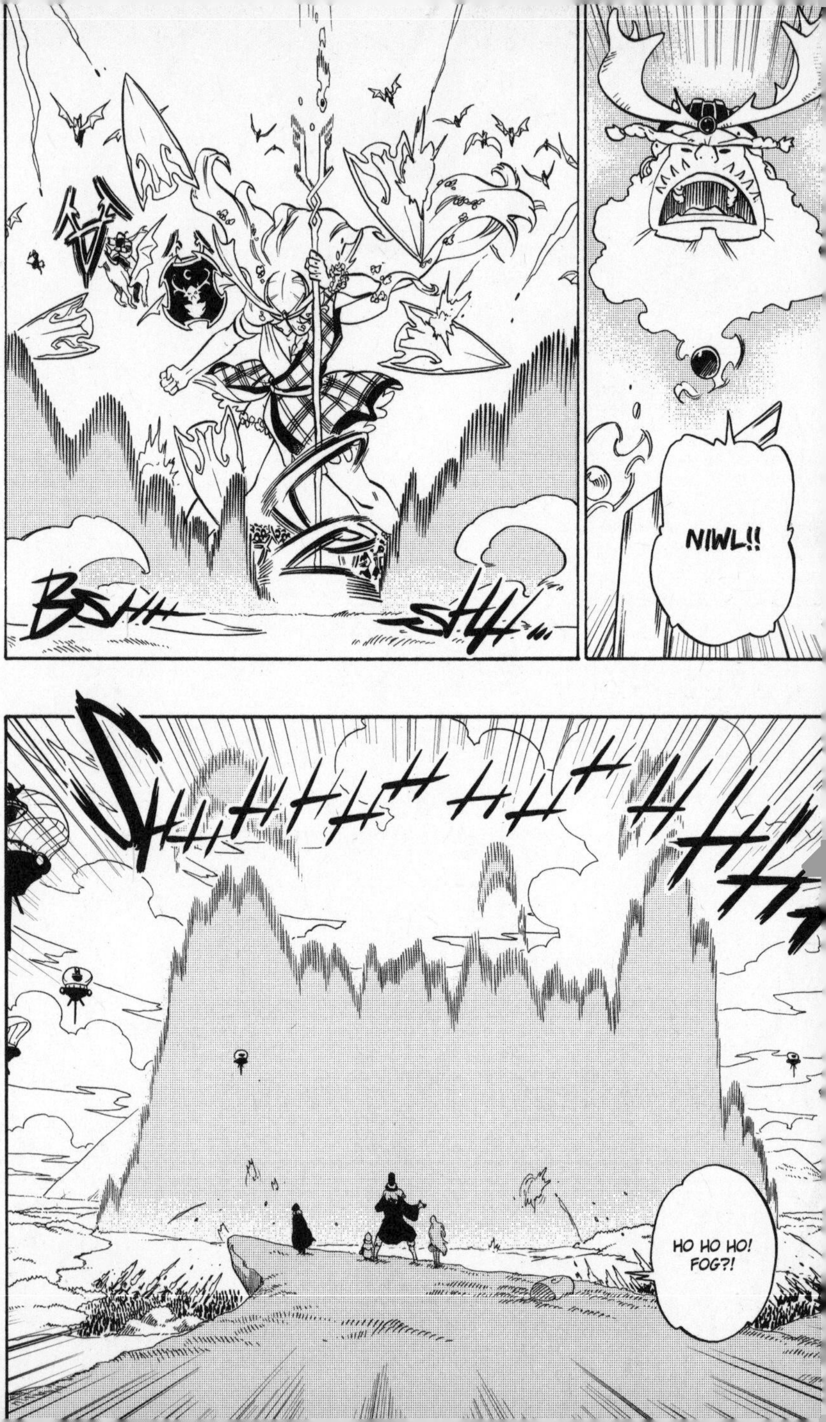
NIWL!!
HO HO HO! FOG?!

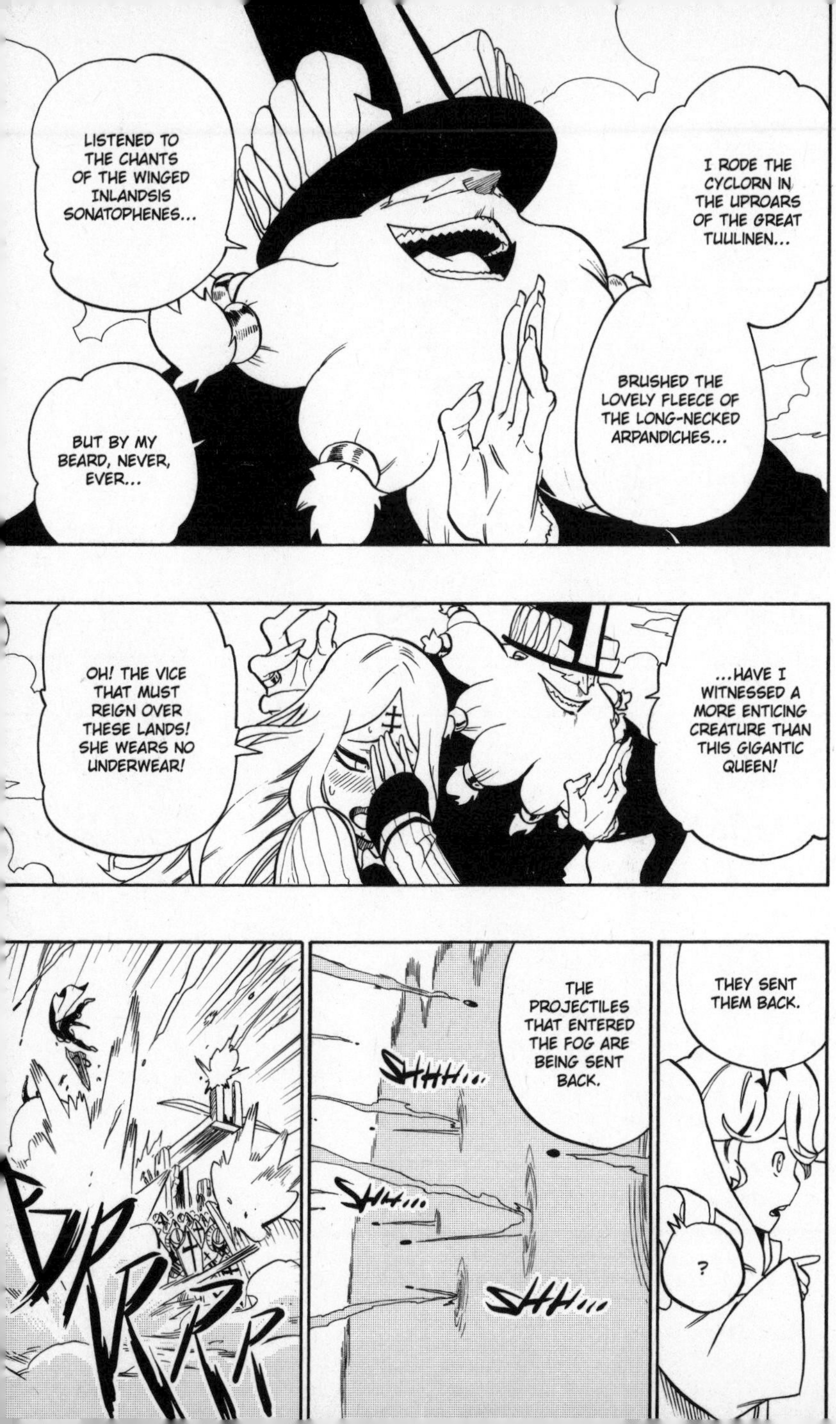
I RODE THE CYCLORN IN THE UPROARS OF THE GREAT TUULINEN...
LISTENED TO THE CHANTS OF THE WINGED INLANDSIS SONATOPHENES...
BRUSHED THE LOVELY FLEECE OF THE LONG-NECKED ARPANDICHES...
BUT BY MY BEARD, NEVER, EVER...
...HAVE I WITNESSED A MORE ENTICING CREATURE THAN THIS GIGANTIC QUEEN!
OH! THE VICE THAT MUST REIGN OVER THESE LANDS! SHE WEARS NO UNDERWEAR!
THEY SENT THEM BACK.
?
THE PROJECTILES THAT ENTERED THE FOG ARE BEING SENT BACK.
SHHH...
SHHH...
SHHH...
BDRRRR

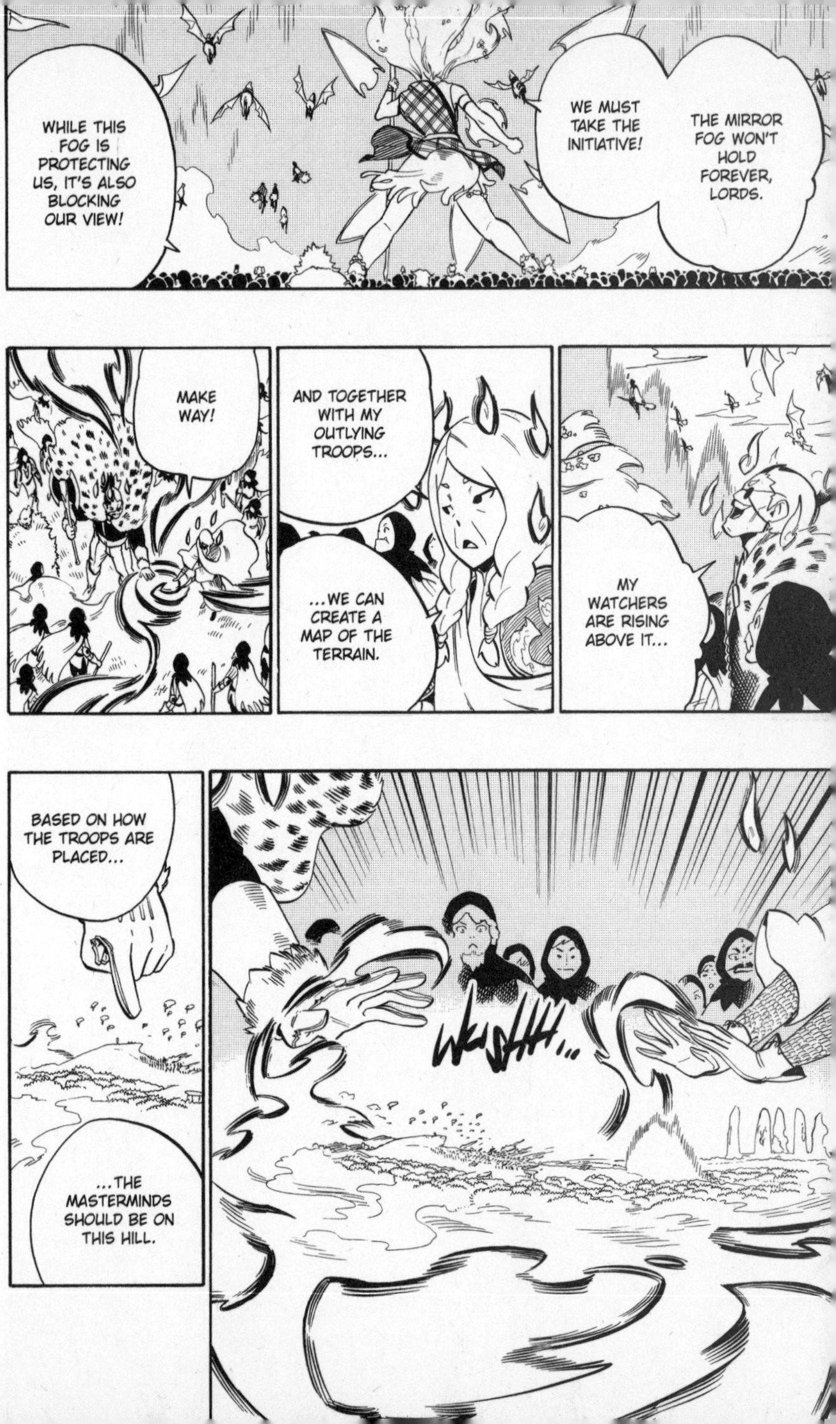
THE MIRROR FOG WON'T HOLD FOREVER, LORDS.
WE MUST TAKE THE INITIATIVE!
WHILE THIS FOG IS PROTECTING US, IT'S ALSO BLOCKING OUR VIEW!
MY WATCHERS ARE RISING ABOVE IT...
AND TOGETHER WITH MY OUTLYING TROOPS...
...WE CAN CREATE A MAP OF THE TERRAIN.
MAKE WAY!
WHSHH...
BASED ON HOW THE TROOPS ARE PLACED...
...THE MASTERMINDS SHOULD BE ON THIS HILL.

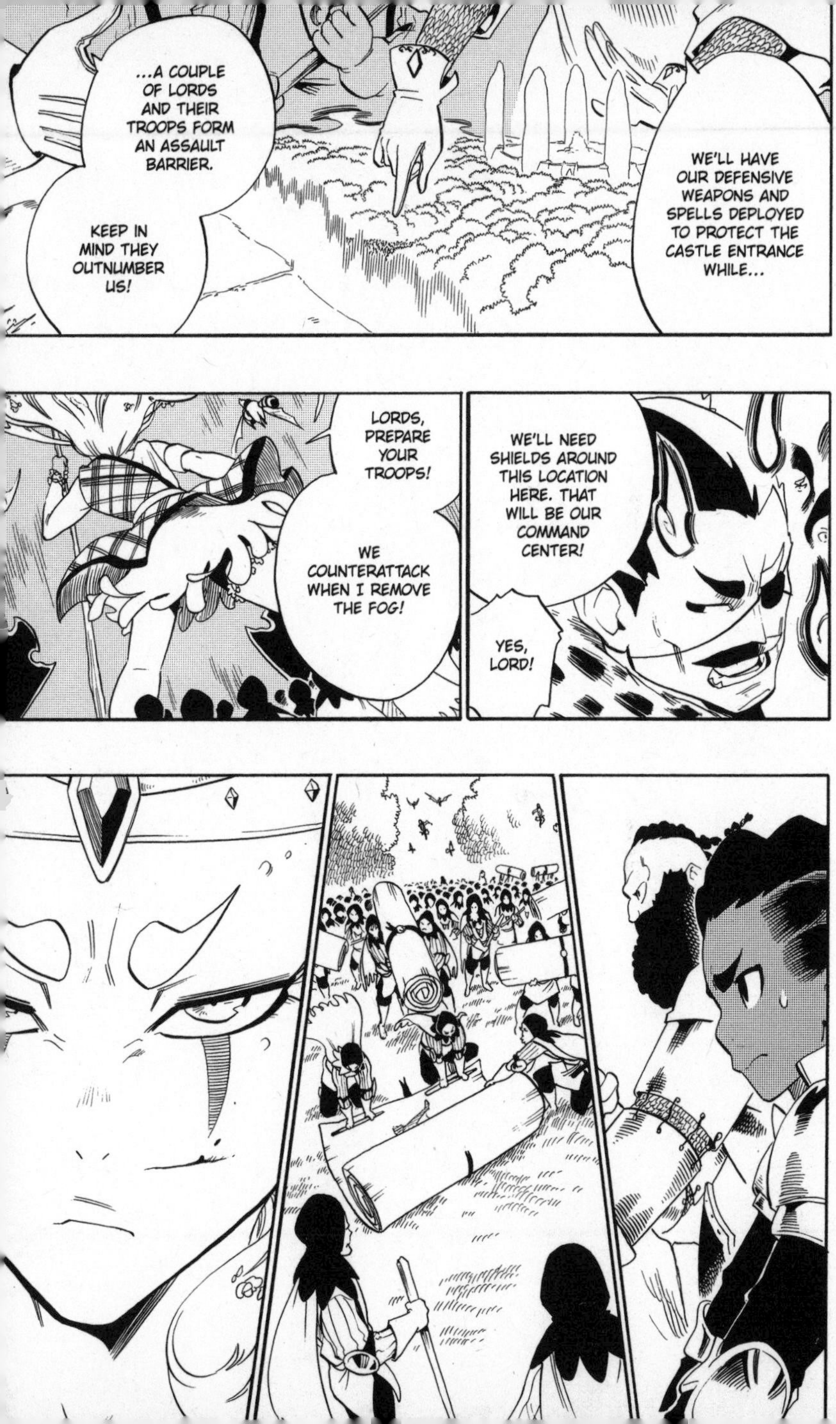
WE'LL HAVE OUR DEFENSIVE WEAPONS AND SPELLS DEPLOYED TO PROTECT THE CASTLE ENTRANCE WHILE...
...A COUPLE OF LORDS AND THEIR TROOPS FORM AN ASSAULT BARRIER.
KEEP IN MIND THEY OUTNUMBER US!
WE'LL NEED SHIELDS AROUND THIS LOCATION HERE. THAT WILL BE OUR COMMAND CENTER!
YES, LORD!
LORDS, PREPARE YOUR TROOPS!
WE COUNTERATTACK WHEN I REMOVE THE FOG!

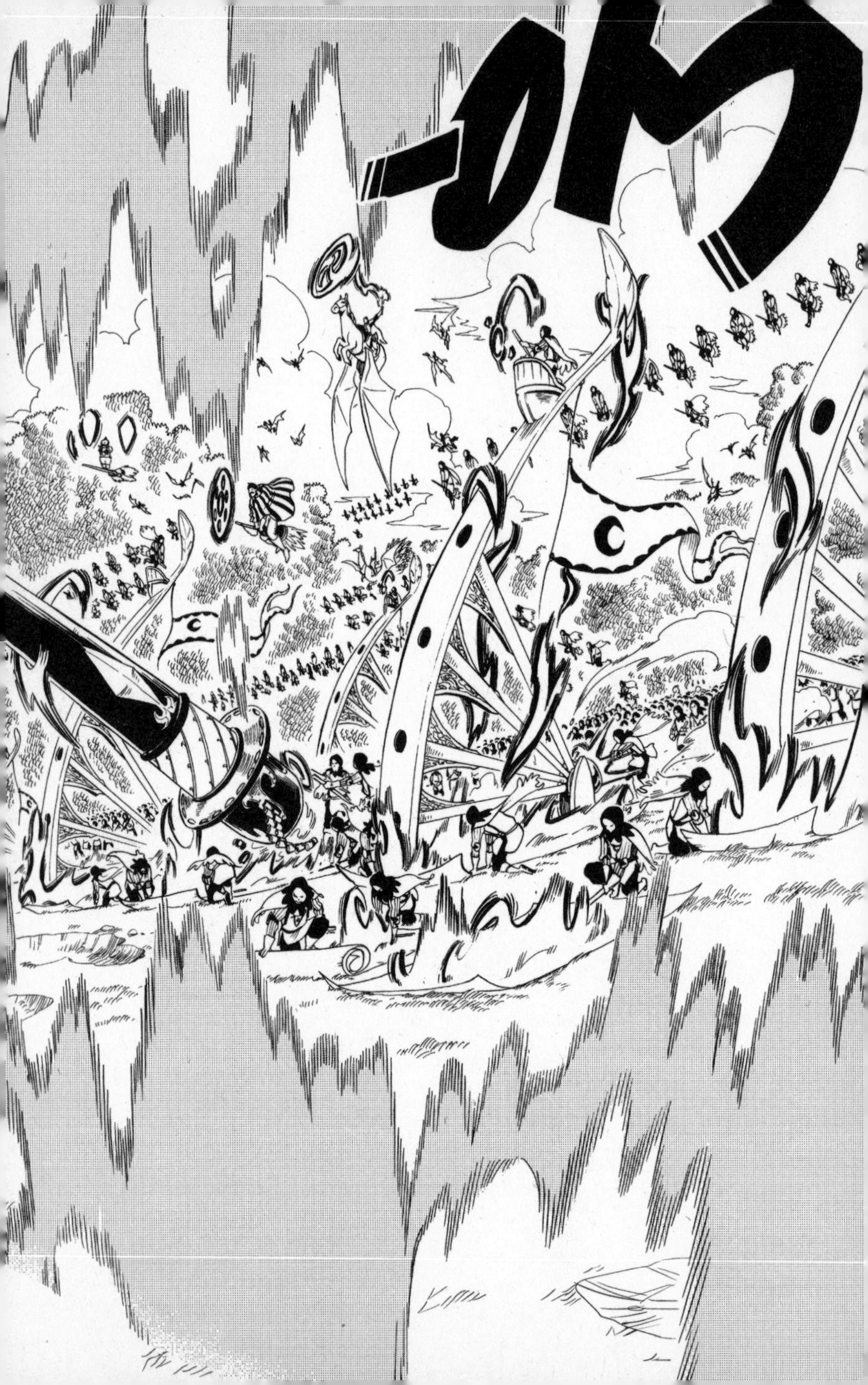

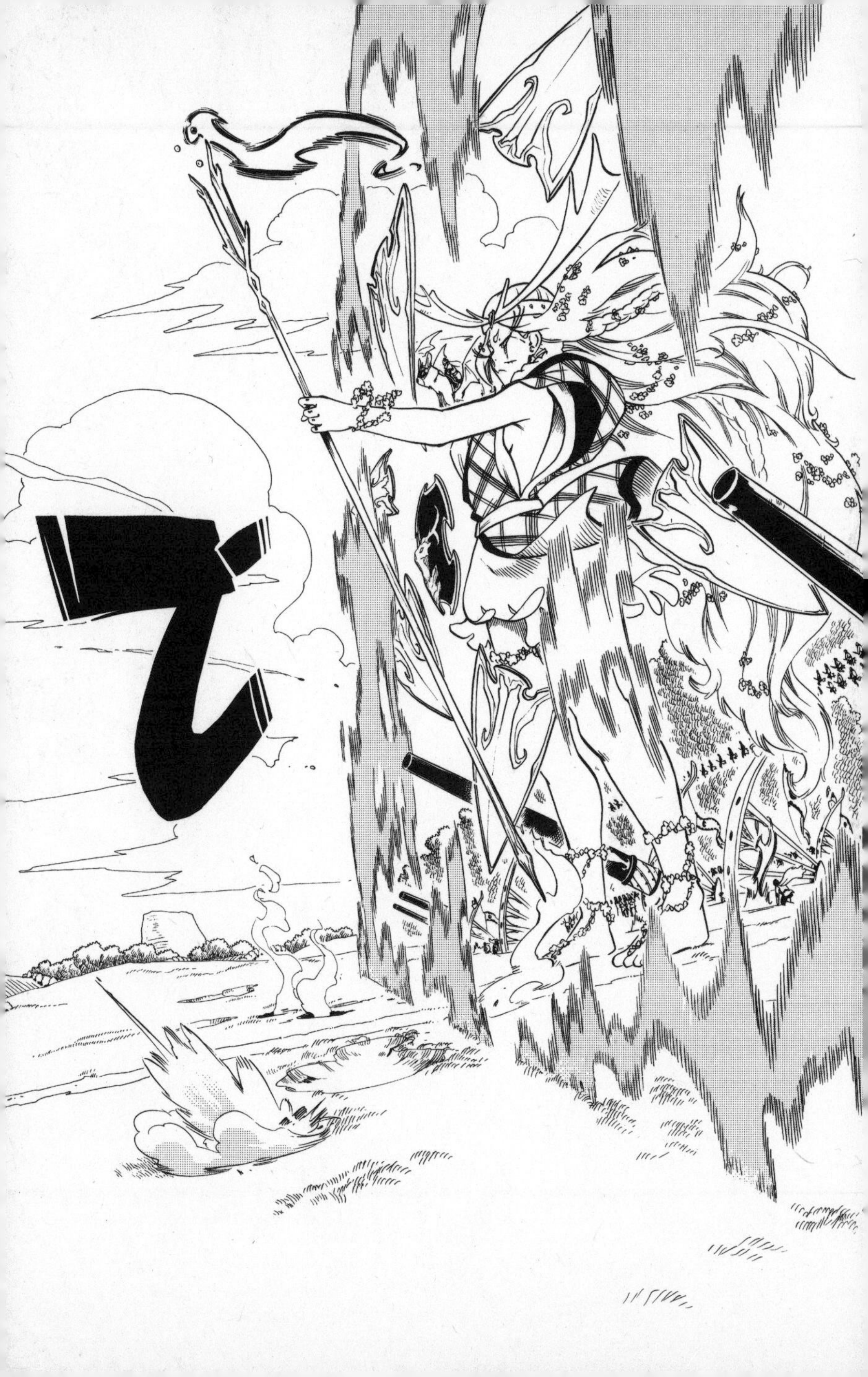

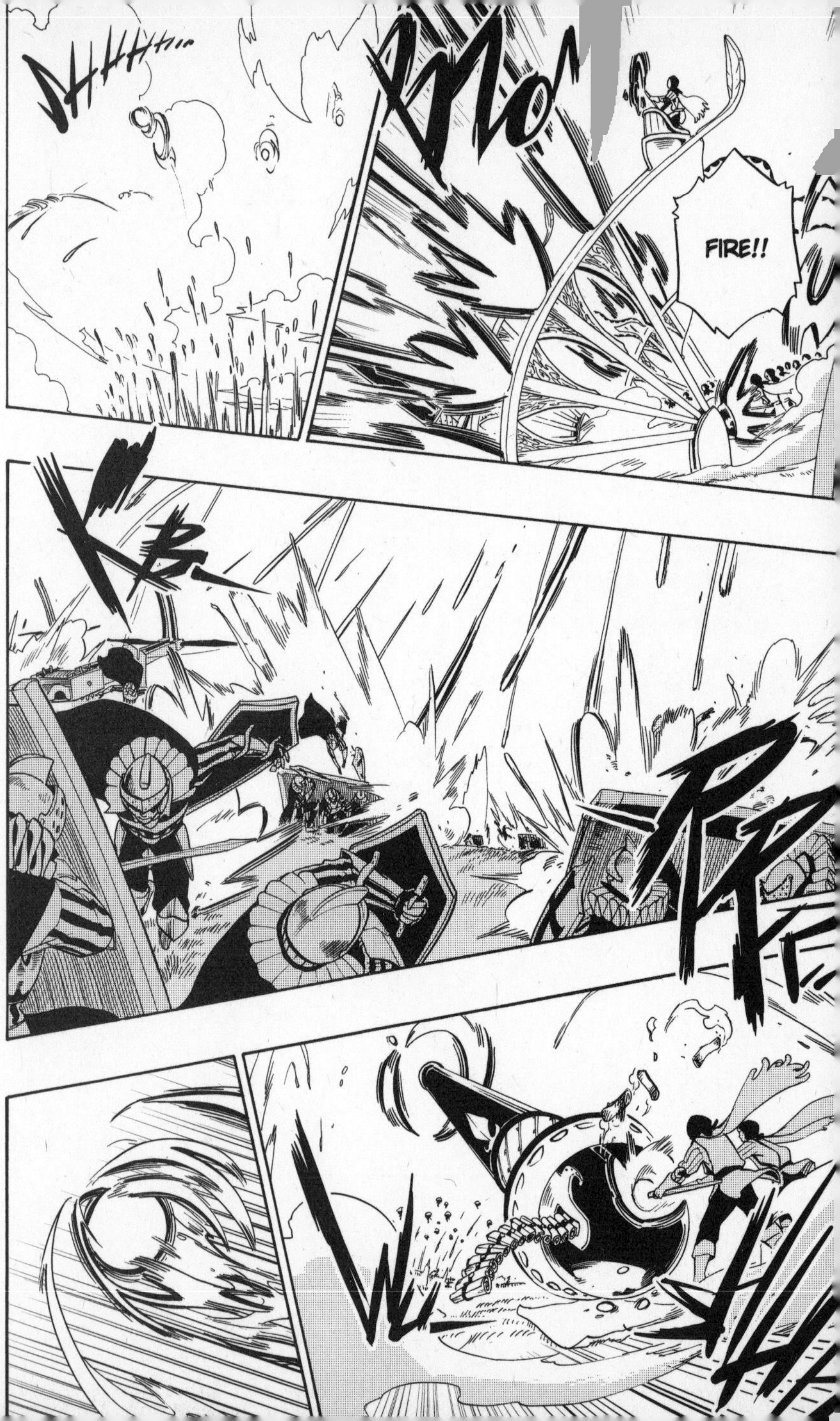
FIRE!!

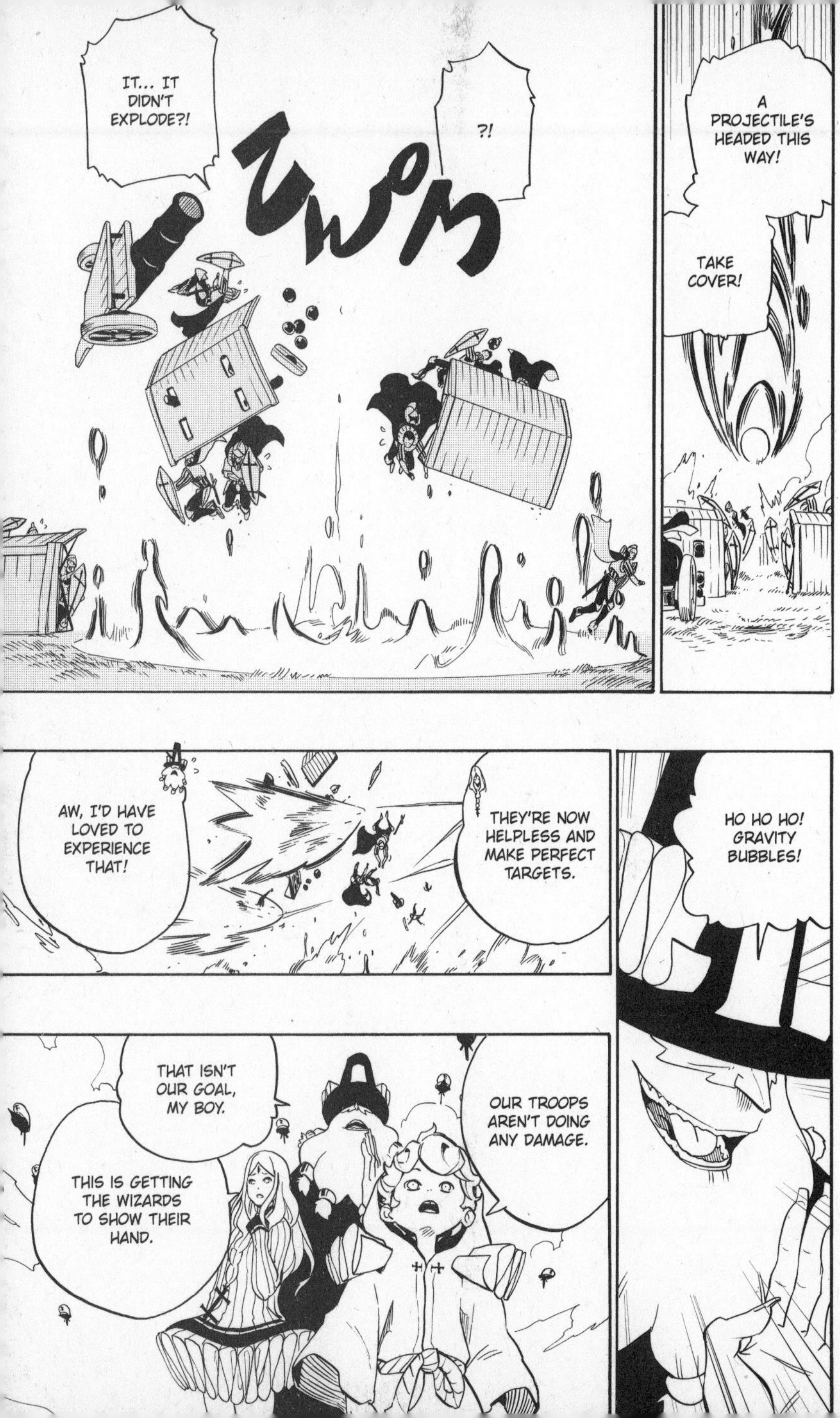
A PROJECTILE'S HEADED THIS WAY!
TAKE COVER!
?!
IT... IT DIDN'T EXPLODE?!
HO HO HO! GRAVITY BUBBLES!
THEY'RE NOW HELPLESS AND MAKE PERFECT TARGETS.
AW, I'D HAVE LOVED TO EXPERIENCE THAT!
OUR TROOPS AREN'T DOING ANY DAMAGE.
THAT ISN'T OUR GOAL, MY BOY.
THIS IS GETTING THE WIZARDS TO SHOW THEIR HAND.

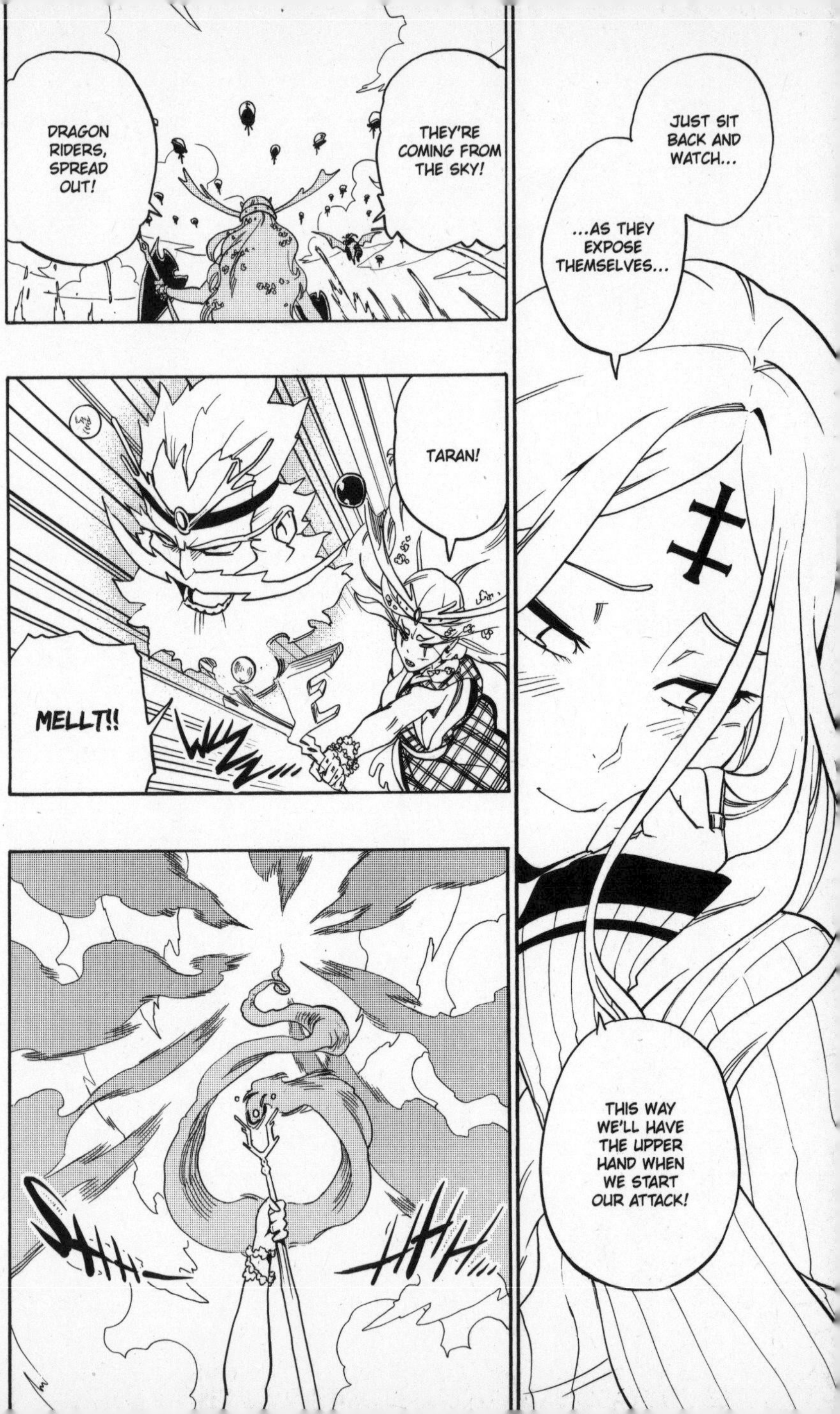
JUST SIT BACK AND WATCH...
...AS THEY EXPOSE THEMSELVES...
THIS WAY WE'LL HAVE THE UPPER HAND WHEN WE START OUR ATTACK!
THEY'RE COMING FROM THE SKY!
DRAGON RIDERS, SPREAD OUT!
TARAN!
MELLT!!

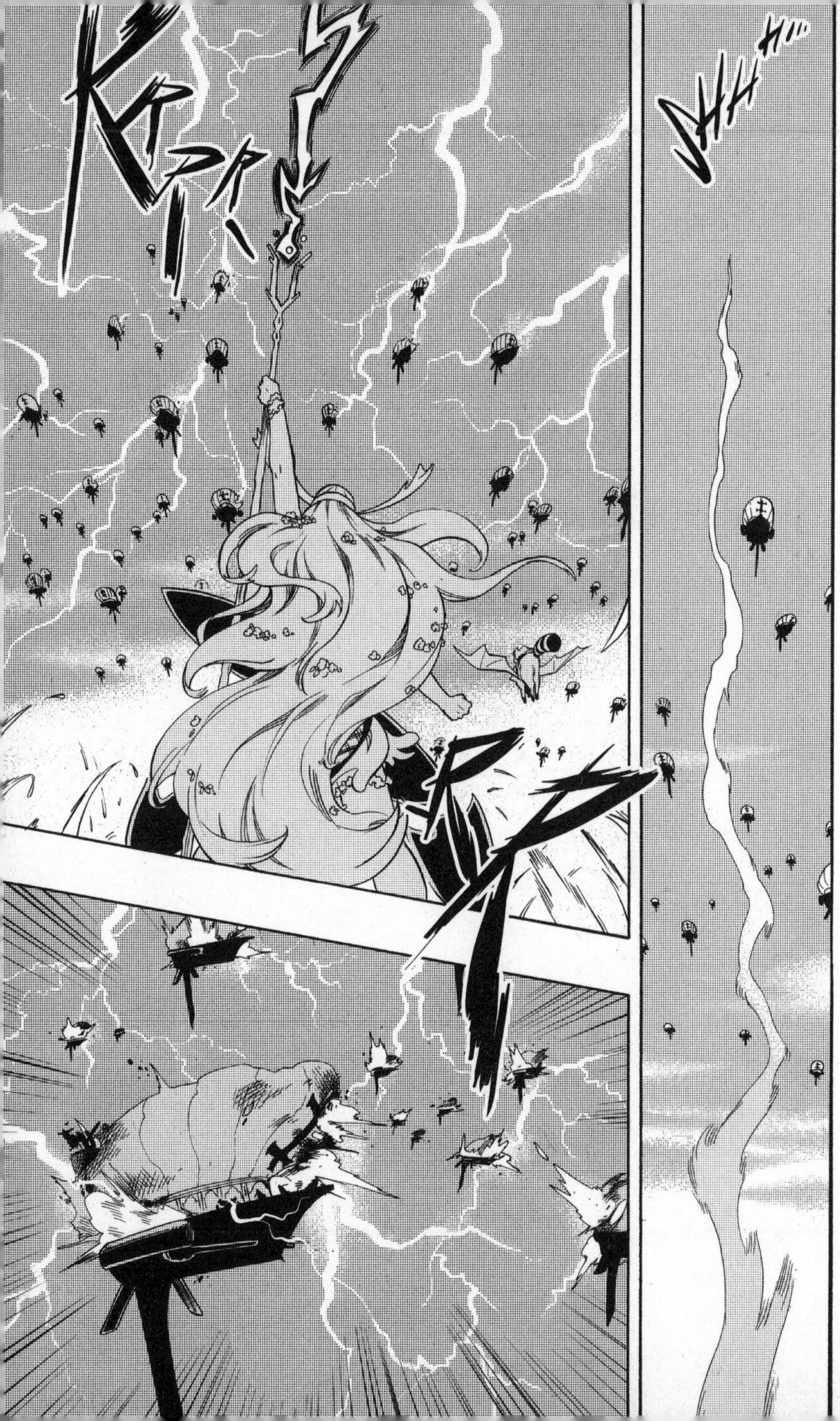

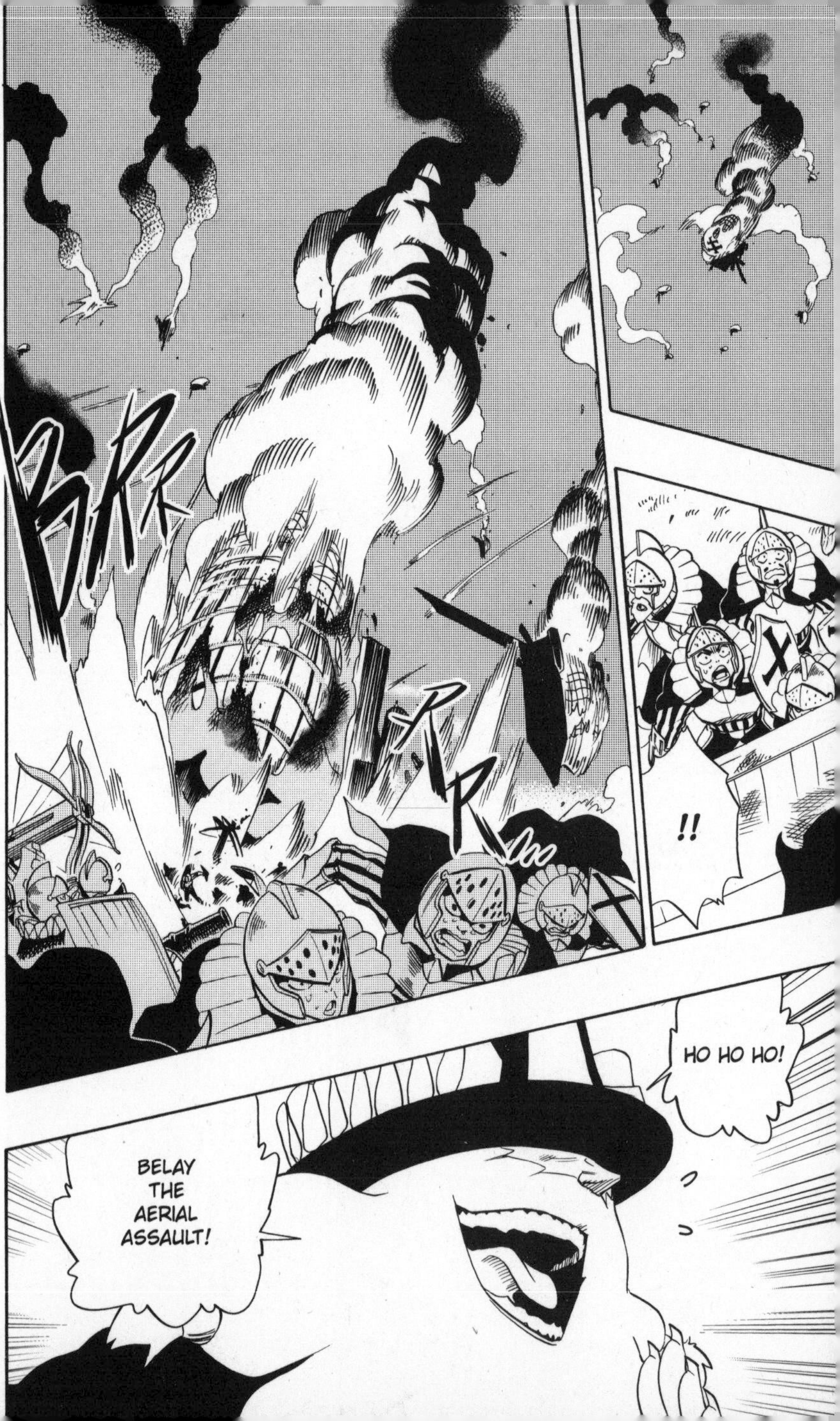
BRR
RRR
!!
HO HO HO!
BELAY THE AERIAL ASSAULT!

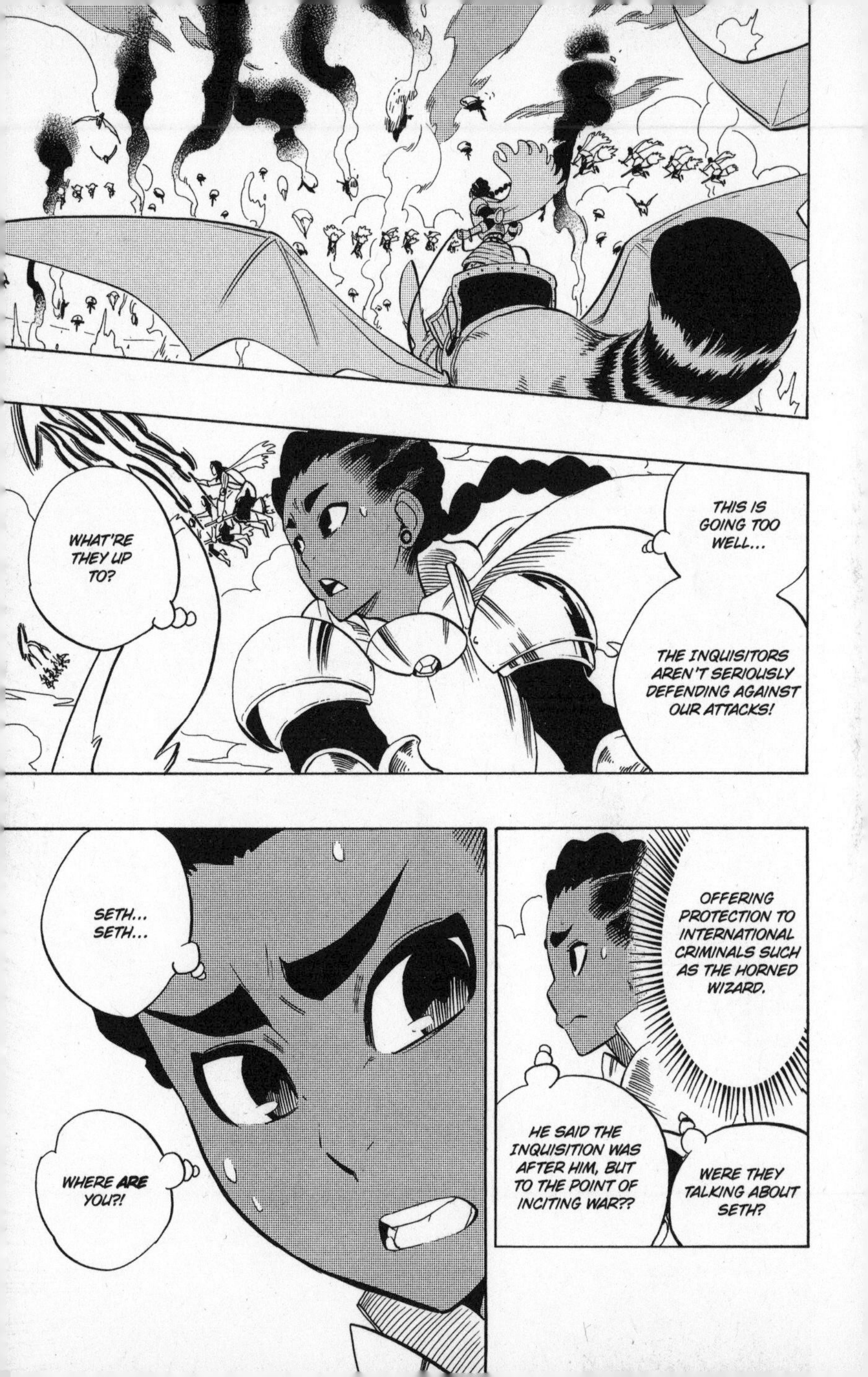
THIS IS GOING TOO WELL...
THE INQUISITORS AREN'T SERIOUSLY DEFENDING AGAINST OUR ATTACKS!
WHAT'RE THEY UP TO?
OFFERING PROTECTION TO INTERNATIONAL CRIMINALS SUCH AS THE HORNED WIZARD.
WERE THEY TALKING ABOUT SETH?
HE SAID THE INQUISITION WAS AFTER HIM, BUT TO THE POINT OF INCITING WAR??
SETH... SETH...
WHERE **ARE** YOU?!

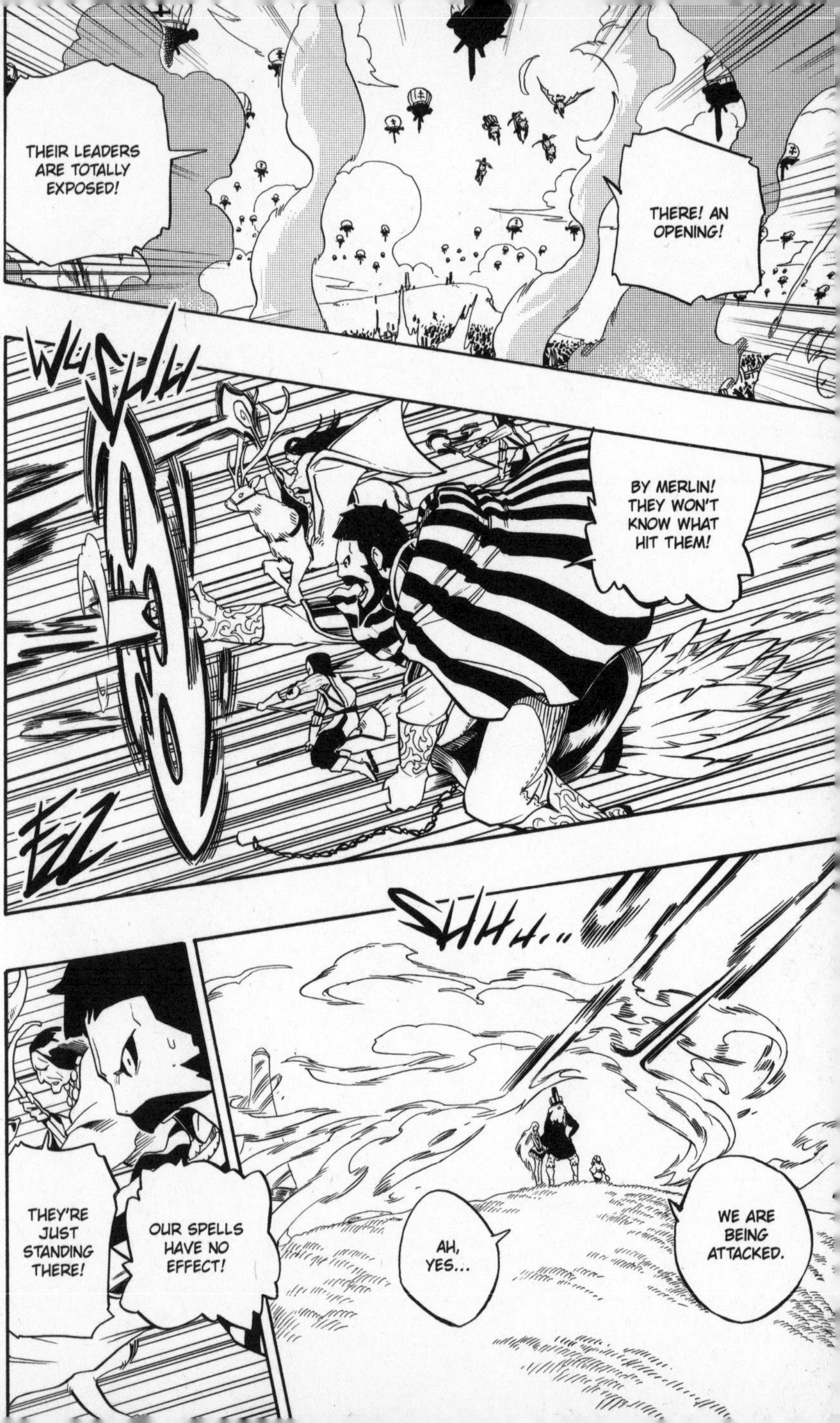
THERE! AN OPENING!
THEIR LEADERS ARE TOTALLY EXPOSED!
BY MERLIN! THEY WON'T KNOW WHAT HIT THEM!
WE ARE BEING ATTACKED.
AH, YES...
OUR SPELLS HAVE NO EFFECT!
THEY'RE JUST STANDING THERE!

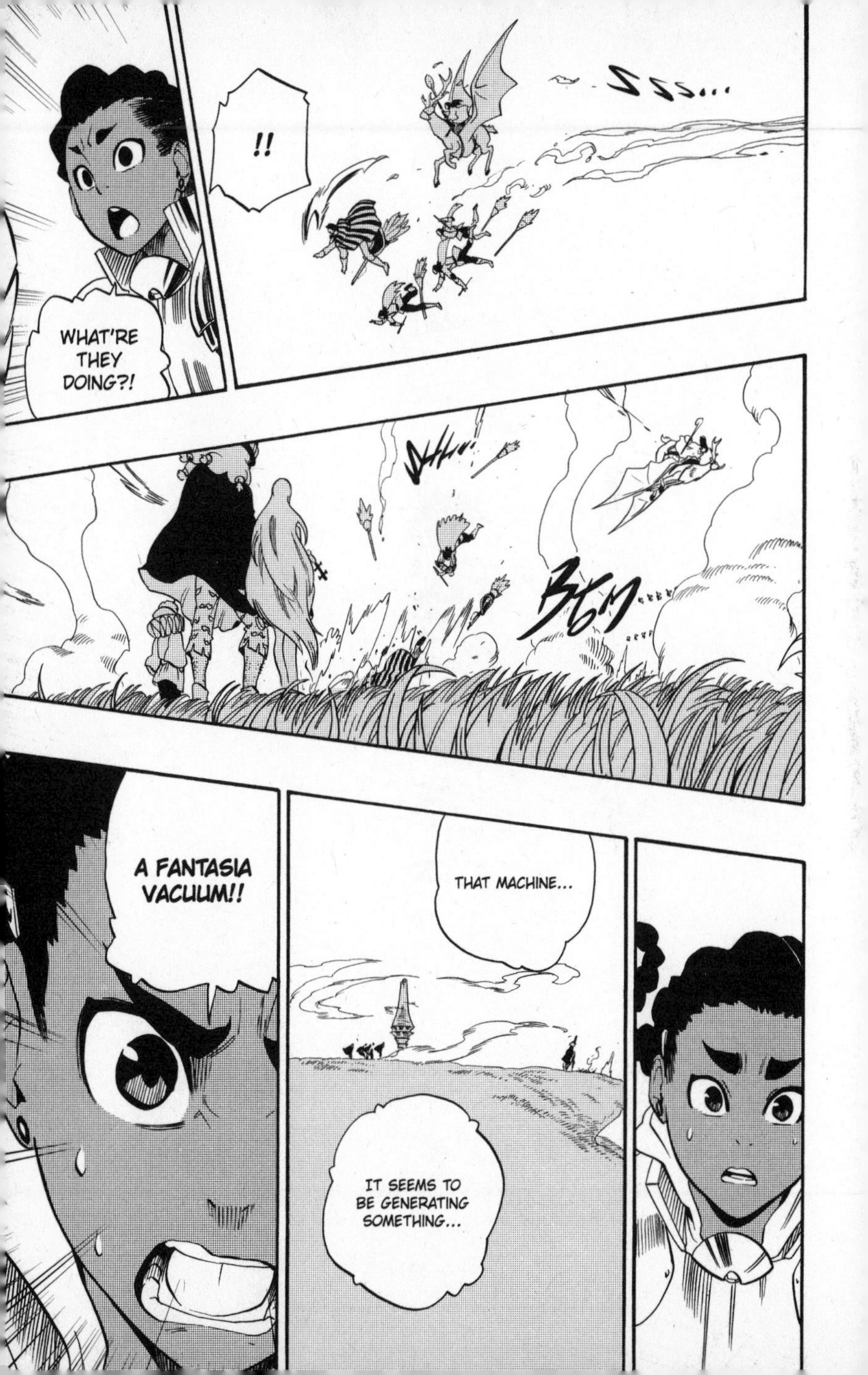
SSS...
!!
WHAT'RE THEY DOING?!
THAT MACHINE...
IT SEEMS TO BE GENERATING SOMETHING...
A FANTASIA VACUUM!!

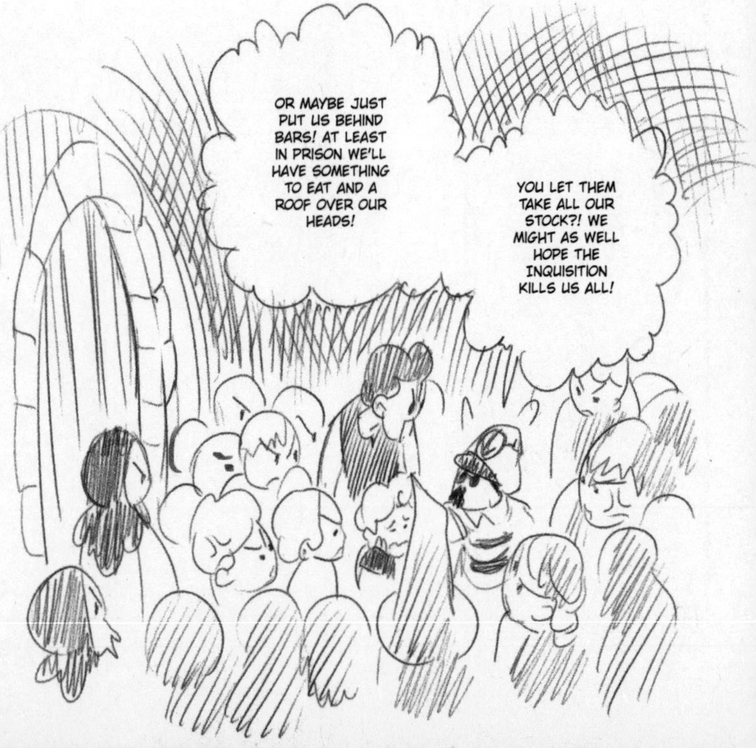
YOU LET THEM TAKE ALL OUR STOCK?! WE MIGHT AS WELL HOPE THE INQUISITION KILLS US ALL!
OR MAYBE JUST PUT US BEHIND BARS! AT LEAST IN PRISON WE'LL HAVE SOMETHING TO EAT AND A ROOF OVER OUR HEADS!

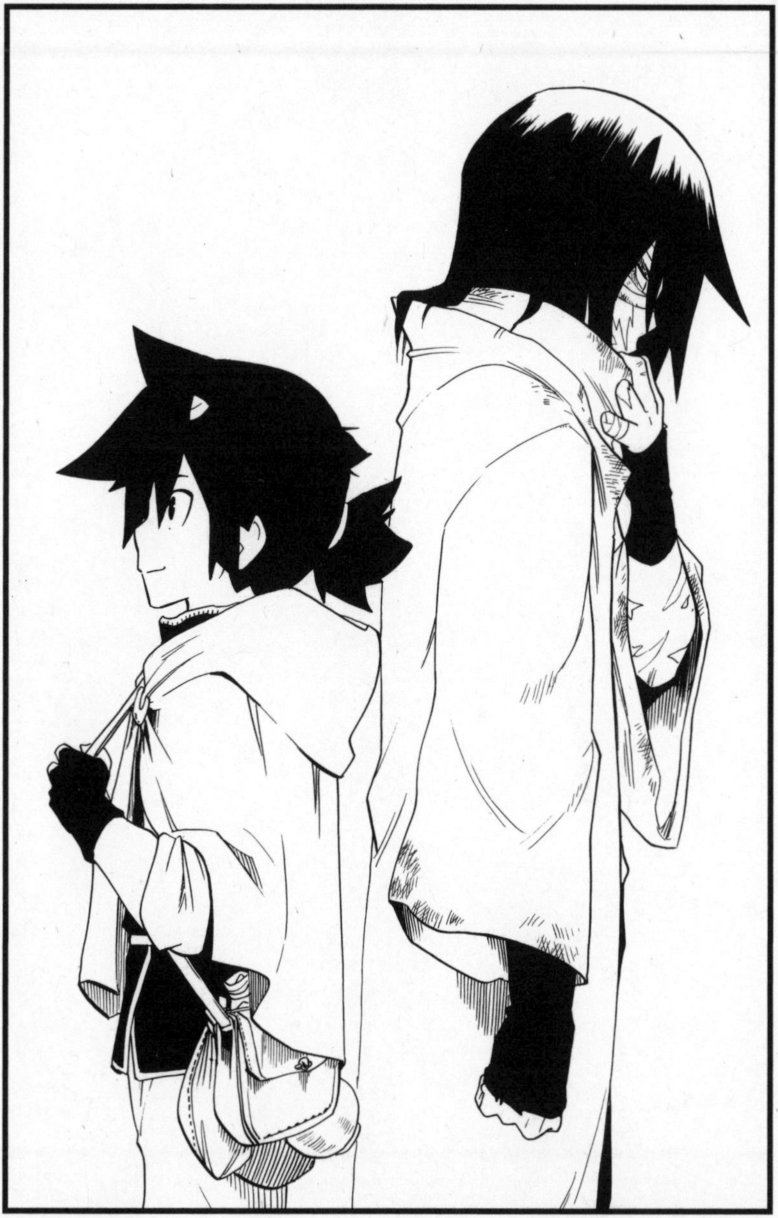

Chapter 58

Memories

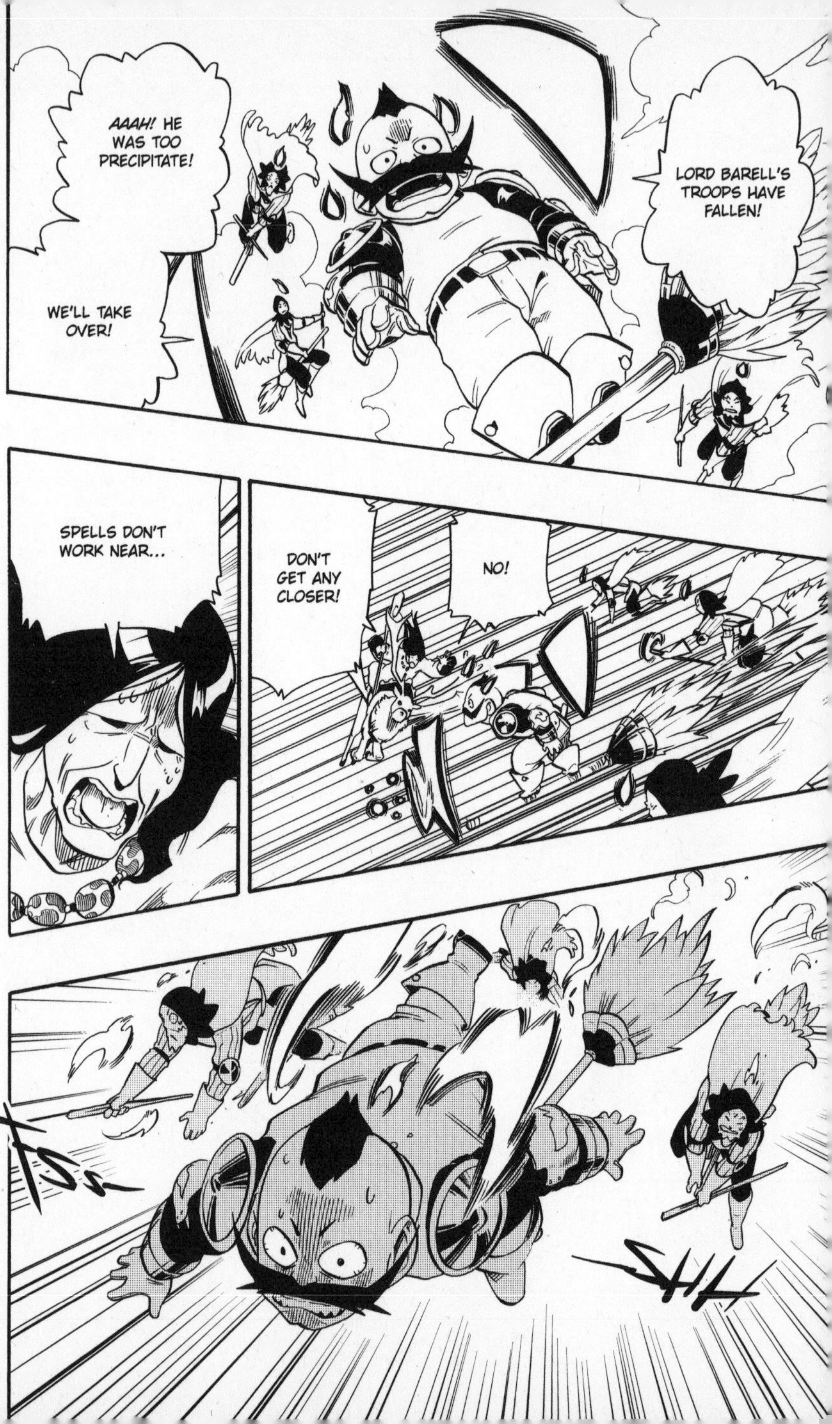
LORD BARELL'S TROOPS HAVE FALLEN!
AAAH! HE WAS TOO PRECIPITATE!
WE'LL TAKE OVER!
NO!
DON'T GET ANY CLOSER!
SPELLS DON'T WORK NEAR...

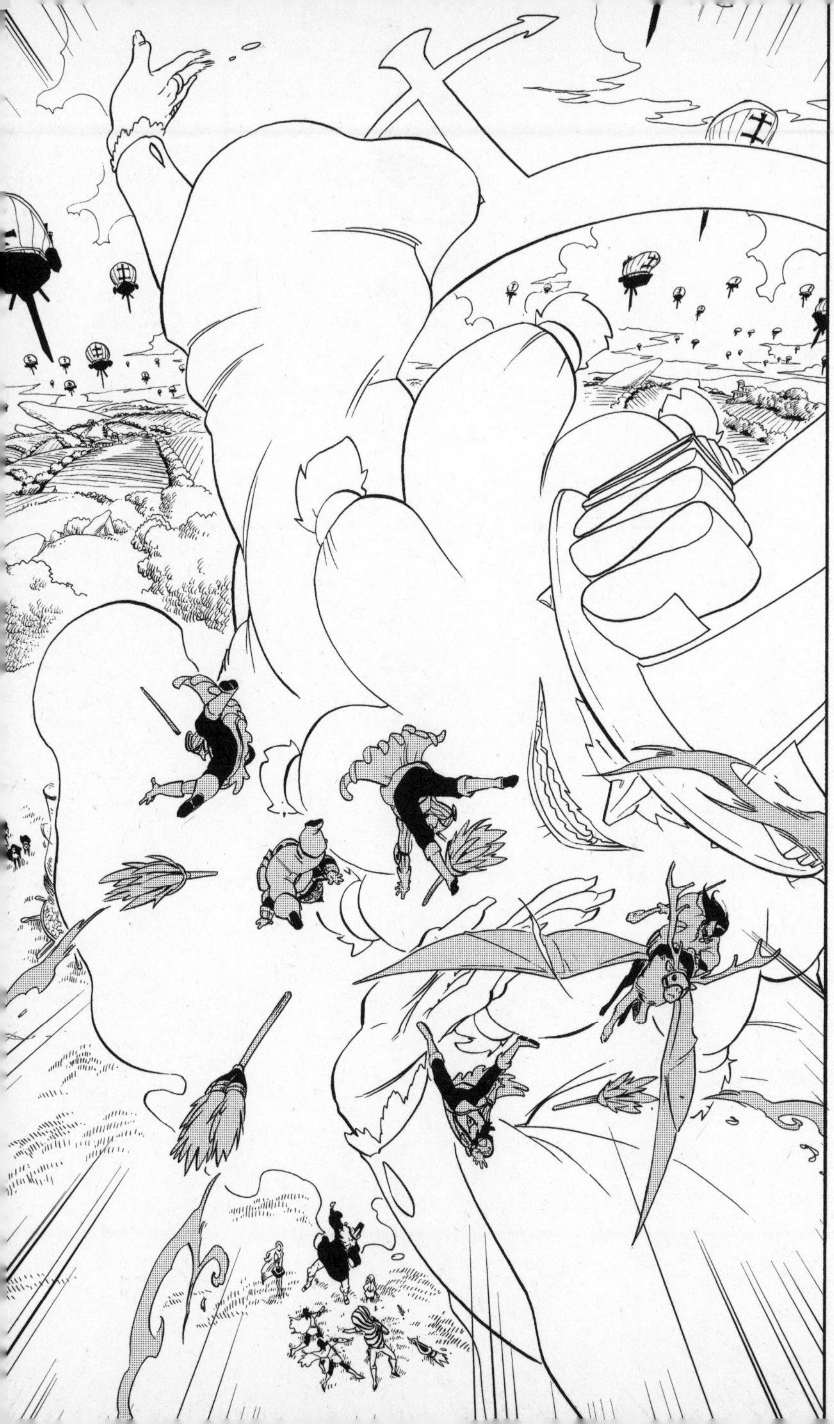

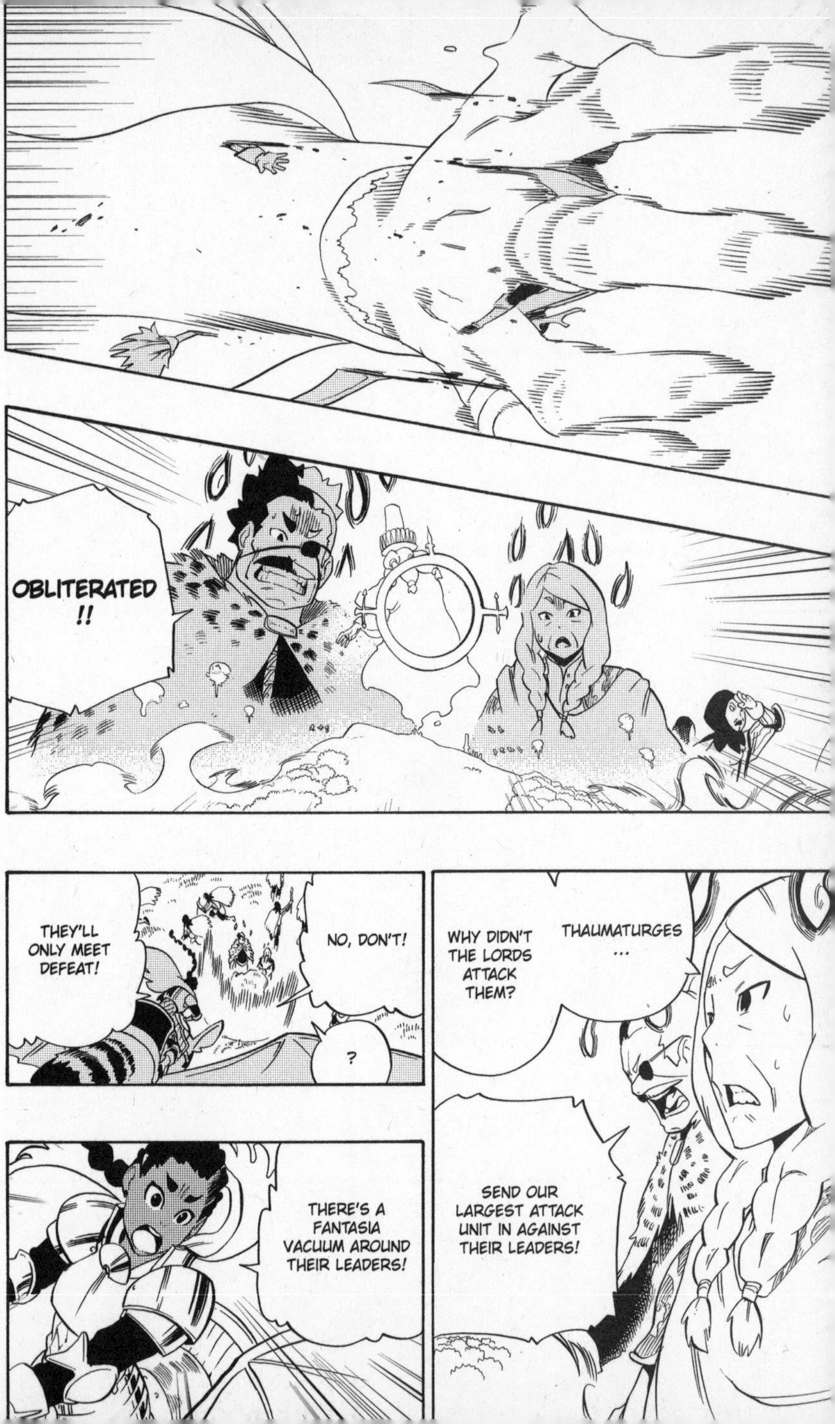
OBLITERATED !!
THAUMATURGES ...
WHY DIDN'T THE LORDS ATTACK THEM?
SEND OUR LARGEST ATTACK UNIT IN AGAINST THEIR LEADERS!
NO, DON'T!
THEY'LL ONLY MEET DEFEAT!
?
THERE'S A FANTASIA VACUUM AROUND THEIR LEADERS!

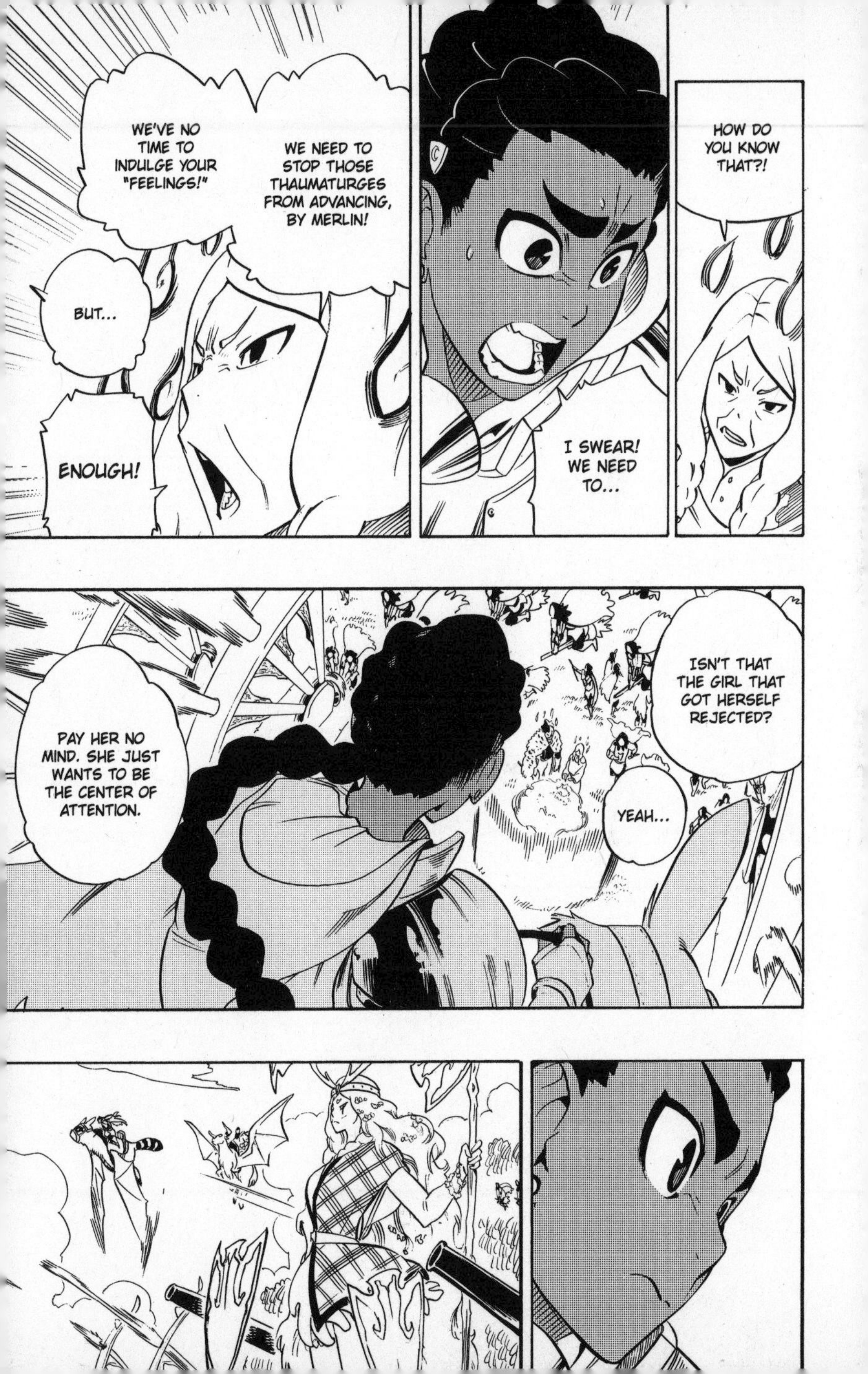
HOW DO YOU KNOW THAT?!
I SWEAR! WE NEED TO...
WE NEED TO STOP THOSE THAUMATURGES FROM ADVANCING, BY MERLIN!
WE'VE NO TIME TO INDULGE YOUR "FEELINGS!"
BUT...
ENOUGH!
ISN'T THAT THE GIRL THAT GOT HERSELF REJECTED?
YEAH...
PAY HER NO MIND. SHE JUST WANTS TO BE THE CENTER OF ATTENTION.

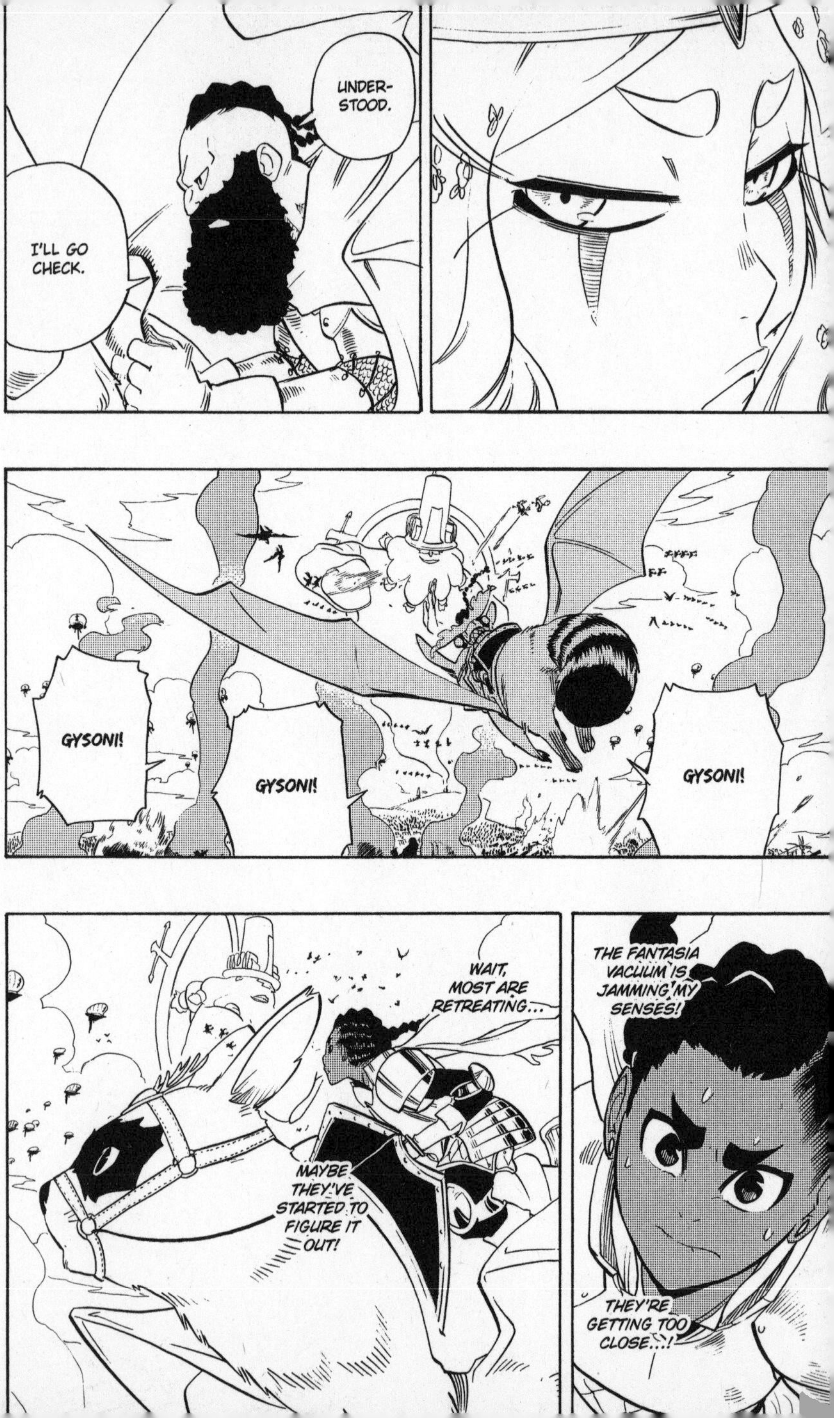
UNDER-STOOD.
I'LL GO CHECK.
GYSONI!
GYSONI!
GYSONI!
THE FANTASIA VACUUM IS JAMMING MY SENSES!
THEY'RE GETTING TOO CLOSE...!
WAIT, MOST ARE RETREATING...
MAYBE THEY'VE STARTED TO FIGURE IT OUT!

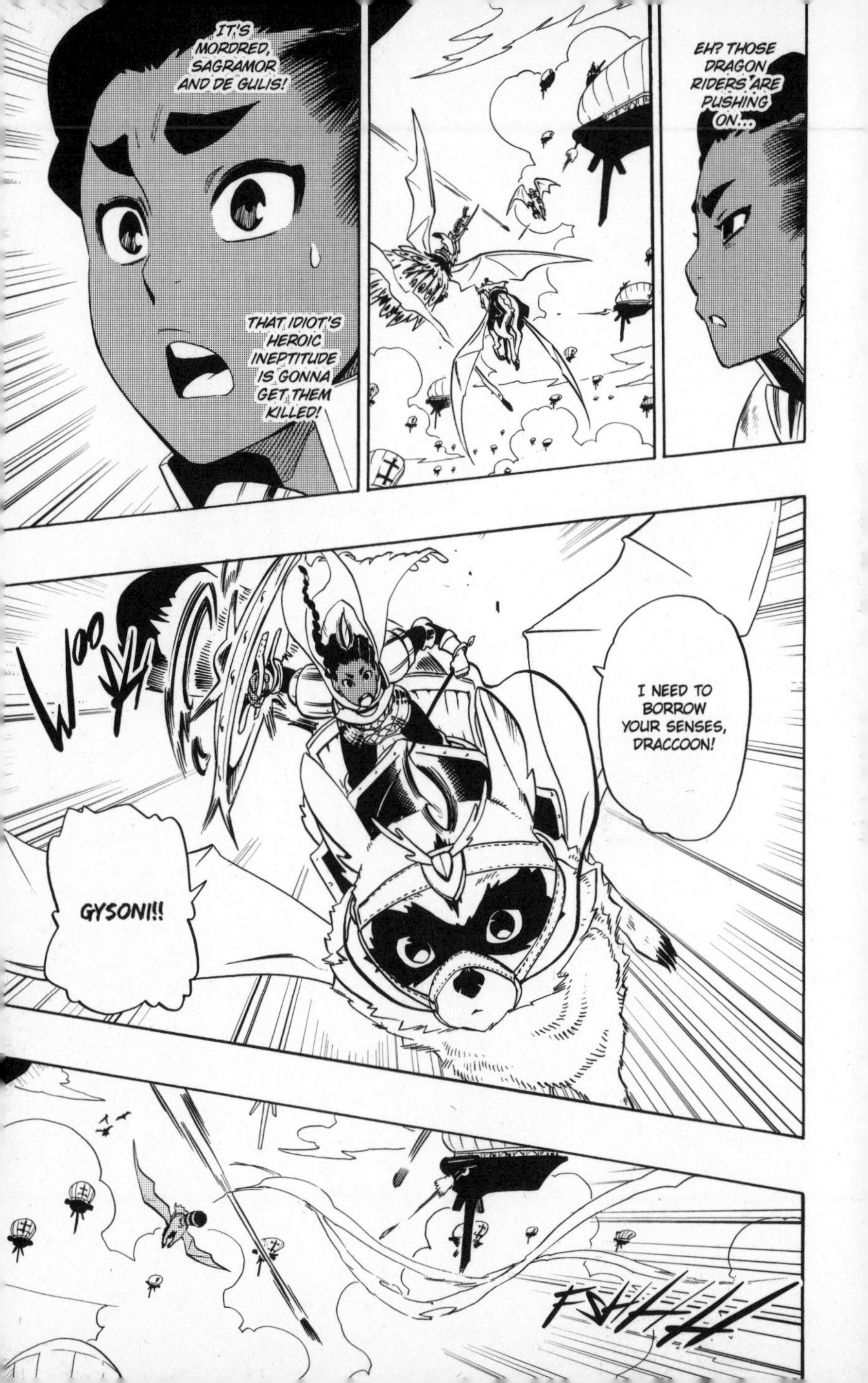
EH? THOSE DRAGON RIDERS ARE PUSHING ON...
IT'S MORDRED, SAGRAMOR AND DE GULIS!
THAT IDIOT'S HEROIC INEPTITUDE IS GONNA GET THEM KILLED!
I NEED TO BORROW YOUR SENSES, DRACCOON!
GYSONI!!
WOO
FSHHH

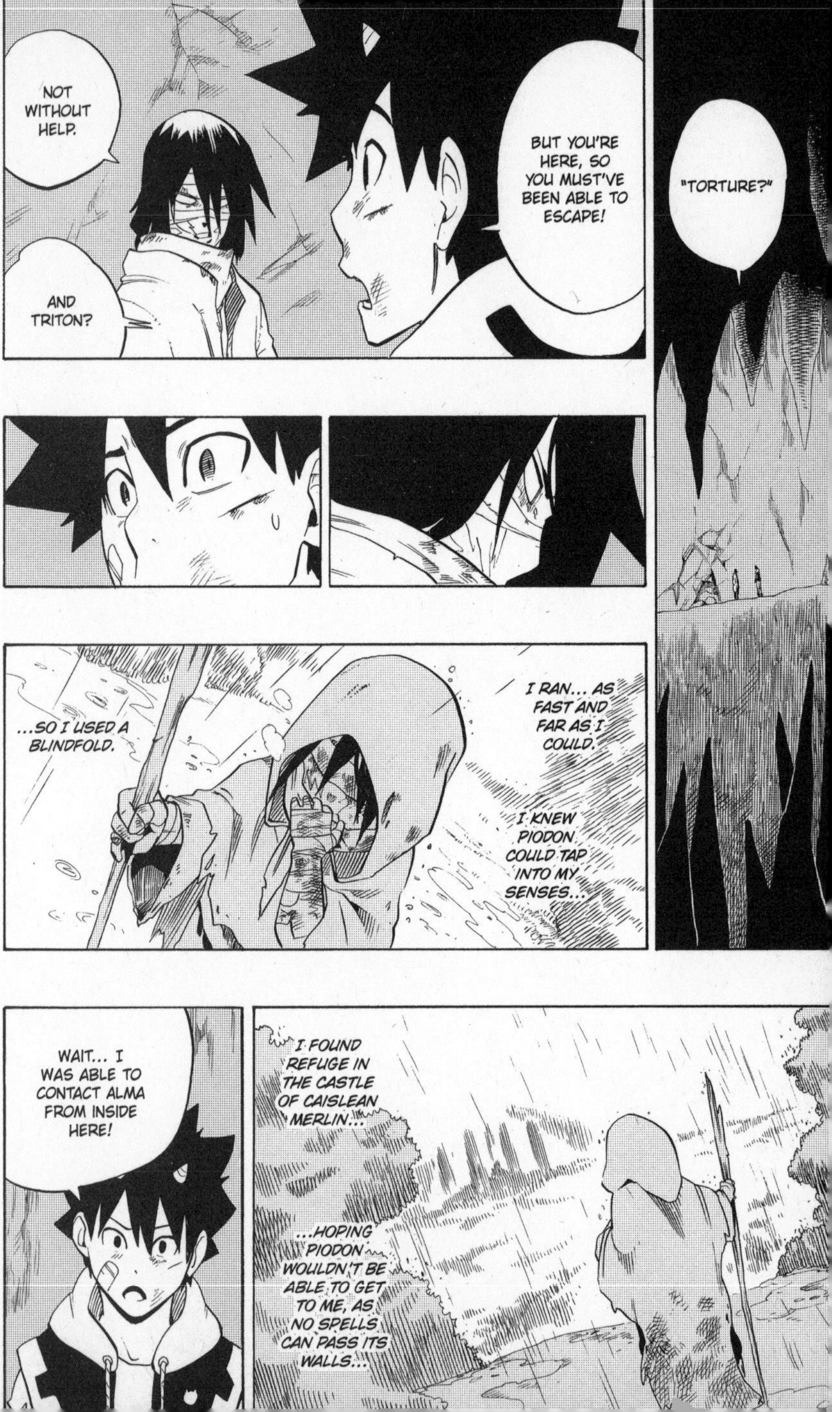
"TORTURE?"
BUT YOU'RE HERE, SO YOU MUST'VE BEEN ABLE TO ESCAPE!
NOT WITHOUT HELP.
AND TRITON?
I RAN... AS FAST AND FAR AS I COULD.
I KNEW PIODON COULD TAP INTO MY SENSES...
...SO I USED A BLINDFOLD.
I FOUND REFUGE IN THE CASTLE OF CAISLEAN MERLIN...
...HOPING PIODON WOULDN'T BE ABLE TO GET TO ME, AS NO SPELLS CAN PASS ITS WALLS...
WAIT... I WAS ABLE TO CONTACT ALMA FROM INSIDE HERE!

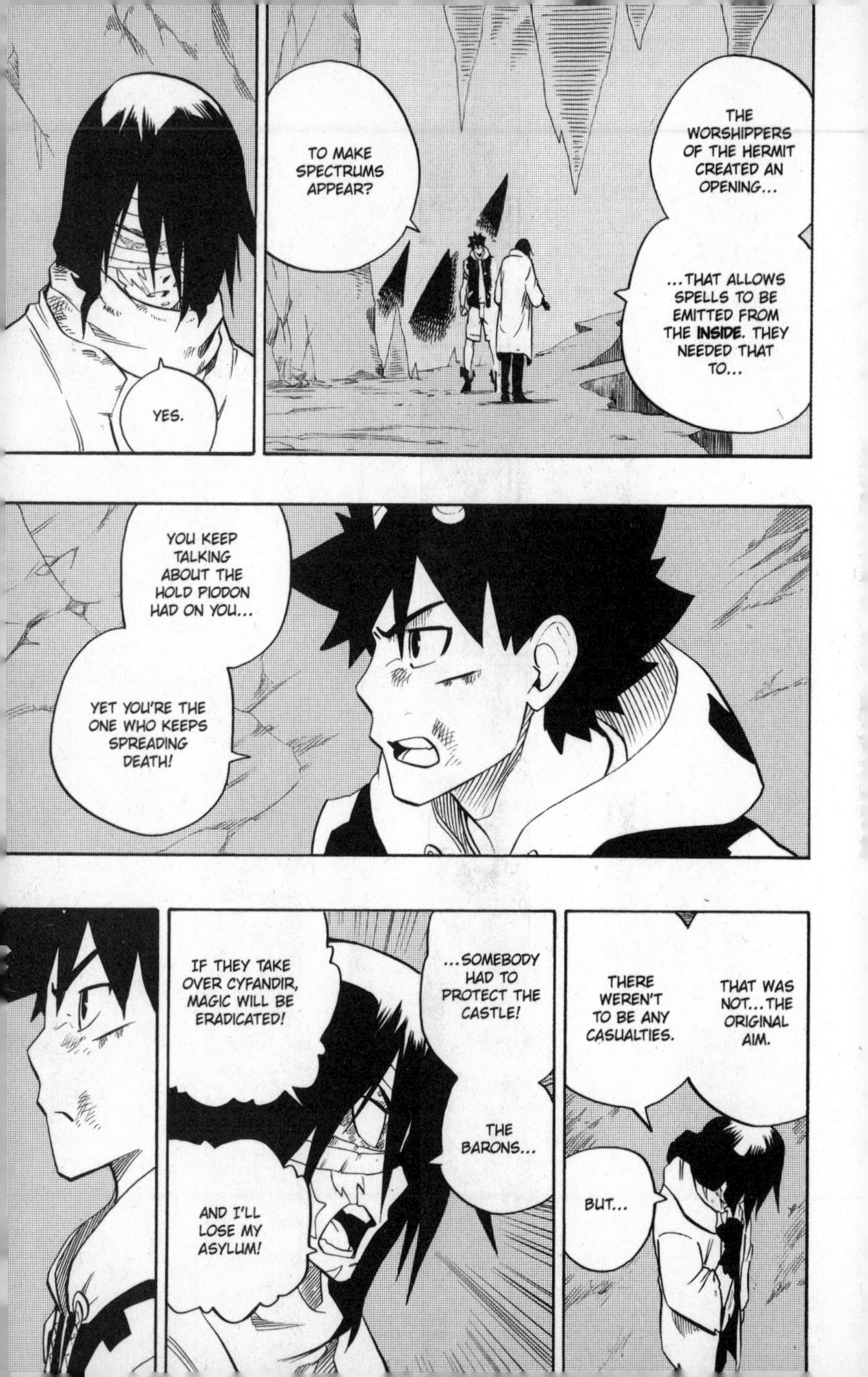
THE WORSHIPPERS OF THE HERMIT CREATED AN OPENING...
...THAT ALLOWS SPELLS TO BE EMITTED FROM THE **INSIDE**. THEY NEEDED THAT TO...
TO MAKE SPECTRUMS APPEAR?
YES.
YOU KEEP TALKING ABOUT THE HOLD PIODON HAD ON YOU...
YET YOU'RE THE ONE WHO KEEPS SPREADING DEATH!
THAT WAS NOT...THE ORIGINAL AIM.
THERE WEREN'T TO BE ANY CASUALTIES.
BUT...
...SOMEBODY HAD TO PROTECT THE CASTLE!
THE BARONS...
IF THEY TAKE OVER CYFANDIR, MAGIC WILL BE ERADICATED!
AND I'LL LOSE MY ASYLUM!

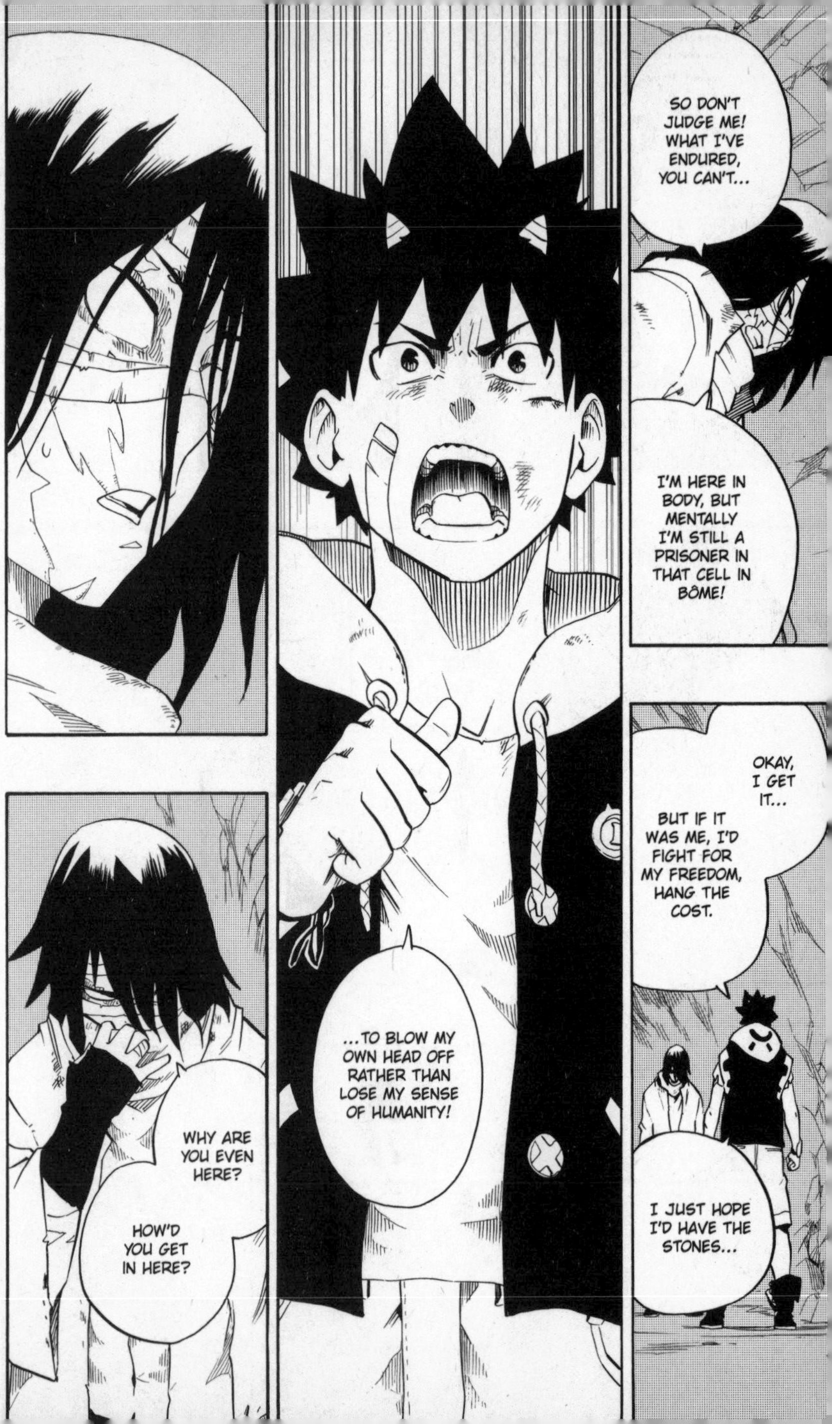
SO DON'T JUDGE ME! WHAT I'VE ENDURED, YOU CAN'T...
I'M HERE IN BODY, BUT MENTALLY I'M STILL A PRISONER IN THAT CELL IN BÔME!
OKAY, I GET IT...
BUT IF IT WAS ME, I'D FIGHT FOR MY FREEDOM, HANG THE COST.
I JUST HOPE I'D HAVE THE STONES...
...TO BLOW MY OWN HEAD OFF RATHER THAN LOSE MY SENSE OF HUMANITY!
WHY ARE YOU EVEN HERE?
HOW'D YOU GET IN HERE?

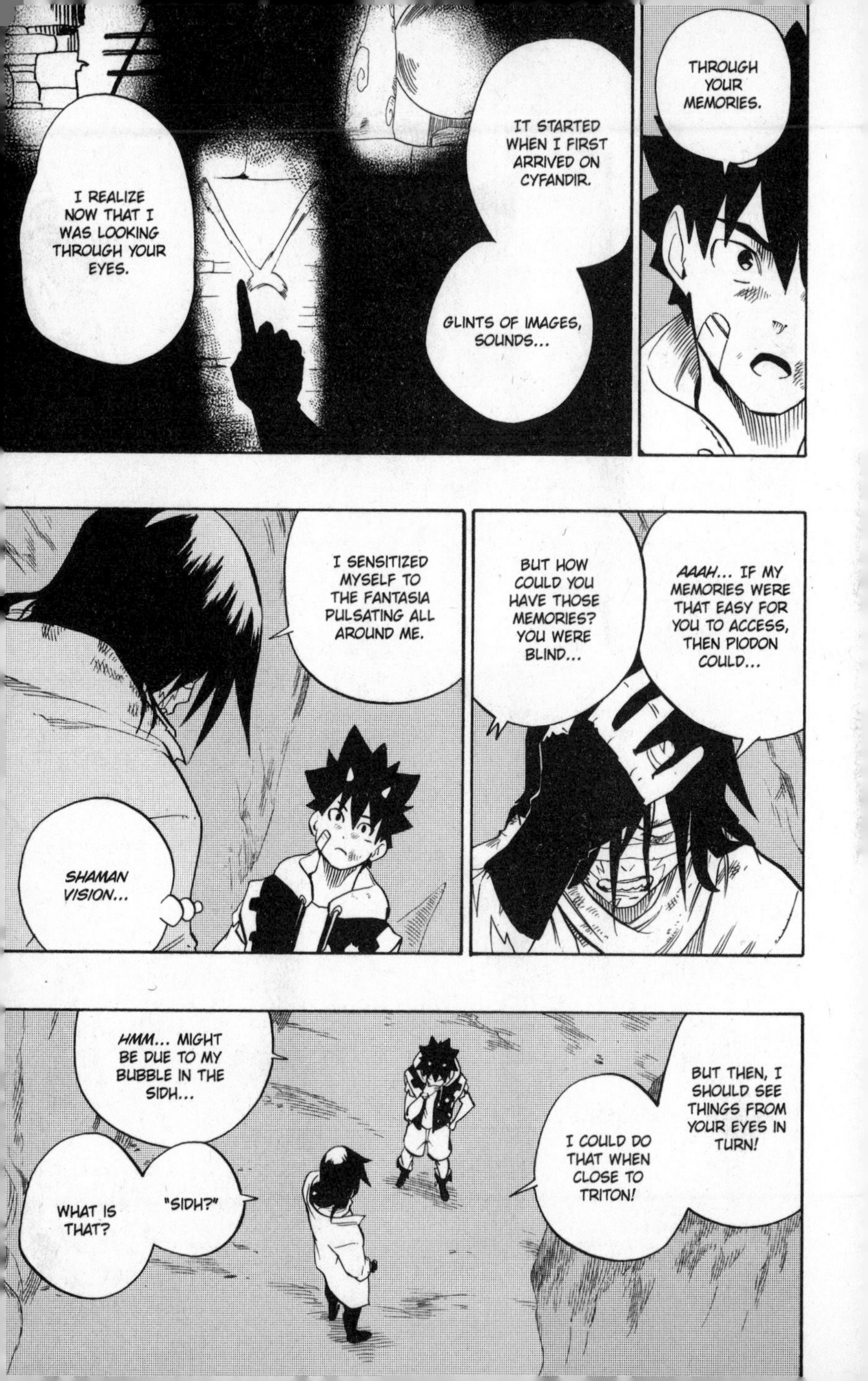
THROUGH YOUR MEMORIES.
IT STARTED WHEN I FIRST ARRIVED ON CYFANDIR.
GLINTS OF IMAGES, SOUNDS...
I REALIZE NOW THAT I WAS LOOKING THROUGH YOUR EYES.
AAAH... IF MY MEMORIES WERE THAT EASY FOR YOU TO ACCESS, THEN PIODON COULD...
BUT HOW COULD YOU HAVE THOSE MEMORIES? YOU WERE BLIND...
I SENSITIZED MYSELF TO THE FANTASIA PULSATING ALL AROUND ME.
SHAMAN VISION...
BUT THEN, I SHOULD SEE THINGS FROM YOUR EYES IN TURN!
I COULD DO THAT WHEN CLOSE TO TRITON!
HMM... MIGHT BE DUE TO MY BUBBLE IN THE SIDH...
"SIDH?"
WHAT IS THAT?

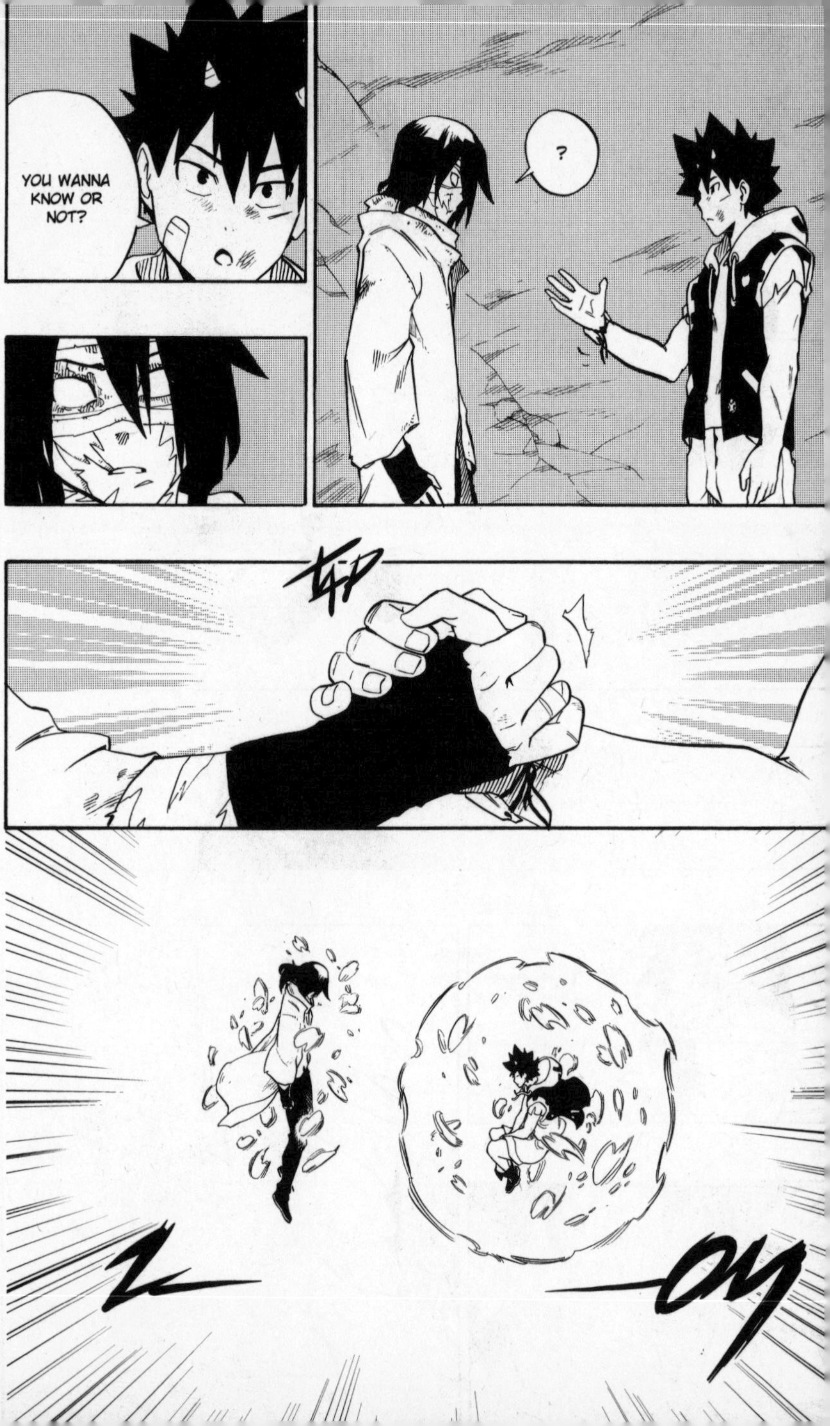
?
YOU WANNA KNOW OR NOT?
TAP

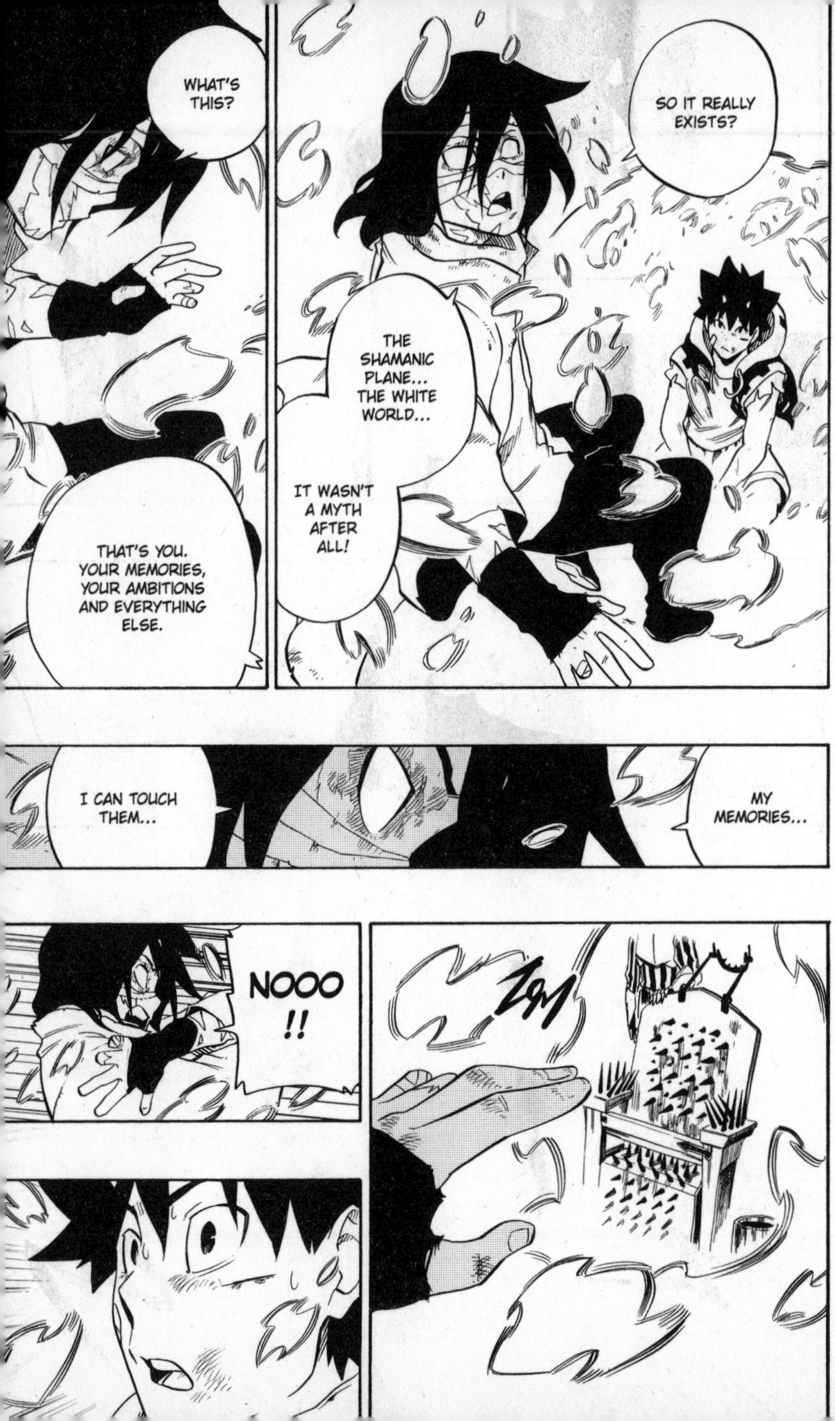
SO IT REALLY EXISTS?
THE SHAMANIC PLANE... THE WHITE WORLD...
IT WASN'T A MYTH AFTER ALL!
WHAT'S THIS?
THAT'S YOU. YOUR MEMORIES, YOUR AMBITIONS AND EVERYTHING ELSE.
MY MEMORIES...
I CAN TOUCH THEM...
NOOO !!

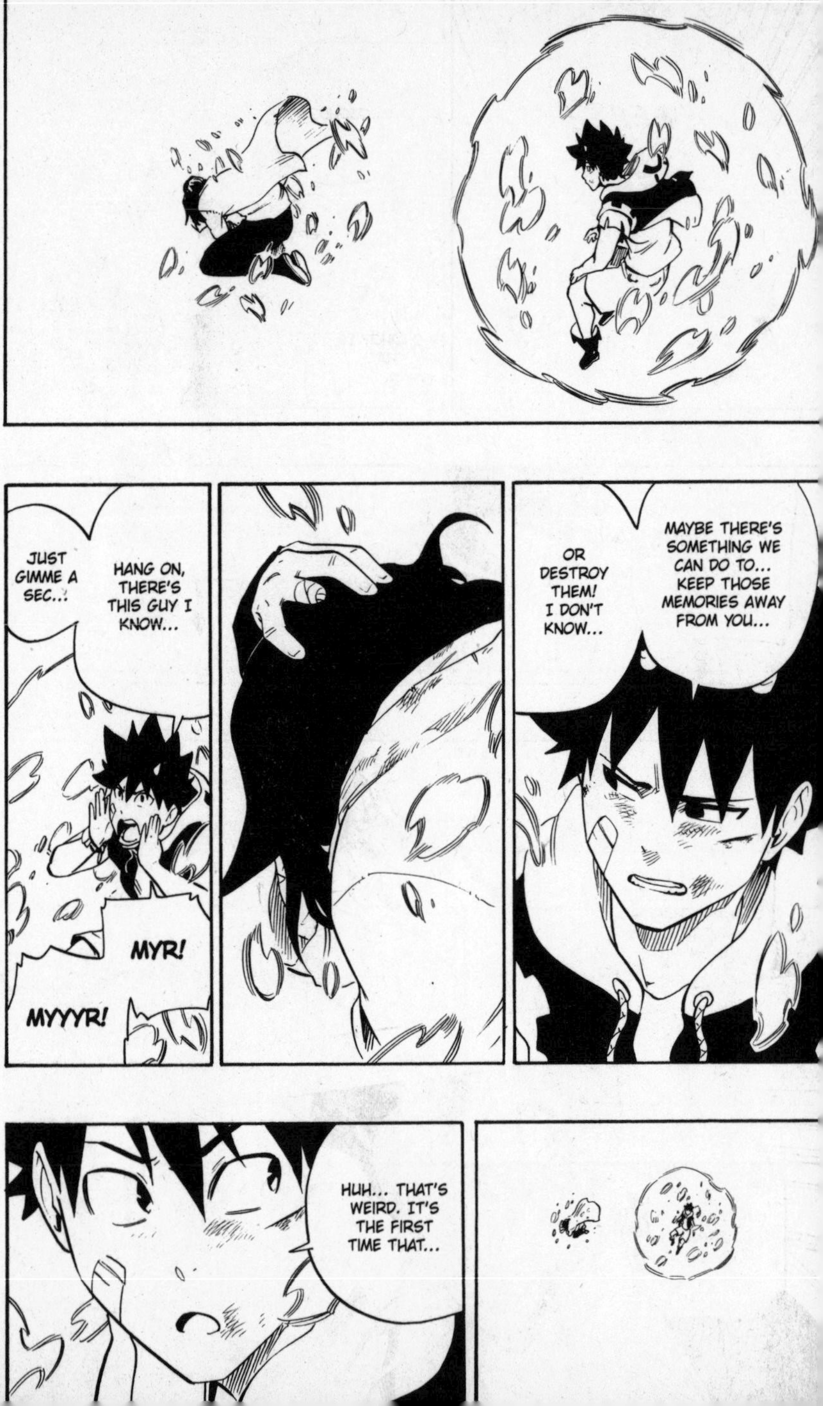
MAYBE THERE'S SOMETHING WE CAN DO TO... KEEP THOSE MEMORIES AWAY FROM YOU...
OR DESTROY THEM! I DON'T KNOW...
HANG ON, THERE'S THIS GUY I KNOW...
JUST GIMME A SEC...
MYR!
MYYYR!
HUH... THAT'S WEIRD. IT'S THE FIRST TIME THAT...

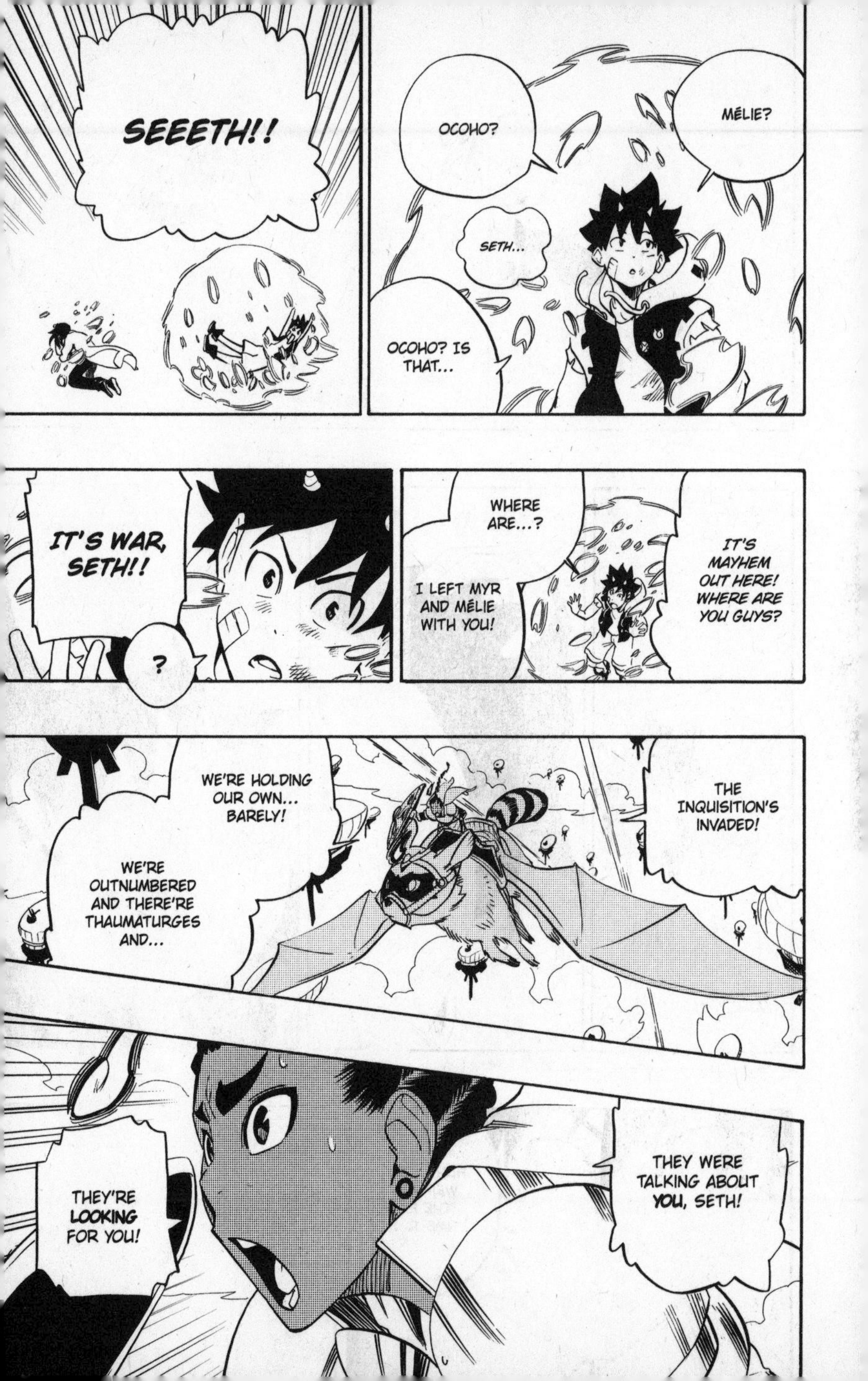
MÉLIE?
OCOHO?
SETH...
OCOHO? IS THAT...
SEEETH!!
IT'S MAYHEM OUT HERE! WHERE ARE YOU GUYS?
WHERE ARE...?
I LEFT MYR AND MÉLIE WITH YOU!
IT'S WAR, SETH!!
?
THE INQUISITION'S INVADED!
WE'RE HOLDING OUR OWN... BARELY!
WE'RE OUTNUMBERED AND THERE'RE THAUMATURGES AND...
THEY WERE TALKING ABOUT **YOU**, SETH!
THEY'RE **LOOKING** FOR YOU!

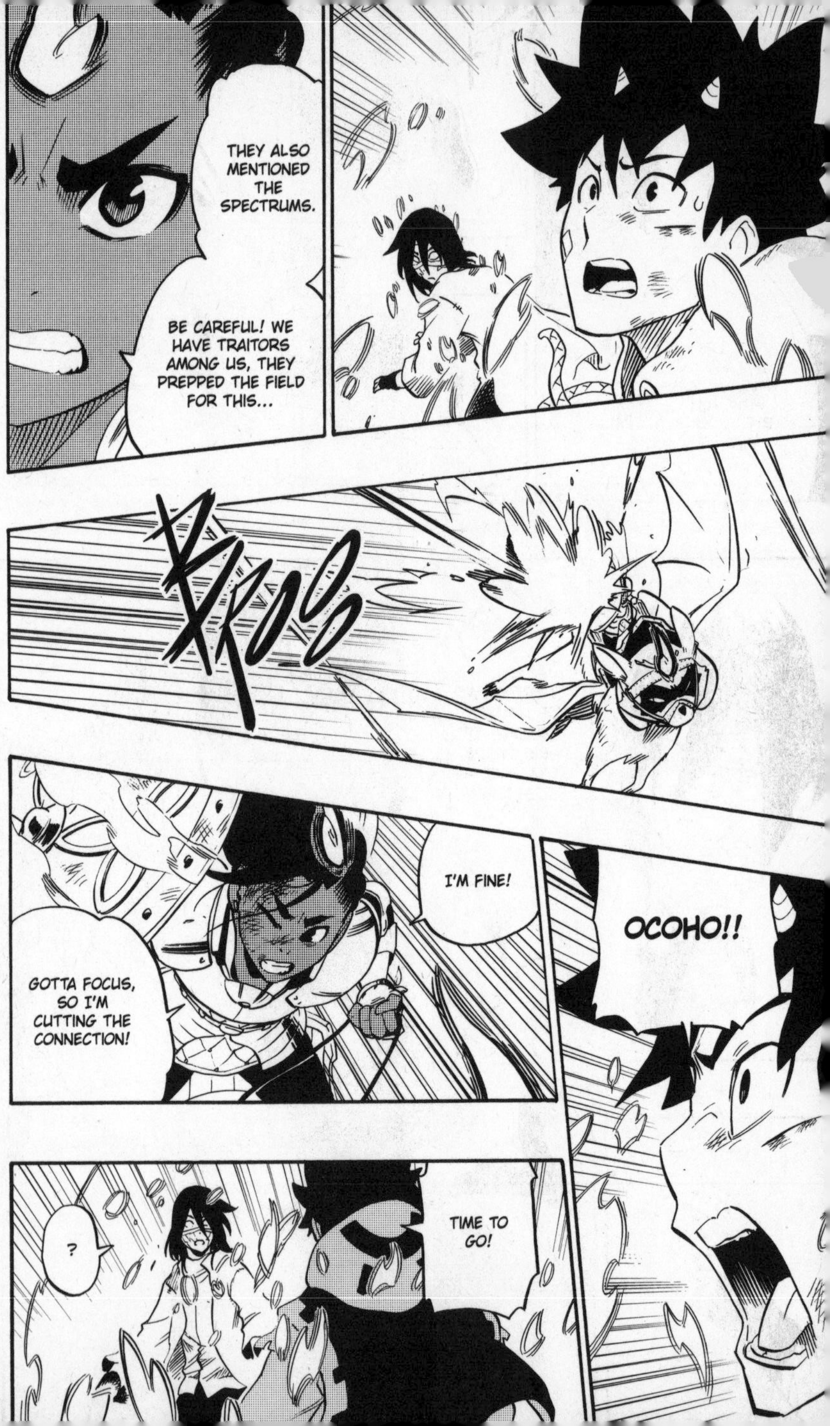
THEY ALSO MENTIONED THE SPECTRUMS.
BE CAREFUL! WE HAVE TRAITORS AMONG US, THEY PREPPED THE FIELD FOR THIS...
BKROOS
OCOHO!!
I'M FINE!
GOTTA FOCUS, SO I'M CUTTING THE CONNECTION!
TIME TO GO!
?

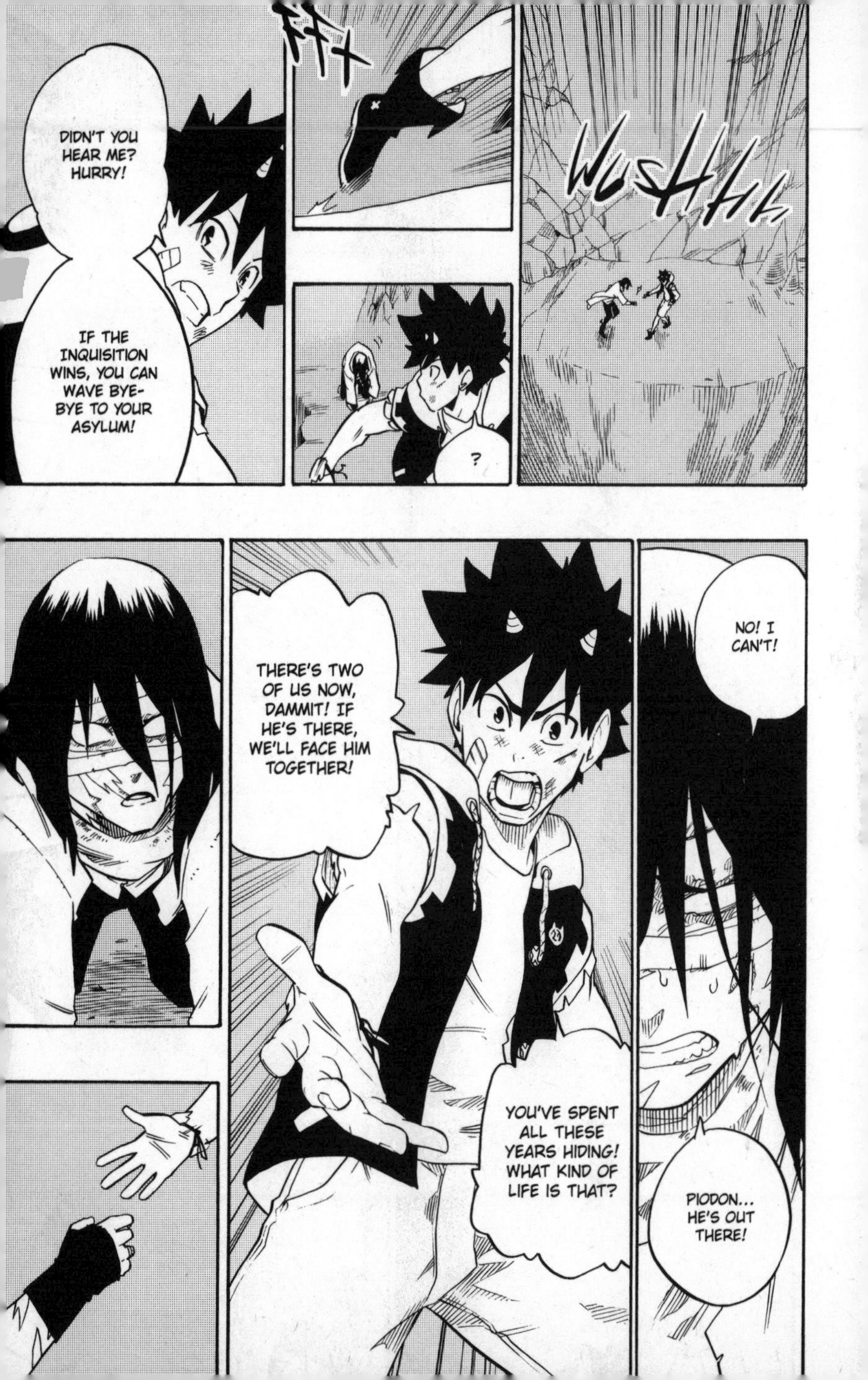
FFT
?
DIDN'T YOU HEAR ME? HURRY!
IF THE INQUISITION WINS, YOU CAN WAVE BYE-BYE TO YOUR ASYLUM!
NO! I CAN'T!
PIODON... HE'S OUT THERE!
THERE'S TWO OF US NOW, DAMMIT! IF HE'S THERE, WE'LL FACE HIM TOGETHER!
YOU'VE SPENT ALL THESE YEARS HIDING! WHAT KIND OF LIFE IS THAT?

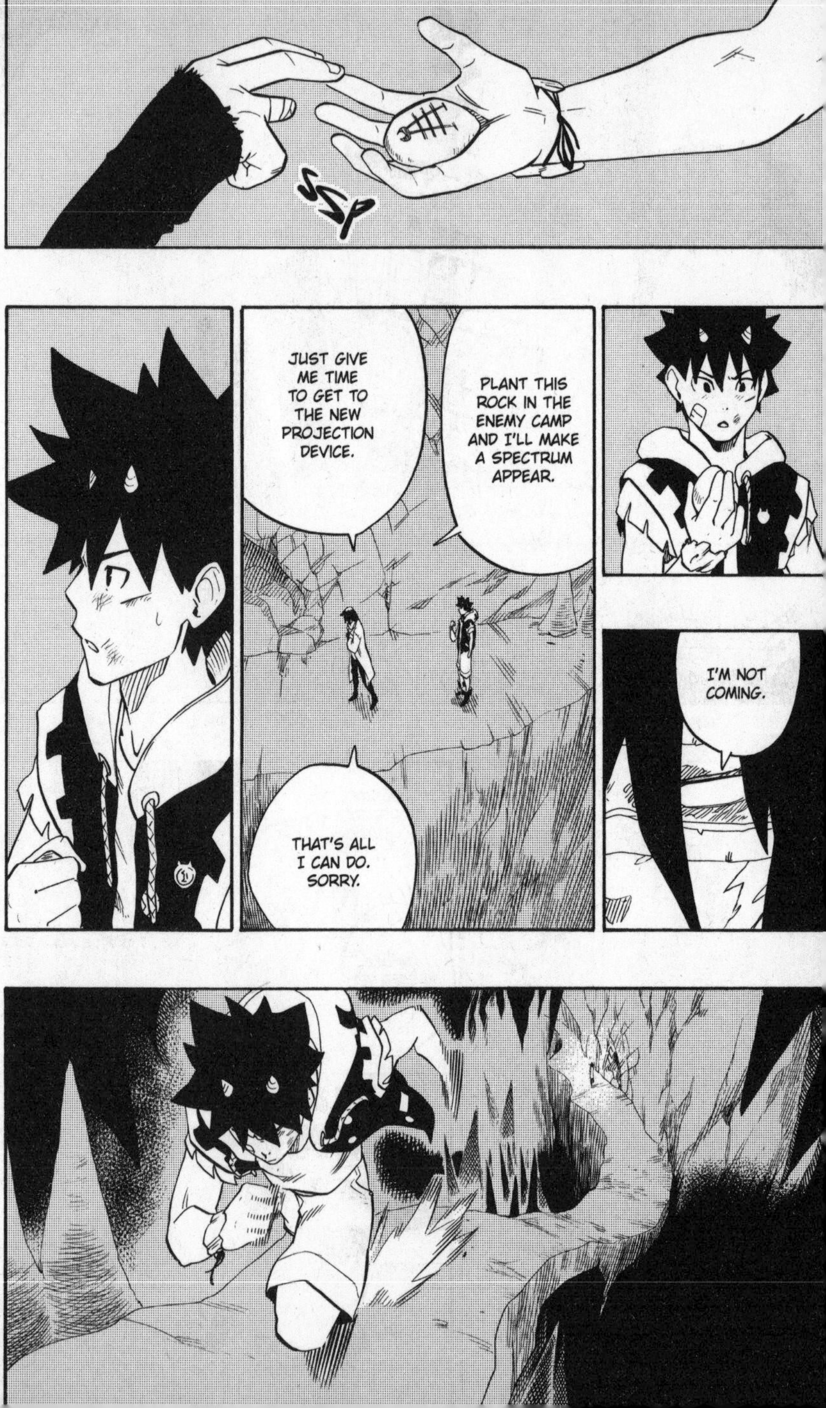
SSP
I'M NOT COMING.
PLANT THIS ROCK IN THE ENEMY CAMP AND I'LL MAKE A SPECTRUM APPEAR.
JUST GIVE ME TIME TO GET TO THE NEW PROJECTION DEVICE.
THAT'S ALL I CAN DO. SORRY.

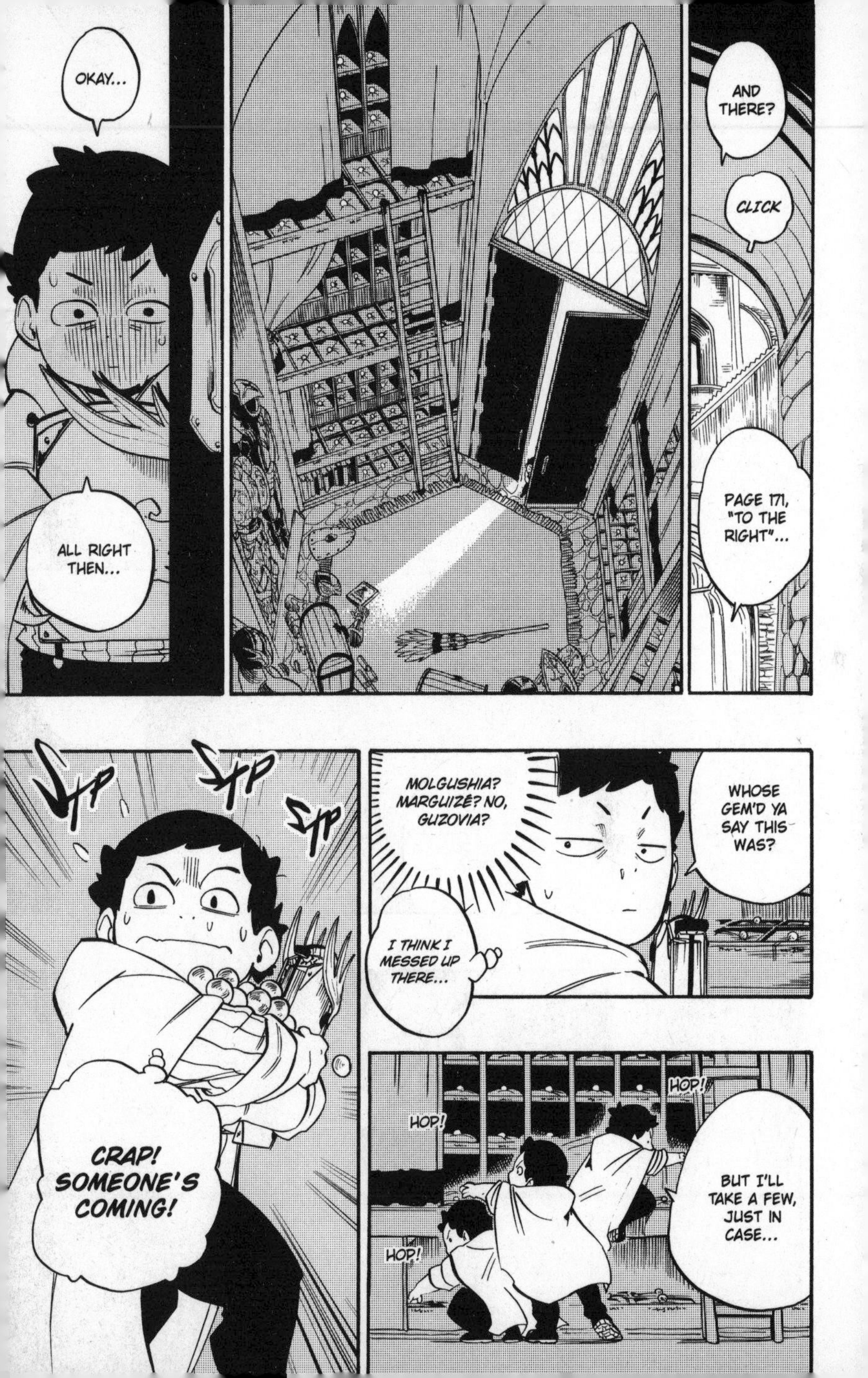
AND THERE?
CLICK
PAGE 171, "TO THE RIGHT"...
OKAY...
ALL RIGHT THEN...
WHOSE GEM'D YA SAY THIS WAS?
MOLGUSHIA? MARGUIZE? NO, GUZOVIA?
I THINK I MESSED UP THERE...
HOP!
HOP!
HOP!
BUT I'LL TAKE A FEW, JUST IN CASE...
CRAP! SOMEONE'S COMING!

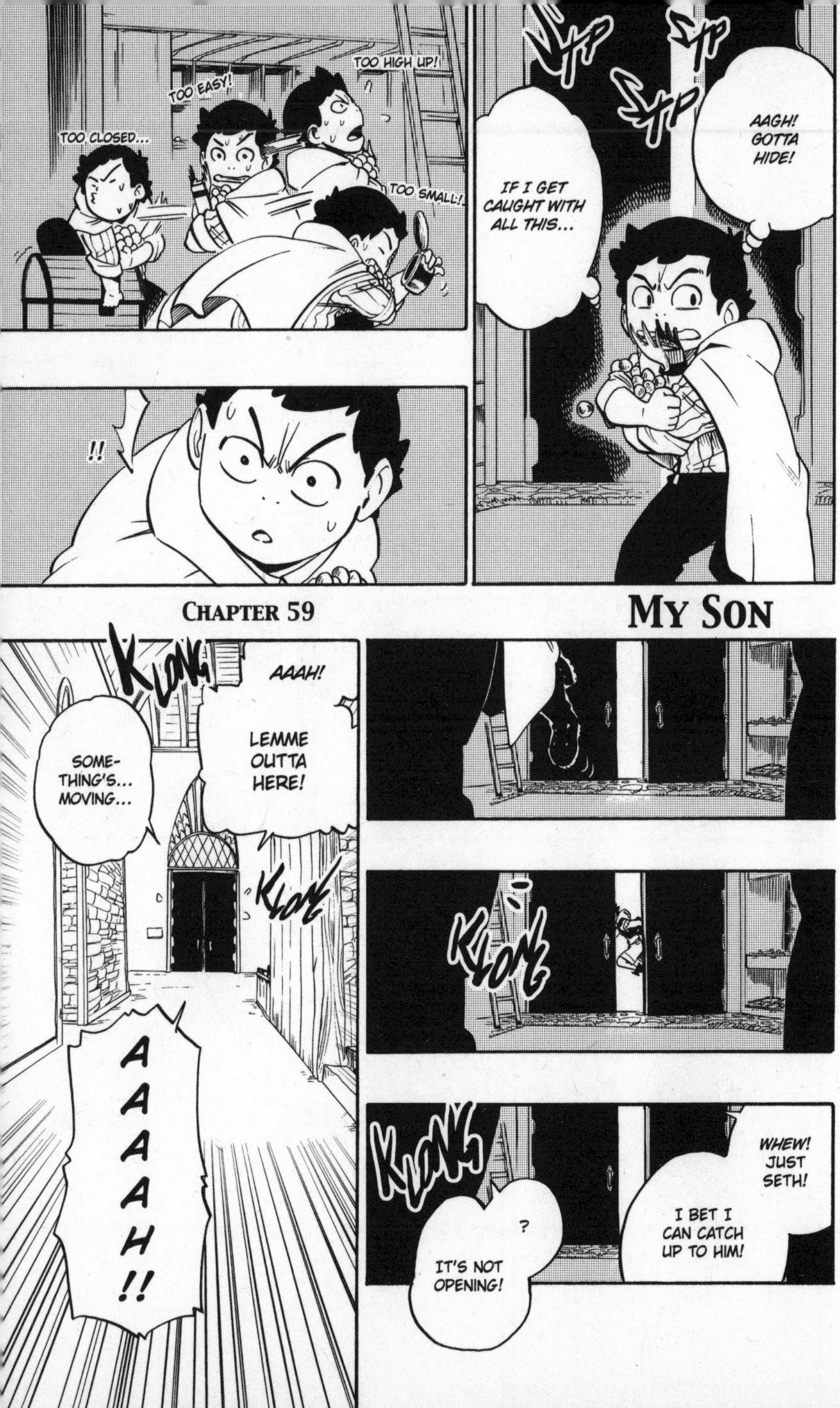
Stp Stp Stp
AAGH! GOTTA HIDE!
IF I GET CAUGHT WITH ALL THIS...
TOO HIGH UP!
TOO SMALL!
TOO EASY!
TOO CLOSED...
!!

Chapter 59 My Son

KLONG
WHEW! JUST SETH!
I BET I CAN CATCH UP TO HIM!
KLONG
?
IT'S NOT OPENING!
KLONG
AAAH!
LEMME OUTTA HERE!
SOME-THING'S... MOVING...
KLONG
AAAAAH!!

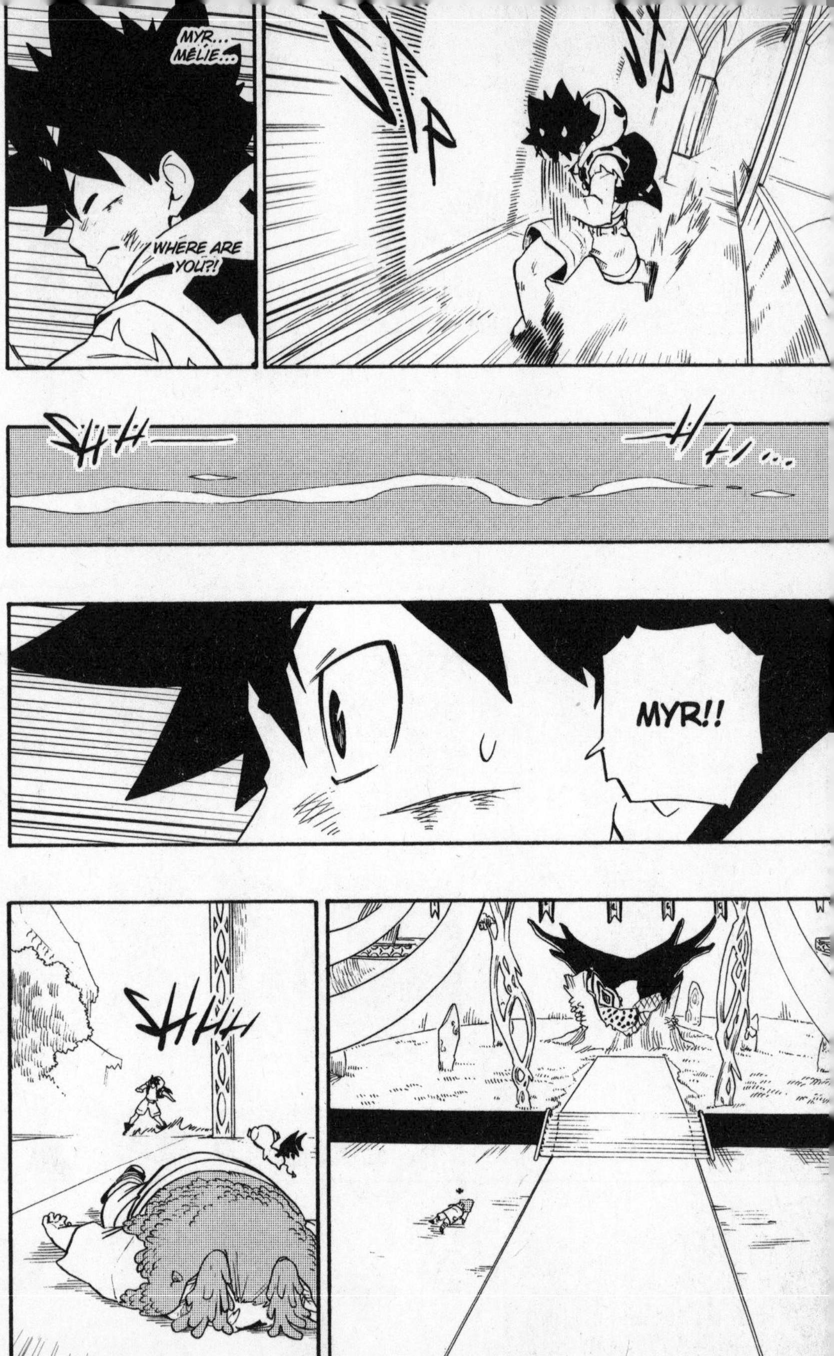
MYR... MÉLIE...
WHERE ARE YOU?!
SHH—
MYR!!
SHHH

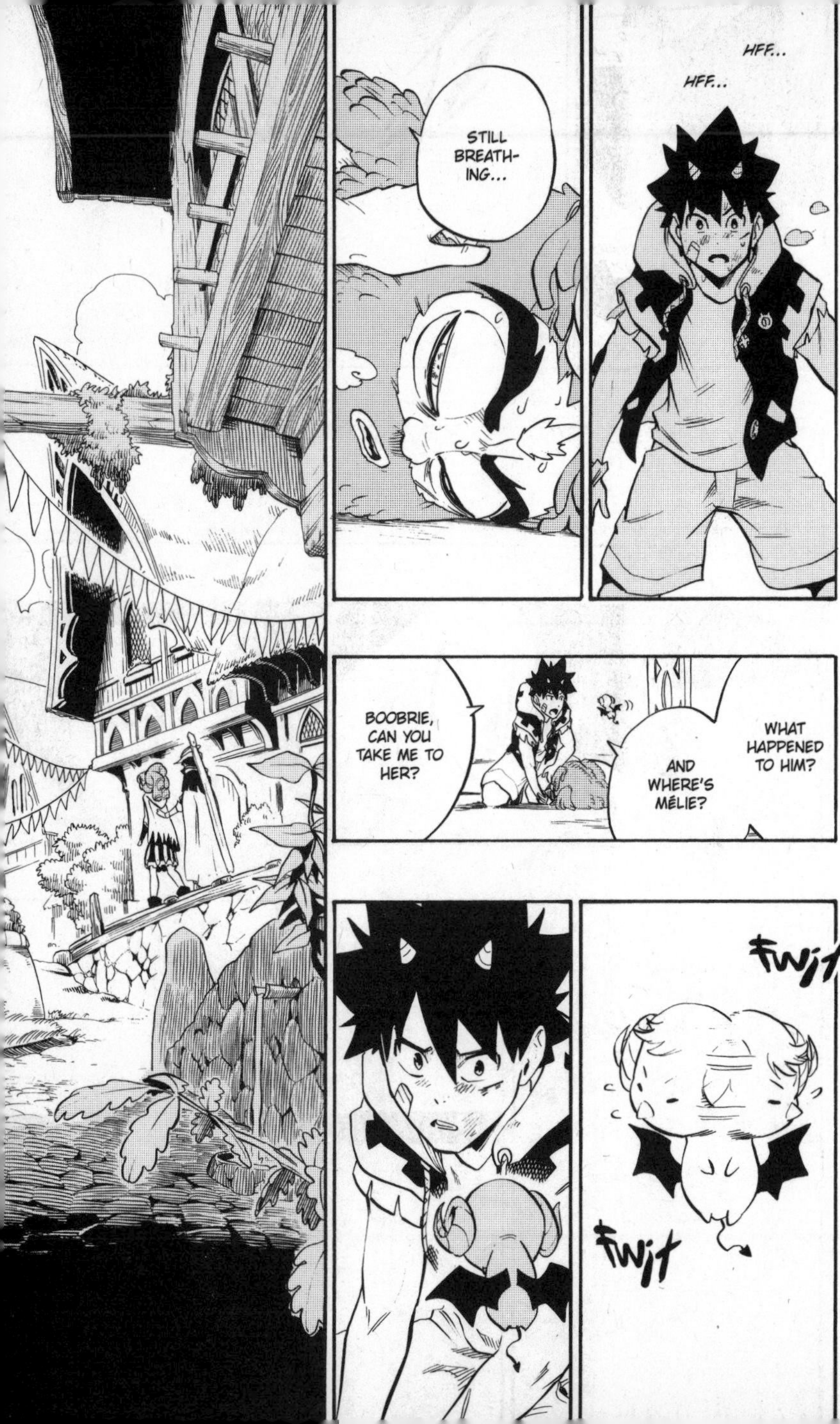
HFF...
HFF...
STILL BREATH-ING...
WHAT HAPPENED TO HIM?
AND WHERE'S MÉLIE?
BOOBRIE, CAN YOU TAKE ME TO HER?
FWIT
FWIT

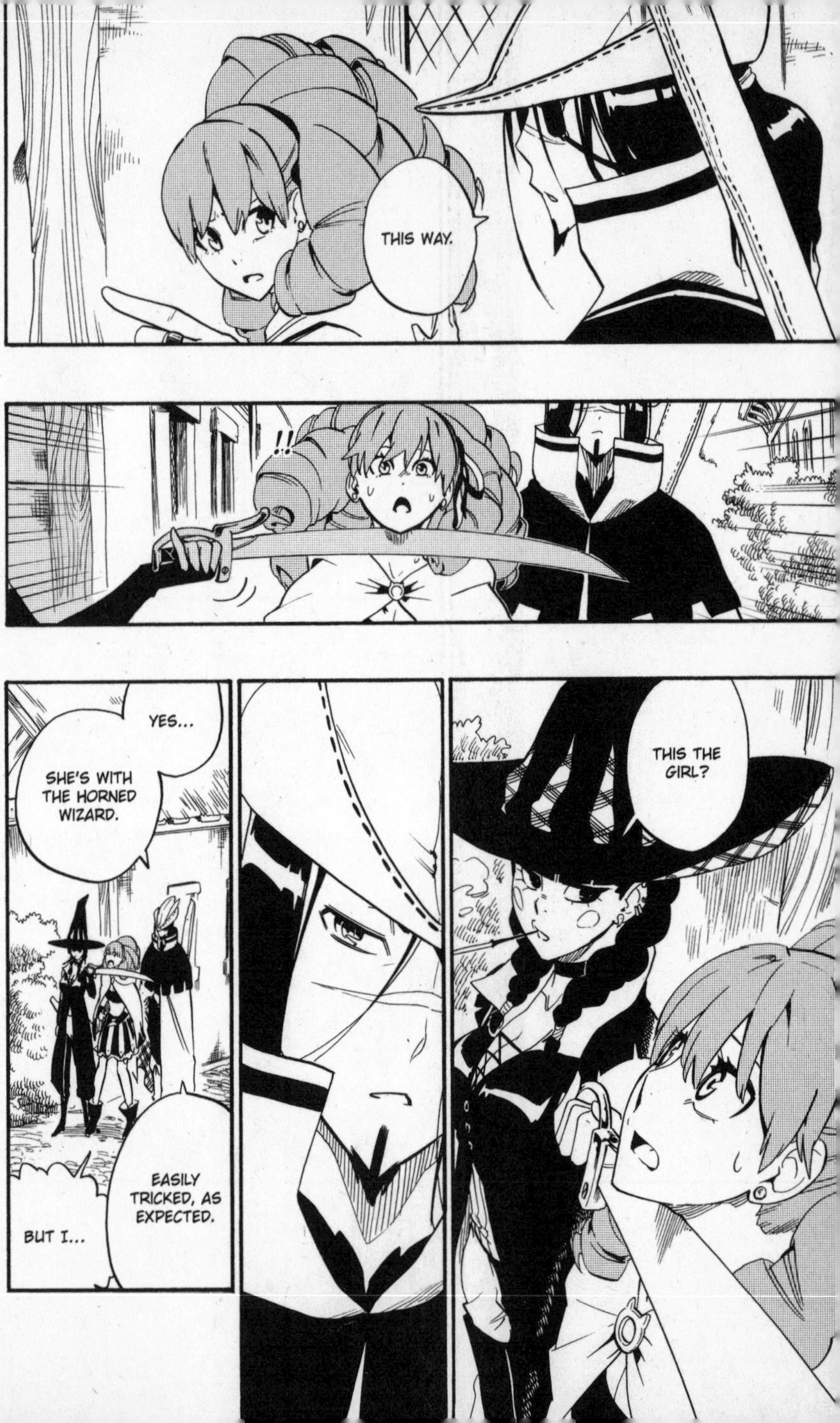
THIS WAY.
!!
THIS THE GIRL?
YES... SHE'S WITH THE HORNED WIZARD.
EASILY TRICKED, AS EXPECTED.
BUT I...

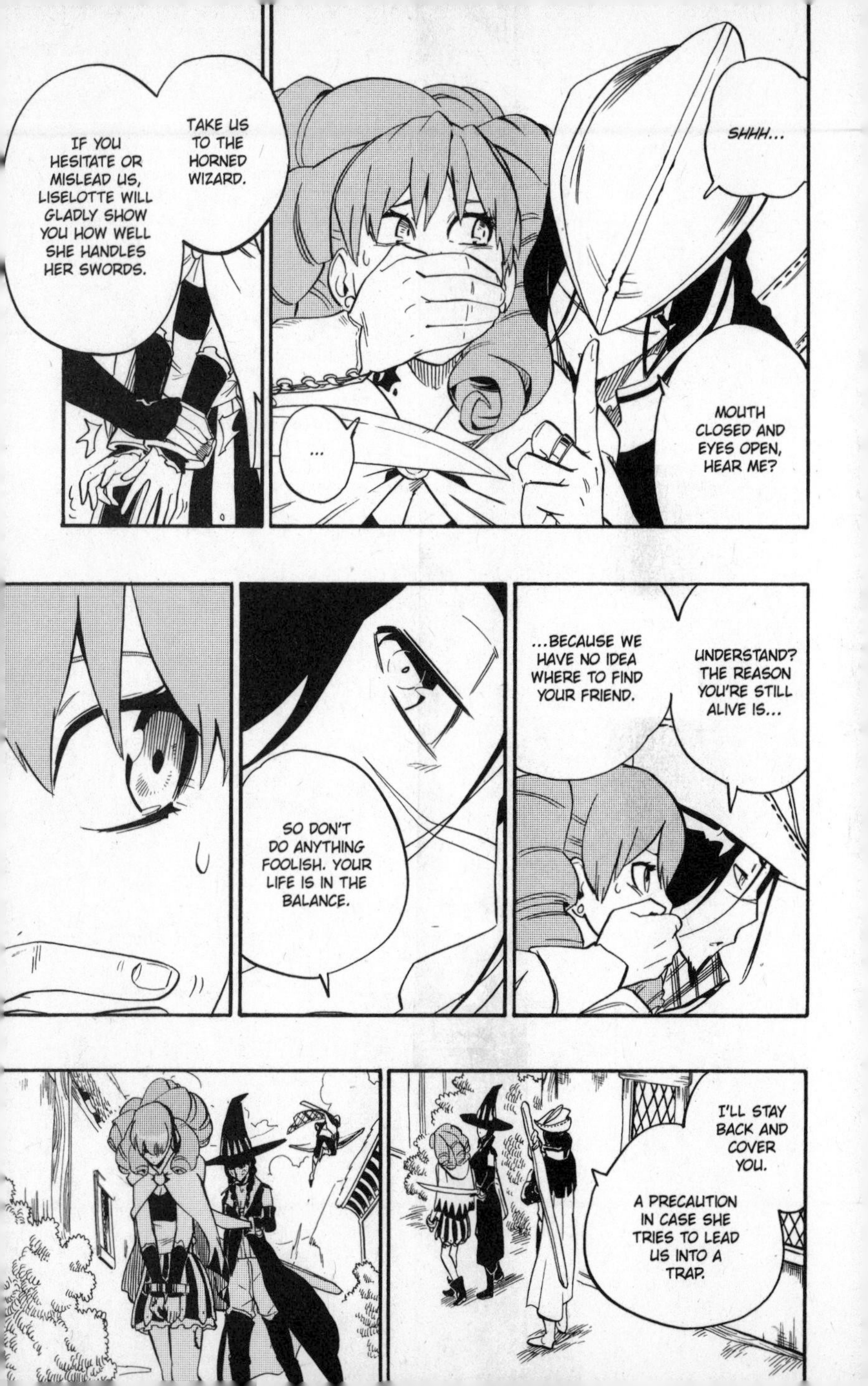
SHHH...
MOUTH CLOSED AND EYES OPEN, HEAR ME?
...
TAKE US TO THE HORNED WIZARD.
IF YOU HESITATE OR MISLEAD US, LISELOTTE WILL GLADLY SHOW YOU HOW WELL SHE HANDLES HER SWORDS.
UNDERSTAND? THE REASON YOU'RE STILL ALIVE IS...
...BECAUSE WE HAVE NO IDEA WHERE TO FIND YOUR FRIEND.
SO DON'T DO ANYTHING FOOLISH. YOUR LIFE IS IN THE BALANCE.
I'LL STAY BACK AND COVER YOU.
A PRECAUTION IN CASE SHE TRIES TO LEAD US INTO A TRAP.

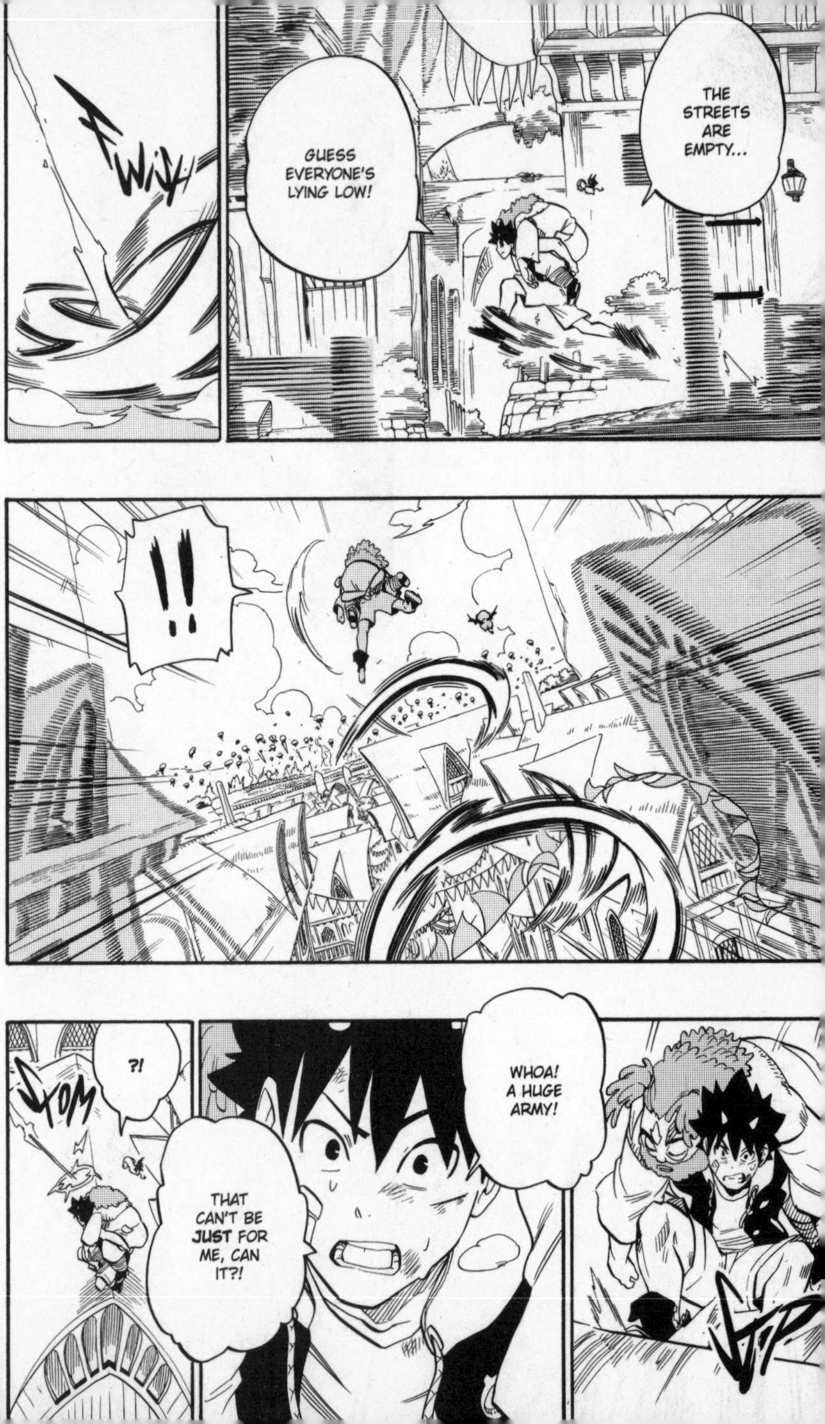
THE STREETS ARE EMPTY...
GUESS EVERYONE'S LYING LOW!
FWISH
!!
WHOA! A HUGE ARMY!
THAT CAN'T BE JUST FOR ME, CAN IT?!
?!

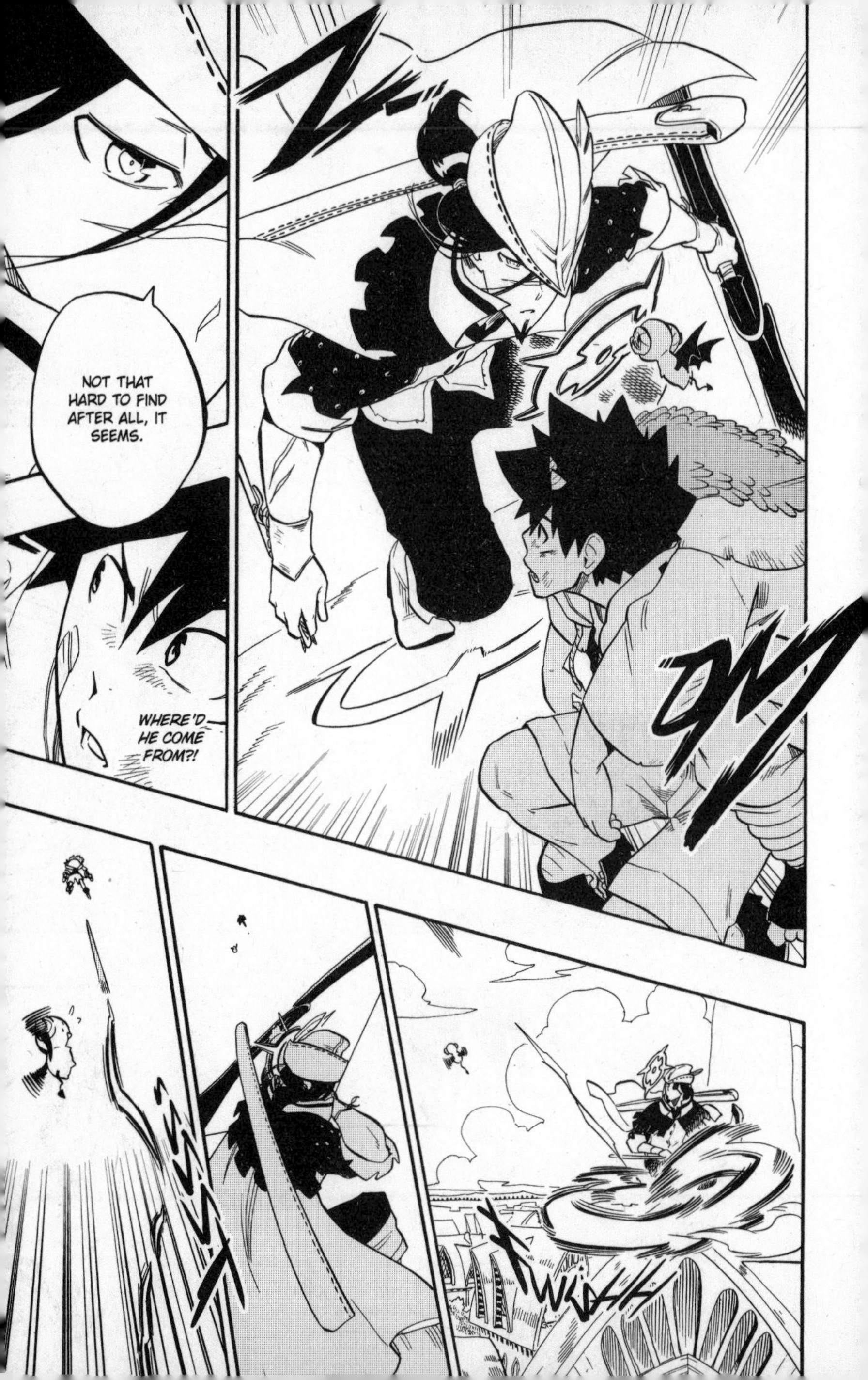
NOT THAT HARD TO FIND AFTER ALL, IT SEEMS.
WHERE'D HE COME FROM?!

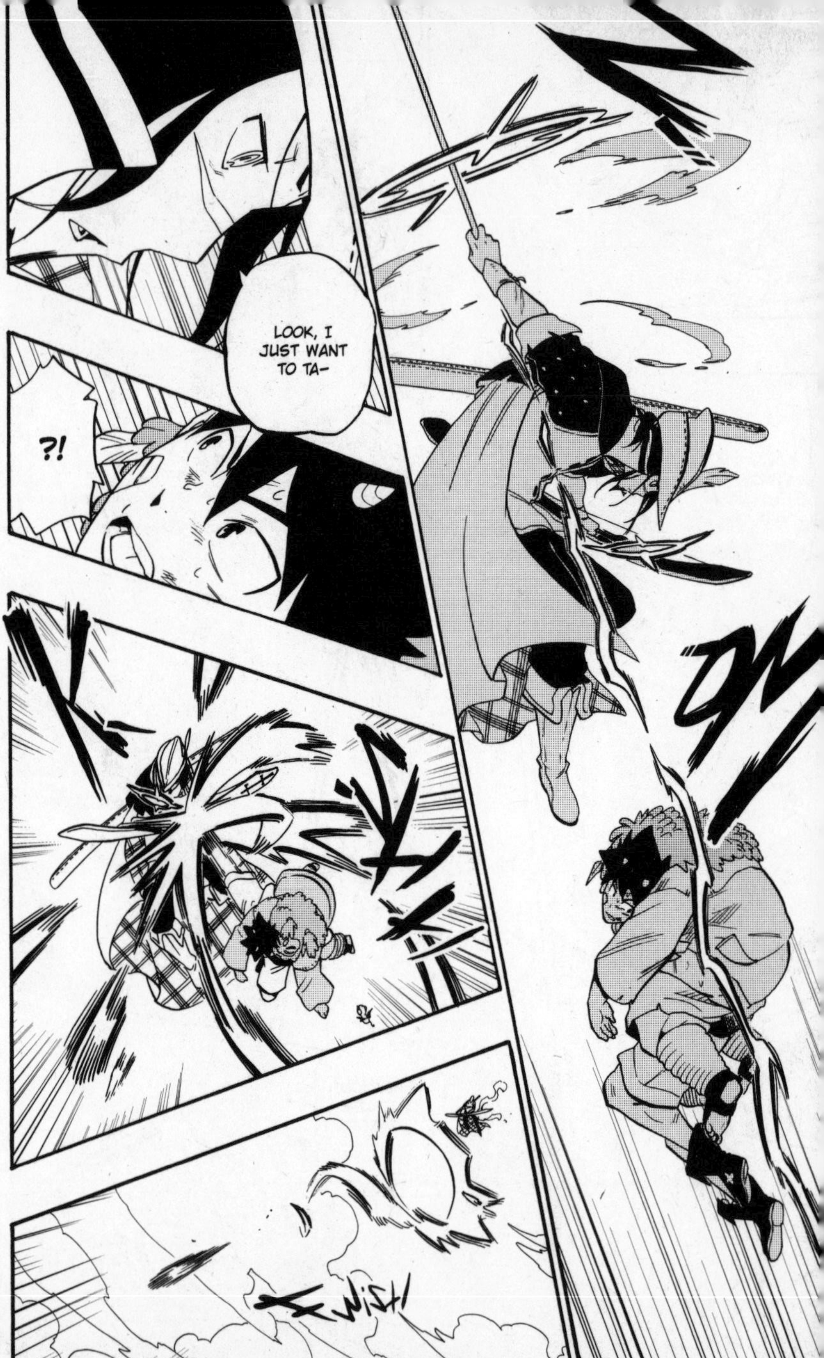
LOOK, I JUST WANT TO TA-
?!

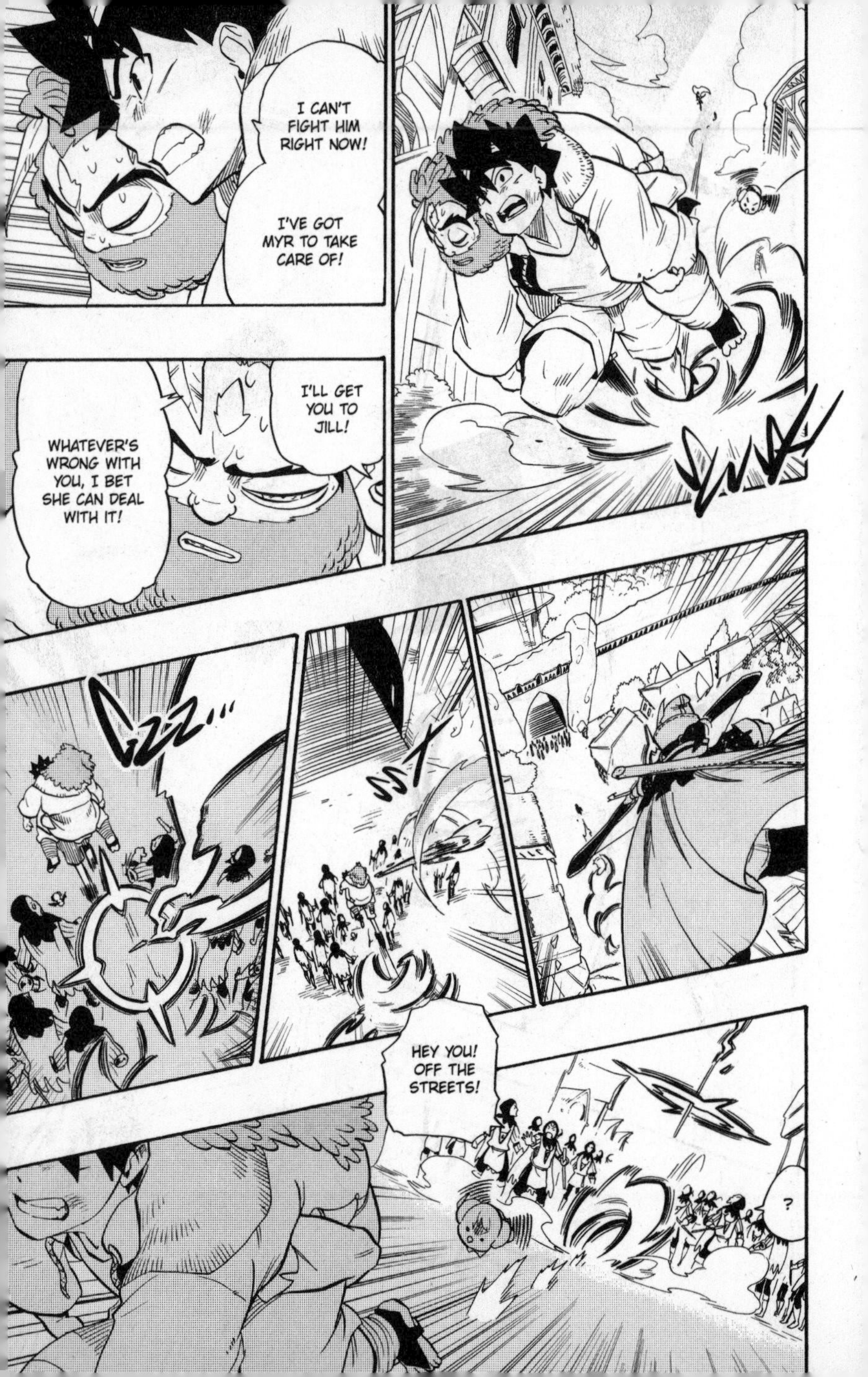
I CAN'T FIGHT HIM RIGHT NOW!
I'VE GOT MYR TO TAKE CARE OF!
I'LL GET YOU TO JILL!
WHATEVER'S WRONG WITH YOU, I BET SHE CAN DEAL WITH IT!
HEY YOU! OFF THE STREETS!
?

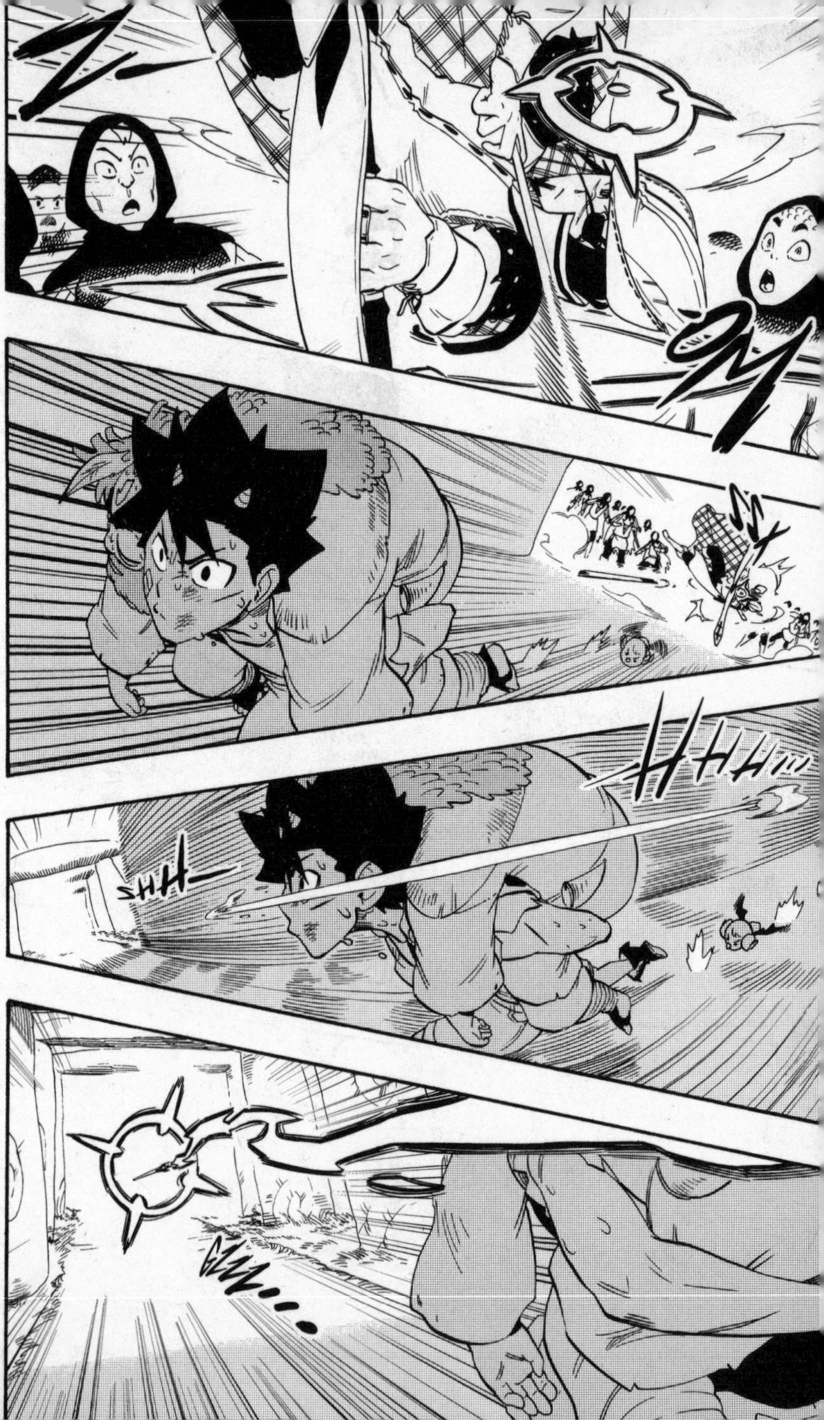
SHHH...
SHH
GZZZ...

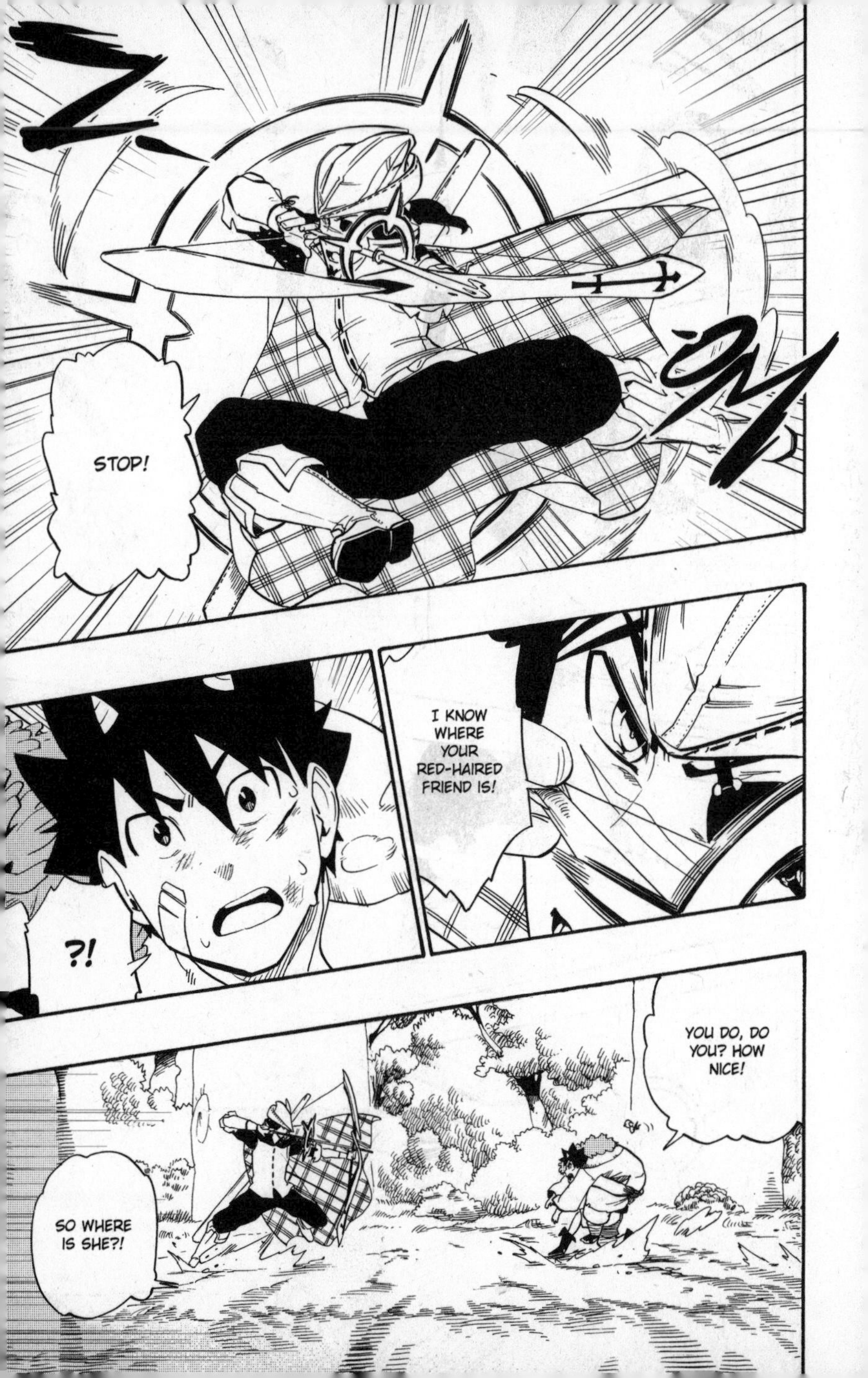
STOP!
I KNOW WHERE YOUR RED-HAIRED FRIEND IS!
?!
YOU DO, DO YOU? HOW NICE!
SO WHERE IS SHE?!

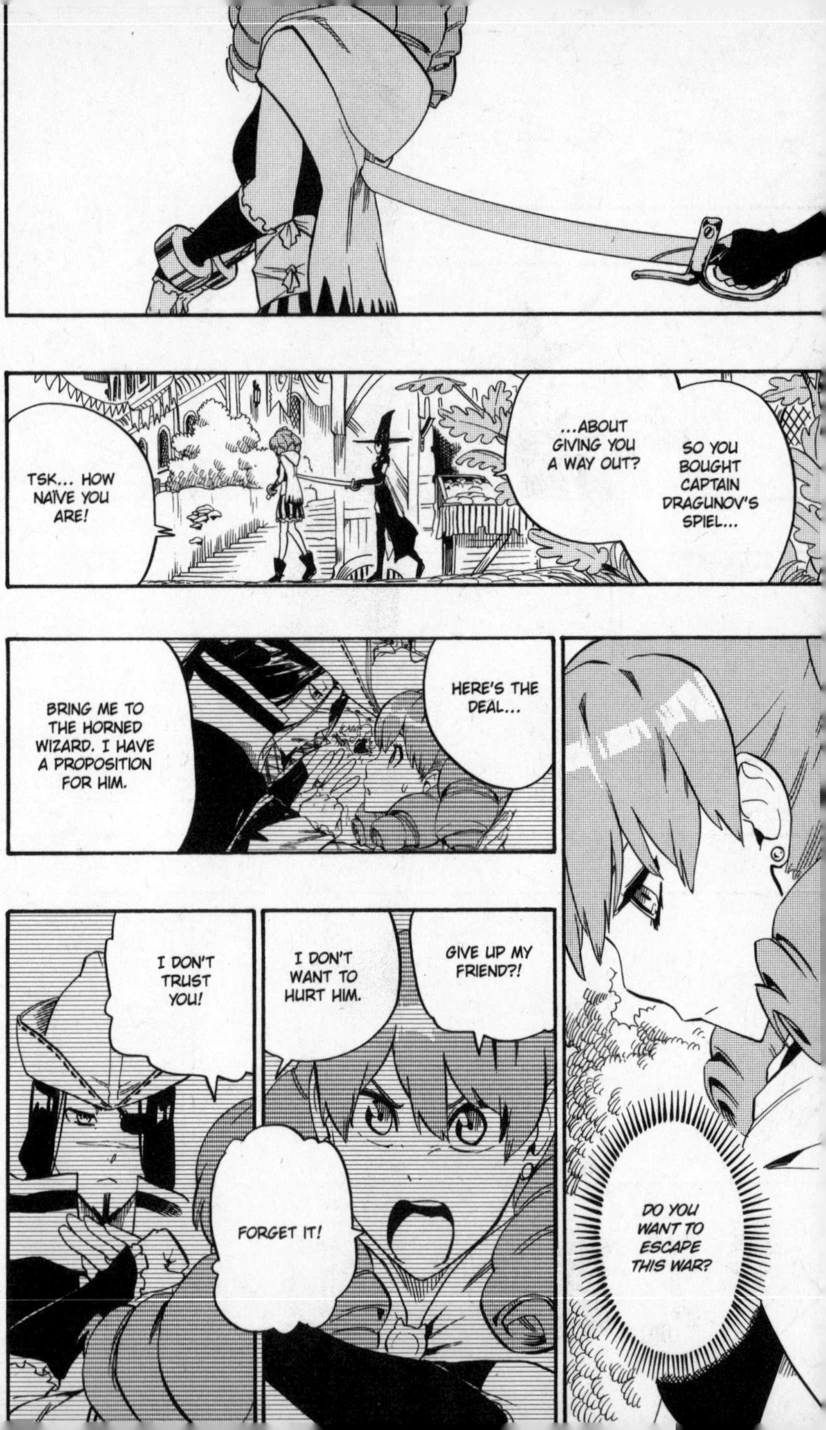
SO YOU BOUGHT CAPTAIN DRAGUNOV'S SPIEL...
...ABOUT GIVING YOU A WAY OUT?
TSK... HOW NAÏVE YOU ARE!
DO YOU WANT TO ESCAPE THIS WAR?
HERE'S THE DEAL...
BRING ME TO THE HORNED WIZARD. I HAVE A PROPOSITION FOR HIM.
GIVE UP MY FRIEND?!
I DON'T WANT TO HURT HIM.
FORGET IT!
I DON'T TRUST YOU!

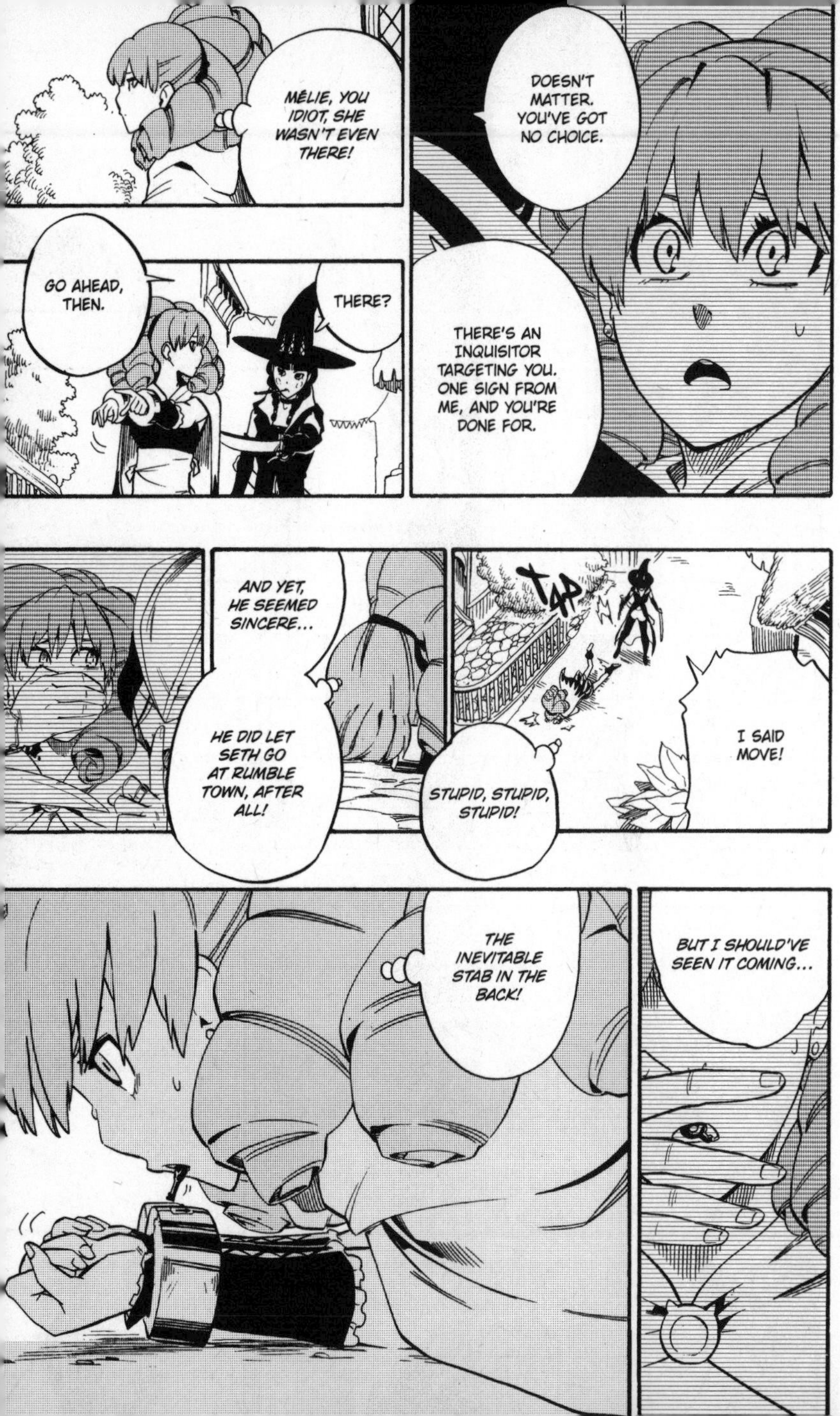
DOESN'T MATTER. YOU'VE GOT NO CHOICE.
THERE'S AN INQUISITOR TARGETING YOU. ONE SIGN FROM ME, AND YOU'RE DONE FOR.
MÉLIE, YOU IDIOT, SHE WASN'T EVEN THERE!
THERE?
GO AHEAD, THEN.
I SAID MOVE!
TAP
STUPID, STUPID, STUPID!
AND YET, HE SEEMED SINCERE...
HE DID LET SETH GO AT RUMBLE TOWN, AFTER ALL!
BUT I SHOULD'VE SEEN IT COMING...
THE INEVITABLE STAB IN THE BACK!

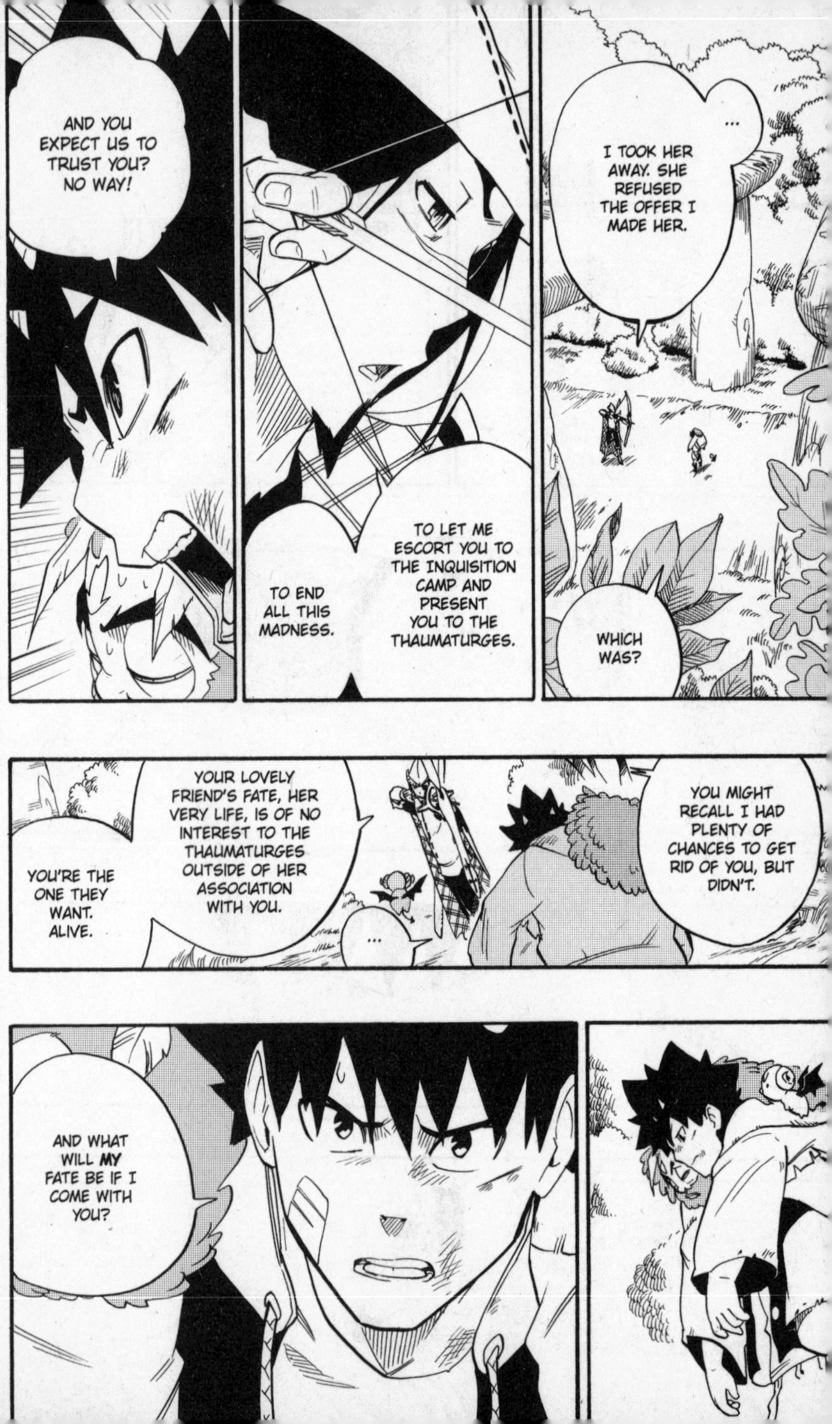
...
I TOOK HER AWAY. SHE REFUSED THE OFFER I MADE HER.
WHICH WAS?
TO LET ME ESCORT YOU TO THE INQUISITION CAMP AND PRESENT YOU TO THE THAUMATURGES.
TO END ALL THIS MADNESS.
AND YOU EXPECT US TO TRUST YOU? NO WAY!
YOU MIGHT RECALL I HAD PLENTY OF CHANCES TO GET RID OF YOU, BUT DIDN'T.
YOUR LOVELY FRIEND'S FATE, HER VERY LIFE, IS OF NO INTEREST TO THE THAUMATURGES OUTSIDE OF HER ASSOCIATION WITH YOU.
YOU'RE THE ONE THEY WANT. ALIVE.
...
AND WHAT WILL **MY** FATE BE IF I COME WITH YOU?

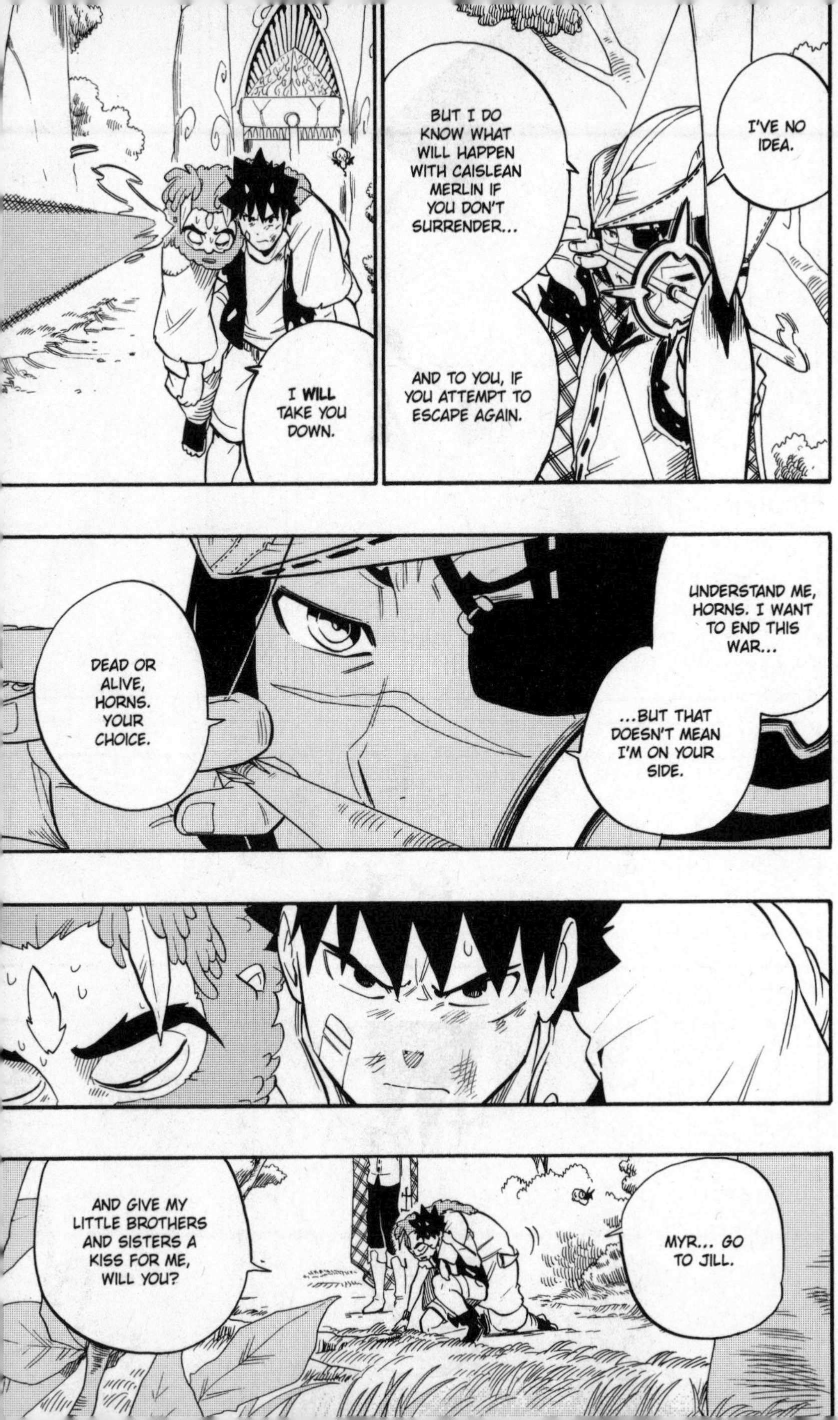
I'VE NO IDEA.
BUT I DO KNOW WHAT WILL HAPPEN WITH CAISLEAN MERLIN IF YOU DON'T SURRENDER...
AND TO YOU, IF YOU ATTEMPT TO ESCAPE AGAIN.
I **WILL** TAKE YOU DOWN.
UNDERSTAND ME, HORNS. I WANT TO END THIS WAR...
...BUT THAT DOESN'T MEAN I'M ON YOUR SIDE.
DEAD OR ALIVE, HORNS. YOUR CHOICE.
MYR... GO TO JILL.
AND GIVE MY LITTLE BROTHERS AND SISTERS A KISS FOR ME, WILL YOU?

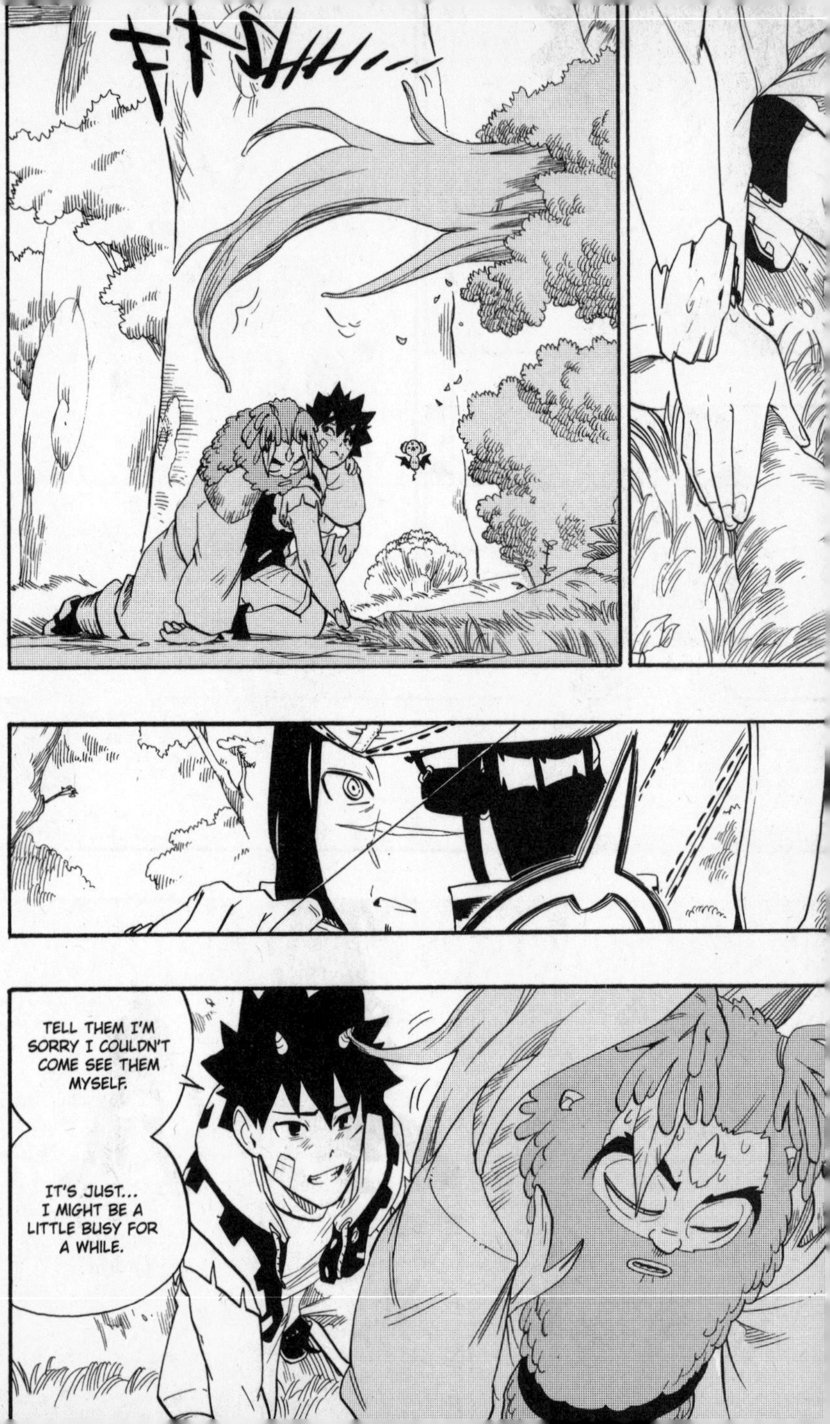
FFSHHH...
TELL THEM I'M SORRY I COULDN'T COME SEE THEM MYSELF.
IT'S JUST... I MIGHT BE A LITTLE BUSY FOR A WHILE.

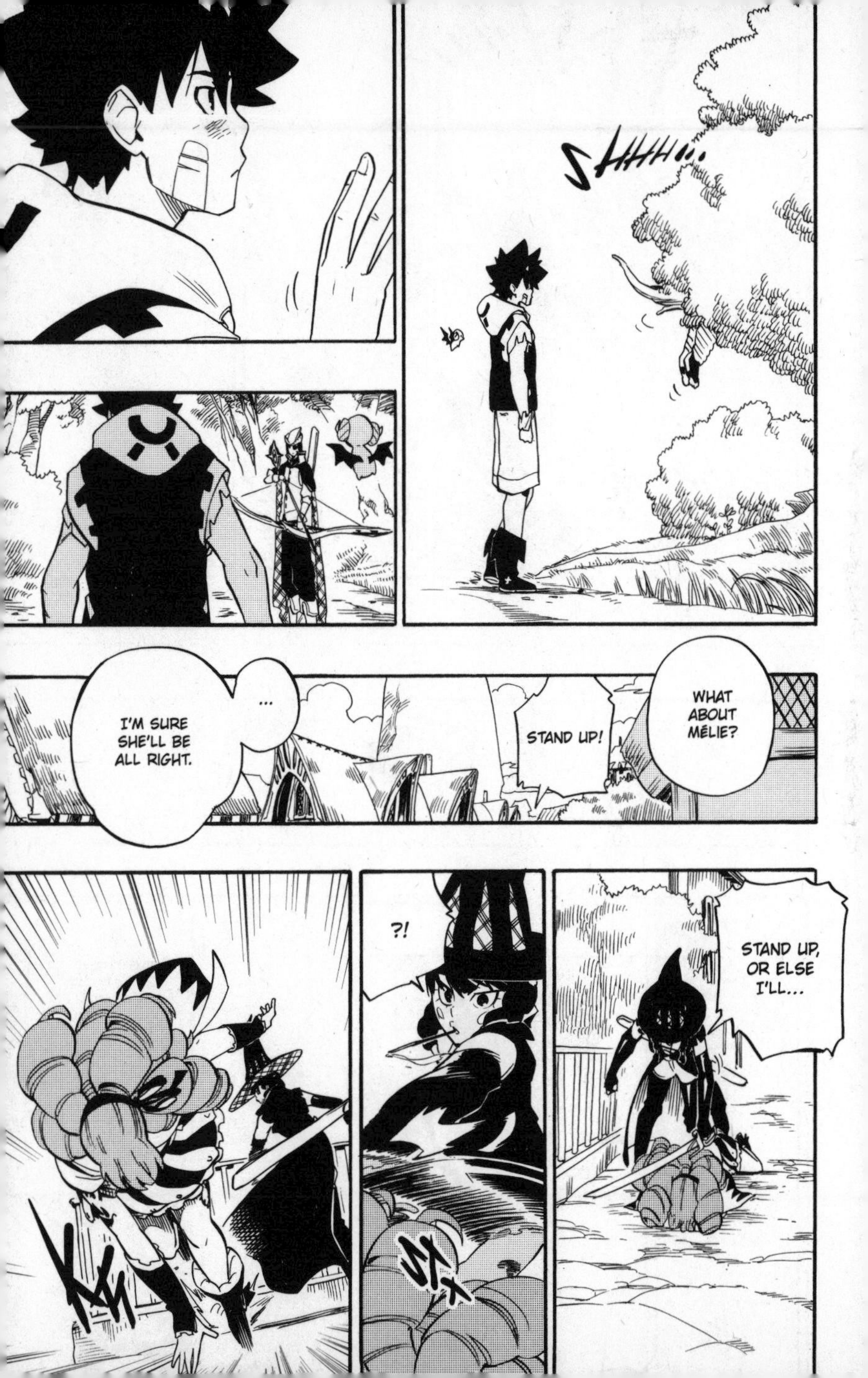
WHAT ABOUT MÉLIE?
STAND UP!
...
I'M SURE SHE'LL BE ALL RIGHT.
STAND UP, OR ELSE I'LL...
?!

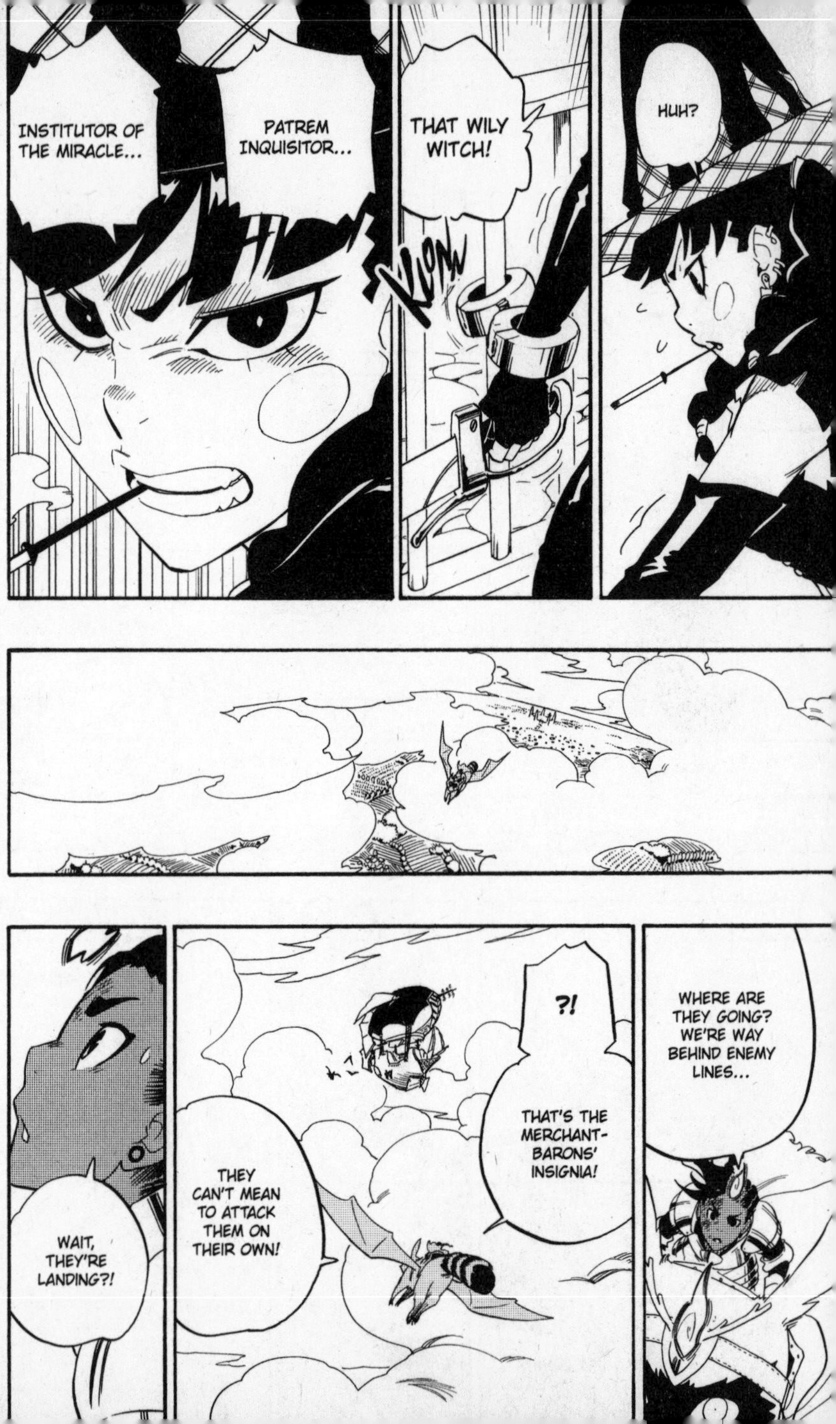
HUH?
THAT WILY WITCH!
PATREM INQUISITOR...
INSTITUTOR OF THE MIRACLE...
WHERE ARE THEY GOING? WE'RE WAY BEHIND ENEMY LINES...
?!
THAT'S THE MERCHANT-BARONS' INSIGNIA!
THEY CAN'T MEAN TO ATTACK THEM ON THEIR OWN!
WAIT, THEY'RE LANDING?!

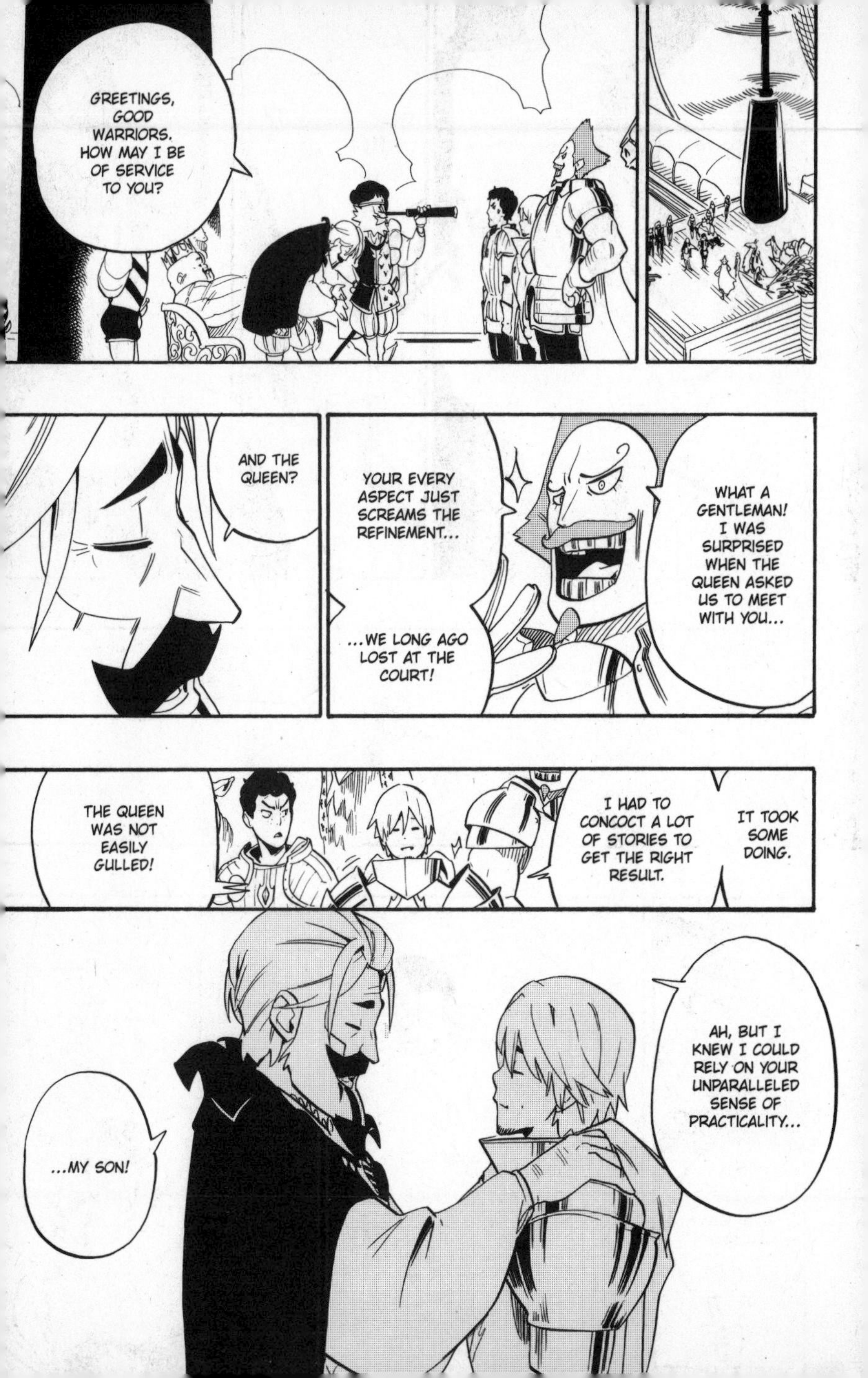
GREETINGS, GOOD WARRIORS. HOW MAY I BE OF SERVICE TO YOU?
WHAT A GENTLEMAN! I WAS SURPRISED WHEN THE QUEEN ASKED US TO MEET WITH YOU...
YOUR EVERY ASPECT JUST SCREAMS THE REFINEMENT...
...WE LONG AGO LOST AT THE COURT!
AND THE QUEEN?
IT TOOK SOME DOING.
I HAD TO CONCOCT A LOT OF STORIES TO GET THE RIGHT RESULT.
THE QUEEN WAS NOT EASILY GULLED!
AH, BUT I KNEW I COULD RELY ON YOUR UNPARALLELED SENSE OF PRACTICALITY...
...MY SON!

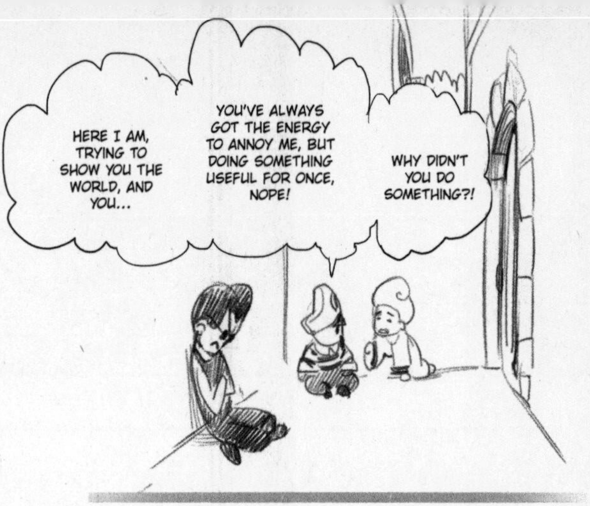
HERE I AM, TRYING TO SHOW YOU THE WORLD, AND YOU...
YOU'VE ALWAYS GOT THE ENERGY TO ANNOY ME, BUT DOING SOMETHING USEFUL FOR ONCE, NOPE!
WHY DIDN'T YOU DO SOMETHING?!

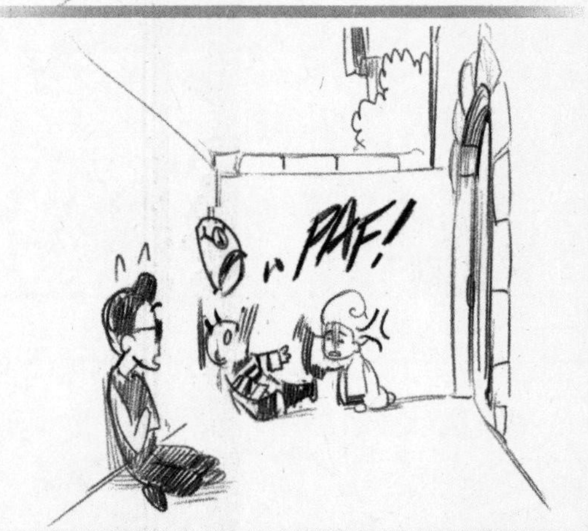
PAF!

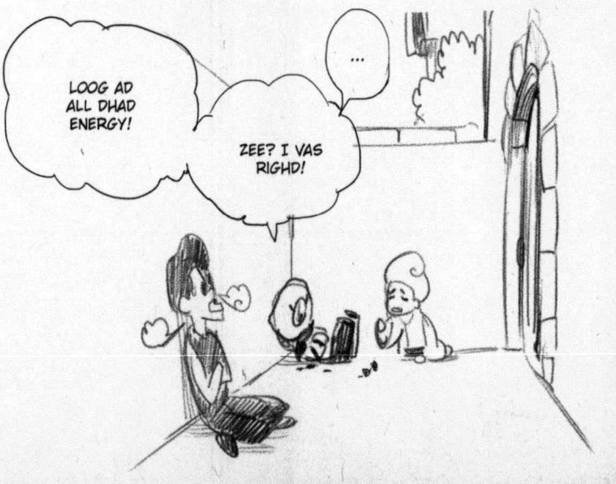
LOOG AD ALL DHAD ENERGY!
ZEE? I VAS RIGHD!
...

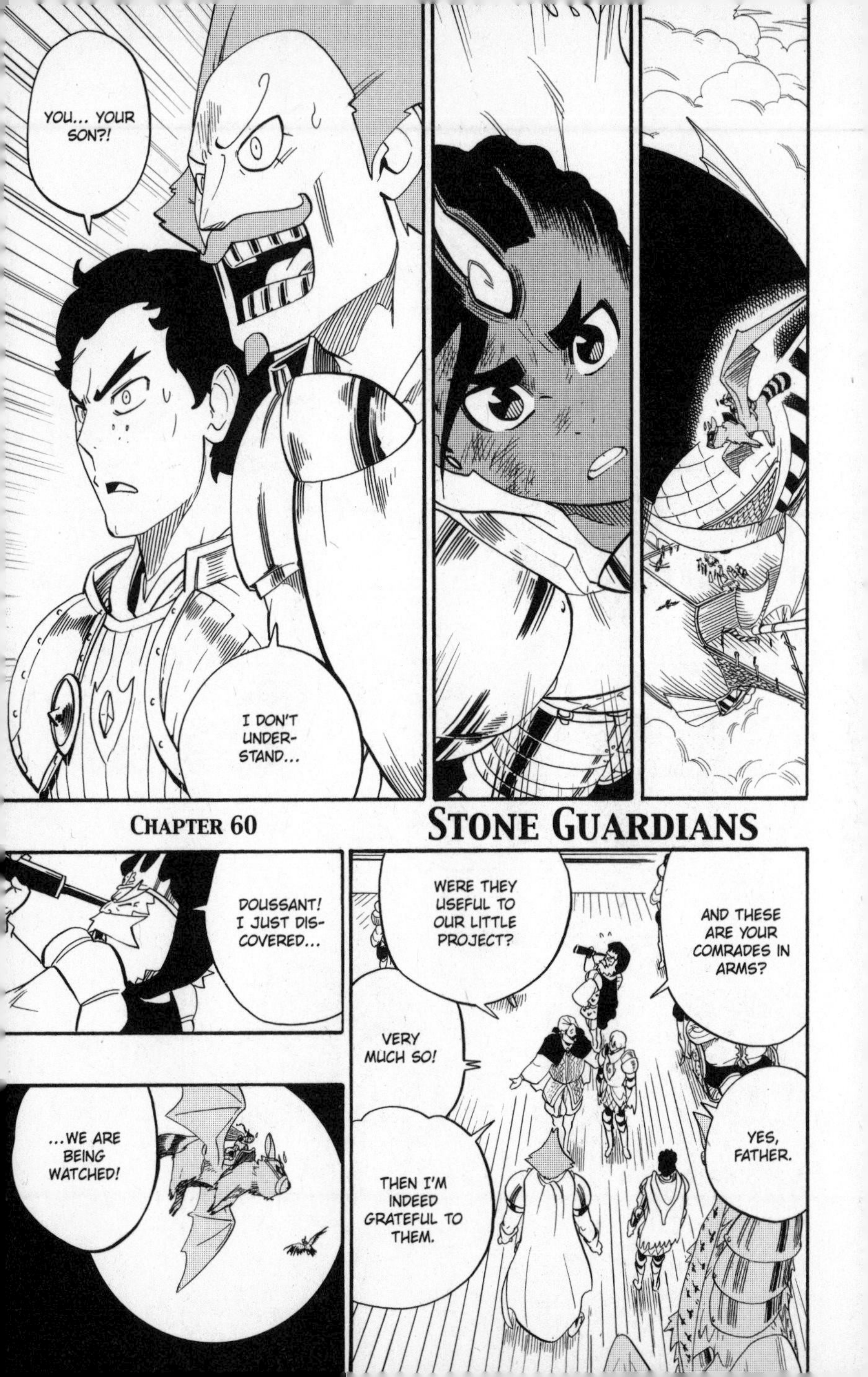
YOU... YOUR SON?!
I DON'T UNDER-STAND...
CHAPTER 60
STONE GUARDIANS
AND THESE ARE YOUR COMRADES IN ARMS?
YES, FATHER.
WERE THEY USEFUL TO OUR LITTLE PROJECT?
VERY MUCH SO!
THEN I'M INDEED GRATEFUL TO THEM.
DOUSSANT! I JUST DIS-COVERED...
...WE ARE BEING WATCHED!

EH?
DAGNABBIT!
THAT WAS MY DISCOVERY!
WHILE YOU WERE INDULGING YOURSELF, BARON CRISTOLOM, I WAS WATCHING OUR BACKS.
TP TAP
GNNN!
HMFF!
WE'RE STUCK!
OUR STRENGTH, FANTASIA, USELESS AGAINST...
...THIS BLACK SILVER BRAIDED NET!

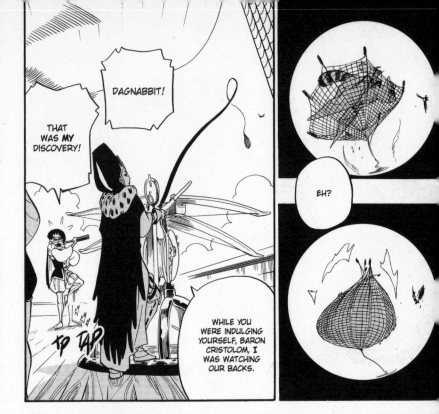

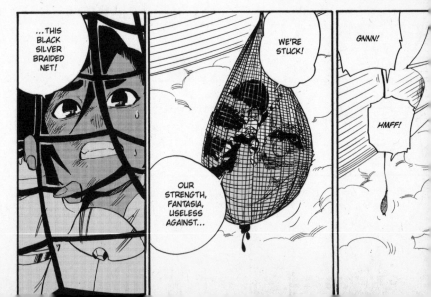

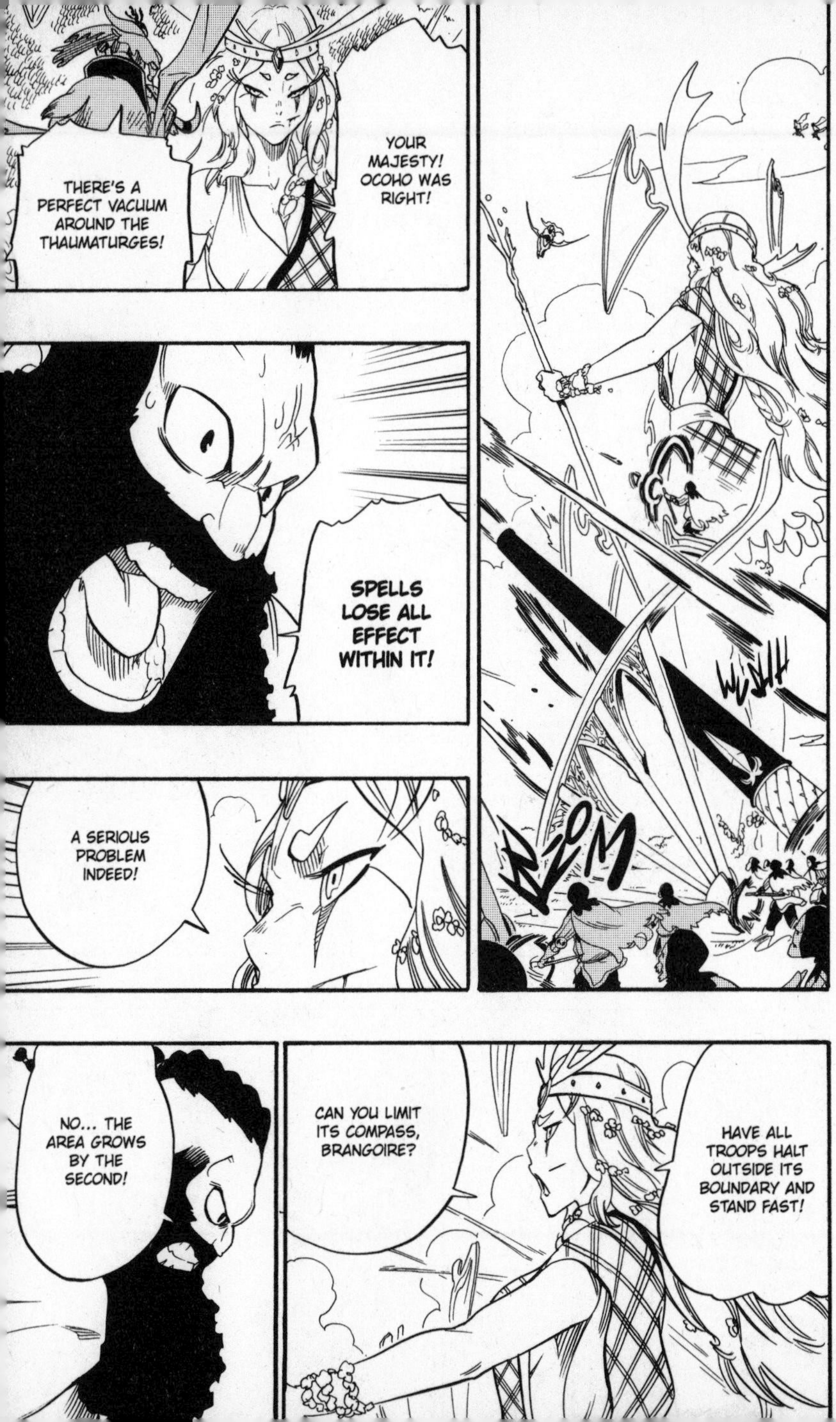
YOUR MAJESTY! OCOHO WAS RIGHT!
THERE'S A PERFECT VACUUM AROUND THE THAUMATURGES!
SPELLS LOSE ALL EFFECT WITHIN IT!
A SERIOUS PROBLEM INDEED!
CAN YOU LIMIT ITS COMPASS, BRANGOIRE?
NO... THE AREA GROWS BY THE SECOND!
HAVE ALL TROOPS HALT OUTSIDE ITS BOUNDARY AND STAND FAST!

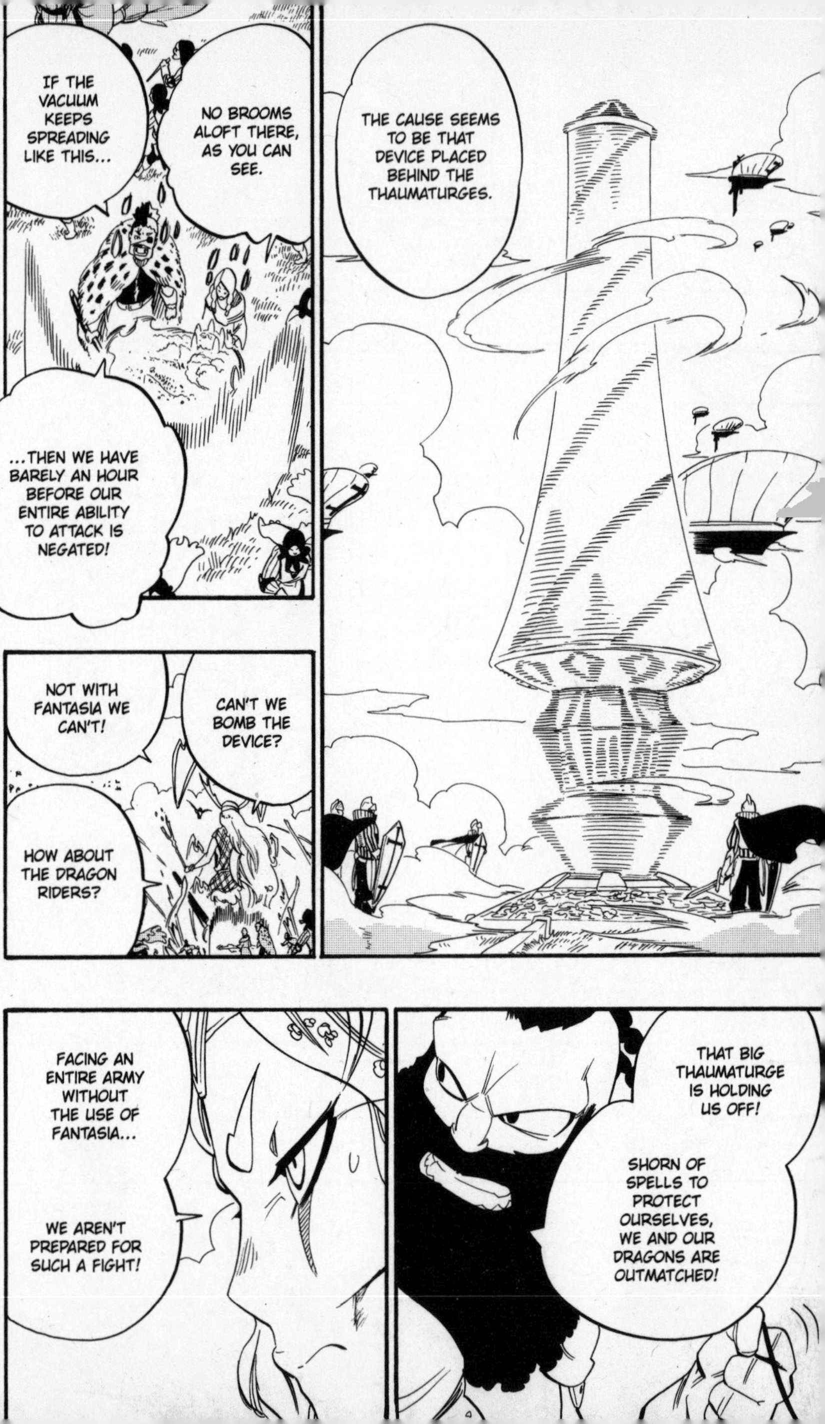
THE CAUSE SEEMS TO BE THAT DEVICE PLACED BEHIND THE THAUMATURGES.
NO BROOMS ALOFT THERE, AS YOU CAN SEE.
IF THE VACUUM KEEPS SPREADING LIKE THIS...
...THEN WE HAVE BARELY AN HOUR BEFORE OUR ENTIRE ABILITY TO ATTACK IS NEGATED!
CAN'T WE BOMB THE DEVICE?
NOT WITH FANTASIA WE CAN'T!
HOW ABOUT THE DRAGON RIDERS?
THAT BIG THAUMATURGE IS HOLDING US OFF!
SHORN OF SPELLS TO PROTECT OURSELVES, WE AND OUR DRAGONS ARE OUTMATCHED!
FACING AN ENTIRE ARMY WITHOUT THE USE OF FANTASIA...
WE AREN'T PREPARED FOR SUCH A FIGHT!

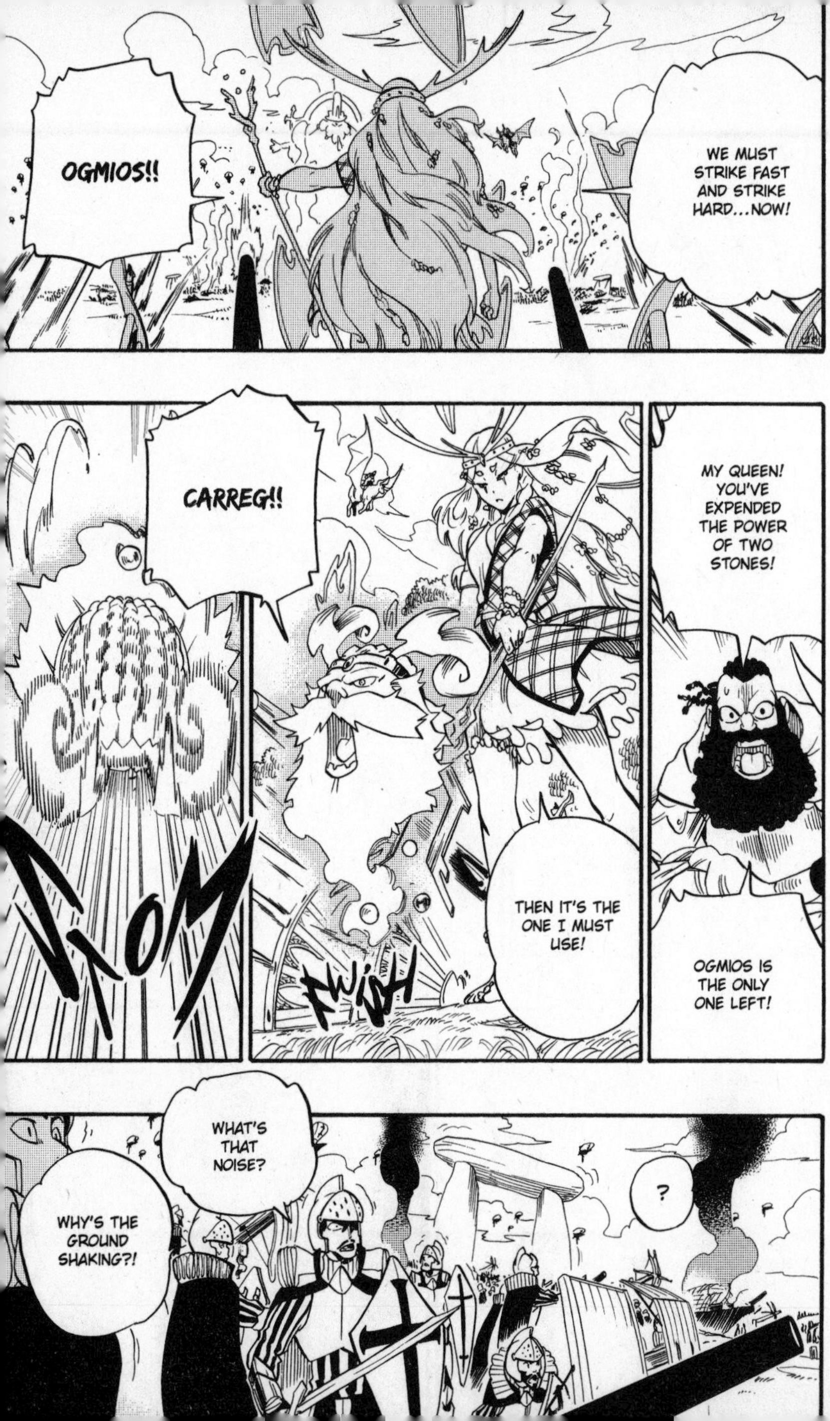
WE MUST STRIKE FAST AND STRIKE HARD...NOW!
OGMIOS!!
MY QUEEN! YOU'VE EXPENDED THE POWER OF TWO STONES!
OGMIOS IS THE ONLY ONE LEFT!
THEN IT'S THE ONE I MUST USE!
FWISH
CARREG!!
?
WHAT'S THAT NOISE?
WHY'S THE GROUND SHAKING?!

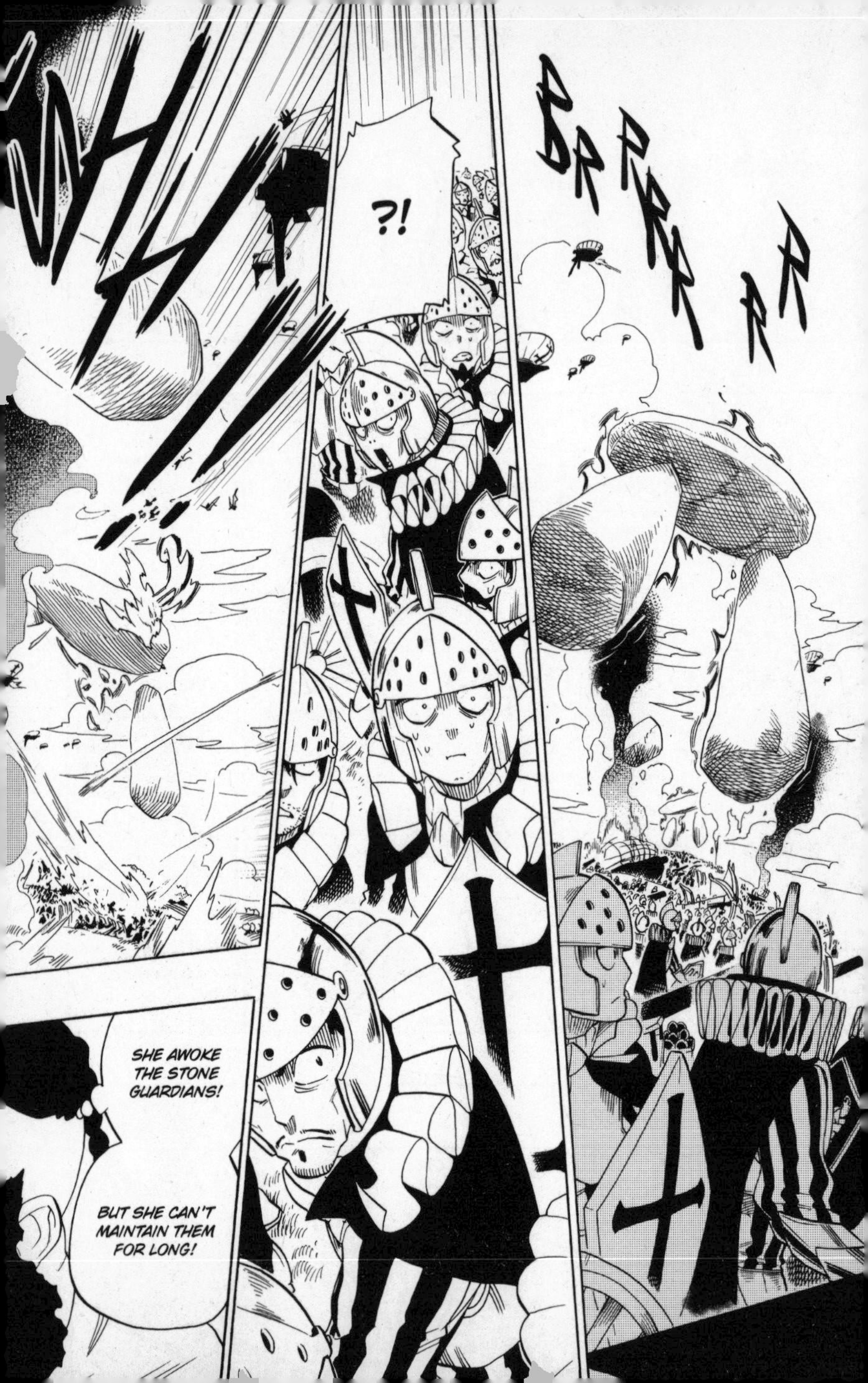
BRRRRRR RR
?!
SHHH
SHE AWOKE THE STONE GUARDIANS!
BUT SHE CAN'T MAINTAIN THEM FOR LONG!

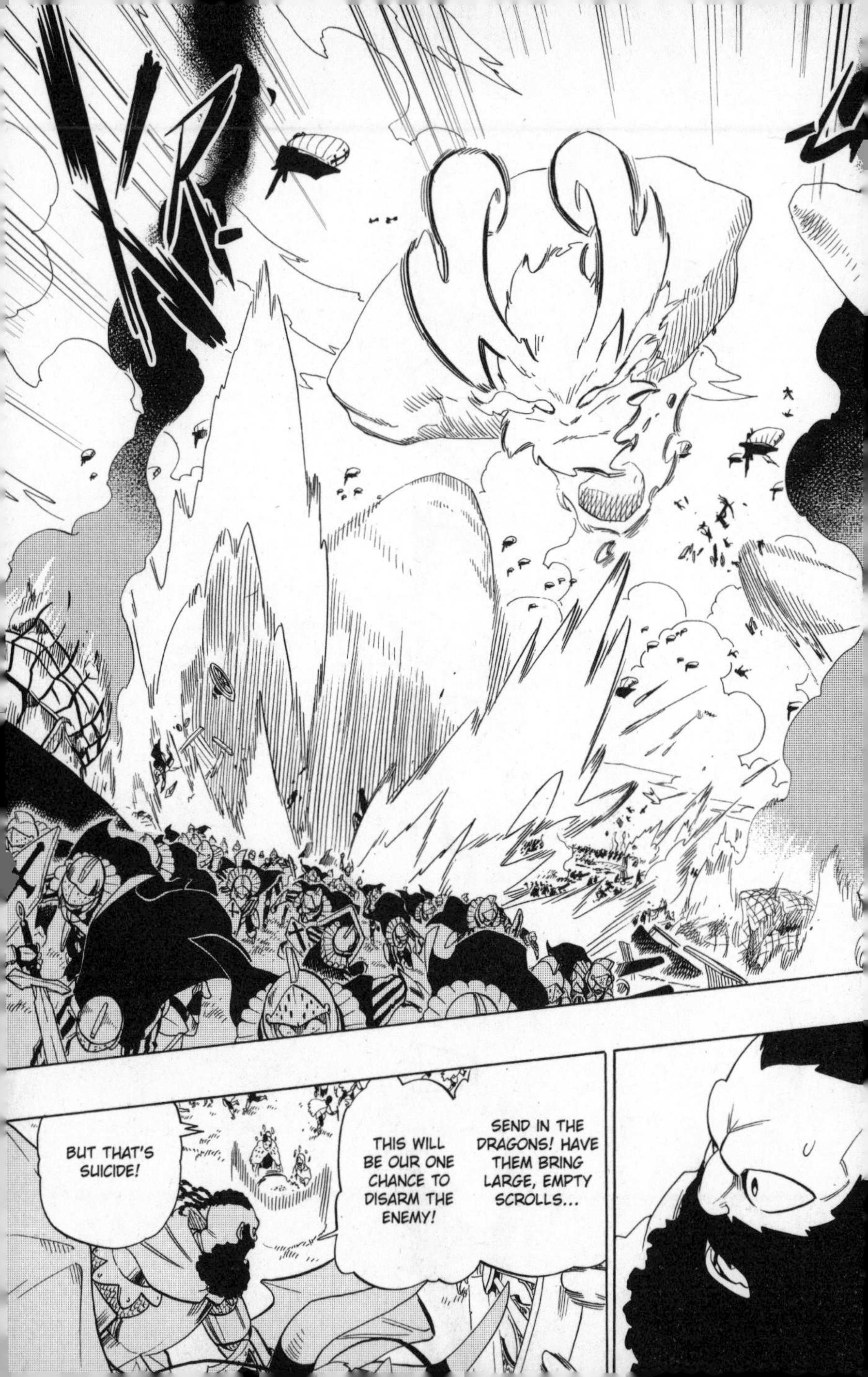
SEND IN THE DRAGONS! HAVE THEM BRING LARGE, EMPTY SCROLLS...
THIS WILL BE OUR ONE CHANCE TO DISARM THE ENEMY!
BUT THAT'S SUICIDE!

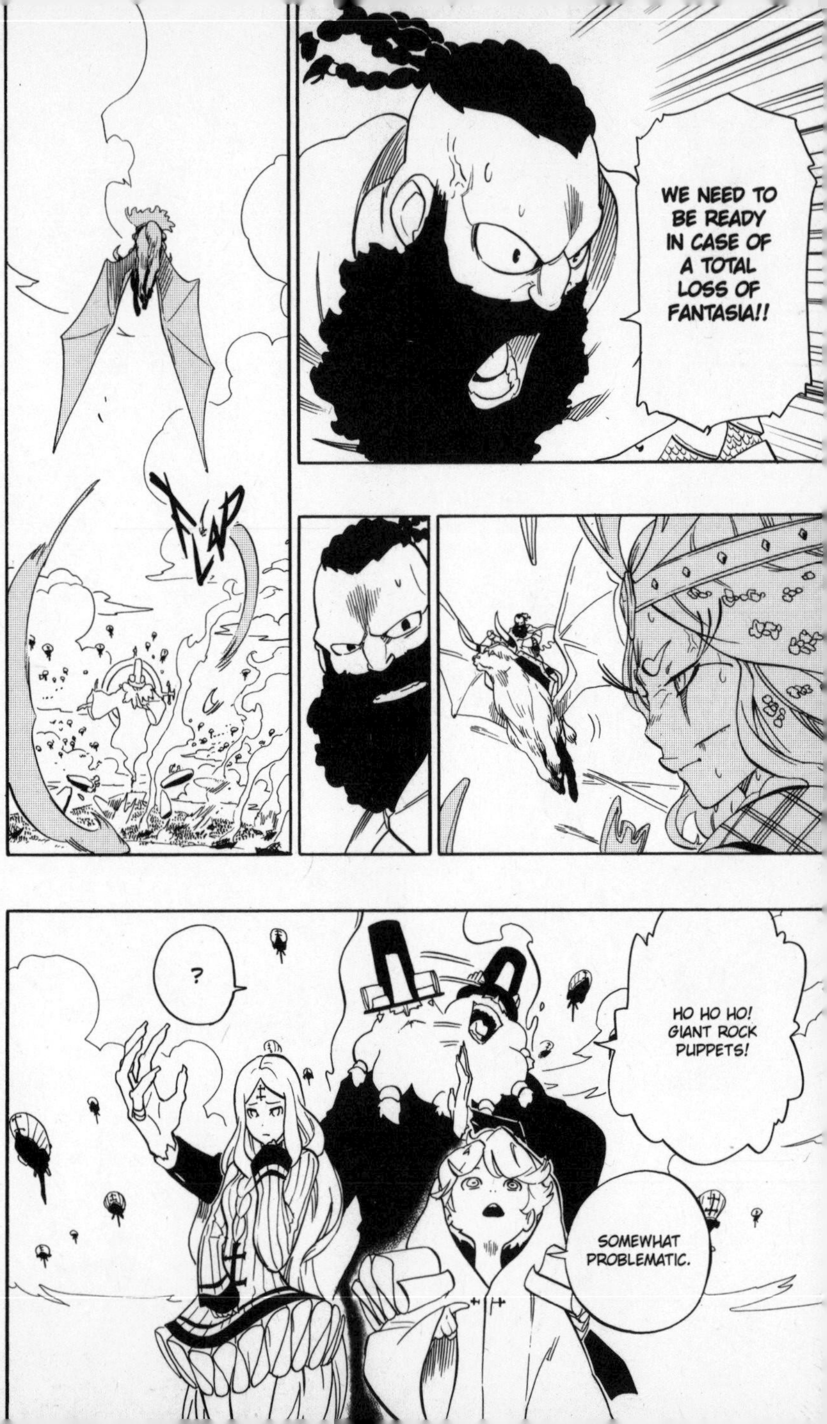
WE NEED TO BE READY IN CASE OF A TOTAL LOSS OF FANTASIA!!
FLAP
HO HO HO! GIANT ROCK PUPPETS!
?
SOMEWHAT PROBLEMATIC.

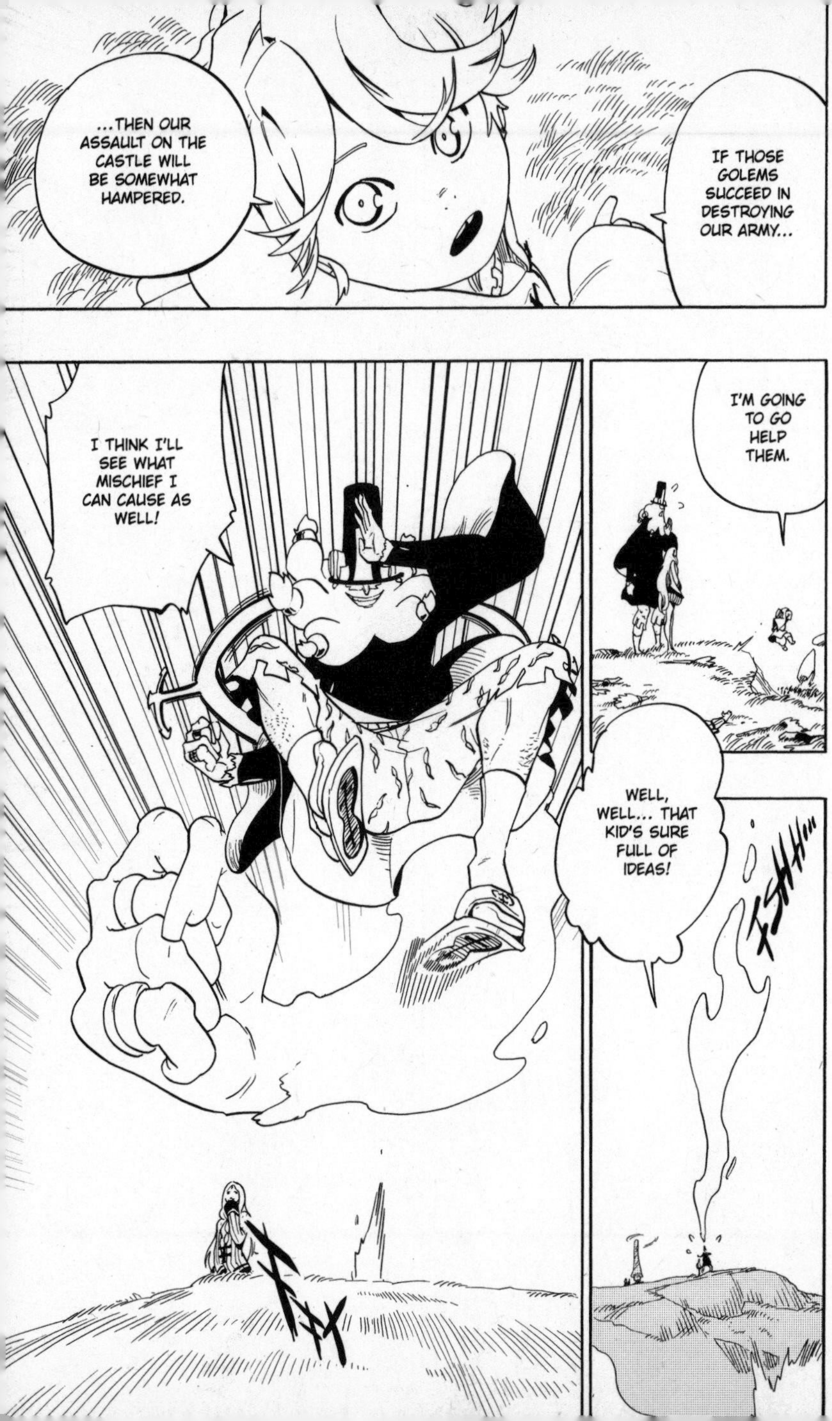
IF THOSE GOLEMS SUCCEED IN DESTROYING OUR ARMY...
...THEN OUR ASSAULT ON THE CASTLE WILL BE SOMEWHAT HAMPERED.
I'M GOING TO GO HELP THEM.
WELL, WELL... THAT KID'S SURE FULL OF IDEAS!
FSHH
I THINK I'LL SEE WHAT MISCHIEF I CAN CAUSE AS WELL!

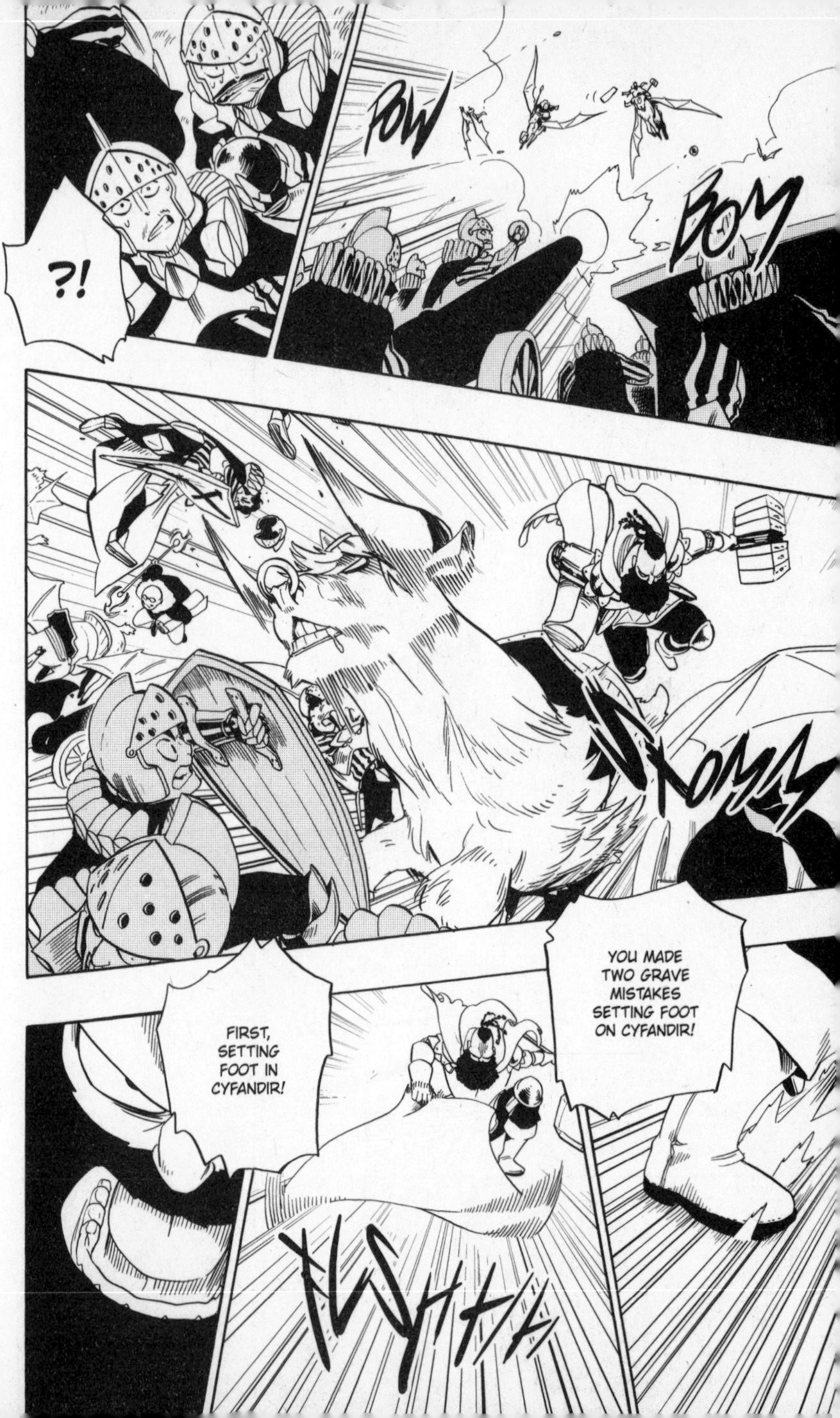
POW
BOOM
?!
STOMP
YOU MADE TWO GRAVE MISTAKES SETTING FOOT ON CYFANDIR!
FIRST, SETTING FOOT IN CYFANDIR!

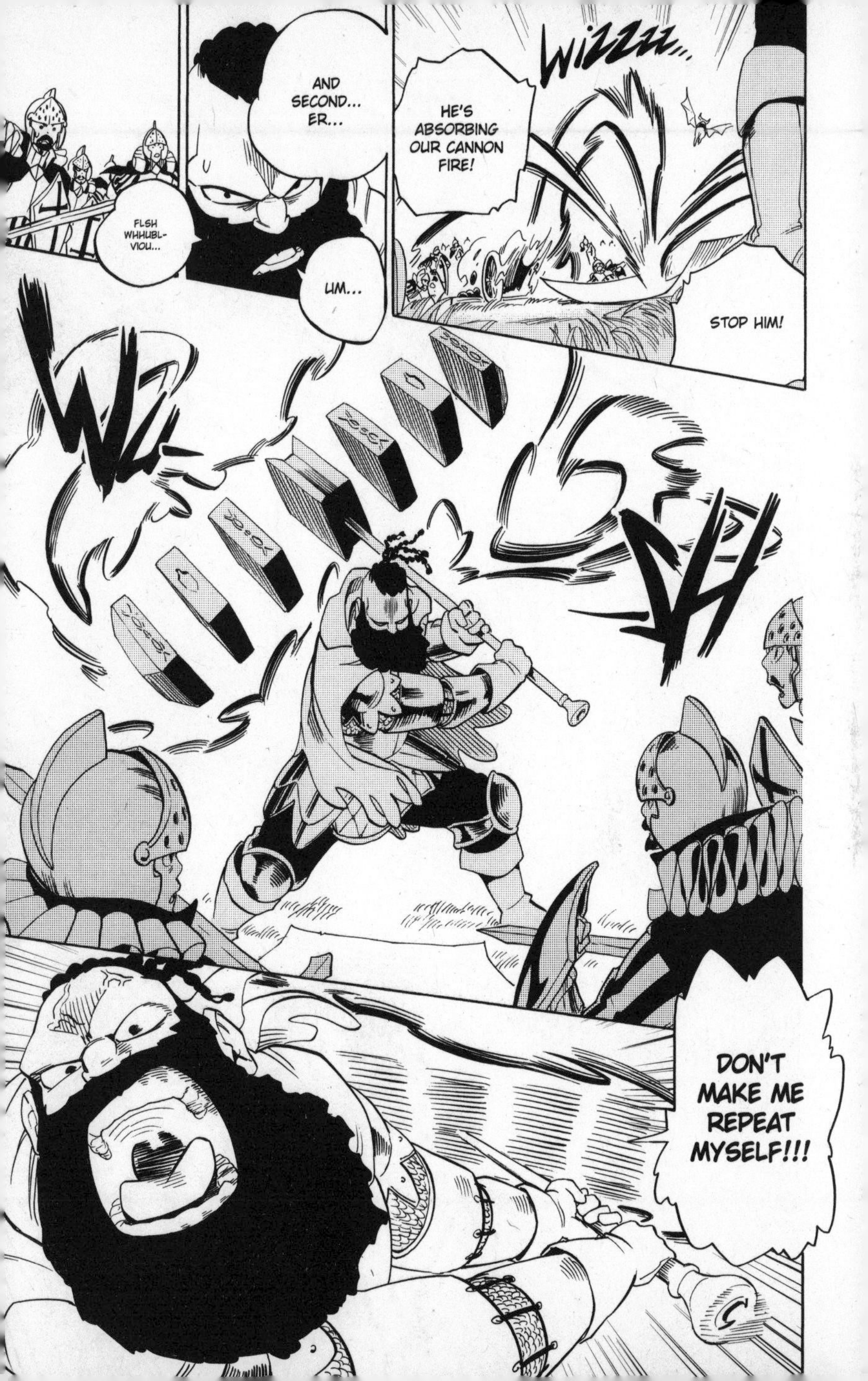
WIZZZZ...
HE'S ABSORBING OUR CANNON FIRE!
STOP HIM!
AND SECOND... ER...
UM...
FLSH WHHUBL-VIOU...
DON'T MAKE ME REPEAT MYSELF!!!

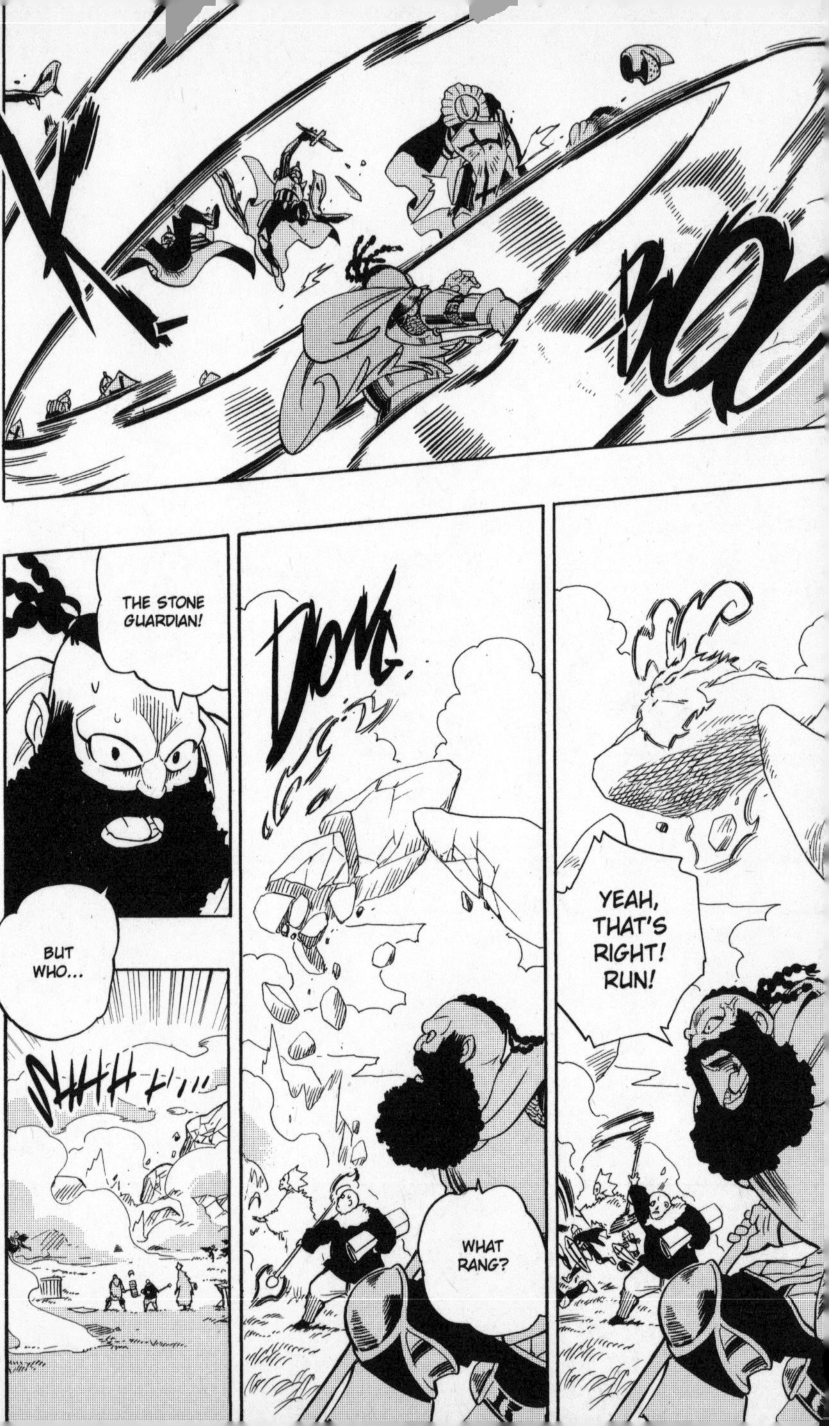
THE STONE GUARDIAN!
BUT WHO...
DONG
WHAT RANG?
YEAH, THAT'S RIGHT! RUN!

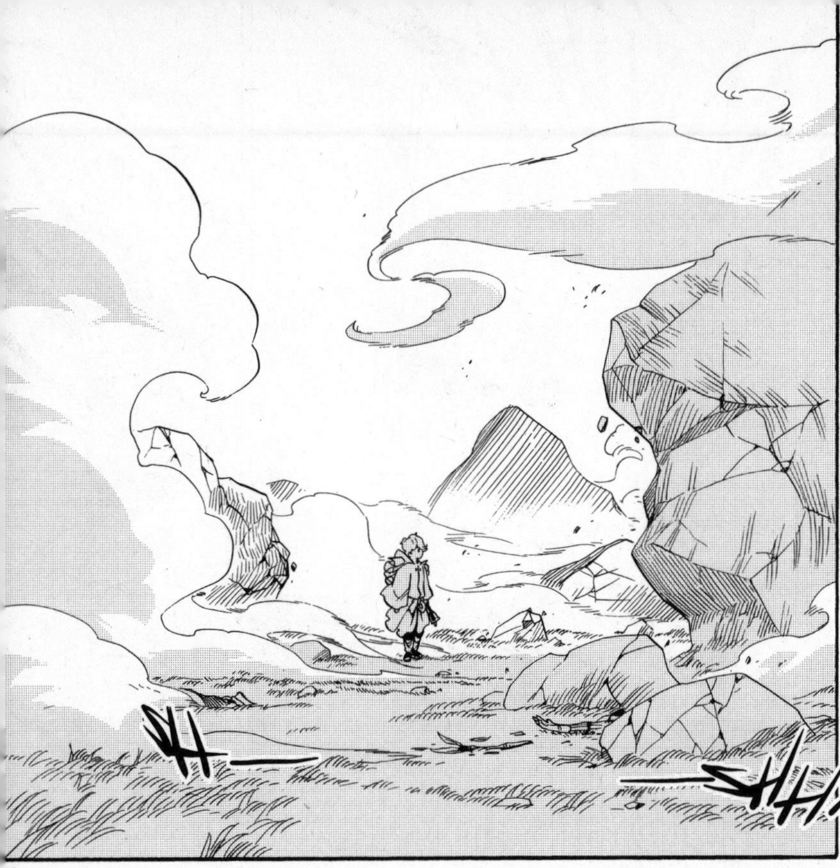
SHH—
—SHHH...
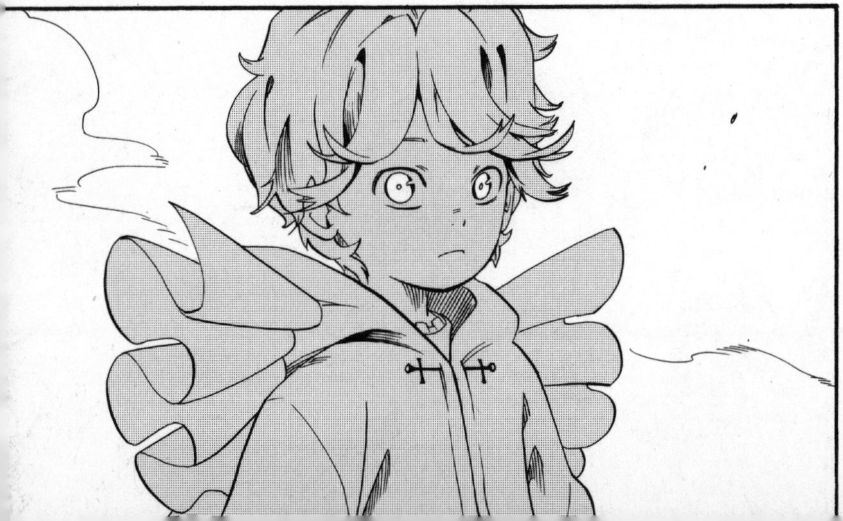

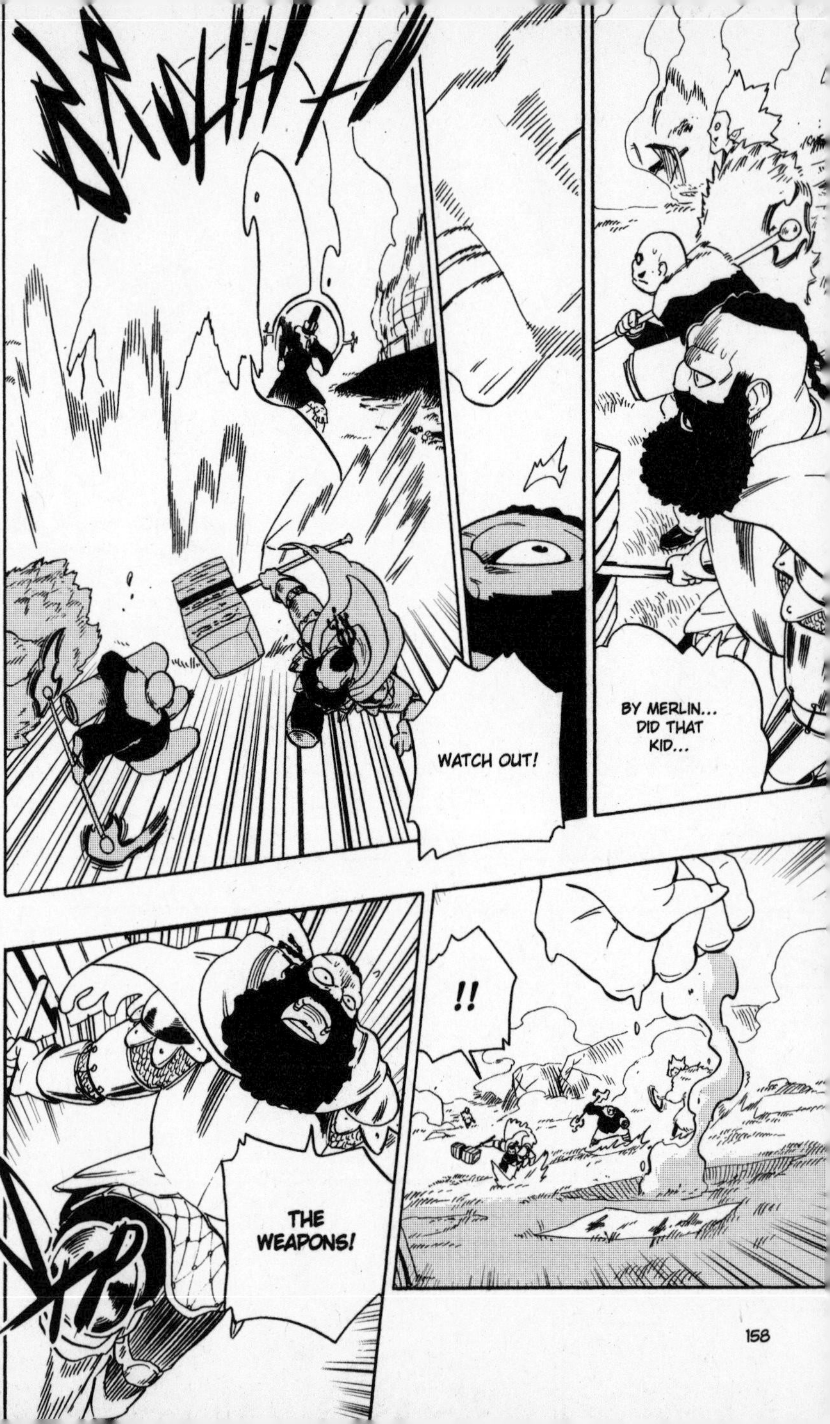
BY MERLIN... DID THAT KID...
WATCH OUT!
!!
THE WEAPONS!

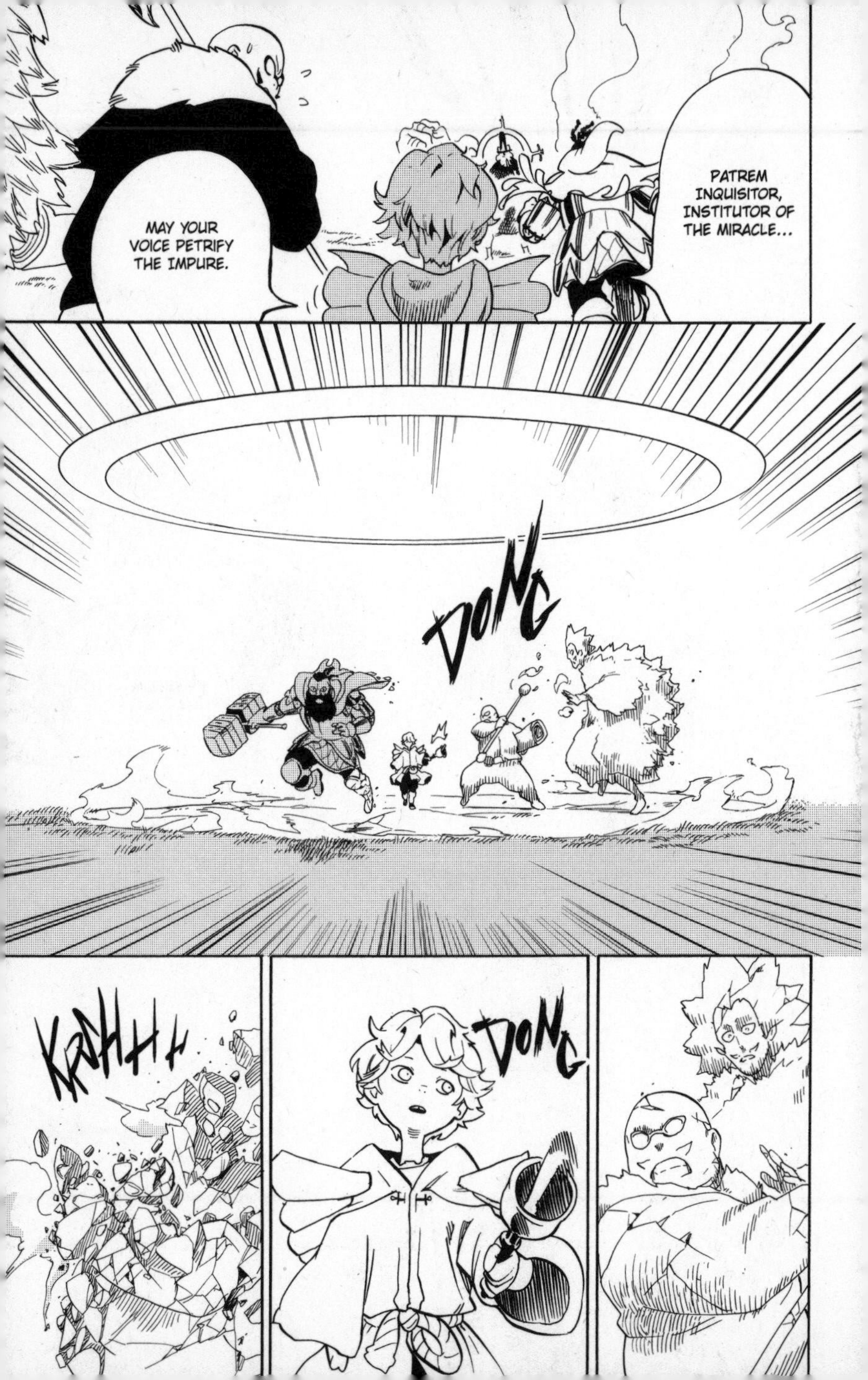
PATREM INQUISITOR, INSTITUTOR OF THE MIRACLE…
MAY YOUR VOICE PETRIFY THE IMPURE.
DONG
DONG
KRSHHH

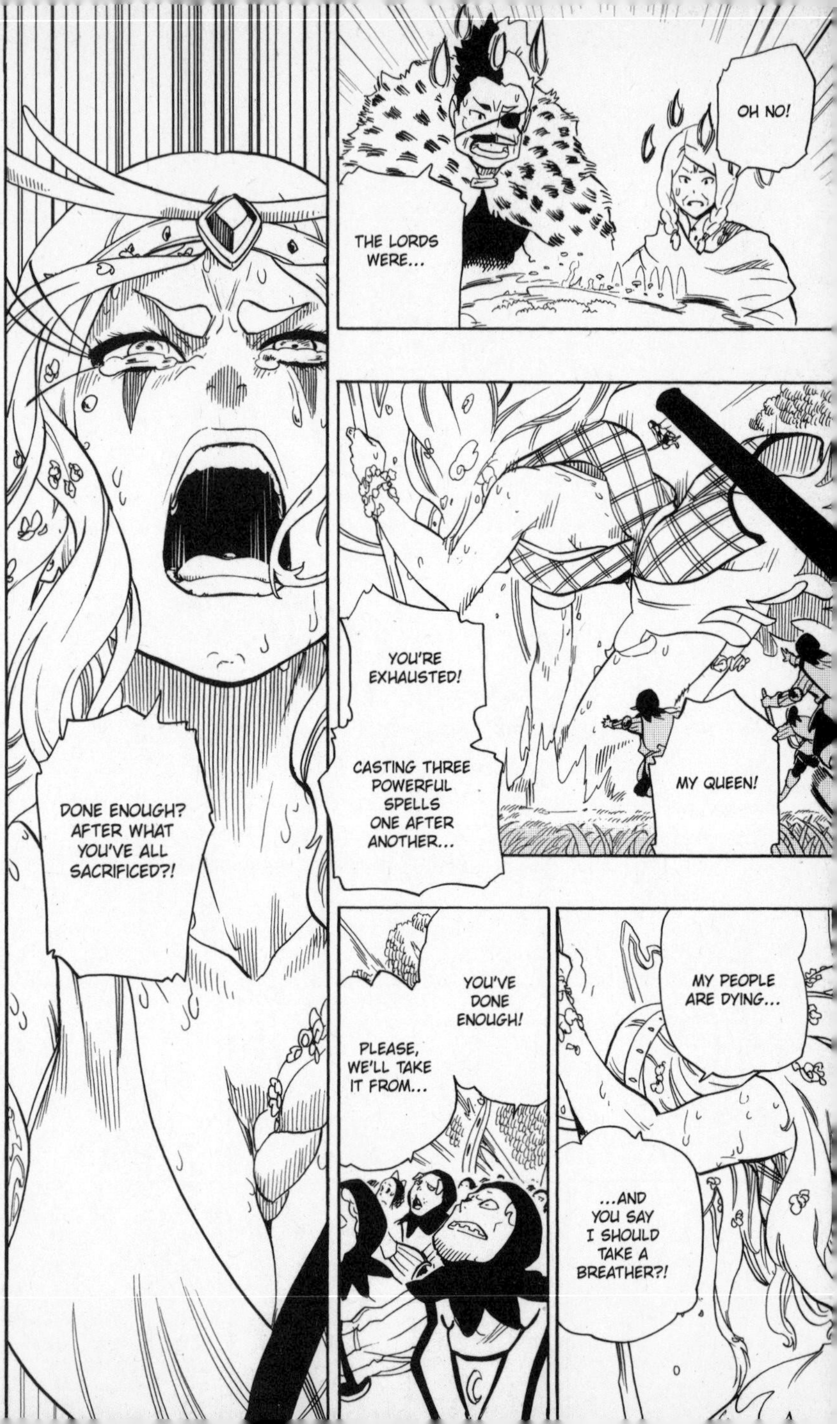
OH NO!
THE LORDS WERE...
MY QUEEN!
YOU'RE EXHAUSTED!
CASTING THREE POWERFUL SPELLS ONE AFTER ANOTHER...
MY PEOPLE ARE DYING...
...AND YOU SAY I SHOULD TAKE A BREATHER?!
YOU'VE DONE ENOUGH!
PLEASE, WE'LL TAKE IT FROM...
DONE ENOUGH? AFTER WHAT YOU'VE ALL SACRIFICED?!

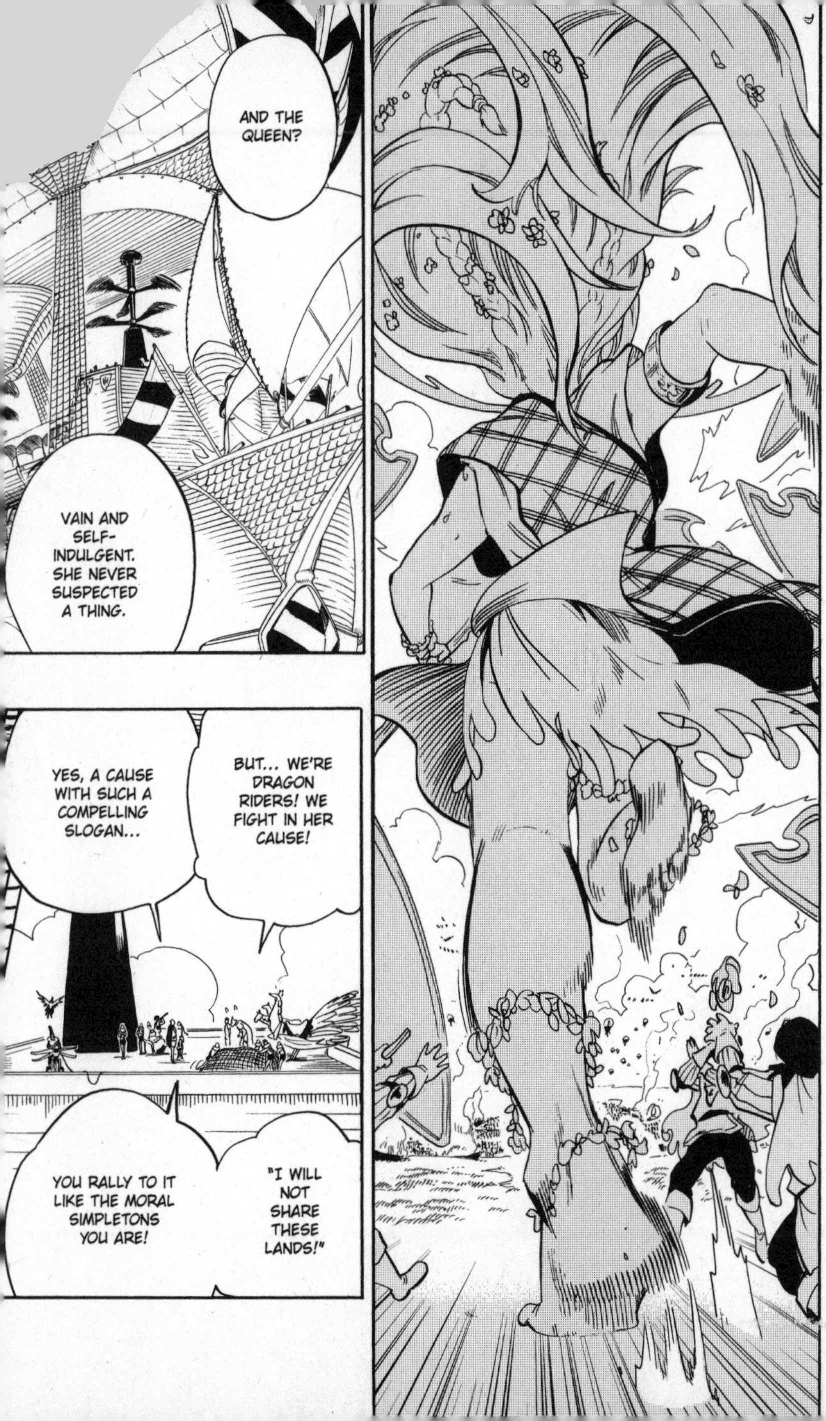
AND THE QUEEN?
VAIN AND SELF-INDULGENT. SHE NEVER SUSPECTED A THING.
BUT... WE'RE DRAGON RIDERS! WE FIGHT IN HER CAUSE!
YES, A CAUSE WITH SUCH A COMPELLING SLOGAN...
"I WILL NOT SHARE THESE LANDS!"
YOU RALLY TO IT LIKE THE MORAL SIMPLETONS YOU ARE!

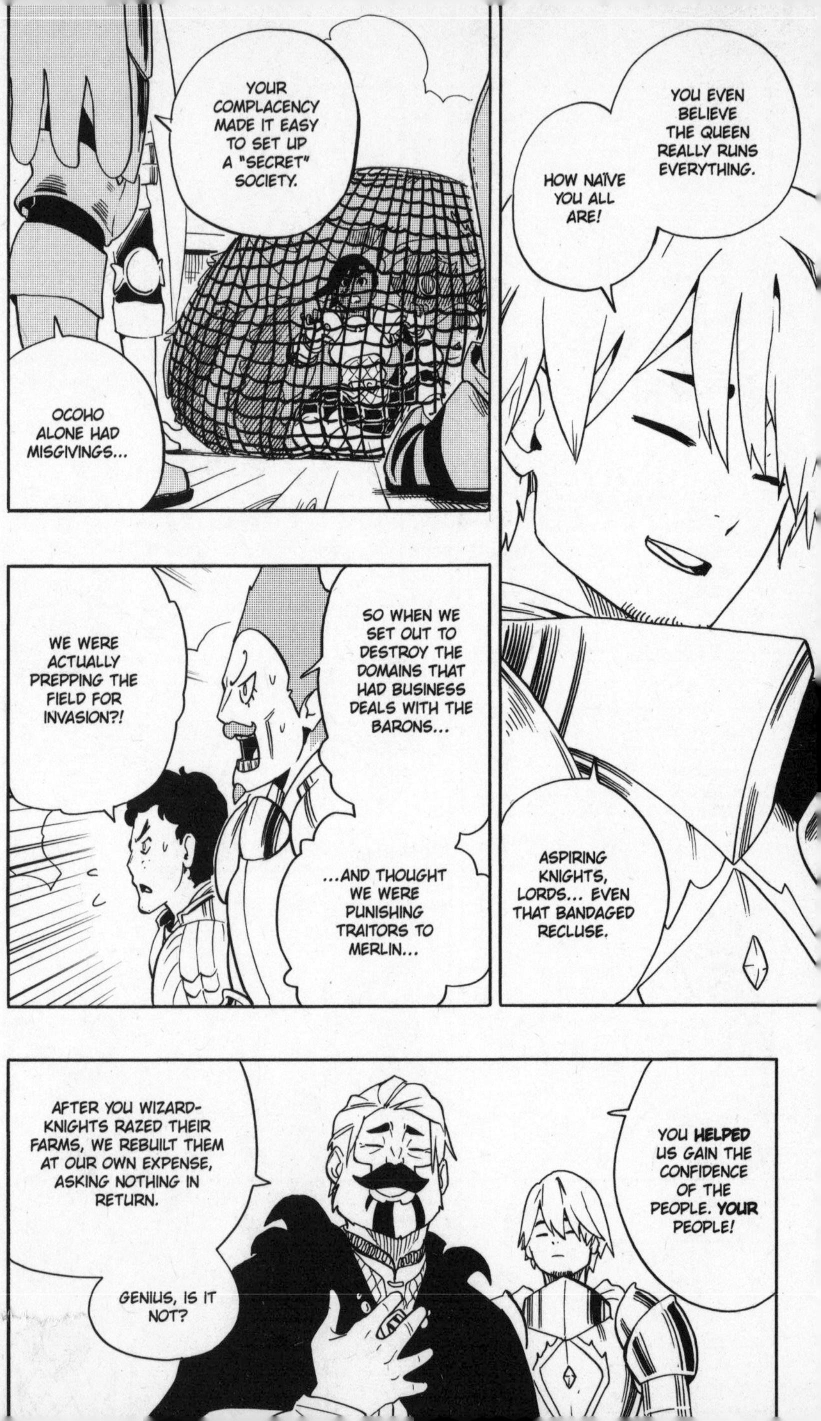
YOU EVEN BELIEVE THE QUEEN REALLY RUNS EVERYTHING.
HOW NAÏVE YOU ALL ARE!
ASPIRING KNIGHTS, LORDS... EVEN THAT BANDAGED RECLUSE.
YOUR COMPLACENCY MADE IT EASY TO SET UP A "SECRET" SOCIETY.
OCOHO ALONE HAD MISGIVINGS...
SO WHEN WE SET OUT TO DESTROY THE DOMAINS THAT HAD BUSINESS DEALS WITH THE BARONS...
...AND THOUGHT WE WERE PUNISHING TRAITORS TO MERLIN...
WE WERE ACTUALLY PREPPING THE FIELD FOR INVASION?!
YOU **HELPED** US GAIN THE CONFIDENCE OF THE PEOPLE. **YOUR** PEOPLE!
AFTER YOU WIZARD-KNIGHTS RAZED THEIR FARMS, WE REBUILT THEM AT OUR OWN EXPENSE, ASKING NOTHING IN RETURN.
GENIUS, IS IT NOT?

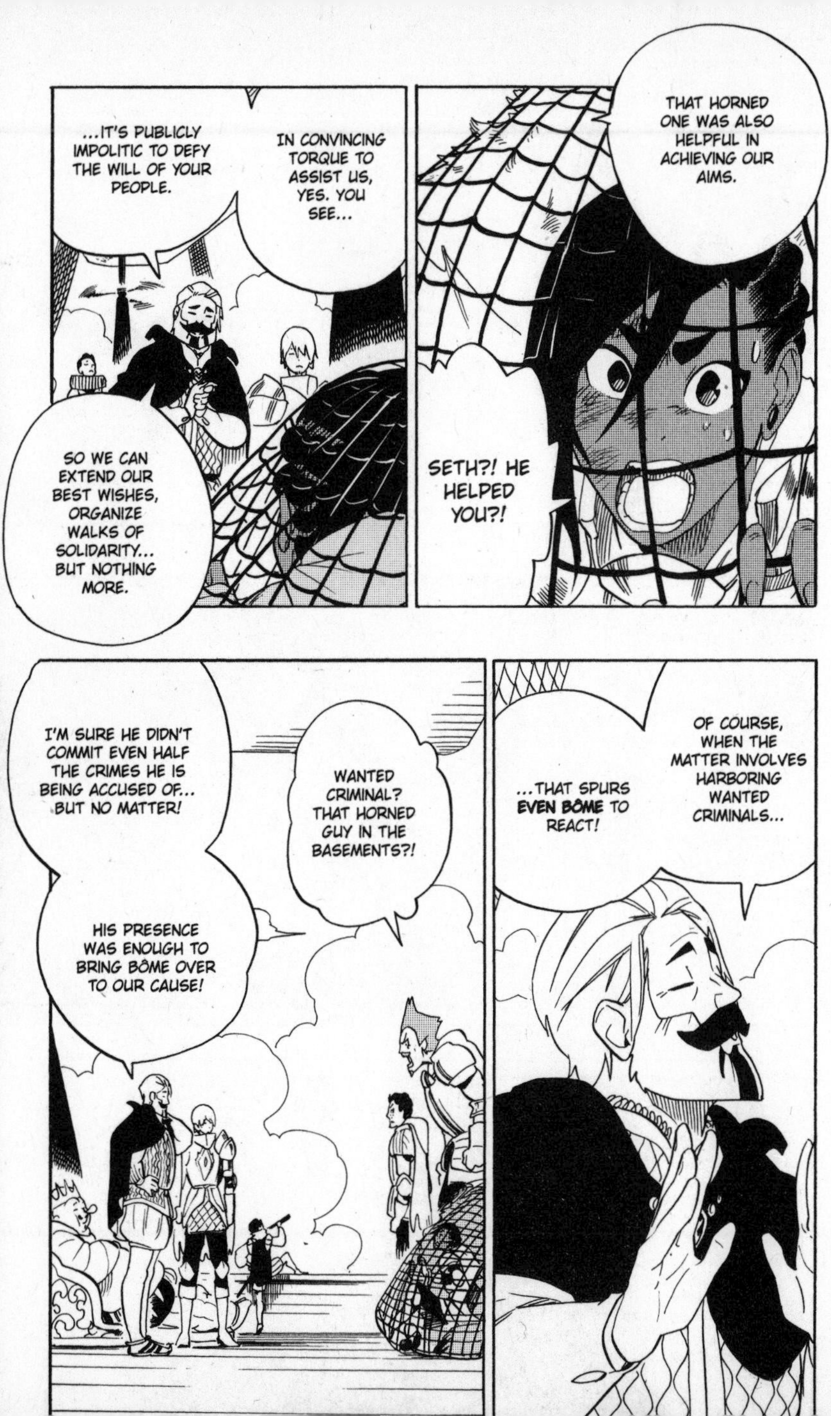
THAT HORNED ONE WAS ALSO HELPFUL IN ACHIEVING OUR AIMS.
SETH?! HE HELPED YOU?!
IN CONVINCING TORQUE TO ASSIST US, YES. YOU SEE...
...IT'S PUBLICLY IMPOLITIC TO DEFY THE WILL OF YOUR PEOPLE.
SO WE CAN EXTEND OUR BEST WISHES, ORGANIZE WALKS OF SOLIDARITY... BUT NOTHING MORE.
OF COURSE, WHEN THE MATTER INVOLVES HARBORING WANTED CRIMINALS...
...THAT SPURS **EVEN BÔME** TO REACT!
WANTED CRIMINAL? THAT HORNED GUY IN THE BASEMENTS?!
I'M SURE HE DIDN'T COMMIT EVEN HALF THE CRIMES HE IS BEING ACCUSED OF... BUT NO MATTER!
HIS PRESENCE WAS ENOUGH TO BRING BÔME OVER TO OUR CAUSE!

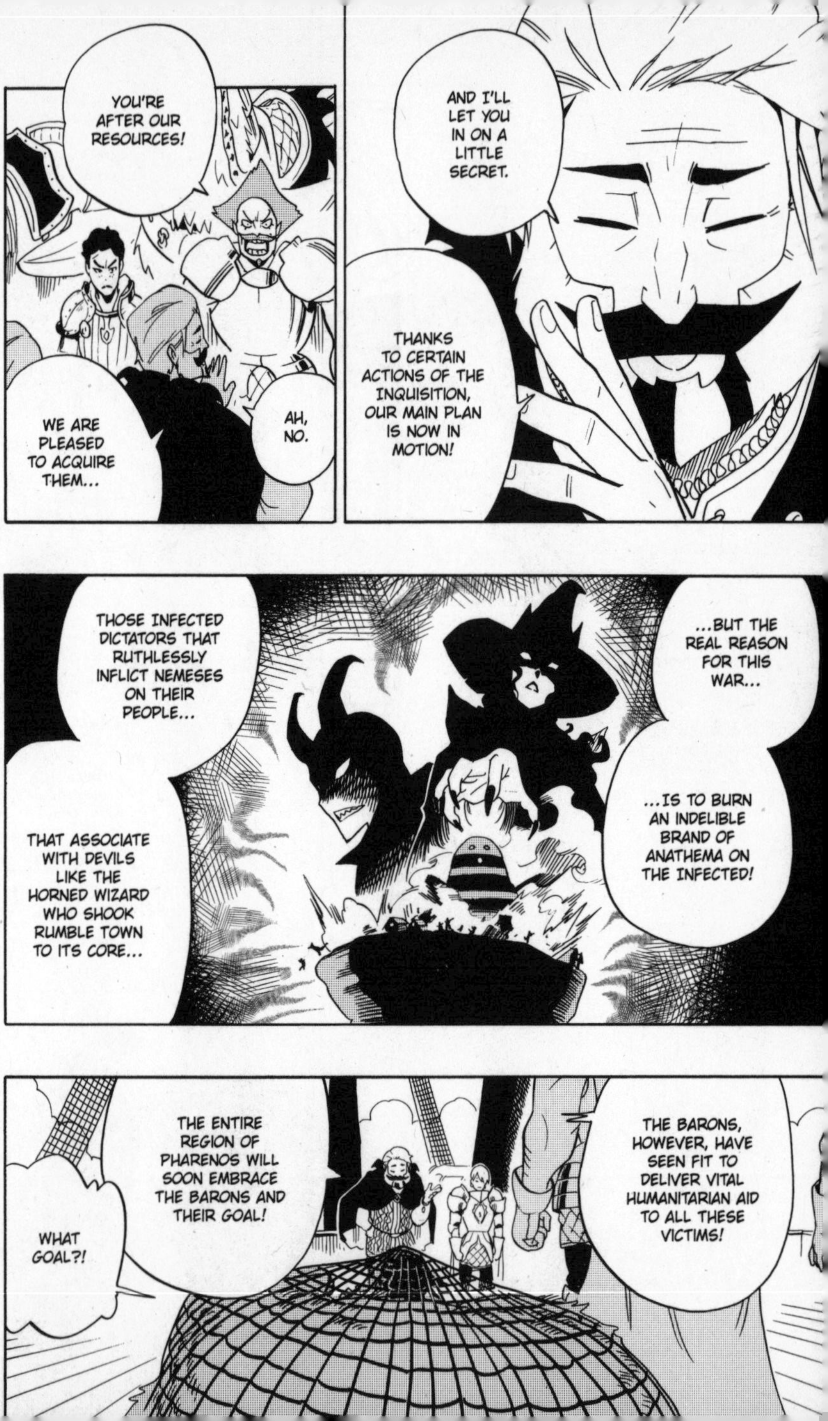
AND I'LL LET YOU IN ON A LITTLE SECRET.
THANKS TO CERTAIN ACTIONS OF THE INQUISITION, OUR MAIN PLAN IS NOW IN MOTION!
YOU'RE AFTER OUR RESOURCES!
AH, NO.
WE ARE PLEASED TO ACQUIRE THEM...
...BUT THE REAL REASON FOR THIS WAR...
...IS TO BURN AN INDELIBLE BRAND OF ANATHEMA ON THE INFECTED!
THOSE INFECTED DICTATORS THAT RUTHLESSLY INFLICT NEMESES ON THEIR PEOPLE...
THAT ASSOCIATE WITH DEVILS LIKE THE HORNED WIZARD WHO SHOOK RUMBLE TOWN TO ITS CORE...
THE BARONS, HOWEVER, HAVE SEEN FIT TO DELIVER VITAL HUMANITARIAN AID TO ALL THESE VICTIMS!
THE ENTIRE REGION OF PHARENOS WILL SOON EMBRACE THE BARONS AND THEIR GOAL!
WHAT GOAL?!

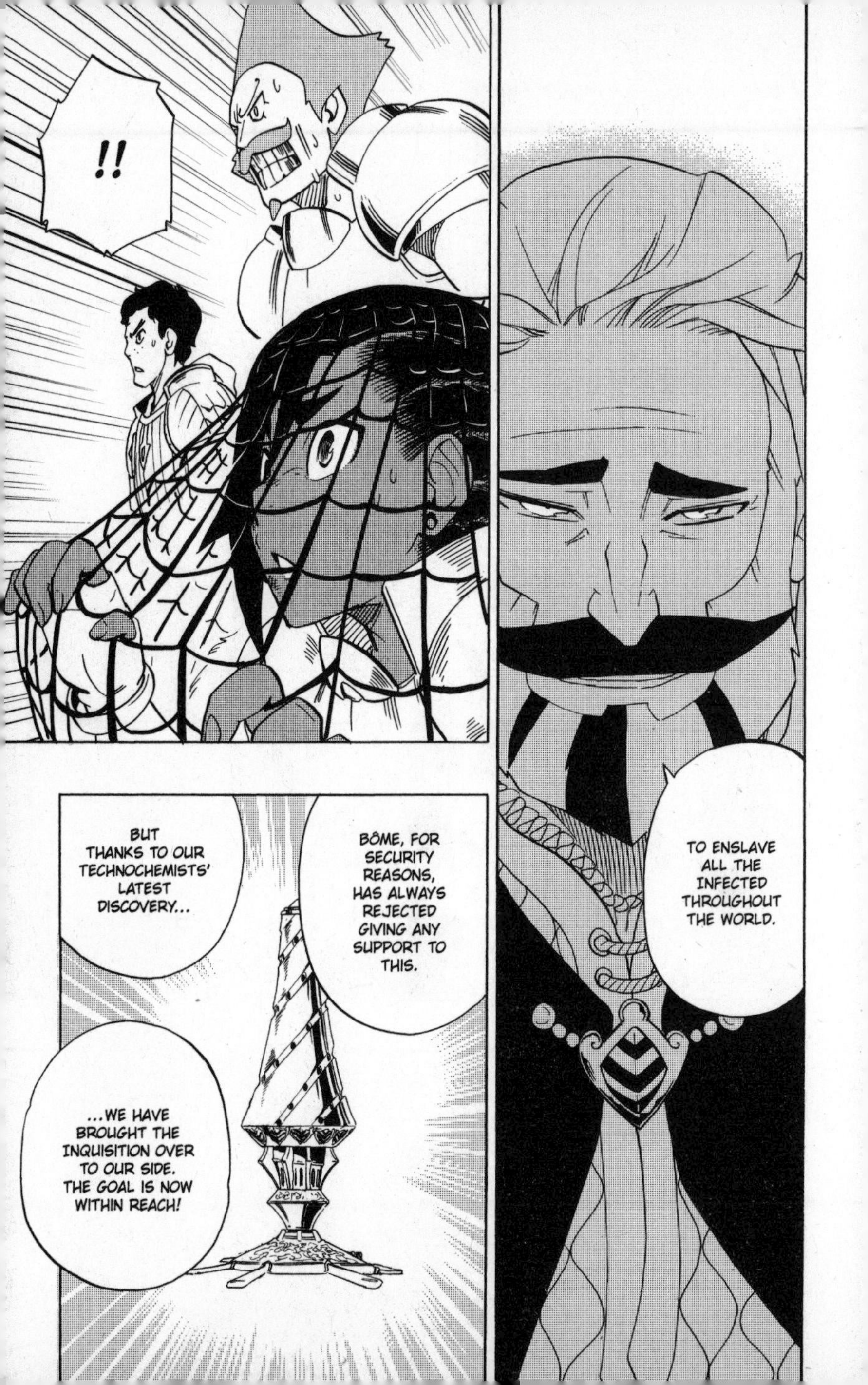
TO ENSLAVE ALL THE INFECTED THROUGHOUT THE WORLD.
!!
BÔME, FOR SECURITY REASONS, HAS ALWAYS REJECTED GIVING ANY SUPPORT TO THIS.
BUT THANKS TO OUR TECHNOCHEMISTS' LATEST DISCOVERY...
...WE HAVE BROUGHT THE INQUISITION OVER TO OUR SIDE. THE GOAL IS NOW WITHIN REACH!

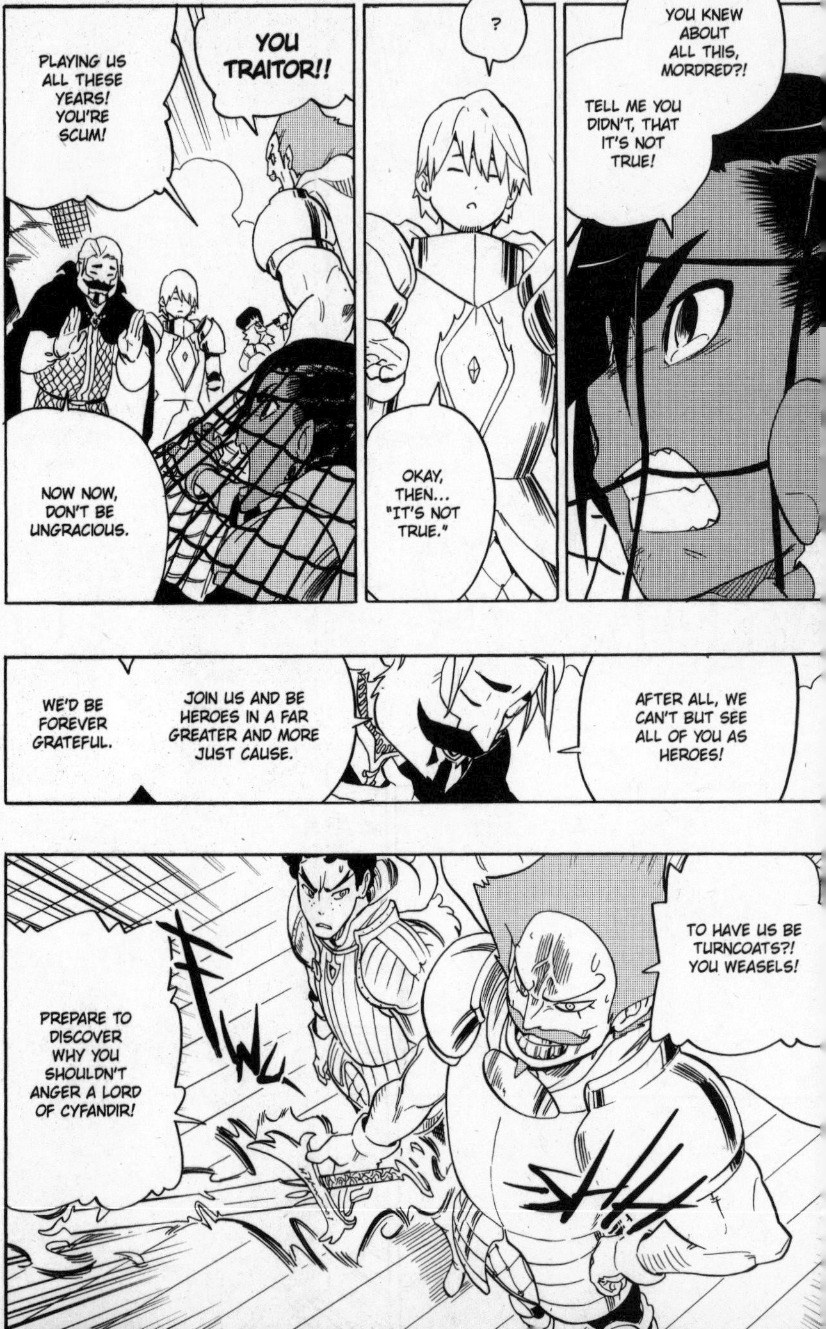
YOU KNEW ABOUT ALL THIS, MORDRED?!
TELL ME YOU DIDN'T, THAT IT'S NOT TRUE!
?
OKAY, THEN... "IT'S NOT TRUE."
YOU TRAITOR!!
PLAYING US ALL THESE YEARS! YOU'RE SCUM!
NOW NOW, DON'T BE UNGRACIOUS.
AFTER ALL, WE CAN'T BUT SEE ALL OF YOU AS HEROES!
JOIN US AND BE HEROES IN A FAR GREATER AND MORE JUST CAUSE.
WE'D BE FOREVER GRATEFUL.
TO HAVE US BE TURNCOATS?! YOU WEASELS!
PREPARE TO DISCOVER WHY YOU SHOULDN'T ANGER A LORD OF CYFANDIR!

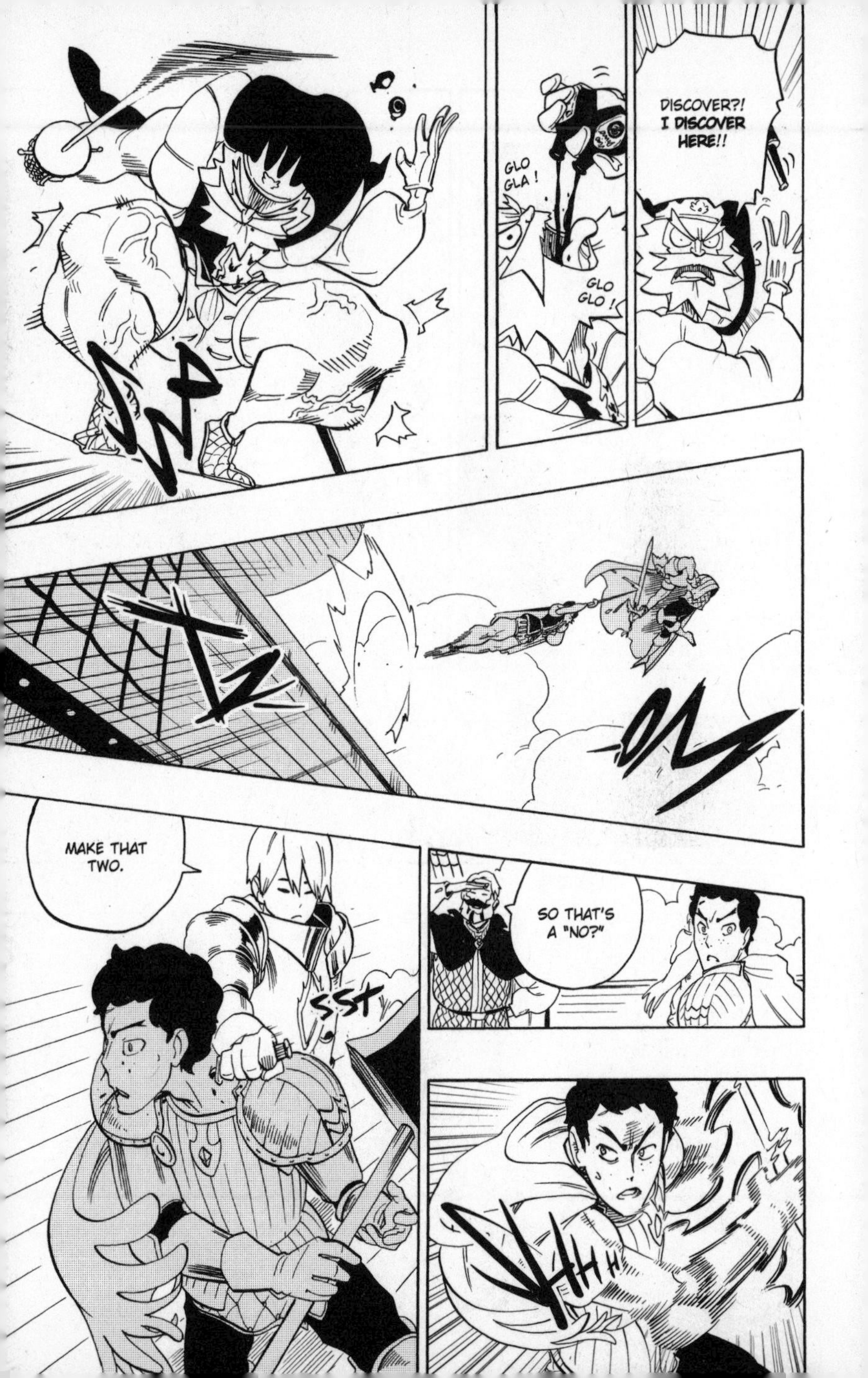
DISCOVER?! I DISCOVER HERE!!
GLO GLA !
GLO GLO !
SO THAT'S A "NO?"
MAKE THAT TWO.
SSK

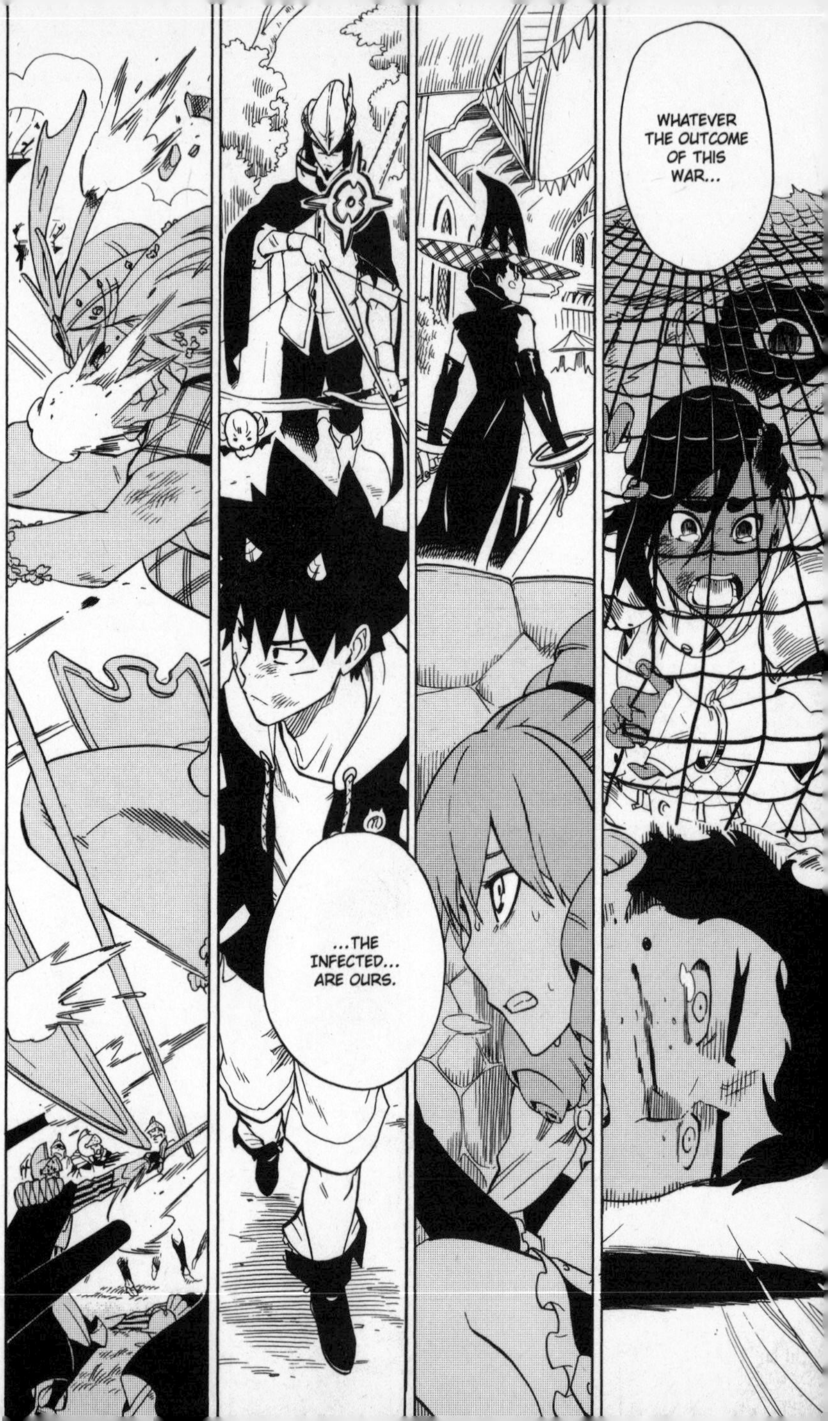
WHATEVER THE OUTCOME OF THIS WAR...
...THE INFECTED... ARE OURS.

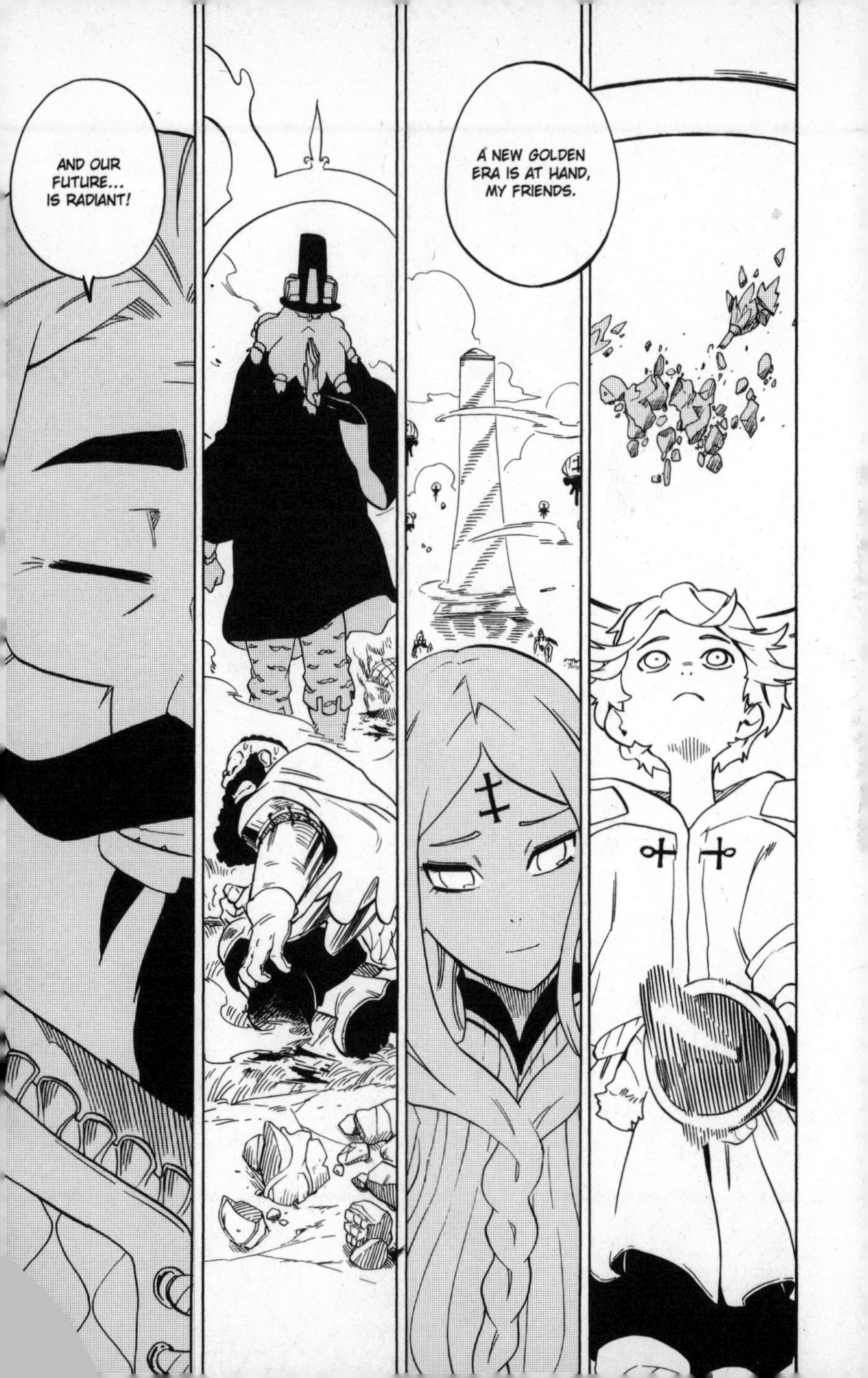
A NEW GOLDEN ERA IS AT HAND, MY FRIENDS.
AND OUR FUTURE... IS RADIANT!

TO BE CONTINUED...

Toum'STAK!!!

QUESTIONS... ANSWERS!

<u>Victor Bonnet</u>: **Toum!!! New question for you, Mister Valente: Do you have any hobbies/ interests or anything else in real life?**

<u>Tony Valente</u>: In real life? Oh, you mean that thing that happens when I'm not working on *Radiant*? Hmm... I read manga and novels. Oh, and castles. Caaastllleees!!! That's my interest! And you know how it manifests itself? I just see a castle and I go /(#°O°#)/

There you go. And because I rarely have the opportunity to see any castles in real life, I play *Witcher* or *Skyrim* in order to walk around fake castles.

- Will the main characters also have their own "Miracle"?
Isn't Dragunov basically almost a main character by now?

- Stak? I hope! Anyway, thanks in advance! Oh and by the way.............. I LOVE *RADIANT*!!!!!!!!
Yeah! And castles!!!!

....

<u>Valentin GRZELAK</u>: **In Grimm's hideout (which is, by the way, super badass), how come the screen tone is so dark? Is it because there's a giant cloud covering the sun? Does he live in a place so far off that the sun can't reach it, like for example underneath the sea of clouds beneath all the Islets?**
<u>Tony Valente</u>: Nice eye for detail!

- When Myr says he's 853 years old in human time, what does he mean by that? Is that the time that passed outside of the forest?
Yup! Just keep in mind that Myr is kind of all over the place in terms of dates, he thinks that Seth spent two years in that cocoon, when Jill says it was at least three years...

- Where did Ocoho get that nonapproved armor of hers?
Oh, just there, on the right.

....

<u>Random Lassie</u>: **Hello sir! This question might seem a little strange, but it's been bugging me for a while now. So here goes: are you by any chance a fan of the French TV show *Kaamelott*? There are a few scenes here and there that seem to mention some expressions, terminology that seems to be from the series! I like it! Anyway, eh, wanted to also say thank you. What you're doing is just amazing! Good luck for the future!**
<u>Tony Valente</u>: Oh, totally!! Alexandre Astier is amongst my all-time favorite creators, besides Eiichiro Oda, Akira Toriyama, Robin Hobb... and a couple others who influenced my work in a lot of ways!!

....

Killian Motto: If the Fantasia was really overflowing, then how did people survive if they normally burn when touching it barehanded?

Tony Valente: The Fantasia used by wizards nowadays is very concentrated and basically made to conjure attack spells, thus its destructive effects. Back when the world was overflowing with Fantasia, it was just a lot easier for wizards to concentrate a bigger quantity and with much less effort… and not necessarily by using any other tools either! And the human body was also a lot more accustomed to it! In other words, the wizards from back then: ULTIMATE BADASS-NESS!!

- Did the Nemesis appear before the Little People disappeared?

No, the Nemeses came after.

- Myr says he trained Seth because Yaga asked him to. Was this before he joined the Coven of Thirteen? Will we learn more about all of its members?

I'm sure we'll see the members someday. I say I'm sure because I want to go through every small detail of this universe and the Coven is one part of it… but time goes by and I've barely even scratched the surface! So, yes, we will see the Coven. It's in the works. Just a matter of "when"… v(°-°)v

....

Florine Antignac: Hi, I've got a small technical question that's been troubling me a lot in my comic book project: do you have any kind of method for the page layout, or even "mise en scène" of your work? Coming from video, I'm trying to tackle the problem via the storyboard, but I can't seem to make the reading very dynamic, to efficiently use my panels. Any tips?

Tony Valente: It's difficult to talk about anything visual without showing any actual examples… but here are some things I discovered while working:

-Unlike with video, a panel can take any shape or form we want it to. I try to use that to my advantage, to guide the reader's eyes to where I want them to go and to create a reading pace (longer on long horizontal panels, shorter on the small ones) to break the rhythm.

-I try to not go against the direction of reading: In Radiant, I decided to go from right to left, the Japanese way… so most of the time, my heroes will be coming from the right and will be following the direction of reading and move forward to the left where there're obstacles: enemies, events, new places, etc.

-The word balloons also follow the direction of reading. A reader's gaze must be able to pick up on the useful elements to the narration in between two word balloons, especially because in black and white comics a reader's eyes will quickly switch from one text to the other. Not placing these elements at the right place can cause your readers to skip on some useful piece of information!

-I try not to focus on the action, but on the characters that go through the action. They're the ones creating the story, not the other way around. Reverting to wider shots, showing their mental state in a certain action rather than just the action itself…reading a story is all about sharing experiences of someone else's life, whether they're fictional or not. Don't forget that this is all a subjective thing!

These are some really generic comments (-_-') but I hope it helps anyway!

....

Aurèle Del-mi: In volume 6, chapter 41, pages 17-18, we can see the same fruits present in Seth's cocoon, all around Yggdrajill. Are these eggs? Does the leprechaun with the "briefs in his beard" need to "inseminate" these for new babies to be born? Or are they just regular pieces of fruit?

Tony Valente: It's a combo of eggs and a bud, actually. And, yes, they are the result of the union between Myr and Yggdrajill. As to how this happens…Myr?

Myr: To better address this issue, I decided to write a little song:

"To fertilize a nice little bud,

First your beloved stud,

Must climb higher

the bark of his beloved to extinguish the fire

set off in her bush so thick,

by repeatedly thrusting his own …"

Tony: WHOAA! ALRIGHT THAT'S ALL THE TIME WE HAD LEFT, THANK YOU FOR ALL YOUR QUESTIONS (°-°')/

Please send your questions to: radiant@ankama.com

Look out for my sausage glove!

Sometimes, I just like to imagine parallel universes for *Radiant*:
• What if Torque had been the hero?
• What if Seth had been a girl?
• What if Seth had to sing to be able to control Fantasia? Or hold his breath or sing while holding his... What?!
• What if instead of trees with feathers, you'd have trees with... sausages? No doubt that the story would have been a little different...

—Tony Valente

Tony Valente began working as a comic artist with the series *The Four Princes of Ganahan*, written by Raphael Drommelschlager. He then launched a new three-volume project, *Hana Attori*, after which he produced *S.P.E.E.D. Angels*, a series written by Didier Tarquin and colored by Pop.

In preparation for *Radiant*, he relocated to Canada. Through confronting caribou and grizzlies, he gained the wherewithal to train in obscure manga techniques. Since then, his eating habits have changed, his lifestyle became completely different and even his singing voice has changed a bit!

RADIANT VOL. 8
VIZ MEDIA Manga Edition

STORY AND ART BY **TONY VALENTE**

Translation/(´・∀・`)ｻﾌﾟ?
Touch-Up Art & Lettering/**Erika Terriquez**
Design/**Julian [JR] Robinson**
Editor/**Gary Leach**

Published by arrangement with MEDIATOON LICENSING/Ankama.
RADIANT T08
© ANKAMA EDITIONS 2017, by Tony Valente
All rights reserved

The stories, characters and incidents mentioned in this publication are entirely
fictional.

No portion of this book may be reproduced or transmitted in any form or by any
means without written permission from the copyright holders.

Printed in the U.S.A.

Published by VIZ Media, LLC
P.O. Box 77010
San Francisco, CA 94107

10 9 8 7 6 5 4 3 2 1
First printing, November 2019

viz.com

PARENTAL ADVISORY
RADIANT is rated T for Teen and is
recommended for ages 13 and up. This
volume contains fantasy violence.
ratings.viz.com

YOU'RE READING THE WRONG WAY

RADIANT reads from right to left, starting in the upper-right corner, meaning that action, sound effects, and word-balloon order are completely reversed from English order.

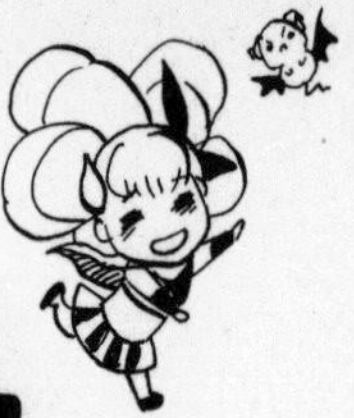

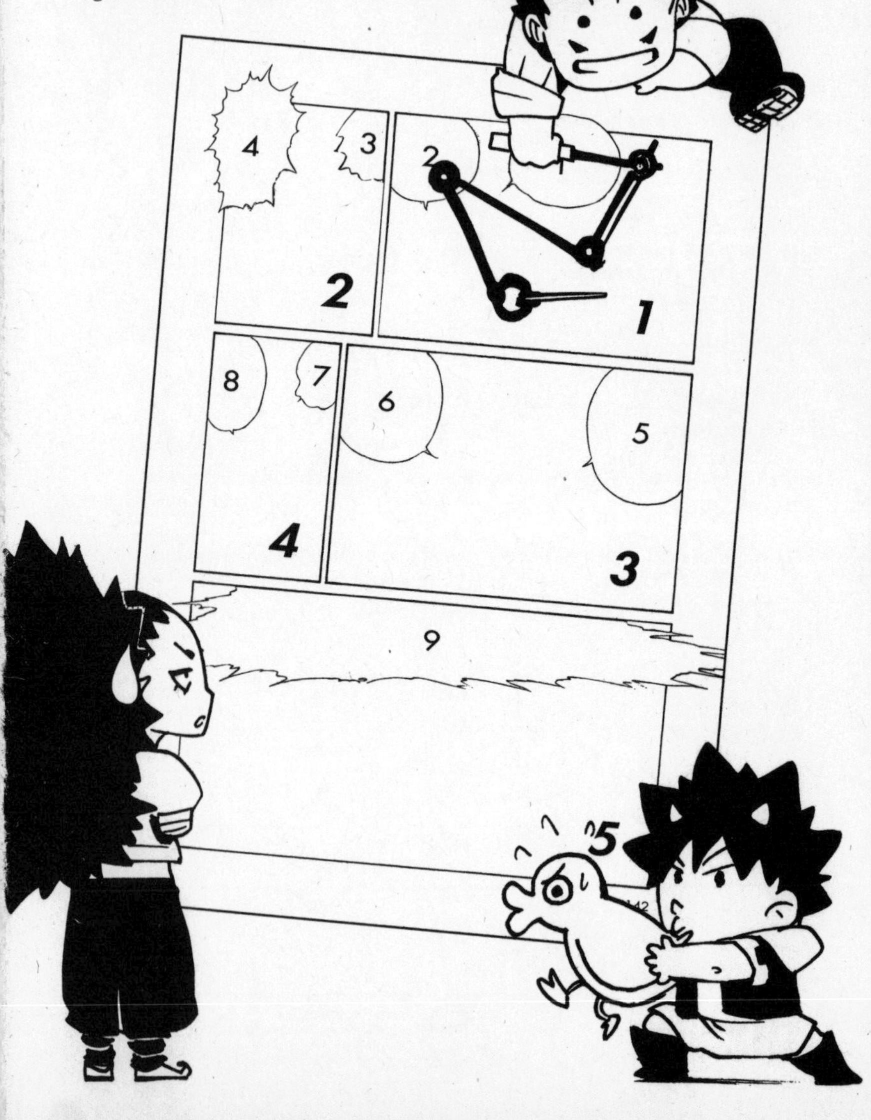